D0402500

Jiffy
Phrasebook
ITALIAN

Langenscheidt
NEW YORK

Phonetic Transcriptions: Walter Glanze Word Books
(The Glanze Intersound System)

Jiffy Phrasebooks are also available for many other languages.

Jiffy Travel Packs combine the Jiffy Phrasebooks with a travel-oriented 60-minute cassette. Each can be used independently of the other.
(Jiffy Travel Pack Italian ISBN 0-88729-978-4)

For detailed information please contact
Langenscheidt Publishers, Inc.
46-35 54th Road, Maspeth, NY 11378
(718) 784-0055

© 1986 by Langenscheidt Publishers, Inc., Maspeth, N.Y. 11378
Printed in Germany

INFORMATION

GUIDE TO THE USE OF THE PHRASEBOOK

This Italian phrasebook offers you all the important words and phrases you may need on a visit to Italy. The phonetic transcriptions which follow the Italian expressions are designed as an aid to correct pronunciation, and the systematic arrangement of the phrasebook will help you to find what you are looking for in the shortest possible time.

Structure of the phrasebook

The phrasebook is divided into 20 chapters. It begins with general words and phrases, followed by sections on transportation, accommodations, food and drink, and many other important aspects of travel abroad. There are chapters on shopping, health, cultural activities, and entertainment; the appendix gives you lists of common signs and abbreviations, weights and measures, and colors. For easy reference, English words and phrases are printed in heavy black type, while the Italian translations are in blue. Following these are the phonetic transcriptions of the Italian phrases in normal black type.

Occasionally two or more phrases have been combined and the interchangeable elements given in italics. For example, the sentence "Is it going to *rain (snow)?*" corresponds to the Italian "Pioverà *(Nevicherà?)*". Thus "Is it going to rain?" is translated "Pioverà?" and "Is it going to snow?" becomes "Nevicherà?".

In the boxes you will find help on certain language difficulties, tips on general etiquette, and information on travel, eating out, using the telephone, etc., which will help you get by in everyday situations you may encounter while traveling abroad.

An asterisk at the beginning of a sentence indicates that this is something someone else might say to you.

Italian pronunciation

On pp. 8–11 you will find a detailed guide to Italian pronunciation. Most of the symbols used in the phonetic system are taken from the Latin alphabet, so you should have no difficulty getting accustomed to the transcriptions.

Italian grammar

If you would like to get to know some important aspects of Italian grammar, the brief survey on pp. 195–202 will give you a basic grounding. Apart from offering you an insight into the structure of the Italian language and helping you to understand the expressions in the phrasebook, this grammatical survey will also enable you to form simple sentences of your own.

Traveler's Dictionary and Index

The glossary at the end of the book is 54 pages long and is for quick reference to words and phrases. The translations are followed by phonetic transcriptions and page references, so that this glossary serves as an index as well.

Carry this phrasebook with you all the time to make the most of your stay.

CONTENTS

PRONUNCIATION GUIDE

Italian pronunciation might pose some difficulties for the beginner. Yet Italian pronunciation is very regular, and once the rules are understood it is easy to pronounce each word correctly.

In this phrase book we have transcribed the words by using the letters of the English alphabet. We have diverged from it in only a few cases in order to direct your attention to particular difficulties or to facilitate your pronunciation. There is a list of phonetic symbols with examples at the end of this chapter. All phonetic symbols and transcriptions have been placed in brackets.

Here are the most important pronunciation rules: The pronunciation of **c** and **g** depends on the letter which follows it. **c** before a, o, u and before consonants has a sound similar to the English **k**, before e and i a sound similar to the English **ch** as in **ch**urch; **g** before a, o, u and before consonants sounds like the **g** in good, before e and i like the **g** in general. Should the pronunciation of **c** or **g** diverge from the norm, a silent **i** or **h** is added in the Italian word. Thus:

c	before a, o, u and consonants like the English **k** [k]: **c**ome.
c	before e and i like **ch** [tsh] in **ch**urch: *cinema*.
ci	before a, o and u like **ch** [tsh] in **ch**urch: *cioccolata* (silent i!).
ch	(only before e and i) like English **k** [k]: *chiesa, benché*.
g	before a, o, u and consonants like the English **g** [g] in good: *gamba*.
g	before e and i like the English **g** [j] in general: *Germania*.
gi	before e, o and u like the English **g** [j] in general: *Giovanni* (silent i!)
gh	(only before e and i) like the English **g** [g] in good: *ghiaccio*.

Combinations with the letter **s** are pronounced similarly:

sc	before a, o and u like **s** with the English **k** [sk]: *scala*.
sc	before e and i like the **sh** [sh] in **sh**ip: *sci*.
sci	before a, o and u like the **sh** [sh] in **sh**ip (silent i!): *sciarpa*.
sch	(only before e and i) like **sk** [sk] in **sk**irt: *scheda*.

In addition:

Initial *s* before vowels and unvoiced consonants (c, f, p, q, s, t) is pronounced like the **s** [s] in sun: *sera*.

s before voiced consonants (b, d, g, l, m, n, r, v) like the **s** [z] in rose: *sdegno, smentita*.

gli like **lli** [ly] in million: *figlio*.

gn like the **ni** [ny] in onion: *bagno, gnocchi*.

z can be voiced [dz] or unvoiced [ts].

Italian is known as a musical language and this is because every sound is pronounced clearly and precisely but remains soft rather than hard. Although syllables and words are linked together, they never lose their fundamental sound value. Vowels (*a, e, i, o, u*) always retain their value in diphthongs: for example *ei* is pronounced **e-i** [e′ē], *eu* is pronounced **e-u** [e′o͞o] and so on with other vowel combinations.

Although Italian pronunciation is regular, accentuation is less so. In this phrase book, we always place the accent mark [′] after the accented syllable: *mia* [mē′ä], *niente* [nyen′te]. To avoid ambiguity as to phonetic syllabification, a dot has been placed between two consecutive vowels: *qui* [ko͞o·ē′] here, *questo* [ko͞o·e′stō] this, *Europa* [e·o͞orō′pä] Europe.

The Italian Alphabet

a	=	[ä]	n	=	[e′ne]
b	=	[bē]	o	=	[ō]
c	=	[tshē]	p	=	[pē]
d	=	[dē]	q	=	[ko͞o]
e	=	[e]	r	=	[e′re]
f	=	[e′fe]	s	=	[e′se]
g	=	[dzhē]	t	=	[tē]
h	=	[ä′kä]	u	=	[o͞o]
i	=	[ē]	v	=	[vo͞o]
l	=	[e′le]	z	=	[ze′tä]
m	=	[e′me]			

The letters j = i [ē] lungo, w = doppio vu [vo͞o], x = ics and y = ipsilon [ēpsēlōn] are found only in words of foreign origin. h is never pronounced.

Description of Phonetic Symbols
A. Vowels and Diphthongs

Symbol	Pronunciation	Italian Example
[ä]	like **a** in path	cameriere [kämerye′re] waiter mare [mä′re] sea
[e]	has two sounds: short vowel like **e** in pen: long vowel, similar to **ai** in fair:	bello [be′lō] beautiful mese [me′se] month
[ē]	like **ea** in tea or **i** in machine:	invitare [ēnvētä′re] to invite vino [vē′nō] wine
[ō]	has two sounds: like **o** in not: similar to **o** in order:	notte [nō′te] night, buono [boo·ō′nō] good orario [ōrär′yō] schedule, ora [ō′rä] hour
[oo]	has two sounds: like **oo** in book or **ui** in fruit: like **w** in wait or **qu** in quick:	tutto [too′tō] all, muro [moo′rō] wall questo [koo·e′stō] this
[ī]	like **i** in time:	mai [mī] never
[ou]	like **ou** in cloud or **o** in how:	auto [ou′tō] car, ciao [tschou′] hi

B. Consonants

I. Special attention should be given to:

[s]	sharp s like in sun:	sempre [sem'pre] always
[z]	soft s like in cheese:	rosa [rō'zä] rose
[j]	like g in general:	gentile [jentē'le] kind

II. Grouped Consonants

[ts]	like ts in hats:	grazie [grä'tsye] thank you
[dz]	like ds in maids:	mezzo [me'dzō] half
[sh]	like sh in ship:	sciopero [shō'perō] strike
[tsh]	like ch in chair:	ci [tshē] here, there
[ly]	like lli in billiards:	figlia [fēl'yä] daughter
[ny]	like ni in onion:	signore [sēnyō're] Mr., Sir

III. Similar to English are:

[b]	like b in bell	bagno [bä'nyō] bath
[d]	like d in deep	due [dōō'e] two
[f]	like f in fat	forte [fōr'te] strong
[g]	like g in go	gonna [gō'nä] skirt
[k]	like c in can	casa [kä'sä] house
[l]	like "clear" l in long, lip	lago [lä'gō] lake
[m]	like m in more	madre [mä'dre] mother
[n]	like n in no	naso [nä'zō] nose
[p]	like p in pen	pera [pe'rä] pear
[r]	is always trilled	
[t]	like t in tea	tutto [tōō'tō] all
[v]	like v in vest	vaso [vä'zō] vase
[y]	like y in yet	gennaio [jenä'yō] January

GENERAL WORDS AND PHRASES

Greetings

Good morning!	**Good afternoon!**	**Good evening!**
Buon giorno!	Buon giorno!	Buona sera!
bōō·ōn′ jōr′nō	bōō·ōn′ jōr′nō	bōō·ō′nä se′rä

Hello!	**Hello!** *(on answering phone)*	*Hi! (Bye, bye!)*
Salve!	Pronto!	Ciao!
säl′ve	prōn′tō	tshou

Particularly in the Tuscany one uses the expression Buona sera *after noon. Further forms of greeting are* Addio! *much like the French* Adieu!, *also* Ciao *is an informal greeting.*

---

*Welcome! (Glad to see you!)
   Benvenuto! (Sono felice di *vederLa/vederti!*)
   benvenōō′tō (sō′nō felē′tshe dē veder′lä) (veder′tē)

*Did you have a good trip?
*Ha fatto buon viaggio?
 ä fä′tō bōō·ōn′ vyä′jō

I'm delighted to see you.
Mi fa molto piacere *vederLa (vederti).*
mē fä mōl′tō pyätshe′re veder′lä (veder′tē)

How are you?
Come sta?
kō′me stä

How're you doing?	**And you?**	**How's the family?**
Come va?	E Lei?	Come sta la Sua famiglia?
kō′me vä	e le′ē	kō′me stä lä sōō′ä fämē′lyä

My . . . is sick.
Mio (-a) è *malato (-a).*
mē′ō (mē′ä) . . . e mälä′tō (mälä′tä)

Did you sleep well?
Ha dormito bene?
ä dōrmē′tō be′ne

Thanks, just fine.
Grazie, *bene (non c`è male).*
grä′tsye, be′ne (nōn tshe mä′le)

We're feeling fine.
Ci sentiamo bene.
tshē sentyä′mō be′ne

Thanks for your cordial welcome.
Grazie per la cordiale accoglienza!
grä′tsye per lä kōrdyä′le äkōlyen′tsä

Forms of Address

Mr. *(name)*	Signor *(nome)*	sēnyōr′
Mrs. *(name)*	Signora *(nome)*	sēnyō′rä
Madam/Sir	Signora/Signore	sēnyō′rä/sēnyō′re
Miss	Signorina	sēnyōrē′nä
Ladies and Gentle-men!	Signore e signori!	sēnyō′re e sēnyō′rē
Your wife	Sua moglie	sōō′ä mō′lye
Your husband	Suo marito	sōō′ō märē′tō
Doctor (when addres-sing him or her)	Dottore, Dottoressa	dōtō′re dōtōre′sä
Professor	Professore, Professoressa	prōfesō′re prōfesōre′sä

When using the Dottore *or* Professore *form of address, in person or in a letter, the proper name is usually omitted.* Signore *becomes* Signor *when followed by a name.* Signore *is not used in front of relatives' names, and most titles are used without* Signore.

Letters

Mr. Carlo Varini	Signor Carlo Varini	sēnyōr′ värē′nē
Mrs. Gianna Ravone	Signora Gianna Ravone	sēnyō′rä rävō′ne
Dear Mr. Busoni,	Caro Signor Busoni,	kä′rō sēnyōr′ bōōzō′nē
Dear Mrs. Busoni	Cara Signora Busoni,	kä′rä sēnyō′rä bōōzō′nē
Dear Miss Busoni	Cara Signorina Busoni,	kä′rä sēnyōrē′nä bōōzō′nē
Dear Gianni,	Caro Gianni,	kä′rō jä′nē
Dear Graziella,	Cara Graziella,	kä′rä grätsye′lä
Dear Sirs, Gentlemen,	Egregi Signori,	egre′jē sēnyō′rē
Dear Mr. Busoni *(to a respected friend)*	Egregio Signor Busoni,	egre′jō sēnyōr′ bōōzō′nē
Dear Mrs. Busoni *(to a respected friend)*	Gentile Signora Busoni,	jentē′le sēnyō′rä bōōzō′nē
Yours sincerely, Cordially yours,	Cordiali saluti,	kōrdyä′lē sälōō′tē

Introductions

My name is	Il mio nome è	ēl mē'ō nō'me e ...
my son	mio figlio	mē'ō fēl'yō
my daugther	mia figlia	mē'ä fēl'yä
my friend (*male*)	il mio amico	ēl mē'ō ämē'kō
my friend (*female*) ..	la mia amica	lä mē'ä ämē'kä
my friends	i miei amici	ē mye'ē ämē'tshē

> *In Italian, a young man speaks of his girl friend – and only his girl friend – as „la mia ragazza", a young woman refers to her boy friend – and only her boy friend – as "il mio ragazzo". They will refer to non-intimate friends as "un amico" for a male and "un' amica" for a female friend.*

my fiancé/boyfriend .	il mio fidanzato	ēl mē'ō fēdäntsä'tō
my fiancée/girlfriend	la mia fidanzata	lä mē'ä fēdäntsä'tä

Glad to meet you. (How do you do?)
Che piacere incontrarLa. (Come sta?)
ke pyätshe're ēnkōnträr'lä (kō'me stä)

Haven't we seen one another before?
Non ci conosciamo già di vista?
nōn tshē kōnōshä'mō jä dē vē'stä

Do you live here?   **Are you Mr. (Mrs., Miss) Ponti?**
Lei abita qui?   Lei è *il signor (la signora, la signorina)* ...?
le'ē ä'bētä kōo·ē'   le'ē e ēl sēnyōr' (lä sēnyō'rä, lä sēnyōrē'nä) ...

What is your name, please?
Com'è il Suo nome?
kōme' ēl sōo·ō nō'me

We've been here for a week.
Siamo qui da una settimana.
syä'mō kōo·ē' dä ōo'nä setēmä'nä

Do you like it here?
Le (ti) piace qui?
le (tē) pyä'tshe kōo·ē'

This is my husband.
Questo è mio marito.
kōo·e'stō e mē'ō märē'tō

This is my wife.
Questa è mia moglie.
kōo·e'stä e mē'ä mō'lye

Where are you from?
Di dove è?
dē dō've e

Are you here alone?
E' *(Sei)* qui da solo?
e (se'ē) kōo·ē' dä sō'lō

Where do you work?
Dove lavora (lavori)?
dō′ve lävō′rä (lävō′rē)

What do you do for a living?
Qual è la Sua professione?
kōō·äle′ lä sōō′ä prōfesyō′ne

What are you studying?
(What's your major?)
Che cosa studia?
ke kō′sä stōō′dyä

Got some time?
Ha un po' di tempo?
ä ōōn pō dē tem′pō

Shall we go to the ...?
Vogliamo andare al ...?
vōlyä′mō ändä′re äl ...

What time shall we meet?
Quando ci incontriamo?
kōō·än′dō tshē ēnkōntrē·ä′mō

May I pick you up?
Posso venire a prenderLa?
pō′sō venē′re ä pren′derlä

Please leave me alone!
Mi lasci in pace, per favore!
mē lä′shē ēn pä′tshe, per fàvō′re

Get lost! (Buzz off!)
Va al diavolo!
vä äl dyä′vōlō

A Visit

Is *Mr. (Mrs., Miss)* ... at home?
E' in casa il signor *(la signora, la signorina)* ...?
e ēn kä′sä ēl sēnyōr′ (lä sēnyō′rä, lä sēnyōrē′nä) ...

Could I speak to Mr. (Mrs., Miss) ...?
Posso parlare con il signor *(la signora, la signorina)* ...?
pō′sō pärlä′re kōn ēl sēnyōr′ (lä sēnyō′rä, lä sēnyōrē′nä)

Does *Mr. (Mrs., Miss)* ... live here?
Abita qui il signor *(la signora, la signorina)* ...?
ä′bētä kōō′ē′ ēl sēnyōr′ (lä sēnyō′rä, lä sēnyōrē′nä)

I'm looking for ...
Cerco ...
tsher′kō ...

When will *he (she)* be home?
Quando sarà a casa?
kōō·än′dō särä′ ä kä′sä

I'll drop by again later.
Ritornerò più tardi.
rētōrnerō′ pyōō tär′dē

When *can I (shall we)* come?
A che ora *posso (dobbiamo)* venire?
ä ke ō′rä pō′sō (dōbyä′mō) venē′re

I'd (We'd) love to come.
Vengo (Veniamo) molto volentieri.
ven'gō (venyä'mō) mōl'tō vōlentye're

*Come in!
Avanti!
ävän'tē

*Please have a seat!
Prego, si accomodi!
pre'gō, sē äkō'mōdē

*Just a minute, please.
Un momento, per favore.
ōōn mōmen'tō, per fävō're

*Come right in.
Si avvicini, per favore.
sē ävētshē'nē, per fävō're

Thanks so much for the invitation.
Tante grazie per il Suo invito.
tän'te grä'tsye per ēl sōō'ō ēnvē'tō

Would you like ...?
Desidera ...?
desē'derä ...?

Am I bothering you?
Disturbo?
dēstōōr'bō

Please don't go to a lot of trouble.
Non si disturbi, La prego!
nōn sē dēstōōr'bē, lä pre'gō

*What'll you have? (What may I offer you?)
Che cosa preferisce? (Che cosa posso offrirLe?)
ke kō'sä preferē'she (ke kō'sä pō'sō ōfrēr'le)

Mr. (Mrs.) Smith sends you *his (her) regards (love)*.
Le porto i saluti del signor (della signora) ...
le pōr'tō ē sälōō'tē del sēnyōr' (de'lä sēnyō'rä) ...

I'm afraid I've got to go now.
Mi dispiace, ma ora devo andare.
mē dēspyä'tshe, mä ō'rä de'vō ändä're

Thanks so much for a *lovely evening (coming)*.
Tante grazie per la simpatica serata (visita).
tän'te grä'tsye per lä sēmpä'tēkä serä'tä (vē'zētä)

Please give *Mr. (Mrs.)* ... my best regards.
Saluti il signor (la signora) ... da parte mia.
sälōō'tē ēl sēnyōr' (lä sēnyō'rä) ... dä pär'te mē'ä

I'll tell *him (her)* you said hello.
Lo (La) saluterò da parte Sua.
lō (lä) sälōōterō' dä pär'te sōō'ä

I hope we'll meet again soon!
Spero che ci rivedremo presto!
spe'rō ke tshē rēvedre'mō pre'stō

Farewells

Italian farewells vary according to the degree of the relationship and the finality of the parting. Among friends, especially among younger people the informal "Ciao" is appropriate. For more formal situations "Arrivederci" and "Auguri" are more appropriate. For more final partings the expression "Addio" can be used.

Good-bye!	**See you soon.**	**Good night!**
Arrivederci!	A presto!	Buonanotte!
ärēveder'tshē	ä pre'stō	bōō·ō'nä nō'te

See you tomorrow.	**All the best.**	***Have a good trip.**
A domani!	Auguri!	Buon viaggio!
ä dōmä'nē	ougōō'rē	bōō·ōn' vyä'jō

I'd like to say good-bye!
Vorrei congedarmi!
vōre'ē kōnjedär'mē

I'm afraid we have to go.
Purtroppo dobbiamo andare.
pōōrtrō'pō dōbyä'mō ändä're

Thanks so much for coming.
Grazie per essere venuto.
grä'tsye per e'sere venōō'tō

Come again soon!
Torni presto!
tōr'nē pre'stō

When can we get together again?
Quando ci rivedremo?
kōō·än'dō tshe rēvedre'mō

I'll give you a call tomorrow.
Le (ti) telefono domani.
le (tē) tele'fōnō dōmä'nē

Can I give you a lift home?
Posso accompagnar*La (-ti)* a casa?
pō'sō äkōmpänyär'lä (tē) ä kä'sä

It's pretty late.
E' già tardi.
e jä tär'dē

Give ... my best!	**Thanks very much.**	**I had a lovely time.**
Saluti ...	Tante grazie.	E' stato molto bello.
sälōō'tē ...	tän'te grä'tsye	e stä'tō mōl'tō be'lō

I enjoyed myself very much.
Mi è piaciuto molto.
mē e pyätshōō'tō mōl'tō

I'll *take you to (give you a lift to)* the ...
La (ti) accompagno al (alla) ...
lä (tē) äkōmpä'nyō äl (ä'lä) ...

General Questions

When?	Why?	What?	What kind of...?
Quando?	Perchè?	Che cosa?	*Quale (Quali)...?*
kōo·än'dō	perke'	ke kō'sä	kōo·ä'le (kōo·ä'lē)...

Which?	To whom?	With whom?	Whom?
Quale...?	A chi?	Con chi?	Chi?
kōo·ä'le...	ä kē	kōn kē	kē

Who?	*Why? (How come?)*	How?	How long?
Chi?	*Perchè? (Come mai?)*	Come?	Quanto tempo?
kē	*perke' (kō'me mī)*	kō'me	kōo·än'tō tem'pō

How *much (many)*?	Where?	Where from?	Where to?	What for?
Quanto/-a (quanti/-e)?	Dove?	Da dove?	Dove?	Per che cosa?
kōo·än'tō/-ä (kōo·än'tē/-e)	dō've	dä dō've	dō've	per ke kō'sä

Is... allowed here?	Can I...?	Do you need...?
Si può... qui?	Posso...?	Ha bisogno di...?
sē pōo·ō'... kōo·ē	pō'sō...	ä bēzō'nyō dē...

Have you (got)...?	When can I get...?
Ha...?	Quando posso avere...?
ä...	kōo·än'dō pō'sō äve're...

What time do you open (close)?	*What would you like? (What can I do for you? May I help you?)*
A che ora apre (chiude)?	*Cosa desidera? (Posso fare qualcosa per Lei? Posso aiutarLa?)*
ä ke ō'rä ä'pre (kyōo'de)	kō'sä desē'derä (pō'sō fà're kōo·älkō'sä per le'ē / pō'sō äyōotär'lä)

What's that?	What happened?	What does that mean?
Che cos'è questo?	Cos'è successo?	Cosa significa?
ke kōze' kōo·e'stō	kōze' sōotshe'so	kō'sä sēnyē'fēkä

How much does that cost?	What are you looking for?
Quanto costa questo?	Che cosa *cerca (cerchi)?*
kōo·än'tō kō'stä kōo·e'stō	ke kō'sä tsher'kä (tsher'kē)

Whose is that?
Di chi è questo?
dē kē e koo·e'stō

*Whom do you wish to see?
Chi desidera?
kē desē'derä

Who's there?
Chi è?
kē e

Who can (Can anyone) ...?
Chi può (Può qualcuno) ...?
kē poo·ō' (poo·ō' koo·älkoo'nō...

What do you call ...?
Come si dice ...?
kō'me sē dē'tshe ...

What's your name?
Come si chiama (ti chiami)?
kō'me sē kyä'mä (tē kyä'mē)

How do I get to ...?
Qual è la strada per ...?
koo·äle' lä strä'dä per ...

How does that work?
Come funziona?
kō'me foontsyō'nä

How long does it take?
Quanto tempo ci vuole?
koo·än'tō tem'pō tshē voo·ō'le

How much do I get?
Quanto ricevo?
koo·än'tō rētshe'vō

How much is it?
Quant'è?
koo·änte'

Where can I find ... (is ... located)?
Dove posso trovare ... (è situato ...)?
dō've pō'sō trōvä're ... (e sētoo·ä'tō)

Where is (are) ...?
Dov'è (Dove sono) ...?
dōve' (dō've sō'nō) ...

Where's the nearest ...?
Dov'è il prossimo (la prossima) ...?
dōve' ēl prō'sēmō (lä prō'sēmä) ...

Where can I ...?
Dove posso ...?
dō've pō'sō ...

Where can I get (find) ...?
Dove posso avere (trovare) ...?
dō've pō'sō äve'rē (trōvä're) ...

Where is (are) ...?
Dove si può (possono) avere ...?
dō've sē poo·ō' (pō'sōnō) äve're
...

Where do you live?
Dove abita (abiti)?
dō've ä'bētä (ä'bētē)

Where are we?
Dove siamo?
dō've syä'mō

Where do you come from?
Da dove viene (vieni)?
dä dō've vye'ne (vye'nē)

Where are you going?
Dove va (vai)?
dō've vä (vī)

Where does this road (path) lead?
Dove porta questa strada (questo cammino)?
dō've pōr'tä koo·e'stä strä'dä (koo·e'stō kämē'nō)

Wishes, Requests

> *The Italian word* "prego" *like the English word* please *expresses a number of different concepts. The most widely used meanings of* "prego" *are* "please", "excuse me" *(as used when one says* "excuse me" *or* "sorry, I didn't hear *or* understand you"*). "Prego" is also used to express* "you're welcome" *as well as* "here you are" *and* "please go ahead" *as when one is holding a door or helping someone.*

Would you please bring (give, show) me ...?
Potrebbe *portarmi (darmi, mostrarmi) ...?*

pōtre′be pōrtär′mē (där′mē, mōsträr′mē) ...

Would you please tell me...?
Potrebbe dirmi ...?

pōtre′be dēr′mē ...

Would you please get (fetch) ...?
Potrebbe andare a prendere ...?

pōtre′be ändä′re a pren′dere ...

Beg your pardon? (What did you say?)
Come dice? (Scusi?)

kō′me dē′tshe (skōō′zē)

What can I do for you? (May I help you?)
Che cosa posso fare per Lei?
(Posso aiutarLa?)

ke kō′sä pō′sō fä′re per le′ē
(pō′sō äyōōtär′lä)

I'd (We'd) like ...
Vorrei (Vorremmo) ...

vōre′ē (vōre′mō) ...

I need ...
Ho bisogno di ...

ō bēzō′nyō dē ...

I'd rather have ...
Preferirei ...

preferēre′ē ...

Could I have (get) ...?
Potrei *avere (ricevere) ...?*

pōtre′ē äve′re (rētshe′vere) ...

Please help me!
Per favore, mi aiuti!

per fävō′re, mē äyōō′tē

Certainly!
Certamente!

tshertämen′te

Allow me? (Excuse me?)
Permette? (Mi scusi.)

perme′te (mē skōō′zē)

Get well soon!
Buona guarigione!

bōō·ō′nä gōō·ärējō′ne

All the best!
(Tanti) Auguri!

(tän′tē) ougōō′rē

Have *a good time (fun)!*
Buon divertimento!

bōō·ōn′ dēvertēmen′tō

I wish you ...
Le (ti) auguro ...

le (tē) ou′gōōrō ...

Thanks

Thanks!	**Thanks very much!**	**Thanks a lot!**	**No, thanks.**
Grazie!	Tante grazie!	Mille grazie!	No, grazie.
grä′tsye	tän′te grä′tsye	mē′le grä′tsye	nō, grä′tsye

Thank you too!	**Don't mention it.**	**Glad to do it.**
Grazie, altrettanto!	Di niente.	E un piacere.
grä′tsye, ältretän′tō	dē nyen′te	e ōōn pyätshe′re

I'm very grateful to you.
La *(Ti)* ringrazio molto.
lä (tē) rēn·grä′tsyō mōl′tō

You're welcome.
Prego, non c'è di che.
pre′gō, nōn tshe dē ke

Thanks very much for *your help (all your trouble)*!
Tante grazie per *il Suo aiuto (la Sua gentilezza)*!
tän′te grä′tsye per ēl sōō′ō äyōō′ō (lä sōō′ä jentēle′tsä)

I *(We)* thank you so much for ...
La *ringrazio (ringraziamo)* molto per ...
lä rēn·grä′tsyō (rēn·grätsyä′mō) mōl′tō per ...

Yes and no

Yes.	**Certainly.**	**Of course.**	**I'd be glad to.**
Sì.	Certamente.	Naturalmente.	Molto volentieri.
sē	tshertämen′te	nätōōrälmen′te	mōl′tō vōlentye′rē

Good! (Fine!)	**Right!**	**Terrific!**	**With pleasure!**
(Molto) bene!	Esatto!	Magnifico!	Con piacere!
(mōl′tō) be′ne	ezä′tō	mänyē′fēkō	kōn pyätshe′re

No.	**Never.**	**Nothing.**	**Certainly not! (No way!)**
No.	Mai.	Niente.	In nessun caso!
nō	mī	nyen′te	ēn nesōōn′ kä′zō

Out of the question!	**I'd rather not!**
Impossibile!	Preferirei di no!
ēmpōsē′bēle	preferēre′ē dē nō

I *don't want to (can't)*.	**Perhaps (Maybe).**	**Probably.**
Non *voglio (posso)*.	*Forse (Può darsi)*.	Probabilmente.
nōn vō′lyō (pō′sō)	fōr′se (pōō·ō′ där′sē)	prōbäbēlmen′te

Pardon

Excuse me!	**I beg your pardon!**	**Please excuse me!**
Scusi!	Scusi!	Mi scusi, per favore!
skōō´zē	skōō´zē	mē skōō´zē, per fävō´re

I'm very sorry.
Mi dispiace tanto.
mē dēspyä´tshe tän´tō

I'm extremely sorry.
Mi dispiace molto.
mē dēspyä´tshe mōl´tō

I must apologize to you.
La (ti) prego di scusarmi.
lä (tē) pre´gō dē skōōzär´mē

Please don't be angry!
Non se l´abbia a male!
nōn se lä´byä ä mä´le

Regrets

What a pity! (Too bad!)
Che peccato!
ke pekä´tō

I'm afraid that can't be done.
Mi dispiace, ma non si può fare.
mē dēspyä´tshe, mä nōn sē pōō·ō´ fä´re

I´m so very sorry about that.
Sono veramente spiacente.
sō´nō verämen´te spyätshen´te

To my (great) regret . . .
Con mio (grande) dispiacere . . .
kōn mē´ō (grän´de) dēspyätshe´re . . .

I'm afraid that isn't possible.
Purtroppo è impossibile.
pōōrtrō´pō e ēmpōsē´bele

What a shame that . . .
E´ peccato che . . .
e pekä´tō ke . . .

Congratulations and Condolences

Congratulations!	**I congratulate you . . .**
Auguri!	I miei migliori auguri. . .
ougōō´rē	ē mye´ē mēlyō´rē ougōō´rē

on your birthday	per il compleanno	per ēl kōmple·ä´nō
on your engagement .	per il fidanzamento . . .	per ēl fēdäntsämen´tō
on your marriage	per il matrimonio	per ēl mätrēmō´nyō

The Italian expressions for congratulations of course vary according to the situation but usually begin with the expression "Auguri!". Also used somewhat less formally is the phrase "Tante buone cose!"

All the best! (Best wishes!)

Tante buone cose! (I miei migliori auguri!)
tän'te bōō·ō'ne kō'se (ē mye'ē mēlyō'rē
ougōō'rē)

Happy birthday!

Buon compleanno!
bōō·ōn' kōmple·ä'nō

Merry Christmas!

Buon Natale!
bōō·ōn' nätä'le

Happy New Year!

Felice Anno Nuovo!
felē'tshe ä'nō nōō·ō'vō

Happy Easter!

Buona Pasqua!
bōō·ōnä päs'kōō·ä

I (We) wish you ...

Le *auguro (auguriamo)* ...
le ou'gōōrō (ougōōryä'mō) ...

Good luck!

Buona fortuna!
bōō·ō'nä fōrtōō'nä

All the best!

Tanto successo! (Auguri!)
tän'to sōōtshe'sō (ougōō'rē)

My sincerest condolences.

Le mie sentite condoglianze.
le mē'e sentē'te kōndōlyän'tse

Our warmest sympathy.

Vivissime condoglianze da parte
nostra.
vēvē'sēme kōndōlyän'tse dä
pär'te nō'strä

Complaints

I'd like to register a complaint.

Devo fare un reclamo.
de'vō fä're ōōn reklä'mō

I'd like to speak to the manager.

Vorrei parlare con il direttore.
vōre'ē pärlä're kōn ēl dēretō're

I'm afraid I'll have to make a complaint about ...

Devo fare un reclamo riguardo a ...
de'vō fä're ōōn reklä'mō rēgōō·är'dō ä ...

... is (are) missing.

Manca (mancano) ...
män'kä (män'känō) ...

I haven't got any ...

Non ho ...
nōn ō ...

... doesn't work.

... non funziona.
... nōn fōōntsyō'nä

... is not in order.

... non è in ordine.
... nōn e ēn ōr'dēne

... is out of order.

... non è a posto.
... nōn e ä pō'stō

... is broken.

... è rotto.
... e rō'tō

... is torn.

... è strappato.
... e sträpä'tō

That's very annoying.

Questa è una vera seccatura (E` veramente spiacevole).
kōo·e'stä e ōo'nä ve'rä sekätōo'rä (e verämen'te spyätshe'vōle)

Do you speak English?	**Italian?**	**French?**
Parla inglese?	italiano?	francese?
pär'lä ēn·gle'se	ētälyä'nō	fräntshe'se

Can you understand me?	**I understand.**	**I can't understand a thing.**
Mi capisce?	Capisco.	Non capisco niente.
mē käpē'she	käpē'skō	nōn käpē'skō nyen'te

Would you please speak a little slower?

Parli un po' più lentamente, per piacere.
pär'lē ōon pō pyōo lentämen'te, per pyätshe're

What do you call . . . in Italian?

Come si dice . . . in italiano?
kō'me sē dē'tshe . . . ēn ētälyä'nō

What does that mean?

Cosa significa questo?
kō'sä sēnyē'fēkä kōo·e'stō

How do you say that in Italian?

Come dice questo in italiano?
kō'me dē'tshe kōo·e'stō ēn ētälyä'nō

I beg your pardon? (Say again?)

Come dice? / Scusi? (Può ripetere?)
kō'me dē'tshe / skōo'zē (pōo·ō' rēpe'tere)

How do you pronounce this word?

Come si pronuncia questa parola?
kō'me sē prōnōon'tshä kōo·e'stä pärō'lä

Would you please translate this for me?

Può tradurre questo per me, per favore?
pōo·ō' trädōo're kōo·e'stō per me, per fävō're

Would you please write that down for me?

Me lo scriva, per favore.
me lō skrē'vä, per fävō're

Would you spell that please?

Come si scrive, per favore?
kō'me sē skrē've, per fävō're

Weather

How's the weather going to be?
Che tempo farà?
ke tem'pō färä'

What's the weather report?
Cosa dice la previsione del tempo?
kō'sä dē'tshe lä prevēzyō'ne del
tem'pō

The barometer's *rising (falling)*.
Il barometro *sale (scende)*.
ēl bärō'metrō sä'le (shen'de)

We're going to have …
Avremo …
ävre'mō …

fine weather ……	bel tempo ……………	bel tem'pō
bad weather ……	brutto tempo ………	broo'tō tem'pō
changeable weather …	tempo variabile ……	tem'pō väryä'bēle

Is it going to *rain (snow)*?
Pioverà (Nevicherà)?
pyōverä' (nevēkerä')

It looks like rain.
Pare che voglia piovere.
pä're ke vōlyä pyō'vere

How are the road conditions between here and …?
Come è la viabilità delle strade tra qui e …?
kō'me e lä vyäbēlētä' de'le strä'de trä koo·ē' e …

It's very slippery.	**– very hot.**	**– *foggy (misty)*.**
Si scivola.	Fa molto caldo.	C'è nebbia.
sē shē'vōlä	fä mōl'tō käl'dō	tshe ne'byä
– very muggy.	**– very windy.**	**– stormy.**
C'è afa.	C'è vento.	C'è tempesta.
tshe ä'fä	tshe ven'tō	tshe tempe'stä

What's the temperature?
Quanti gradi ci sono?
koo·än'tē grä'dē tshē sō'nō

It's … *above (below)* zero.
Ci sono … gradi *sopra (sotto)* lo zero.
tshē sō'nō … grä'dē sō'prä (sō'tō) lō
dze'rō

It's *cold (hot)*.
Fa *freddo (caldo)*.
fä fre'dō (käl'dō)

Is the weather going to stay nice?
Il tempo rimane bello?
ēl tem'pō rēmä'ne be'lō

Since the Italian expression for "hot" (caldo) sounds much like the English word "cold" be careful not to confuse the two.
Remember: hot = caldo *and* cold = freddo!

The weather's going to change.
Il tempo cambierà.
ēl tem'pō kämbyerä'

It'll be nice again.
Il tempo torna bello.
ēl tem'pō tōr'nä be'lō

The wind has dropped.
Il vento si è calmato.
ēl ven'tō sē e kälmä'tō

The wind has changed.
Il vento ha girato.
ēl ven'tō ä jērä'tō

We're going to have a thunderstorm.
Ci sarà un temporale.
tshē särä' ōōn tempōrä'le

There's going to be a storm.
Ci sarà una burrasca.
tshē särä' ōō'nä bōōräs'kä

Is the fog going to lift?
La nebbia si alzerà?
lä ne'byä sē ältserä'

It's stopped raining.
Ha smesso di piovere.
ä zme'sō dē pyō'vere

It's clearing up.
Si sta schiarendo.
sē stä skyären'dō

The sun is shining.
C'è sole.
tshe sō'le

The sun is burning hot.
Il sole scotta.
ēl sō'le skō'tä

The sky is clear.
Il cielo è sereno.
ēl tshe'lō e sere'nō

Italian temperatures are always measured in degrees Centigrade (Celsius). Here's a handy conversion table:

Fahrenheit to Celsius = $(x-32)$ $5/9$ = $°C$
Celsius to Fahrenheit = $32+9/5x$ = $°F$

---

air	(l') aria *f*	är'yä
atmospheric pressure	(la) pressione atmosferica	presyō'ne ätmōsfe'rēkä
barometer	(il) barometro	bärō'metrō
blizzard	(la) tormenta	tōrmen'tä
climate	(il) clima	klē'mä
cloud	(la) nuvola	nōō'vōlä
cloudburst	(il) temporale	tempōrä'le
cloud cover, cloudy skies	(il) cielo coperto, nuvoloso	tshe'lō kōper'tō, nōōvōlo'sō
cloudy	nuvoloso	nōōvōlo'sō
dew	(la) rugiada	rōōjä'dä
dusk	(il) crepuscolo	krepōō'skōlō
earth quake	(il) terremoto	teremō'tō

fog	(la) nebbia	ne'byä
frost	(il) gelo	je'lō
hail	(la) grandine	grän'dēne
heat	(il) calore	kälō're
high pressure (system)	(l') alta pressione *f*	äl'tä presyō'ne
ice	(il) ghiaccio, gelo	gyä'tshō, je'lō
icy road	(la) strada ghiacciata	strä'dä gyätshä'tä
it's freezing	gela	je'lä
it's hailing	grandina	grän'dēnä
it's raining	piove	pyō've
it's snowing	nevica	ne'vēkä
it's thawing	sgela	zje'lä
it's windy	c'è vento	tshe ven'tō
lightning	(il) lampo	läm'pō
low pressure (system)	(la) bassa pressione	bä'sä presyō'ne
mist	(la) foschia	fōskē'ä
moon	(la) luna	lōō'nä
***north (east)* wind**	*(la) tramontana*	trämōntä'nä
	(il) vento di levante	ven'tō dē levän'te
precipitation	(la) precipitazione	pretshēpētätsyō'ne
rain *(noun)*	(la) pioggia	pyō'jä
road conditions	(la) viabilità	vyäbēlētä'
snow	(la) neve	ne've
snow flurries	(la) tempesta di neve	tempe'stä dē ne've
***south (west)* wind**	*(il) vento australe*	ven'tō ousträ'le
	(il) vento di ponente	ven'tō dē pōnen'te
star	(la) stella	ste'lä
storm	(la) tempesta	tempe'stä
sun	(il) sole	sō'le
sunrise	(il) sorgere del sole	sōr'jere del sō'le
sunset	(il) tramonto (del sole)	trämōn'tō (del sō'le)
temperature	(la) temperatura	temperätōō'rä
thaw	(il) tempo di sgelo	tem'pō dē zje'lō
thunder	(il) tuono	tōō·ō'nō
thunderstorm	(il) temporale	tempōrä'le
weather	(il) tempo	tem'pō
weather prediction	(le) previsioni del	prevēzyō'nē del
	tempo	tem'pō
weather report	(il) bollettino	bōletē'nō
	meteorologico	mete·ōrōlō'jēkō
wind	(il) vento	ven'tō

Numbers		*Cardinal Numbers*	

0	zero	dze′rō	**5**	cinque	tshēn′kōo·e
1	uno	ōo′nō	**6**	sei	se′ē
2	due	dōo′e	**7**	sette	se′te
3	tre	tre	**8**	otto	ō′tō
4	quattro	kōo·ä′trō	**9**	nove	nō′ve

10	dieci	dye′tshē
11	undici	ōon′dētshē
12	dodici	dō′dētshē
13	tredici	tre′dētshē
14	quattordici	kōo·ätōr′dētshē
15	quindici	kōo·ēn′dētshē
16	sedici	se′dētshē
17	diciassette	dētshäse′te
18	diciotto	dētshō′tō
19	diciannove	dētshänō′ve
20	venti	ven′tē
21	ventuno	ventōo′nō
22	ventidue	ventēdōo′e
23	ventitré	ventētre′
24	ventiquattro	ventēkōo·ä′trō
25	venticinque	ventētshēn′kōo·e
26	ventisei	ventēse′ē
27	ventisette	ventēse′te
28	ventotto	ventō′tō
29	ventinove	ventēnō′ve
30	trenta	tren′tä
40	quaranta	kōo·ärän′tä
50	cinquanta	tshēnkōo·än′tä
60	sessanta	sesän′tä
70	settanta	setän′tä
80	ottanta	ōtän′tä
90	novanta	nōvän′tä
100	cento	tshen′tō
200	duecento	dōo·etshen′tō
1.000	mille	mē′le
2.000	duemila	dōo·emē′lä
10.000	diecimila	dyetshēmē′lä
1.000.000	un milione	ōon mēlyō′ne
1.000.000.000	un miliardo	ōon mēlyär′dō

When writing numbers in Italian, the function of periods and commas is reversed from that in English. Thus, the number 1.000 = one thousand ("mille") and 1,5 = one point five or one and five tenths or, in Italian, "uno virgola cinque".

Ordinal Numbers

In Italian, as in English, the ordinal numbers are slightly different from the cardinal numbers. With the exception of the first ten digits the basic rule is to take the desired number, delete its ending and add the suffix "-esimo". When not written out in full form the ordinal numbers are shortened to the cardinal number plus the correct ending. For example: first = 1° (primo), tenth = 10° (dècimo) or, in the case of female gender, 1ª (prima), and likewise 10ᵗʰ = 10ª (decima).

1°	primo	prē′mō	6°	sesto	ses′tō
2°	secondo	sekōn′dō	7°	settimo	se′tēmō
3°	terzo	ter′tsō	8°	ottavo	otä′vō
4°	quarto	kōō·är′tō	9°	nono	nō′nō
5°	quinto	kōō·ēn′tō	10°	decimo	de′tshēmō

11°	undicesimo	ōōndētshe′zēmō
12°	dodicesimo	dōdētshe′zēmō
13°	tredicesimo	tredētshe′zēmō
14°	quattordicesimo	kōō·ätōrdētshe′zēmō
15°	quindicesimo	kōō·ēndētshe′zēmō
16°	sedicesimo	sedētshe′zēmō
17°	diciassettesimo	dētshäsete′zēmō
18°	diciottesimo	dētshōte′zēmō
19°	diciannovesimo	dētshänōve′zēmō
20°	ventesimo	vente′zēmō
21°	ventunesimo	ventōōne′zēmō
22°	ventiduesimo	ventēdōō·e′zēmō
23°	ventitreesimo	ventētre·e′zēmō
24°	ventiquattresimo	ventēkōō·ätre′zēmō
30°	trentesimo	trente′zēmō
100°	centesimo	tshente′zēmō
200°	duecentesimo	dōō·etshente′zēmō
1.000°	millesimo	mēle′zēmō
10.000°	diecimillesimo	dyetshēmēle′zēmō
1.000.000°	milionesimo	mēlyōne′zēmō

Time

What time is it?
Che ore sono?
ke ō're sō'nō

Have you got the exact time?
Ha l'ora esatta?
ä lō'rä ezä'tä

It's one o'clock.
E' l'una.
e lōō'nä

It's about two o'clock.
Sono quasi le due.
sō'nō kōō·ä'zē le dōō'e

It's exactly three o'clock.
Sono le tre in punto.
sō'nō le tre ēn pōōn'tō

It's quarter past five.
Sono le cinque e un quarto.
sō'nō le tshēn'kōō·e e ōōn kōō·är'tō

It's half past seven.
Sono le sette e mezzo.
sō'nō le se'te e me'dzō

It's quarter to nine.
Sono le nove meno un quarto.
sō'nō le nō've me'nō ōōn kōō·är'tō

It's five (minutes) past four.
Sono le quattro e cinque.
sōn'ō le kōō·ä'trō e tshēn'kōō·e

It's ten (minutes) to eight.
Sono le otto meno dieci.
sō'nō le ō'tō me'nō dye'tshē

When?
Quando?
kōō·än'dō

At ten o'clock (10 : 00).
Alle dieci.
ä'le dye'tshē

At eleven sharp.
Alle undici in punto.
ä'le ōōn'dētshē ēn pōōn'tō

At *half-past nine (nine-thirty)*.
Alle *nove e mezzo (nove e trenta)*.
ä'le nō've e me'dzō (nō've e tren'tä)

At eight-fifteen P.M.
Alle otto e un quarto di sera.
ä'le ō'tō e ōōn kōō·är'tō dē se'rä

From eight to nine A.M.
Dalle otto alle nove di mattina.
dä'le ō'tō ä'le nō've dē mätē'nä

At five P.M.
Alle cinque di pomeriggio.
ä'le tshēn'kōō·e dē pōmerē'jō

Between ten and twelve A.M.
Tra le dieci e le dodici di mattina.
trä le dye'tshē e le dō'dētshē dē mätē'nä

At seven P.M.
Alle sette di sera.
ä'le se'te dē se'rä

In Italy as in most of Europe, time is based on the 24 hour day and not on the 12 hour clock. Thus 1 pm is expressed as 13:00, 5:30 pm as 17:30, etc. That means an appointment or invitation for 19:30 is meant for 7:30 pm.

In half an hour.
Fra mezz'ora.
frä medzō'rä

In two hours.
Fra due ore.
frä dōō'e ō're

Not before seven.
Non prima delle sette.
nōn prē'mä de'le se'te

Shortly after eight.
Poco dopo le otto.
pō'kō dō'pō le ō'tō

It's (too) late.
E' (troppo) tardi.
e (trō'pō) tär'dē

It's still too early.
E' ancora troppo presto.
e änkō'rä trō'pō pre'stō

Is this clock right?
Quest' orologio va bene?
kōō·estōrōlō'jō vä be'ne

It's too *fast (slow)*.
Va avanti (rimane indietro).
vä ävän'tē (rēmä'ne ēndye'trō)

Times of the Day

During the day.
Di giorno.
dē jōr'nō

In the morning.
Di mattina.
dē mätē'nä

During the morning.
In mattinata.
ēn mätēnä'tä

At noon.
A mezzogiorno.
ä medzōjōr'nō

Around noon.
Verso mezzogiorno.
ver'sō medzōjōr'nō

In the afternoon.
Nel pomeriggio.
nel pōmerē'jō

In the evening.
Di sera.
dē se'rä

At night.
Di notte.
dē nō'te

At midnight.
A mezzanotte.
ä medzänō'te

Daily (Every day).
Ogni giorno.
ō'nye jōr'nō

Hourly (Every hour).
Tutte le ore (ogni ora)
tōō'te le ō're (ō'nye ō'rä)

The day before yesterday.
Ieri l'altro.
ē·e'rē läl'trō

Yesterday.
Ieri.
ē·e'rē

Today.
Oggi.
ō'jē

Tomorrow.
Domani.
dōmä'nē

Tomorrow morning.
Domani mattina.
dōmä'nē mätē'nä

The day after tomorrow.
Dopodomani.
dōpōdōmä'nē

Tonight.
Stanotte.
stänō'te

This *morning (afternoon, evening)*.
Stamattina (oggi pomeriggio, stasera).
stämätē'nä (ō'jē pōmerē'jō, stäse'rä)

A week from now.
Oggi fra una settimana.
ō'jē frä ōō'nä setēmä'nä

This noon.	**A month ago.**	**Within a week.**
Oggi a mezzogiorno.	Un mese fa.	Entro una settimana.
ō′jē ä medzōjōr′nō	ōon me′se fä	en′trō ōo′na setēmä′nä

For the last ten days.	**This coming weekend.**	**At the moment.**
Da dieci giorni.	Il prossimo weekend.	Adesso.
dä dye′tshē jōr′nē	el prō′sēmō ōo·ē′kend	äde′sō

Last (Next) year.	***Every year.***	***Every week (Weekly).***
L'anno *scorso (prossimo)*.	Ogni anno.	Ogni settimana.
lä′nō skōr′sō (prō′sēmō)	ō′nyē ä′nō	ō′nyē setēmä′nä

From time to time.	**Now and then.**
Di tanto in tanto.	Di quando in quando.
dē tän′tō ēn tän′tō	dē kōo·än′dō ēn kōo·än′dō

About this time.	***During this time (Meanwhile).***
Verso quest'ora.	*Durante questo periodo (Nel frattempo).*
ver′sō kōo·estō′rä	dōorän′te kōo·e′stō perē′ōdō (nel frätem′pō)

a little while ago	poco fa	pō′kō fä
any time	in ogni tempo	ēn ō′nyē tem′pō
earlier	prima	prē′mä
later	più tardi	pyōo tär′dē
now	adesso (ora)	äde′sō (ō′rä)
on time	in punto	ēn pōon′tō
previously (before) ...	prima	prē′mä
recently	recentemente	retshentemen′te
since	da	dä
sometimes	qualche volta	kōo·äl′ke vōl′tä
soon	presto, fra poco	pre′sto, frä pō′kō
temporarily (for the		
time being)	per ora	per ō′rä
until	fino a	fē′nō ä
second	(il) secondo	sekōn′dō
minute	(il) minuto	mēnōo′tō
hour	(l') ora *f*	ō′rä
day	(il) giorno	jōr′nō
week	(la) settimana	setēmä′nä
month	(il) mese	me′se
year	(l') anno *m*	ä′nō
half year	(il) semestre	seme′stre
quarter, three months	(il) trimestre	trēme′stre

Days of the Week

Monday	(il) lunedì	loonedē′
Tuesday	(il) martedì	märtedē′
Wednesday	(il) mercoledì	merkōledē′
Thursday	(il) giovedì	jōvedē′
Friday	(il) venerdì	venerdē′
Saturday	(il) sabato	sä′bätō
Sunday	(la) domenica	dōme′nēkä

Months

January	Gennaio	jenä′yō
February	Febbraio	febrä′yō
March	Marzo	mär′tsō
April	Aprile	äprē′le
May	Maggio	mä′jō
June	Giugno	joo′nyō
July	Luglio	loo′lyō
August	Agosto	ägō′stō
September	Settembre	setem′bre
October	Ottobre	ōtō′bre
November	Novembre	nōvem′bre
December	Dicembre	dētshem′bre

Seasons

Spring	(la) primavera	prēmäve′rä
Summer	(l') estate *f*	estä′te
Fall/Autumn	(l') autunno *m*	outoo′nō
Winter	(l') inverno *m*	ēnver′nō

Holidays

New Year's Eve	(il) Capodanno	käpōdä′nō
New Year's Day	(il) Primo dell'anno . . .	prē′mō delä′nō
Good Friday	Venerdì Santo	venerdē′ sän′tō
Easter	(la) Pasqua	päs′koo·ä
Easter Monday	(la) Pasquetta	päskoo·e′tä
Christmas	(il) Natale	nätä′le

Boxing Day ....　San Stefano ....　sän ste′fäno
Liberation Day .....　Festa della Liberazione　fe′stä de′lä lēberä-
　(April 25th)　　　　　　　　　　　　　　　 tsyō′ne

> *Another holiday, which sends families crowding to beaches and*
> *mountains, is "Ferragosto" and commemorates Ascension Day of*
> *the Virgin Mary. The first of May is also a full holiday and*
> *commemorates all workers. April 25th is the national holiday of Italy*
> *celebrating Italy's freedom from fascism.*

The Date

What's the date today?　　　**It's the second of July.**
Quanti ne abbiamo oggi?　　　 E' il due luglio.
koo′än′tē ne äbyä′mō ō′jē　　　 e ēl doo′e loo′lyō

On *the fifteenth of May (May fifteenth)*, 19 ...
Il quindici maggio millenovecento ...
ēl koo-ēn′dētshē mä′jō mēlenōvetshen′tō ...

On April first of last year.　　　**Until the 10th of March.**
Il primo aprile dell'anno scorso.　　Fino al dieci marzo.
el prē′mō äprē′le delä′nō skōr′sō　 fē′no äl dye′tshē mär′tsō

We leave on *the twentieth of September (September twentieth)*.
Partiamo il venti settembre.
pärtyä′mō ēl ven′tē setem′bre

We arrived on *the twelfth of August (August the twelfth)*.
Siamo arrivati il dodici agosto.
syä′mo arēvä′tē ēl dō′dētshē ägō′stō

Age

I'm twenty years old.　　　　**I'm over 18.**
Ho venti anni (Ho vent`anni).　Ho più di diciotto anni.
ō ventē ä′nē (ō ventä′nē)　　　 ō pyoo dē dētshō′tō ä′nē

Children under 14.　　　　　**I was born on the ...**
Ragazzi inferiori ai quattordici anni.　Sono nato (*f:* nata) il ...
rägä′tsē ēnferyō′rē ī koo·ätōr′dētshē ä′nē　sō′nō nä′tō (nä′tä) ēl ...

He's *younger (older)*.
E' più *giovane (vecchio)*.
e pyōō jō'väne (pyōō ve'kyō)

– **under age.**
– minorenne
– mēnōre'ne

– **grown up.**
– maggiorenne.
– mäjōre'ne

At the age of ...
All'età di ...
äletä' dē ...

At my age.
Alla mia età.
ä'lä mē'ä etä'

Family

aunt	(la) zia	tsē'ä
boy	(il) ragazzo	rägä'tsō
brother	(il) fratello	fräte'lō
brother-in-law	(il) cognato	kōnyä'tō
cousin *(female)*	(la) cugina	kōōjē'nä
cousin *(male)*	(il) cugino	kōōjē'nō
daughter	(la) figlia	fē'lyä
daughter-in-law	(la) nuora	nōō-ō'rä
family	(la) famiglia	fämē'lyä
father	(il) padre	pä'dre
father-in-law	(il) suocero	sōō-ō'tsherō
girl	(la) ragazza	rägä'tsä
grandchild	(il) nipote	nēpō'te
granddaughter	(la) nipote	nēpō'te
grandfather	(il) nonno	nō'nō
grandmother	(la) nonna	nō'nä
grandparents	(i) nonni	nō'nē
grandson	(il) nipote	nēpō'te
husband	(il) marito	märē'tō
mother	(la) madre	mä'dre
mother-in-law	(la) suocera	sōō-ō'tsherä
nephew	(il) nipote	nēpō'te
niece	(la) nipote	nēpō'te
parents	(i) genitori	jenētō'rē
relative	(il) parente	pären'te
sister	(la) sorella	sōre'lä
sister-in-law	(la) cognata	kōnyä'tä
son	(il) figlio	fē'lyō
son-in-law	(il) genero	je'nerō
uncle	(lo) zio	tsē'ō
wife	(la) moglie	mō'lye

Occupations

apprentice	(l') apprendista m/f	äprendē'stä
artist	(l') artista m/f	ärtē'stä
auto mechanic	(il) meccanico d'auto	mekä'nēkō dou'tō
baker	(il) fornaio	fōrnä'yō
bank teller	(il) cassiere	käsye're
bookkeeper	(il) contabile	kōntä'bēle
bookseller	(il) libraio	lēbrä'yō
bricklayer	(il) muratore	mōōrätō're
butcher	(il) macellaio	mätshelä'yō
cabinetmaker	(l') ebanista m	ebänē'stä
carpenter	(il) carpentiere	kärpentye're
chef	(il) cuoco	kōō·ō'kō
civil servant	(il) funzionario statale	fōōntsyōnär'yō stätä'le
cobbler	(il) calzolaio	kältsōlä'yō
doctor	(il) dottore (medico)	dōtō're (me'dēkō)
dressmaker	(là) sarta	sär'tä
driver	(l') autista m	outē'stä
druggist (pharmacist)	(il) farmacista, (il) droghiere	färmätshē'stä, drōgē·e're
electrician	(l') elettricista m	eletrētshē'stä
engineer (scientific)	(l') ingegnere m	ēnjenye're
engineer (railroad)	(il) macchinista	mäkēnē'stä
farmer	(l') agricoltore m	ägrēkōltō're
fisherman	(il) pescatore	peskätō're
forester	(la) guardia forestale	gōō·är'dyä fōrestä'le
gardener	(il) giardiniere	järdēnye're
glazier	(il) vetraio	veträ'yō
interpreter	(l') interprete m	ēnter'prete
journalist	(il) giornalista	jōrnälē'stä
judge	(il) giudice	jōō'dētshe
lawyer	(l') avvocato m	ävōkä'tō
librarian	(il) bibliotecario	bēblē·ōtekär'yō
locksmith	(il) fabbro	fä'brō
mailman	(il) postino	pōstē'nō
mechanic	(il) meccanico	mekä'nēkō
metalworker	(l') operaio metal-meccanico	ōperä'yō metäl-mekä'nēkō

midwife	(la) levatrice	levätrē'tshe
miner	(il) minatore	mēnätō're
musician	(il) musicista	mōozētshē'stä
notary	(il) notaio	nōtä'yō
nurse *(female)*	(l') infermiera *f*	ēnfermye'rä
nurse *(male)*	(l') infermiere *m.*	ēnfermye're
optician	(l') ottico *m*	ō'tēkō
painter	(l') imbianchino *m*	ēmbyänkē'nō
painter *(artist)*	(il) pittore	pētō're
pharmacist	(il) farmacista	färmätshē'stä
plumber	(il) stagnino	stänyē'nō
postal clerk	(l') impiegato *m* postale	ēmpyegä'tō pōstä'le
pupil *(including high school students)*	(il) discente, (lo) scolaro	dēshen'te, skōlä'rō
railroad man	(il) ferroviere	ferōvye're
representative	(il) rappresentante	räprezentä'nte
retailer	(il) commerciante	kōmertshän'te
retiree	(il) pensionato	pensyōnä'tō
salesperson *(female)*	(la) commessa	kōme'sä
salesperson *(male)*	(il) commesso	kōme'sō
scholar	(lo) scienziato	shentsyä'tō
sculptor	(lo) scultore	skōoltō're
secretary	(la) segretaria	segretär'yä
shoemaker	(il) calzolaio	kältsōlä'yō
storekeeper	(il) magazziniere	mägädzēnye're
student	(lo) studente	stōoden'te
tailor	(il) sarto	sär'tō
teacher	(l') insegnante *m/f.*	ēnsenyän'te
technician	(il) tecnico	tek'nēkō
trainee	(l') apprendista *m/f.*	äprendē'stä
translator	(il) traduttore	trädōotō're
truck driver	(il) camionista	kämyōnē'stä
veterinarian	(il) veterinaio	veterēnä'yō
waiter	(il) cameriere	kämerye're
waitress	(la) cameriera	kämerye'rä
watchmaker	(l') orologiaio *m*	ōrōlōjä'yō
wholesaler	(il) grossista	grōsē'stä
worker	(l') operaio *m*	ōperä'yō
writer	(lo) scrittore	skrētō're

> *The European school system in general and the Italian in particular differ in a number of ways from the British and American systems. The most obvious difference from the American system is the separation into different schools at the highschool level and the university qualifying exams which are (is) called the "esame di maturità".*

Education

Where are you studying? (What college or university do you attend?
Dove studia? (Che scuola/università frequenta?)
dō've stoo·ō'dyä? (ke skoo·ō'lä/oonēversētä' frekoo·e·'ntä?)

I am at ... *college (university).*
Studio *a ... (all' Università di ...)*
stoo'dyō ä ... (äloonēversētä' dē ...)

I'm *studying (majoring in) ...*
Mi sto specializzando in ...
mē stō spetshälēdzän'dō ēn ...

I *go to (am attending)* **the ...** *school.*
Frequento la scuola ...
frekoo·en'tō lä skoo·ō'lä ...

lecture	(la) lezione	letsyō'ne
major	(la) materia	mäte'ryä
school	(la) scuola	skoo·ō'lä
– boarding school ...	(il) collegio	kōle'jō
– business school	(la) scuola commerciale	skoo·ō'lä kōmer-tshä'le
– grammar school ...	(la) scuola elementare .	skoo·ō'lä elementä're
– high school	(la) scuola superiore, (il) liceo, ginnasio	skoo·ō'lä sooperyō're, lētshe'ō, jēnä'zyō
– school of applied arts	(la) scuola dell' arti-gianato	skoo·ō'lä delärtē-jänä'tō
– vocational school ..	(la) scuola d'avviamento professionale	skoo·ō'lä dävyä-men'tō prōfesyō-nä'le

subject	(la) materia	mäter′yä
– American studies	(l') americanistica	ämerēkänē′stēkä
– archaeology	(l') archeologia	ärke·ōlōjē′ä
– architecture	(l') architettura	ärkētetoo′rä
– art history	(la) storia dell'arte	stō′ryä delär′te
– biology	(la) biologia	bē·ōlōjē′ä
– business administration	(la) amministrazione contabile	ämēnēsträtsyō′ne kōntä′bēle
– chemistry	(la) chimica	kē′mēkä
– dentistry	(l') odontologia	ōdōntōlōjē′ä
– economics	(l') economia	ekōnōmē′ä
– education	(la) pedagogia	pedägōjē′ä
– English	(l') anglistica	änglē′stēkä
– geology	(la) geologia	je·ōlōjē′ä
– history	(la) storia	stō′ryä
– journalism	(il) giornalismo	jōrnälēz′mō
– law	(la) legge	le′je
– mathematics	(la) matematica	mätemä′tēkä
– mechanical engineering	(l') industria meccanica	ēndoo′strē·ä mekä′nēkä
– medicine	(la) medicina	medētshē′nä
– musicology	(la) musica	moo′zēkä
– painting	(la) pittura	pētoo′rä
– pharmacy	(la) farmacia	färmätshē′ä
– physics	(la) fisica	fē′zēkä
– political science	(le) scienze politiche	shen′tse pōlē′tēke
– psychology	(la) psicologia	psēkōlōjē′ä
– Romance languages	(le) lingue romanze	lēn′goo·e rō- män′dze
– Slavic languages	(le) lingue slave	lēn′goo·e slä′ve
– sociology	(la) sociologia	sōtshōlōjē′ä
– veterinary medicine	(la) veterinaria	veterēnär′yä
– zoology	(la) zoologia	dzō·ōlōjē′ä
technical college	(l') istituto *m* tecnico	ēstētoo′tō tek′nēkō
university	(l') università *f*	oonēversētä′

ON THE ROAD

Asking the Way

Where is (are) ...?
Dov'è (Dove sono) ...?
dōve' (dō've sō'nō) ...

How do I get to ...?
Qual è la strada per ...?
kōō·äle' lä strä'dä per ...

How many kilometers is it to the next town?
A quanti chilometri è la città più vicina?
ä kōō·än'tē kēlō'metrē e lä tshētä' pyōō vētshē'nä

---

8 kilometers (km) = 5 miles

Is this the road to ...?
E' questa la strada per ...?
e kōō·e'stä lä strä'dä per ...

Is this the right way to ...?
E' giusta questa strada per ...?
e jōō'stä kōō·e'stä strä'dä per ...

Do I have to go ...?
Devo proseguire ...?
de'vō prōsegōō·ē're ...

Right.	**Left.**	**Straight ahead.**	**Back.**
A destra.	A sinistra.	Sempre diritto.	Indietro.
ä de'strä	ä sēnē'strä	sem'pre dērē'tō	ēndye'trō

Here.	**There.**	**This way.**	**As far as** ...
Qui.	Là.	In questa direzione.	Fino a ...
kōō·ē'	lä	ēn kōō·e'sta dēretsyō'ne	fē'nō ä ...

How long?	**Where (to)?**	**How far is it to ...?**
Quanto tempo?	Dove?	Che distanza c'è a ...?
kōō·än'tō tem'pō	dō've	ke dēstän'tsä tshe ä ...

Would you please show me that on the map?
Me lo indichi sulla carta, per favore.
me lō ēn'dēkē sōō'lä kär'tä, per fàvō're

Vehicles

camping trailer	(la) roulotte	rōōlōt'
car	(la) macchina	mä'kēnä
– delivery truck	(il) furgoncino	fōōrgōntshē'nō

– passenger car	(l') autovettura *f*	outōvetoō′rä
– station wagon	(la) macchina familiare	mä′kēnä fämēlyä′re
– truck	(l') autocarro *m*	outōkä′rō
bicycle	(la) bicicletta	bētshēkle′tä
moped	(il) motorino	mōtōrē′nō
motorcycle	(la) motocicletta	mōtōtshēkle′tä
motor scooter	(la) motoretta	mōtōre′tä
trailer	(il) rimorchio	rēmōr′kyō
vehicle	(il) veicolo	ve·ē′kōlō

Renting a Car

Where can I rent a car?
Dove posso noleggiare una
macchina?
dō′ve pō′sō nōlejä′re oō′nä
mä′kēnä

I'd like to rent a car.
Vorrei noleggiare una macchina.
vōre′ē nōlejä′re oō′nä mä′kēnä

... with chauffeur.
... con autista.
... kōn outē′stä

... for *2 (6)* people.
... per *due (sei)* persone.
... per doō′e (se′ē) persō′ne

... for *one day (one week, two weeks)*.
... per *un giorno (una settimana, due settimane)*.
... per oōn jōr′nō (oō′nä setēmä′nä, doō′e setēmä′ne)

How much will it cost?
Quanto costa?
koō·än′tō kō′stä

... including full coverage insurance?
... compresa l'assicurazione integrale?
... kōmpre′sä läsēkoōrätsyō′ne ēntegrä′le

Will I have to pay for the gasoline myself?
La benzina la devo pagare io?
lä bendzē′nä lä de′vō pägä′re ē′ō

How much will I have to deposit?
Quanto devo dare come cauzione?
koō·än′tō de′vō dä′re kō′me koutsyō′ne

***When (Where)* can I pick up the car?**
Quando (Dove) posso ritirare la macchina?
koō·än′dō (dō′ve) pō′sō rētērä′re lä mä′kēnä

Will somebody be there when I bring the car back?
Ci sarà qualcuno quando riporto la macchina?
tshē särä′ koō·älkoō′nō koō′än′dō rēpōr′tō lä mä′kēnä

On a Drive

I'm going (driving) to ...
Vado a ...
vä′dō ä ...

Are you going to ...?
Va a ...?
vä ä ...

To go by car (motorcycle, bicycle).
Andare in macchina (motocicletta, bicicletta)
ändä′re ēn mä′kēnä (mōtōtshēkle′tä, bētshē-
kle′tä)

Fast. – Slow.
Veloce. – Adagio.
velō′tshe – ädä′jō

access road	(la) strada d'accesso	strä′dä dätshe′sō
bike lane	(la) ciclopista	tshēklōpē′stä
bridge	(il) ponte	pōn′te
center strip	(la) linea di mezzo	lē′ne·ä dē med′zō
city limits sign	(il) cartello di	kärte′lō dē
	località	lōkälētä′
curve	(la) curva	koͦor′vä
detour	(la) deviazione	devyätsyō′ne
direction sign	(l') indicatore m stradale	ēndēkätō′re
		strädä′le
driver's license	(la) patente	päten′te
driveway	(l') entrata f	enträ′tä
exit	(l') uscita f	ooshē′tä
falling rocks	(la) caduta massi	kädoo′tä mä′se
highway	(l') autostrada f	outōsträ′dä
intersection	(l') incrocio m	ēnkrō′tshō
lane	(la) corsia	kōrse′ä
limited parking zone	(la) zona disco	dzō′nä dēs′kō
maximum speed	(la) velocità massima	velōtshētä′
		mä′sēmä
(mountain) pass	(il) passo	pä′sō
no parking	(il) divieto di	dēvye′tō dē
	parcheggio	pärke′jō
no passing	(il) divieto di sorpasso	dēvye′tō dē
		sōrpä′sō
no stopping	(il) divieto di sosta	dēvye′tō dē sō′stä
parking disc	(il) disco orario	dē′skō ōrär′yō
parking lot	(il) parcheggio	pärke′jō
parking meter	(il) parcometro	pärkō′metrō
path, footpath	(il) sentiero	sentye′rō
railroad crossing	(il) passaggio a livello	päsä′jō ä lēve′lō

registration	(l') immatricolazione f .	ēmätrēkōlätsyō'ne
right of way	(la) precedenza	pretsheden'tsä
road	(la) strada	strä'dä
– coastal road	(la) strada costiera	strä'dä kōstye'rä
– country road	(la) strada di campagna	strä'dä dē kämpä'nyä
– cross road	(la) strada trasversale	strä'dä träzversä'le
– main *road (street)*	(la) strada principale	strä'dä prēntshepä'le
– one way	(il) senso unico	sen'sō ōō'nēkō
road sign	(il) segnale stradale	senyä'le strädä'le
road under construction	(i) lavori in corso	lävō'rē ēn kōr'sō
route	(l') itinerario m	ētēnerär'yō
side wind	(il) vento di traverso	ven'tō dē träver'sō
slippery road	(la) strada sdrucciolevole	strä'dä zdrōōtshōle'vōle
speed limit	(il) limite di velocità	lē'mēte dē velōtshetä'
steep downgrade	(la) discesa	dēshe'sä
steep upgrade	(la) salita	sälē'tä
traffic	(il) traffico	trä'fēkō
traffic circle	(la) rotatoria	rōtätō'ryä
traffic light	(il) semaforo	semä'fōrō
traffic regulations	(il) codice della strada	kō'dētshe de'lä strä'dä
trip (journey)	(la) gita; (il) viaggio	jē'tä; vyä'jō
– brake	frenare	frenä're
– drive	guidare	gōō·ēdä're
– get in lane	inserirsi	ēnserēr'sē
– get out (of the car) .	uscire	ōōshē're
– hitch-hike	fare l'autostop	fä're loutōstōp'
– overtake, pass	sorpassare	sōrpäsä're
– park	parcheggiare	pärkejä're
– pass, cross	traversare	träversä're
– stop	fermare	fermä're
– turn (the car)	girare	jērä're
– turn (into a road) .	voltare	vōltä're
– turn off (a road)	cambiare strada	kämbyä're strä'dä
winding road	(la) serpentina	serpentē'nä
zebra crossing	(le) strisce pedonali	strē'she pedōnä'lē

Garage, Parking Lot

Where can I leave my car? (for safekeeping)

Dove posso lasciare la macchina? (in custodia)
dō've pō'sō läshä're lä mä'kēnä (ēn kōōstō'dyä)

Is there a garage near here?

C'è un garage qui vicino?
tshe ōōn gäräzh' kōō·e' vētshē'nō

Have you still got a vacant *garage (parking space)*?

C'è ancora *un posto libero (un box)*?
tshe änkō'rä ōōn pō'stō lē'berō (ōōn bōks)

Where can I leave the car?

Dove posso mettere la macchina?
dō've pō'sō me'tere lä mä'kēnä

Can I leave it here?

Posso metterla qui?
pō'sō me'terlä kōō·e'

Can I park here?

Posso parcheggiare qui?
pō'sō pärkejä're kōō·e'

Is this parking lot guarded?

Questo parcheggio è custodito?
kōō·e'stō pärke'jō e kōōstōdē'tō

Is there a space free?

C'è un posto libero?
tshe ōōn pō'stō lē'berō

How long can I park here?

Quanto tempo posso parcheggiare qui?
kōō·än'tō tem'pō pō'sō pärkejä're kōō·e'

How much does it cost to park here *overnight (until . . .)*?

Quanto costa il posteggio *per una notte (fino a . . .)*?
kōō·än'tō kō'stä ēl pōste'jō per ōō'nä nō'te (fē'nō ä . . .)

Is the garage open all night?

Il garage è aperto tutta la notte?
ēl gäräzh' e äper'tō tōō'tä lä nō'te

When do you close?

Quando chiude?
kōō·än'dō kyōō'de

I'll be leaving *this evening (tomorrow morning at eight)*.

Riparto *questa sera (domani mattina alle otto)*.
rēpär'tō kōō·e'stä se'rä (dōmä'nē mätē'nä ä'le ō'tō)

I'd like to take my car out of the garage.

Vorrei uscire con la mia macchina dall'autorimessa.
vōre'ē ōōshē're kōn lä mē'ä mä'kēnä däloutōrēme'sä

Gas Station, Car Repair

Where's the nearest gas station?
Dov'è il distributore di benzina più vicino?
dōve' ēl dēstrēboōotō're dē bendzē'nä pyoō
vētshē'nō

How far is it?
Quanto dista?
kōōän'tō dē'stä

Fifteen liters of *regular (high test)*, please.
Quindici litri di *benzina normale (Super)*, per favore.
kōō·ēn'dētshē lē'trē dē bendzē'nä nōrmä'le (dē soō'per) per fävō're

> *In Italy gasoline is heavily taxed, diesel fuel is somewhat cheaper. To compensate the foreign tourists for the expensive gasoline prices the government offers coupons for gasoline at a lower price than the normal tank price. These coupons are called "buoni-benzina" and can be bought at the ENIT (Ente Nazionale Industrie Turistiche) in most areas. If you are planning to drive or rent a car in Italy, try to make arrangements for the coupons in advance with your travel agent or automobile club.*

I'd like 20 liters of diesel, please.
Vorrei venti litri di diesel.
vōre'ē ven'tē lē'trē dē dē'zel

Fill her up, please.
Il pieno, per favore.
ēl pye'nō, per fävō're

I need *water (coolant)*.
Ho bisogno di acqua per il radiatore.
ō bēzō'nyō dē ä'koō·ä per ēl rädyätō're

A road map, please.
Una carta stradale,
per favore.
oō'nä kär'tä strädä'le,
per fävō're

Would you please fill up the radiator?
Può riempire il radiatore per favore?
poō·ō' rē·empē're ēl rädyätō're per fävō're

Would you please check the brake fluid?
Può controllare il liquido per i freni?
poō·ō' kōntrolä're ēl lē'koō·ēdō per ē fre'nē

car repair service	(il) servizio ripara-zioni auto	servē'tsyō rēpärä-tsyō'nē ou'tō
gasoline	(la) benzina	bendzē'nä
gas tank	(il) serbatoio	serbätō'yō
spark plug	(la) candela	kände'lä
distilled water	(l') acqua distillata	ä'koō·ä dēstēlä'tä

Oil

Please check the oil.
Controlli il livello dell'olio, per favore.
kontrō'lē ēl lēve'lō delō'lyō, per fàvō're

Please change the oil.
Cambi l'olio, per favore.
käm'bē lō'lyō, per fàvō're

Please fill up the oil tank.
Aggiunga dell'olio, per favore.
äjōōn'gä delō'lyō, per fàvō're

1¹/₂ liters of oil, please.
Un litro e mezzo di olio.
ōōn lē'tro e me'dzō dē ō'lyō

1 gallon = approx. 4 liters		1 liter = approx. 2 pints

gear oil	(l') olio *m* per il cambio	ō'lyō per ēl käm'byō
lubrication	(il) servizio lubrificazione	servē'tsyō lōōbrēfēkätsyō'ne
motor oil	(l') olio *m* motore	ō'lyō mōtō're
oil level	(il) livello dell'olio	lēve'lō delō'lyō

In Italy the hours of business of most gas stations is rather short. Generally they are from 9:30 or 10 am until between 12:30 and 1:30 pm. Be sure to find out the hours of the gas stations you will be needing. The gas stations along the autostrada are open all the time except for two to three hours between 2 and 5 am.

Tires

Can you repair this tire?
Può riparare questa gomma?
pōō·ō' rēpärä're kōō·e'stä gō'mä

One of my tires had a blow-out.
Ho bucato una gomma.
ō bōōkä'tō ōō'nä gō'mä

Can this inner tube be patched?
Può aggiustare questa camera d'aria?
pōō·ō' äjōōstä're kōō·e'stä kä'merä där'yä

Please change this tire.
Cambi questa gomma,
per favore.
käm'bē kōō·e'stä gō'mä,
per fàvō're

A new inner tube please.
Una nuova camera d'aria,
per favore.
ōō'nä nōō·ō'vä kä'merä där'yä,
per fàvō're

Would you please check the tire pressure?
Controlli la pressione delle gomme, per favore.
ōntrō'lē lä presyō'ne de'le gō'me, per fävōre

The front tires are 22.7, and the rear ones are 28.4.
Quelle davanti sono 1,6 (uno e sei) e quelle dietro sono 2 (due).
ōō·e'le dävän'tē sō'nō ōō'nō e se'ē e kōō·e'le dye'trō so'nō dōō'e

Tire Pressure Conversion Table					
lbs./sq. in.	atr	lbs./sq. in.	atr	lbs./sq. in.	atr
17.0	1,2	22.7	1,6	28.4	2,0
18.5	1,3	24.2	1,7	29.9	2,1
19.9	1,4	25.6	1,8	31.3	2,2
21.3	1,5	27.1	1,9	32.7	2,3
atr = atmosphere excess pressure					

blow-out	(la) foratura	fōrätōō'rä
inner tube	(la) camera d'aria	kä'merä där'yä
jack	(il) cric	krēk
puncture	(la) foratura	fōrätōō'rä
tires *(in general)*	(le) ruote	rōō·ō'te
tire	(la) gomma	gō'mä
tire change	(il) cambio di una	käm'byō dē ōō'nä
	gomma	gō'mä
tire pressure	(la) pressione delle	presyō'ne de'le
	gomme	gō'me
valve	(la) valvola	väl'vōlä
wheel	(la) ruota	rōō·ō'tä
– back wheel	(la) ruota di dietro	rōō·ō'tä dē dye'tro
– front wheel	(la) ruota davanti	rōō·ō'tä dävän'tē
– reserve wheel	(la) ruota di scorta	rōō·ō'tä dē skōr'tä

Car Wash

Please wash the *windshield (the windows)*.
Pulisca il *parabrezza (i vetri)*.
pōōlēs'kä ēl päräbre'dzä (ē ve'trē)

I'd like my car washed, please.
Vorrei far lavare la macchina.
vōre'ē fär lävä're lä mä'kēnä

Breakdown, Accident

I've (We've) had a breakdown.
Ho (abbiamo) avuto un guasto.
ō (äbyä'mō) ävoo'tō ōon goo·ä'stō

... is *broken (not working)*.
... è guasto (non funziona).
... e goo·ä'stō (nōn foontsyō'nä)

I've had an accident.
Ho avuto un incidente.
ō ävoo'tō ōon ēntshēden'te

May I use your phone?
Posso telefonare?
pō'sō telefōnä're

Would you please call the police?
Può chiamare la polizia, per favore.
poo·ō' kyämä're lä pōlētsē'ä, per fävō're

Get a doctor!
Chiami un medico!
kyä'mē ōon me'dēkō

Please call an ambulance, quickly.
Per piacere, chiami un'autoambulanza, presto.
per pyätshe're, kyä'mē ōon outō·ämboolän'tsä, pre'stō

Please help me!
Per piacere, mi aiuti!
per pyätshe're, mē äyoo'tē

I need bandages.
Ho bisogno di garze.
ō bēzō'nyō dē gär'tse

Could you lend me ...?
Potrebbe imprestarmi...?
pōtre'be ēmprestär'mē ...

Could you ...?
Potrebbe ....?
pōtre'be ...

– give me a lift?
– darmi un passaggio?
– där'mē ōon päsä'jō

– tow my car?
– rimorchiare la mia macchina?
– rēmōrkyä're lä mē'ä mä'kēnä

– get me a *mechanic (a tow truck)*?
– mandarmi un *meccanico (rimorchiatore)*?
– mändär'mē ōon mekä'nēkō (rēmōrkyätō're)

– look after the injured?
– curarsi dei feriti?
– koorär'sē de'ē ferē'tē

Where is there a *service station (repair shop)*?
Dov'è un' *officina riparazioni-auto*?
dōve' ōonōfētshē'nä rēpärätsyō'nē ou'tō

Would you please give me your name and address?
Potrebbe darmi il Suo nome ed indirizzo?
pōtre'be där'mē ēl soo'ō nō'me ed ēndērē'tsō

It's your fault.
E' colpa Sua.
e kōl′pä sŏŏ′ä

You've damaged ...
Lei ha danneggiato ...
le′ē ä däneja′tō ...

I had the right of way.
Avevo la precedenza.
äve′vō lä pretsheden′tsä

... is (badly) injured.
... e ferito(-a) (gravemente).
... e ferē′tō(-ä) (grävemen′te)

Nobody's hurt.
Nessuno è ferito.
nesŏŏ′nō e ferē′tō

Thanks very much for your help.
Tante grazie per il Suo aiuto.
tän′te grä′tsye per ēl sŏŏ′ō äyŏŏ′tō

Will you be my witness?
Può farmi da testimone?
pŏŏ·ō′ fär′mē dä testēmō′ne

Where is your car insured?
Dov'è assicurata la Sua macchina?
dōve′ äsēkŏŏrä′tä lä sŏŏ′ä mä′kēnä

accident	(l') incidente *m*	ēntshēden′te
ambulance	(l') ambulanza *f*	ämbŏŏlän′tsä
bandages	(le) bende, garze	ben′de, gär′tse
body and fender damage	(il) danno alla carrozzeria e al parafango	dä′nō ä′lä kärōtserē′ä e äl päräfän′gō
breakdown	(il) guasto	gŏŏ·ä′stō
damage	(il) danno	dä′nō
danger!	Pericolo!	perē′kōlō
dealership garage	(l') officina *f* concessionaria	ōfētshē′nä kōntshesyōnär′yä
fire department	(i) vigili del fuoco	vē′jēle del fŏŏ·ō′kō
first aid station	(il) posto di pronto soccorso	pō′stō dē prōn′tō sōkōr′sō
head-on collision	(lo) scontro frontale	skōn′trō frōntä′le
help	(l') aiuto *m*	äyŏŏ′tō
hospital	(l') ospedale *m*	ōspedä′le
impact	(l') urto *m*	ŏŏr′tō
injury	(la) ferita	ferē′tä
insurance	(l') assicurazione *f*	äsēkŏŏrätsyō′ne
mechanic	(il) meccanico	mekä′nēkō
police	(la) polizia (stradale)	pōlētsē′ä (strädä′le)
rear-end collision	(il) tamponamento	tämpōnämen′tō
service station	(l') officina *f* per auto	ōfētshē′nä per ou′tō
towing service	(il) servizio traino-auto	servē′tsyō trī′nō-ou′tō
tow line	(il) cavo di rimorchio	kä′vo dē rēmōr′kyo
tow truck	(il) carro attrezzi	kä′rō ätre′tsē

Repair Workshop

Where's the nearest (dealership) garage for . . . cars?
Dov'è l'officina di riparazioni (concessionaria . . .) più vicina?
dōve' lōfētshē'nä dē rēpärätsyō'nē (kōntshesyōnär'ya) pyōō vētshē'nä

. . . isn't working right.	**. . . is out of order (isn't working).**
. . . non è a posto.	. . . non funziona.
. . . nōn e ä pō'stō	. . . nōn fōōntsyō'nä

Can you fix it?
Può ripararlo?
pōō·ō' rēpärär'lō

Where can I have this fixed?
Chi può ripararlo?
kē pōō·o' rēpärär'lō

Would you please check . . .
Per favore, controlli . . .
per fävō're, kontrō'lē . . .

Would you please give me . . .
Per favore, mi dia . . .
per fävō're, mē dē'ä . . .

Would you please fix this.
Me lo ripari, per favore.
me lō rēpä'rē, per fävō're

Have you got manufacturer's spare parts for . . .?
Ha i pezzi di ricambio originali per . . .?
ä ē pe'tsē dē rēkäm'byō ōrējēnä'lē per . . .

How soon can you get the spare parts?
Quando riceverà i pezzi di ricambio?
kōō·än'dō rētsheverä' ē pe'tsē dē rēkäm'byō

I need a new . . .
Ho bisogno di *un nuovo (una nuova)* . . .
ō bēzō'nyō dē ōōn nōō·ō'vō (ōō'nä nōō·ō'vä) . . .

Can I still drive it?
Va così la macchina?
vä kōsē' lä mä'kēnä

Just do the essentials, please.
Faccia solo le riparazioni più urgenti.
fä'tshä sō'lō le rēpärätsyō'nē pyōō ōōrgen'tē

When will it be ready?	**How much *does (will)* it cost?**
Quando sarà pronta?	Quanto costa?
kōō·än'dō särä' prōn'tä	kōō·än'tō kō'stä

Car Parts, Repairs

accelerator	(l') acceleratore *m*	ätshelerätō're
air filter	(il) filtro d'aria	fēl'trō där'yä
anti-freeze	(l') anticongelante *m*	äntēkōnjelän'te
automatic transmission	(il) cambio automatico	käm'byō outōmä'tēkō
axle	(l') asse *f*	ä'se
backfire	(l') accensione *f* a vuoto	ätshensyō'ne ä vŏŏ·ō'tō
ball bearings	(i) cuscinetti a sfere	kŏŏshēne'tē ä sfe're
battery	(la) batteria	bäterē'ä
blinker	(il) lampeggiatore	lämpejätō're
body	(la) carrozzeria	kärōtserē'ä
bolt	(il) bullone	bŏŏlō'ne
– nut	(il) dado	dä'dō
brake drum	(il) tamburo di freno	tämbŏŏ'rō dē fre'nō
brake lights	(i) fanali d'arresto	fänä'lē däre'stō
brake lining	(la) guarnizione dei freni	gŏŏ·ärnētsyō'ne de'ē fre'nē
brake pedal	(il) pedale del freno	pedä'le del fre'nō
brakes	(i) freni	fre'nē
– disc brake	(il) freno a disco	fre'nō ä dē'skō
– foot brake	(il) freno a pedale	fre'nō ä pedä'le
– hand brake	(il) freno a mano	fre'nō ä mä'nō
bulb	(la) lampadina	lämpädē'nä
bumper	(il) paraurti	pärä·ŏŏr'tē
cable	(il) cavo	kä'vō
camshaft	(l') albero *m* a camme	äl'berō ä kä'me

The battery *has run down (needs charging)*.
La batteria *è scarica (bisogna caricarla)*.
lä bäterē'ä e skä'rēkä (bēzōnya kärēkär'lä)

The brakes aren't working right.
I freni non sono a posto.
ē fre'nē nōn sō'nō ä pō'stō

They're *slack (too tight)*.
Non fanno presa (Sono troppo stretti).
nōn fä'nō pre'sä (sō'nō trō'pō stre'tē)

carburetor	(il) carburatore	kärbōōrätō're
carburetor jet ...	(l') ugello *m*	ōōje'lō
car door	(la) portiera	pōrtye'rä
car keys	(le) chiavi della macchina	kyä've de'lä mä'kēnä
chain	(la) catena	käte'nä
– snow chains ...	(le) catene da neve	käte'ne dä ne've
chassis	(il) telaio	telä'yō
clutch	(la) frizione	frētsyō'ne
– clutch pedal ...	(il) pedale della frizione	pedä'le de'lä frētsyō'ne
compression	(la) compressione	kōmpresyō'ne
condenser	(il) condensatore	kōndensätō're
connecting rod ..	(la) biella	bye'lä
– connecting rod bearing	(i) supporti della biella	sōōpōr'tē de'lä bye'lä
contact	(il) contatto	kōntä'tō
crankshaft	(la) manopola	mänō'pōlä
cylinder	(il) cilindro	tshēlēn'drō
– cylinder head ..	(la) testata del cilindro	testä'tä del tshēlēn'drō
diesel nozzle	(il) polverizzatore	pōlverēdzätō're
differential	(il) differenziale	dēferentsyä'le
dip stick	(la) bacchetta misura-olio	bäke'tä mēzōō'rä ōl'yō
distributor	(lo) spinterogeno	spēnterō'jenō
door lock	(la) serratura della portiera	serätōō'rä de'lä pōrtye'rä
drive shaft	(l') albero *m* motore	äl'berō mōtō're
dynamo	(la) dinamo	dē'nämō
exhaust	(lo) scappamento	skäpämen'tō

The dynamo isn't charging.
La dinamo non si carica.
lä dē'nämō non sē kä'rēkä

It won't stay in ... gear.
La ... marcia non rimane innestata.
lä ... mär'tshä nōn rēmä'ne ēnestä'tä

The gearshift needs to be checked over.
Il cambio delle marce deve essere controllato.
ēl käm'byō de'le mär'tshe de've e'sere kōntrōlä'tō

There's oil leaking out of the gear-box.
Il cambio perde olio.
ēl käm'byō per'de ō'lyō

fan	(il) ventilatore	ventēlätō're
fan belt	(la) cinghia	tshēn'gē·ä
fender	(il) parafango	päräfän'gō
fire extinguisher	(l') estintore *m*	estēntō're
fuel injector	(l') iniettore-combustibile *m*	ēnyetō're-kōmbōōstē'bēle
fuel lines	(la) conduttura della benzina	kōndōōtōō'rä de'lä bendzē'nä
fuel pump	(la) pompa della benzina	pōm'pä de'lä bendzē'nä
fuse	(il) fusibile	fōōzē'bēle
gas/gasoline	(la) benzina	bendzē'nä
gasket	(la) guarnizione	gōō·ärnētsyō'ne
gear	(la) marcia	mär'tshä
– neutral	in folle	ēn fō'le
– reverse	(la) retromarcia	retrōmär'tshä
– to put it in gear	innestare la marcia	ēnestä're lä mär'tshä
gear box	(il) cambio	käm'byō
gear lever	(la) leva del cambio	le'vä del käm'byō
gearshift	(il) cambio	käm'byō
handle	(la) maniglia	mänēl'yä
headlight	(il) faro	fä'rō
– dimmed headlights	(la) luce anabbagliante	lōō'tshe änäbälyän'te
– high beam	(i) fari abbaglianti	fä'rē äbälyän'tē
– parking lights	(le) luci di posizione	lōō'tshē dē pōzētsyō'ne
– rear lights	(le) luci posteriori	lōō'tshē pōsteryō'rē
heating system	(il) riscaldamento	rēskäldämen'tō
hood	(il) cofano di motore	kō'fänō dē mōtō're
horn	(il) clacson	kläk'sōn
hub	(il) mozzo di ruota	mō'tsō dē rōō·ō'tä
hub cap	(la) calotta	kälō'tä

The heating doesn't work.
Il riscaldamento non funziona.
ēl rēskäldämen'to nōn fōōntsyō'nä

The radiator has sprung a leak.
Il radiatore perde acqua.
ēl rädyätō're per'de ä'kōō·ä

The clutch *slips (won't disengage)*.
La frizione *slitta (non separa)*.
lä frētsyō'ne zlē'tä (nōn sepä'rä)

ignition	(l') accensione *f*	ätshensyō'ne
ignition cable	(il) cavo d'accensione . .	kä'vō dätshensyō'ne
– **ignition key**	(la) chiavetta d'accensione	kyäve'tä dätshensyō'ne
– **ignition lock**	(la) serratura d'accensione	serätoo'rä dätshensyō'ne
indicator light	(la) spia	spē'ä
insulation	(l') isolante *m*	ēzōlän'te
interrupter	(l') interruttore *m*	ēnteroōtō're
lamp	(la) lampadina	lämpädē'nä
license plate	(la) targa	tär'gä
lighting system	(l') impianto *m* elettrico	ēmpyän'tō ele'trēkō
lubricant	(il) lubrificante	loōbrēfēkän'te
mileage indicator	(il) contachilometri	kōntäkēlō'metrē
motor	(il) motore	mōtō're
– **diesel motor**	(il) motore a diesel	mōtō're ä dē'zel
– **rear motor**	(il) motore a trazione posteriore	mōtō're ä trätsyō'ne pōsteryō're
– **two-stroke motor** . .	(il) motore a due tempi	mōtō're ä doō'e tem'pē
nationality plate	(la) targa della nazionalità	tär'gä de'lä nätsyōnälētä'
oil filter	(il) filtro dell'olio	fēl'trō delō'lyō
oil pump	(la) pompa dell'olio . . .	pōm'pä delō'lyō
paint job	(la) vernice	vernē'tshe
pedal	(il) pedale	pedä'le
piston	(il) pistone	pēstō'ne
– **piston ring**	(la) fascia elastica	fä'shä elä'stēkä
pipe	(la) cannuccia	känoo'tshä
power steering	(il) servo sterzo	ser'vō ster'tsō
radiator	(il) radiatore	rädyätō're
– **radiator grill**	(la) mascherina del radiatore	mäskerē'nä del rädyätō're

The motor lacks power.	– **is overheating.**	– **misses.**
Il motore non tira.	si riscalda troppo.	va a strappi.
ēl mōtō're nōn tē'rä	sē rēskäl'dä trō'pō	vä ä strä'pē

– knocks.	– suddenly stalls.	
batte in testa.	interrompe improvvisamente.	
bä′te ēn te′stä	ēnterōm′pe ēmprōvēzämen′te	

rear view mirror	(lo) specchietto	spekye′tō
	retrovisore	retrōvēzō′re
repair	riparare·········	rēpärä′re
reserve fuel can	(la) tanica di riserva···	tä′nēkä de rēser′vä
roof	(il) tetto	te′tō
screw	(la) vite ·········	vē′te
seat belt	(la) cintura di sicurezza	tshēntoo′rä dē
		sēkoore′tsä
seat	(il) sedile ··········	sedē′le
– back seat	(il) sedile posteriore ···	sedē′le pōsteryō′re
– driver's seat	(il) sedile dell'autista···	sedē′le deloutē′stä
– front seat	(il) sedile anteriore	sedē′le änteryō′re
– front passenger seat	(il) sedile del passeggero	sedē′le del päse-
		je′rō
shock absorber	(l') ammortizzatore *m* ·	ämōrtēdzätō′re
short circuit	(il) corto circuito·····	kōr′tō tshērkoo·ē′tō
sliding (sun) roof	(il) tetto apribile ······	te′tō äprē′bēle
solder	saldare	säldä′re
spare part	(il) pezzo di ricambio··	pe′tsō dē
		rēkäm′byō
spare wheel	(la) ruota di scorta ····	roo·ō′tä dē skōr′tä
spark	(la) scintilla	shēntē′lä
spark plug	(la) candela·········	kände′lä
speedometer	(il) tachimetro ········	täkē′metrō
spoke	(la) razza.............	rä′tsä
spring	(la) molla.............	mō′lä
starter	(lo) starter,	stär′ter,
	(il) motorino d'avvia-	mōtōrē′nō dävyä-
	mento	men′tō

The windshield wiper *smears (is broken off)*.

Il tergicristallo *sporca (è guasto)*.

ēl terjēkrēstä′lō spōr′kä (e goo·ä′stō)

This screw needs *tightening (loosening)*.

Bisogna *stringere (allentare)* questa vite.

bēzō′nyä strēn′jere (älentä′re) koo·e′stä vē′te

The fuse has blown.

Il fusibile è saltato.
ēl foozē'bēle e sältä'tō

steering	(lo) sterzo	ster'tsō
– steering wheel	(il) volante	vōlän'te
switch	(l') interruttore *m*	ēnterootō're
thermostat	(il) termostato	termō'stätō
(screw) thread	(la) madrevite	mädrevē'te
top	(il) tetto	te'tō
transmission	(il) cambio	käm'byō
trunk	(il) portabagagli	pōrtäbägäl'yē
tube	(il) tubo	too'bō
valve	(la) valvola	väl'vōlä
warning triangle	(il) triangolo	trē·än'gōlō
washer	(la) rondella	rōnde'lä
wheel	(la) ruota	roo·ō'tä
windshield	(il) parabrezza	päräbre'dzä
windshield washer	(l') impianto *m* lava-cristallo	ēmpyän'tō lävä-krēstä'lō
windshield wiper	(il) tergicristallo	terjēkrēstä'lō

Would you please straighten out my bumper?

Può mettere a posto il paraurti, per favore.
poo·ō' me'tere ä pō'stō ēl pärä·oor'tē, per fävō're

Would you please *check (clean)* the carburetor?

Per favore, *metta a punto (pulisca)* il carburatore.
per fävō're, me'tä ä poon'tō (poolē'skä) ēl kärboorätō're

Would you please change the spark plugs?

Cambi le candele, per favore.
käm'bē le kände'le, per fävō're

Can you loan me . . . ?

Può prestarmi . . . ?
pōō·ō' prestär'mē . . .

I need . . .

Ho bisogno di . . .
ō bēzō'nyō dē . . .

air pump	(la) pompa dell'aria	pōm'pä delär'yä
bolt	(la) vite	vē'te
– nut	(la) madrevite	mädrevē'te
– bolt and nut	(il) bullone	bōōlō'ne
cable	(il) cavo	kä'vō
chisel	(lo) scalpello	skälpe'lō
cloth	(lo) strofinaccio	strōfēnä'tshō
drill	(il) trapano	trä'pänō
file	(la) lima	lē'mä
funnel	(l') imbuto *m*	ēmbōō'tō
hammer	(il) martello	märte'lō
inspection light	(la) lampada di collaudo	läm'pädä dē kōlou'dō
jack	(il) cric	krēk
pincers	(le) tenaglie	tenä'lye
pliers	(le) pinze	pēn'tse
rag	(lo) straccio	strä'tshō
sandpaper	(la) carta vetrata	kär'tä veträ'tä
screw	(la) vite	vē'te
screwdriver	(il) cacciavite	kätshävē'te
socket wrench	(la) chiave fissa a tubo	kyä've fē'sä ä tōō'bō
string	(lo) spago	spä'gō
tool	(l') utensile *m*	ōōtensē'le
– tool box (kit)	(la) cassa degli utensili	kä'sä de'lyē ōōtensē'lē
wire	(il) filo metallico	fē'lō metä'lēkō
– a piece of wire	un pezzo di filo metallico	ōōn pe'tsō dē fē'lō metä'lēkō
wrench	(la) chiave (inglese/ per viti)	kyä've (ēngle'se/ per vē'tē)

TRAFFIC SIGNS

1 DANGER Pericolo · 2 YIELD RIGHT OF WAY Dare precedenza · 3 INTERSECTION Incrocio · 4 DO NOT ENTER Divieto di accesso · 5 NO VEHICLE ALLOWED Divieto di transito nei due sensi · 6 ONE WAY STREET Senso unico · 7 SPEED LIMIT *(kilometers)* Limitazione di velocità *(chilometri)* · 8 PRIORITY ROAD Inizio diritto di precedenza · 9 PRIORITY CROSSING Incrocio con una strada senza diritto di precedenza · 10 END OF PRIORITY ROAD Fine diritto di precedenza · 11 DETOUR (TRUCKS) Deviazione per autocarri · 12 NO STOPPING Divieto di sosta · 13 RAILROAD CROSSING Passaggio a livello con barriere · 14 TWO WAY TRAFFIC Zona di doppio senso di circolazione su una carreggiata a senso unico · 15 NO PASSING Divieto di sorpasso · 16 CUSTOMS Dogana

Road signs are color and shape-coded. Triangular signs with a red rim are *warning signs*; round blue signs are *regulatory signs*; round signs with a red rim are *prohibit movement signs*; rectangular green signs with white letters are *destination signs* on highways.

ON THE BUS

Where is the next bus stop?
Dov'è la prossima fermata dell'autobus?
dōve' lä prō'sēmä fermä'tä delou'tōbōōs

Where do the buses to ... stop?
Dove si fermano gli autobus per ...?
dō've sē fer'mänō lyē ou'tōbōōs per ...

Is that far?
E' lontano?
e lōntä'nō

When does *a (the first/last)* bus leave for ...?
A che ora parte *un (il primo/l'ultimo)* autobus per ...?
ä ke ō'rä pär'te ōōn (ēl prē'mō/lōōl'tēmō) ou'tōbōōs per ...

Which bus goes to ...?
Quale autobus va a ...?
kōō·ä'le ou'tōbōōs vä ä ...

Where does the bus go?
Dove va l'autobus?
dō've vä lou'tōbōōs

Is there a bus (Does this bus go) to ...?
C'è un autobus che (Questo autobus) va a ...?
tshe ōōn ou'tōbōōs ke (kōō·e'stō ou'tōbōōs) vä ä ...

When do we get to ...?
Quando arriviamo a ...?
kōō·än'dō ärēvyä'mō ä ...

Do I have to change buses for ...?
Devo cambiare per ...?
de'vō kämbyä're per ...

Where do I have to change?
Dove devo cambiare?
dō've de'vō kämbyä're

bus	(l') autobus *m*	ou'tōbōōs
bus terminal	(la) stazione auto-corriera	stätsyō'ne ou'tō-kōrye'rä
conductor	(il) bigliettaio	bēlyetä'yō
direction	(la) direzione	dēretsyō'ne
driver	(l') autista *m*	outē'stä
last stop	(il) capolinea	käpōlē'ne·ä
stop	(la) fermata	fermä'tä
ticket	(il) biglietto	bēlye'tō

In Rome and a number of larger Italian cities it is no longer possible to purchase tickets on the bus. The tickets, (biglietti) must be purchased in advance, either at the larger bus stops or in stationery stores ("cartoleria"). They are often cheaper when bought in packs of ten.

BY TRAIN

At the Station

Where is the *station (main station)*?
Dov'è la stazione? (stazione centrale)?
dove' lä stätsyō′ne (stätsyō′ne tshenträ′le)

Where is (are) ...?
Dov'è (dove sono) ...?
dōve′ (dō′ve sō′nō) ...

the first aid station ..	(il) pronto soccorso ...	prōn′tō sōkōr′sō
the information office	(le) informazioni	ēnfōrmätsyō′nē
the money exchange .	(il) cambio	käm′byō
the rest room	(il) gabinetto	gäbēne′tō
the restaurant	(il) ristorante	rēstōrän′te
the ticket window ...	(la) biglietteria	bēlyeterē′ä
a time table	(l') orario	ōrär′yō
the waiting room	(la) sala d'aspetto	sä′lä däspe′tō

Time Table

arrival/departure	arrivi/partenze........	ärē′vē/pärten′tse
change trains	cambiar treno	kämbyär′ tre′nō
connection..........	(la) coincidenza	kō·ēntshēden′tsä
couchette sleeper	(la) carrozza cuccette ..	kärō′tsä kōōtshe′te
dining car	(il) vagone ristorante ..	vägō′ne rēstōrän′te
express train	(il) direttissimo	dēretē′sēmō
fast train	(il) diretto	dēre′tō
long distance express	(il) rapido	rä′pēdō
motorail service	(la) littorina	lētōrē′nä
platform	(il) binario /	bēnär′yō /
	(il) marciapiede	märtshäpye′de
rail car	(l') automotrice *f*	outōmōtrē′tshe
sleeper/sleeping car ..	(il) vagone letto	vägō′ne le′tō
suburban train	(il) treno suburbano ...	tre′nō suburbano
		sōōbōōrbä′nō

*A couchette car provides overnight travelers with a simple bench and
blanket to stretch out during the night. A sleeping car contains little
bedrooms complete with private washing facilities.*

upplemental fare ...	(il) supplemento	sooplemen'tō
ystem time table ...	(l') orario *m* ferroviario	ōrär'yō ferōvyär'yō
rough car	(la) carrozza diretta ...	kärō'tsä dēre'tä

Information

Vhen is there a *local (express)* train to ...?
uando parte un *accelerato (direttissimo)* per ...?
ōō·än'dō pär'te ōōn ätshelerä'tō (dēretē'sēmō) per ...

here is the train to ...?
ov'è il treno per ...?
ōve' ēl tre'nō per ...

Is this the train to ...?
E' questo il treno per ...?
e kōō·e'stō ēl tre'nō per ...

oes this train go by way of ...?
uesto treno passa per ...?
ōō·e'stō tre'nō pä'sä per ...

Does this train stop in ...?
Il treno si ferma a ...?
ēl tre'nō sē fer'mä ä ...

the train from ... late?
in ritardo il treno da ...?
ēn rētär'dō ēl tre'nō dä ...

How late?
Di quanto?
dē kōō·än'tō

an we make a connection to ...?
è la coincidenza per ...?
he lä kō·ēntshēden'tsä per ...

When does it get to ...?
Quando arriva a ...?
kōō·än'dō ärē'vä ä ...

o we have to change trains?
obbiamo cambiare treno?
ōbyä'mō kämbyä're tre'nō

Where?
Dove?
dō've

there a *dining car (Are there sleepers)* on the train?
treno ha un *vagone ristorante (vagone letto)?*
tre'nō ä ōōn vägō'ne rēstōrän'te (vägō'ne le'tō)

'an I interrupt the trip in ...?
osso interrompere il viaggio a ...?
ō'sō ēnterōm'pere ēl vyä'jō ä ...

Vhat platform does the train from ... come in on?
u quale binario arriva il treno da ...?
ōō kōō·ä'le bēnär'yō ärē'vä ēl tre'nō dä ...

Vhat platform does the train for ... leave from?
a quale binario parte il treno per ...?
ä kōō·ä'le bēnär'yō pär'te ēl tre'nō per ...

Tickets

Two *one way (round trip)* tickets to . . ., please.
Due biglietti *di andata (di andata e ritorno)* per . . ., per favore.
dōō'e bēlye'tē dē ändä'tä (dē ändä'tä e rētōr'nō) per . . . per fävō're

I'd like to reserve a seat on the twelve o'clock train to . . .
Vorrei prenotare un posto sul treno delle dodici per . . .
vōre'ē prenōtä're ōōn pō'stō sōōl tre'nō de'le dō'dētshē per . . .

How long is the ticket valid?	**– first class.**
Fino a quando è valido il biglietto?	di prima classe
fē'nō ä kōō·än'dō e vä'lēdō ēl bēlye'tō	dē prē'mä klä'se

I'd like to interrupt the trip in . . .	**– second class.**
Vorrei interrompere il viaggio a . . .	di seconda classe
vōre'ē ēnterōm'pere ēl vyä'jō ä . . .	dē sekōn'dä klä'se

I'd like to reserve . . .	**Please reserve two seats.**
Vorrei prenotare . . .	Per favore, mi riservi due posti.
vōre'ē prenōtä're . . .	per fävō're, mē rēzer've dōō'e pō'stē

How much is the fare to . . .?
Quanto costa il biglietto per . . .?
kōō·än'tō kō'stä ēl bēlye'tō per . . .

fare	(la) tariffa	tärē'fä
group fare ticket	(il) biglietto per comitiva	bēlye'tō per kōmētē'vä
half fare	(il) biglietto per ragazzi	bēlye'tō per rägät'sē
one-day round-trip	andata e ritorno in giornata	ändä'tä e rētōr'nō ēn jōrnä'tä
seat reservation	(la) prenotazione posti .	prenōtätsyō'ne pō'stē
sleeper reservation . .	(la) prenotazione vagoni letto	prenōtätsyō'ne vägō'nē le'tō
supplemental fare ticket	(il) supplemento	sōōplemen'tō
ticket	(il) biglietto	bēlye'tō
– reduced fare ticket	(il) biglietto tariffa ridotta	bēlye'tō tärē'fä rēdō'tä

Baggage

In European countries, you can check your bag with the railroad, just as you do with an airline, and then pick it up at your destination. If you are checking your baggage to be forwarded, you should go to the "accettazione bagagli". If you are simply checking your luggage within the station, go to the "consegna" or the "deposito bagagli".

I'd like to ...   **... send this luggage on to ...**
Vorrei ...   ... spedire questo bagaglio a ...
vōre′ē ...   ... spedē′re kōō·e′stō bägä′lyō ä ...

– leave this luggage here.
 lasciare qui questo bagaglio.
 lashä′re kōō·ē′ kōō·e′stō bägä′lyō

– insure (claim) my luggage.   **Here's my claim check.**
 assicurare (ritirare) il mio bagaglio.   Ecco lo scontrino.
 äsēkōōrä′re (rētērä′re) ēl mē′ō bägä′lyō   e′kō lō skōntrē′nō

There are two suitcases and a traveling bag.
 Sono due valige e una borsa.
 sō′nō dōō′e välē′je e ōō′nä bōr′sä

Will my baggage be on the same train?   **When does it get to ...?**
 Il bagaglio viaggia con lo stesso treno?   Quando sarà a ...?
 ēl bägä′lyō vyä′jä kōn lō ste′sō tre′nō   kōō·än′dō särä′ ä ...

These aren't mine.   **One *suitcase (bag)* is missing.**
 Queste cose non sono mie.   Manca una *valigia (borsa)*.
 kōō·e′ste kō′ze nōn sō′nō mē′e   män′kä ōō′nä välē′jä (bōr′sä)

baggage, luggage	(il) bagaglio	bägä′lyō
baggage check area ..	(l') accettazione *f*	ätshetätsyō′ne
	bagagli	bägä′lyē
baggage claim area ..	(la) consegna bagagli	kōnse′nyä bägä′lyē
baggage deposit area	(il) deposito bagagli .	depō′sētō bägä′lyē
claim check	(lo) scontrino	skōntrē′nō
hand luggage	(il) bagaglio a mano .	bägä′lyō ä mä′nō
luggage forwarding	(la) spedizione bagagli	spedētsyō′ne
office		bägä′lyē
luggage locker	(gli) armadietti bagagli	ärmädye′tē
	....	bägä′lyē

Porter

porter . . . .   (il) facchino . . . .   fäkē'nō

Please bring this *luggage (suitcase)* . . .
Per favore, porti *questo bagaglio (questa valigia)* . . .
per fävō're, pōr'tē kōō·e'stō bägä'lyō (kōō·e'stä välē'jä) . . .

– **to the . . . train.**	– **to Platform 2 . . .**	– **to the exit.**
al treno per . . .	al marciapiede due.	all'uscita.
äl tre'nō per . . .	äl märtshäpye'de dōō'e	älōōshē'tä

– **to the baggage check area.**	– **to a taxi.**	– **to the . . . bus.**
al deposito.	ai tassi.	all'autobus per . . .
äl depō'zētō	ī täsē'	älou'tōbōōs per . . .

How much does that cost?
Quanto costa?
kōō·än'tō kōs'tä

Italian porters generally charge a flat fee per piece of luggage with extra charges for greater distances. It is a wise idea to clarify the price in advance, to which one can then add a small tip.

On the Platform

Is this the train *to (from)* . . .?	**What time does the train arrive?**
E' questo il treno *per (da)*. . .?	A che ora arriva il treno?
e kōō·e'stō ēl tre'nō per (dä) . . .	ä ke ō'rä ärē'vä ēl tre'nō

Where is . . .?	– **first class?**	– **the through car to . . .?**
Dov'è . . .?	la prima classe?	la carrozza diretta per . . .?
dōve' . . .	lä prē'mä klä'se	lä kärō'tsä dēre'tä per . . .

European express trains frequently get reassembled at major stations with different cars going to different destinations. Make sure before you get aboard that your car will take you where you want to go.

– **the couchette car?**	– **the sleeping car?**	– **the dining car?**
la carrozza cuccette?	il vagone letto?	il vagone ristorante?
lä kärō'tsä kōōtshe'te	ēl vägō'ne le'tō	ēl vägō'ne rēstōrän'te

– the luggage car?	– car number ...?
il bagagliaio?	la carrozza numero ...?
ēl bägälyä'yō	lä kärō'tsä nōō'merō ...

There.	**Up front.**	**In the middle.**	**At the rear.**
Là.	In testa.	Nel mezzo.	In coda.
lä	ēn te'stä	nel me'dzō	ēn kō'dä

CAPOSTAZIONE	USCITA	INFORMAZIONI
käpōstätsyō'ne	ōōshē'tä	ēnfōrmätsyō'nē
Station Master	**Exit**	**Information**

AI BINARI	RINFRESCHI	GIORNALI
ī bēnä'rē	rēnfres'kē	jōrnä'lē
To Trains	**Refreshments**	**Newspapers**

PRONTO SOCCORSO	ACQUA POTABILE
prōn'tō sōkōr'sō	ä'kōō·ä pōtä'bēle
First Aid	**Drinking Water**

GABINETTI	SIGNORI	SIGNORE
gäbēne'tē	sēnyō'rē	sēnyō're
Rest Rooms	**Gentlemen**	**Ladies**

On the Train

Is this seat taken?	**That's my seat.**
E' libero questo posto?	Questo è il mio posto.
e lē'berō kōō·e'stō pō'stō	kōō·e'stō e ēl mē'ō pō'stō

Mind if I *open (close)* the window?
Permette che *apra (chiuda)* il finestrino?
perme'te ke ä'prä (kyōō'dä) ēl fēnestrē'nō

Many trains do have restaurant cars and vendors selling snacks,
however, this is not always the case. It is a good idea, especially for
longer trips, to do some shopping in the many little food shops offering
anything from fruits, sausages and mineral water to spaghetti and
pizza "to go" which is called "per andare via".

Would you mind if we changed places?
Possiamo cambiare i posti?
pōsyä′mō kämbyä′re ē pō′stē

*Tickets, please.
Biglietti, per favore.
bēlye′tē, per fävō′re

I don't like riding backwards.
Non posso star seduto(a) nella direzione contromarcia.
nōn pō′sō stär sedoo′tō(-ä) ne′lä dēretsyō′ne kōntrōmär′tshä

I'd like to pay *the excess fare (the supplement/now).*
Vorrei *pagare il supplemento (fare adesso il biglietto).*
vōre′ē pägä′re ēl sooplemen′tō (fä′re äde′sō ēl bēlye′tō)

How many stations before . . .?
Quante stazioni ci sono fino a . . .?
koo·än′te stätsyō′nē tshē sō′nō fē′nō ä . . .

Where are we now?
Dove siamo adesso?
dō′ve syä′mō äde′sō

Will we get to . . . on time?
Arriviamo in orario a . . .?
ärēvyä′mō ēn ōrär′yō ä . . .

How long do we stop here?
Quanto tempo stiamo fermi qui?
koo·än′tō tem′pō styä′mō fer′mē koo·ē′

Will I make it on time to change trains for . . .?
Faccio in tempo a prendere il treno per . . .?
fä′tshō ēn tem′pō ä pren′dere ēl tre′nō per . . .

*All change, please!
Scendere tutti!
shen′dere too′tē

*Passengers for . . . change at . . .
I viaggiatori diretti a . . . cambiano a . . .
ē vyäjätō′rē dēre′tē ä . . . käm′byänō ä . . .

*Passengers for . . . get on the *front (rear)* **of the train!**
I viaggiatori diretti a . . . vadano *in testa (in coda)* al treno!
ē vyäjätō′rē dēre′tē ä . . . vä′dänō ēn te′stä (ēn kō′dä) äl tre′nō

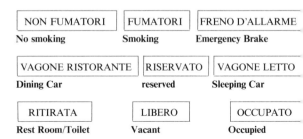

NON FUMATORI	FUMATORI	FRENO D'ALLARME
No smoking	**Smoking**	**Emergency Brake**

VAGONE RISTORANTE	RISERVATO	VAGONE LETTO
Dining Car	**reserved**	**Sleeping Car**

RITIRATA	LIBERO	OCCUPATO
Rest Room/Toilet	**Vacant**	**Occupied**

arrival	(l') arrivo *m*	ärē′vō
arrive	arrivare	ärēvä′re
baggage	(il) bagaglio	bägä′lyō
baggage car	(il) bagagliaio	bägälyä′yō
car	(il) vagone	vägō′ne
change trains	cambiare treno	kämbyä′re tre′nō
compartment	(lo) scompartimento	skōmpärtēmen′tō
conductor	(il) controllore	kōntrōlō′re
– head conductor	(il) capotreno	käpōtre′nō
connection	(la) coincidenza	kō′ēntshēden′tsä
depart	partire	pär′tēre
departure	(la) partenza	pärten′tsä
engine	(la) locomotiva	lōkōmōtē′vä
– engineer	(il) macchinista	mäkēnē′stä
entrance	(l') entrata *f*	enträ′tä
exit	(l') uscita *f*	ōōshē′tä
fare	la tariffa	tärē′fä
– discount	riduzione	rēdōōtsyō′ne
get *in (aboard)*	salire	sälē′re
get off	scendere	shen′dere
heating	(il) riscaldamento	rēskäldämen′tō
– cold	freddo	fre′dō
– warm	caldo	käl′dō
locomotive	(la) locomotiva	lōkōmōtē′vä
luggage rack	(la) rete portabagagli	re′te pōrtäbägä′lye
passenger	(il) passeggero	päseje′rō
platform	(il) marciapiede	märtshäpye′de
railroad	(la) ferrovia	ferōvē′ä
route	(il) percorso	perkōr′sō
station	(la) stazione	stätsyō′ne
station master	(il) capostazione	käpōstätsyō′ne
railroad	(la) ferrovia	ferōvē′ä
route	(il) percorso	perkōr′sō
station	(la) stazione	stätsyō′ne
stop *(noun)*	(la) sosta	sō′stä
stop *(verb)*	fermarsi	fermär′sē
ticket	(il) biglietto	bēlye′tō
track	(il) binario	bēnär′yō
train	(il) treno	tre′nō
window seat	(il) posto al finestrino	pō′stō äl fēne-strē′nō

BY PLANE

Information and Reservations

Is there a (direct) flight to . . . ?
C'è un collegamento (diretto) con . . . ?
tshe ōon kōlegämen'tō (dēre'tō) kōn . . .

When is there a plane *today (tomorrow)* to . . . ?
Quando parte *oggi (domani)* un aereo per . . . ?
kōo·än'dō pär'te ō'jē (dōmä'nē) ōon ä·e're·ō per . . .

When is the next plane to . . . ?
Quando parte il prossimo aereo per . . . ?
kōo·än'dō pär'te ēl prō'sēmō ä·e're·ō per . . .

Does the plane make a stopover in . . . ?
L'aereo fa scalo a . . . ?
lä·e're·ō fä skä'lō ä . . .

Is there a connection to . . . ?
C'è la coincidenza per . . . ?
tshe lä kō·ēntshēden'tsä per . . .

When do we get to . . . ?
Quando arriviamo a . . . ?
kōo·än'dō ärēvyä'mō ä . . .

Are there still seats available?
Ci sono ancora posti liberi?
tshē sō'nō änkō'rä pō'stē lē'berē

How much is a (round-trip) flight to . . . ?
Quanto costa un volo (andata e ritorno) per . . . ?
kōo·än'tō kō'stä ōon vō'lō (ändä'tä e rētōr'nō) per . . .

What's the luggage allowance?
Quanto bagaglio è libero?
kōo·än'tō bägä'lyō e lē'berō

How much does excess baggage cost?
Quanto costa il sovrappeso?
kōo·än'tō kō'stä ēl sōvräpe'sō

How much is the airport service charge?
Quanto costa la tassa d'imbarco?
kōo·än'tō kō'stä lä tä'sä dēmbär'kō

How do I get to the airport?
Come si arriva all'aeroporto?
kō'me sē ärē'vä älä·erōpōr'tō

When is check-in time?
Quando devo essere là?
kōo·än'dō de'vō e'sere lä

I'd like to reserve a seat on the Friday flight to ...
Vorrei prenotare un volo per venerdì per ...
vōre′ē prenōtä′re ōon vō′lō per venerdē′ per ...

I'd like to reserve a round-trip ticket to ... on the 8th of May.
Vorrei prenotare un volo andata e ritorno per ... per l'otto maggio.
vōre′ē prenōtä′re ōon vō′lō ändä′tä e rētōr′nō per ... per lō′tō mä′jō

– First Class.	– Business Class.	– Economy Class.
prima classe	business class.	classe turistica.
prē′mä klä′se	klä′se bōozēnes′	klä′se tōorē′stēkä

How long is the ticket valid?
Per quanto tempo è valido il biglietto?
per kōo·än′tō tem′pō e vä′lēdō ēl bēlye′tō

I have to *cancel (change)* my reservation.
Devo *annullare (rimandare)* il mio volo.
de′vō änōolä′re (rēmändä′re) ēl mē′ō vō′lō

What is the cancellation fee?
Quanto costa l'annullamento?
kōo·än′tō kō′stä länōolämen′tō

Can I take this along as hand luggage?
Posso portare questo come bagaglio a mano?
pō′sō pōrtä′re kōo·e′stō kō′me bägä′lyō ä mä′nō

Where is *the waiting room (Exit B)*?
Dov'è *la sala d'aspetto (l'uscita B)?*
dōve′ lä sä′lä däspe′tō (lōoshē′tä bē)

How much does it cost?
Quanto costa?
kōo·än′tō kō′stä

Where is the information counter?
Dov'è l'ufficio informazioni?
dōve′ lōofē′tshō ēnfōrmätsyō′nē

Is the plane to ... late?
E' in ritardo l'aereo per ...?
e ēn rētär′dō lä·e′re·ō per ...

Where's the duty-free shop?
Dov'è il Duty-shop?
dōve′ ēl dyōo′tē-shōp

Has the plane from ... already landed?
E' già atterrato l'aereo da ...?
e jä äterä′tō lä·e′re·ō dä ...

On the Plane

*Kindly refrain from smoking.
Si prega di non fumare.
sē pre'gä dē nōn foomä're

*Please fasten your seat belts.
Allacciate le cinture di sicurezza.
älätshä'te le tshēntoo're dē
sēkoore'tsä

How high are we flying?
A quanti metri di quota siamo?
ä koo·än'tē me'trē dē koo·ō'tä syä'mō

Where are we now?
Dove siamo adesso?
dō've syä'mō äde'sō

What *mountains are those (river is that)?*
Che montagne sono (che fiume è)?
ke mōntä'nye sō'nō (ke fyoo'me e)

Can I have ...?
Posso avere ...?
pō'sō äve're ...

I feel sick.
Mi sento male.
mē sen'tō mä'le

When do we land?
Quando si atterra?
koo·än'dō sē äte'rä

Have you got an air-sickness remedy?
Ha qualcosa contro il mal d'aria?
ä koo·älkō'sä kōn'trō ēl mäl där'yä

How's the weather in ...?
Che tempo fa a ...?
ke tem'pō fä ä ...

aircraft	(l') aereo *m*	ä·e're·ō
air jet *(over the seat)*	(il) diffusore di aria fresca	dēfoozō're dē är'yä fres'kä
airline	(la) compagnia aerea ..	kompänyē'ä ä·e'ryä
air passenger	(il) passeggero	päseje'rō
airport	(l') aeroporto *m*	ä·erōpōr'tō
airport service charge	(la) tassa d'imbarco ...	tä'sä dēmbär'kō
air sickness	(il) mal d'aria	mäl där'yä
approach	avvicinarsi	ävētshēnär'sē
arrival	(l') arrivo *m*	ärē'vō
charter plane	(il) charter	tshär'ter
climb	alzarsi	ältsär'sē
crew	(l') equipaggio *m*	ekoo·ēpä'jō
destination	(la) destinazione	destēnätsyō'ne
duty-free goods	(le) merci esenti da dogana	mer'tshē ezen'tē dä dōgä'nä
emergency chute	(lo) scivolo d'emergenza	shē'vōlō demer-jen'tsä
emergency exit	(l') uscita *f* d'emergenza	ooshē'tä demerjen'tsä

emergency landing ..	(l') atterraggio *m* di fortuna	äterä'jō dē fōrtoō'nä
engine	(la) macchina	mä'kēnä
excess baggage	(il) bagaglio in eccedenza	bägä'lyō ēn etsheden'tsä
exit	(l') uscita *f*	ooshē'tä
flight	(il) volo	vō'lō
flight attendant	(l') assistente *m* di volo	äsēsten'te dē vō'lō
fly	volare	vōlä're
flying time	(il) tempo di volo	tem'pō dē vō'lō
fog	(la) nebbia	ne'byä
hand luggage	(il) bagaglio a mano ...	bägä'lyō ä mä'nō
helicopter	(l') elicottero *m*	elēkō'terō
information	(le) informazioni	ēnfōrmätsyō'nē
information counter .	(l') ufficio *m* informazioni	oofē'tshō ēnfōrmätsyō'nē
intermediate landing .	(lo) scalo	skä'lō
jet *(plane)*	(il) jet	jet
land *(verb)*	atterrare	äterä're
landing	(l') atterraggio *m*	äterä'jō
landing gear	(il) carrello d'atterraggio	käre'lō däterä'jō
life jacket	(il) giubbetto di salvataggio	joobe'tō dē sälvätä'jō
pilot	(il) pilota	pēlō'tä
plane	(l') aeroplano *m*	ä·erōplä'nō
reservation	(la) prenotazione	prenōtätsyō'ne
return flight	(il) volo di ritorno	vō'lō dē rētōr'nō
scheduled flight	(l') aereo *m* di linea ...	ä·e're·ō dē lē'ne·ä
seat belt	(la) cintura di sicurezza	tshēntoō'rä dē sēkoore'tsä
– fasten seat belts ...	allacciare le cinture di sicurezza	älätshä're le tshēntoō're dē sēkoore'tsä
stopover	(lo) scalo	skä'lō
system timetable	(l') orario *m* del volo ..	ōrär'yō del vō'lō
take-off	(il) decollo	dekō'lō
thunderstorm	(il) temporale	tempōrä'le
ticket	(il) biglietto	bēlye'tō
waiting room	(la) sala d'aspetto	sä'lä däspe'tō
weather	(il) tempo	tem'pō
wing	(l') ala *f*	ä'lä

BY SHIP

When does *a ship (the ferry)* leave for ...?
Quando parte *una nave (il traghetto)* per ...?
kōō·än′dō pär′te ōō′nä nä′ve (ĕl träge′tō) per ...

Where?
Dove?
dō′ve

How often does the car ferry go to ...?
Quante volte fa servizio la nave-traghetto per ...?
kōō·än′te vōl′te fä servē′tsyō lä nä′ve träge′tō per ...

How long does the crossing (from ...) to ... take?
Quanto tempo dura la traversata (da ...) a ...?
kōō·än′tō tem′pō dōō′rä lä träversä′tä (dä ...) ä ...

How far is the railroad station from the harbor?
Quant'è lontana la stazione dal porto?
kōō·änte′ lōntä′nä lä stätsyō′ne däl pōr′tō

What are the ports of call?
In quali porti si fa scalo?
ēn kōō·ä′lē pōr′tē sē fä skä′lō

Can I get a connection to ...?
C'è la coincidenza per ...?
tshe lä kō·ēntshēden′tsä per ...

When do we *dock (land)* at ...?
Quando si fa scalo a ...?
kōō·än′dō sē fä skä′lō ä ...

For how long?
Per quanto tempo?
per kōō·än′tō tem′pō

Can we go ashore at ...?
Si può sbarcare a ...?
sē pōō·ō′ zbärkä′re ä ...

Where can we get tickets?
Dove si comprano i biglietti?
dō′ve sē kōm′pränō ē bēlye′tē

Will there be any land excursions?
Verranno organizzate escursioni a terra?
verä′nō ōrgänēdzä′te eskōōrsyō′nē ä te′rä

When do we have to be back on board?
Quando dobbiamo essere a bordo?
kōō·än′dō dōbyä′mō e′sere ä bōr′dō

I'd like ...
Vorrei ...
vōre′ē ...

– to book passage to ...
– un biglietto per la nave per ...
– ōōn bēlye′tō per lä nä′ve per ...

– two tickets on the ... to ... tomorrow.
due biglietti sulla ... per ... per domani.
dōō'e bēlye'tē sōō'lä ... per ... per dōmä'nē

– a round-trip ticket from ... to ... and back.
un biglietto per il giro da ... a ... e ritorno.
ōōn bēlye'tō per ēl jē'rō dä ... ä ... e rētōr'nō

– a ticket for a *car (motorcycle, bicycle).*
un biglietto per *una macchina (una motocicletta, una bicicletta).*
ōōn bēlye'tō per ōō'nä mä'kēnä (mōtōtshēkle'tä, bētshēkle'tä)

– a single cabin.   **– an** *outside (inside)* **cabin.**
una cabina singola.   una cabina *esterna (interna).*
ōō'nä käbē'nä sēn'gōlä   ōō'nä käbē'nä ester'nä (ēnter'nä)

– a double cabin.   **First Class.**   **Tourist Class.**
una cabina a due letti.   Prima classe.   Classe turistica.
ōōn'ä käbē'nä ä dōō'e le'tē   prē'mä klä'se   klä'se tōōrē'stēkä

In the Harbor

Where is the "..." lying?   **Where does the "..." dock?**
Dove si trova la ...?   Dove fa scalo la ...?
dō've sē trō'vä lä ...   dō've fä skä'lō lä ...

Does this ship sail to ...?   **When does she sail?**
Questa nave va a ...?   A che ora parte?
kōō·e'stä nä've vä ä ...   ä ke ō'rä pär'te

Where is the *shipping company's office (customs office)?*
Dov'è *la compagnia di navigazione (l'amministrazione doganale)?*
dōve' lä kōmpänyē'ä dē nävēgätsyō'ne (lämēnēsträtsyō'ne dōgänä'le)

Where can I pick up my luggage?   **I come from the "...".**
Dove posso ritirare il mio bagaglio?   Vengo dalla "...".
dō've pō'sō rētērä're ēl mē'ō bägä'lyō   ven'gō dä'lä ...

On Board

I'm looking for cabin no ...   **Where's my baggage?**
Cerco la cabina numero ...   Dov'è il mio bagaglio?
tsher'kō lä käbē'nä nōō'merō ...   dōve' ēl mē'ō bägä'lyō

Have you got . . . on board?		**Please, where is . . .?**
Ha . . . a bordo?		Per favore, dov'è . . .?
ä . . . ä bōr'dō		per fävō're, dōve' . . .

the bar	(il) bar	bär
the *barber shop*	(il) barbiere	bärbye're
(beauty parlor)	(il) parrucchiere	pärōōkye're
the dining room	(la) sala da pranzo	sä'lä dä prän'dzō
the lounge	(la) sala di soggiorno . .	sä'lä dē sōjōr'nō
the purser's office . . .	(l') ufficio *m* del	ōōfē'tshō del
	commissario di bordo .	kōmēsär'yō dē
		bōr'dō
the radio room	(la) stazione radiotele-	stätsyō'ne rädyō-
	gramma	telegrä'mä
the reading room	(la) sala di lettura	sä'lä dē letōō'rä
the ship's photo-	(il) fotografo di bordo .	fōtō'gräfō dē bōr'-
grapher		dō
the sick bay	(l') infermeria *f* di	ēnfermerē'ä dē
	bordo	bōr'dō
the swimming pool . .	(la) piscina	pēshē'nä
the tour guide's	(l') ufficio *m* della guida	ōōfēt'shō de'lä
office		gōō·ē'dä

I'd like to speak to the . . .		
Vorrei parlare con . . .		
vōre'ē pärlä're kōn		

– captain	(il) capitano	käpētä'nō
– chief steward	(il) capocameriere di	käpōkämerye're dē
	bordo	bōr'dō
– deck officer	(l') ufficiale *m* di	ōōfētshä'le dē
	coperta	kōper'tä
– luggage master	(il) responsabile del	respōnsä'bēle del
	bagaglio	bägä'lyō
– purser	(il) commissario di	kōmēsär'yō dē
	bordo	bōr'dō
– ship's doctor	(il) medico di bordo . . .	me'dēkō dē bōr'dō
– tour guide	(la) guida	gōō·ē'dä

Steward, please bring me . . .		**What is the voltage here?**
Cameriere, per favore mi porti . . .		Che voltaggio c'è qui?
kämerye're, per fävō're mē pōr'tē . . .		ke vōltä'jō tshe kōō·ē'

Please call the ship's doctor!
Chiami il medico di bordo, per favore!
kyä′mē ēl me′dēkō dē bōr′dō, per fävō′re

Have you got anything for seasickness?
Ha qualcosa contro il mal di mare?
ä kōō·älkō′sä kōn′trō ēl mäl dē mä′re

air conditioning	(l') aria *f* condizionata	är′yä kōndētsyō-nä′tä
anchor	(l') ancora *f*	än′kōrä
bank	(la) sponda	spōn′dä
barge	(la) scialuppa	shälōō′pä
bay	(la) baia	bä′yä
blanket	(la) coperta di lana	kōper′tä dē lä′nä
board	(il) bordo	bōr′dō
– on board	a bordo	ä bōr′dō
boat	(la) barca	bär′kä
– fishing trawler	(la) barca da pesca	bär′kä dä pes′kä
– launch	(la) scialuppa	shälōō′pä
– lifeboat	(la) scialuppa di salvataggio	shälōō′pä dē sälvätä′jō
– motorboat	(il) motoscafo	mōtōskä′fō
– sailboat	(la) barca a vela	bär′kä ä ve′lä
bow	(la) prua	prōō′ä
breeze	(la) brezza	bre′dzä
bridge	(il) ponte	pōn′te
buoy	(la) boa	bō′ä
cabin	(la) cabina	käbē′nä
cable	(il) cavo	kä′vō
call (at port)	fare scalo	fä′re skä′lō
canal	(il) canale	känä′le
captain	(il) capitano	käpētä′nō
captain's table	(la) tavola di capitano	tä′vōlä dē käpētä′nō
coast	(la) costa	kō′stä
course	(la) rotta	rō′tä
crew	(l') equipaggio *m*	ekōō·ēpä′jō
crossing	(la) traversata	träversä′tä
cruise	(la) crociera	krōtshe′rä
deck	(la) coperta	kōper′tä
– boat deck	(il) ponte delle scialuppe	pōn′te de′le shälōō′pe

– foredeck	(il) ponte di prua	pōn'te dē prōō'ä
– main deck	(il) ponte principale	pōn'te prēntshē-pä'le
– poop deck	(il) ponte di poppa	pōn'te dē pō'pä
– promenade deck	(il) ponte di passeggio	pōn'te dē päse'jō
– saloon deck	(il) ponte coperto	pōn'te kōper'tō
– steerage	(il) ponte corridoio	pōn'te kōrēdō'yō
– sun deck	(il) solario	sōlär'yō
– upper deck	(il) ponte superiore	pōn'te sōōperyō're
deck chair	(lo) sdraio di coperta	zdrä'yō dē kōper'tä
disembark	sbarcare	zbärkä're
dock (verb)	approdare	äprōdä're
excursion	(l') escursione f	eskōōrsyō'ne
excursion program	(il) programma d'escursione	prōgrä'mä deskōōrsyō'ne
farewell dinner	(il) pranzo d'addio	prän'dzō dädē'ō
ferry	(il) traghetto	träge'tō
– car ferry	(la) nave-traghetto	nä've träge'tō
– train ferry	(il) traghetto ferroviario	träge'tō ferō-vyär'yō
first officer	(l') ufficiale m in seconda	ōōfētshä'le ēn sekōn'dä
gangway	(la) passerella	päsere'lä
harbor	(il) porto	pōr'tō
harbor police	(la) polizia di porto	pōlētsē'ä dē pōr'tō
helm	(il) timone	tēmō'ne
helmsman	(il) timoniere	tēmōnye're
island	(l') isola f	ē'zōlä
jetty	(il) molo	mō'lō
knot	(il) nodo	nō'dō
lake	(il) lago	lä'gō
land (verb)	far scalo, approdare	fär skä'lō, äprōdä're
landing stage	(il) pontile d'approdo	pōntē'le däprō'dō
life belt	(la) cintura di salvataggio	tshēntōō'rä dē sälvätä'jō
life jacket	(il) giubbetto di salvataggio	jōōbe'tō dē sälvätä'jō
lighthouse	(il) faro	fä'rō
mast	(l') albero m	äl'berō
ocean	(l') oceano m	ōtshe'änō

passenger	(il) passeggero	päseje'rō
pier	(il) pontile	pōntē'le
place on deck	(il) posto in coperta	pō'stō ēn kōper'tä
playroom	(la) sala da gioco	sä'lä dä jō'kō
port *(land)*	(il) porto	pōr'tō
port *(side)*	(il) babordo	bäbōr'dō
port fees	(i) diritti portuali	dērē'tē pōrtoo·ä'lē
quay	(la) banchina	bänkē'nä
railing	(il) parapetto	päräpe'tō
river	(il) fiume	fyoo'me
rope	(la) fune	foo'ne
rough seas	(il) mare mosso	mä're mō'sō
rudder	(il) timone	tēmō'ne
sailor	(il) marinaio	märēnä'yō
sea	(il) mare	mä're
– on the high seas	in alto mare	ēn äl'tō mä're
seasickness	(il) mal di mare	mäl dē mä're
ship	(la) nave	nä've
– freighter	(la) nave mercantile	nä've merkäntē'le
– passenger ship	(la) nave passeggeri	nä've päseje'rē
– warship	(la) nave da guerra	nä've dä goo·e'rä
ship's doctor	(il) medico di bordo	me'dēkō dē bōr'dō
shipboard party	(la) festa a bordo	fe'stä ä bōr'dō
shipping agency	(l') agenzia *f* di navigazione	äjentsē'ä dē nävēgätsyō'ne
shipping company	(la) compagnia di navigazione	kōmpänyē'ä dē nävēgätsyō'ne
shore	(la) terra	te'rä
starboard	(il) tribordo	trēbōr'dō
steamer	(il) vaporetto	väpōre'tō
stern	(la) poppa	pō'pä
steward	(il) cameriere	kämerye're
strait	(lo) stretto	stre'tō
tourist class	(la) classe turistica	klä'se toorē'stēkä
tug	(il) rimorchiatore	rēmōrkyätō're
voyage	(il) viaggio in nave	vyä'jō ēn nä've
wave	(l') onda *f*	ōn'dä
yacht	(lo) yacht	yäkt

AT THE BORDER

Passport Control

When do we get to the border?
Quando arriviamo alla frontiera?
kōō·än'dō ärēvyä'mō ä'lä frōntye'rä

*Your passport, please.
Il Suo passaporto.
ēl sōō'ō päsäpōr'tō

*Your papers, please.
I Suoi documenti, per favore.
ē sōō·o'ē dōkōōmen'tē per fàvōr're

Here they are.
Eccoli.
e'kōlē

I'll be staying *a week (two weeks, until the . . .).*
Mi fermo *una settimana (due settimane, fino al . . .).*
mē fer'mō ōō'nä setēmä'nä (dōō'e setēmä'ne, fē'nō äl . . .)

I'm here *on business (on vacation).*
Sono qui *per affari (come turista).*
sō'nō kōō·ē' per äfä're (kō'me tōōrē'stä)

I am visiting (We are visiting) . . .
Visito (visitiamo) . . .
vē'zētō (vēzētyä'mō) . . .

Do I have to fill in this form?
Devo riempire il modulo?
de'vō rē·empē're ēl mō'dōōlō

I haven't got a vaccination certificate.
Non ho il certificato di vaccinazione.
nōn ō ēl tshertēfēkä'tō dē vätshēnätsyō'ne

What should I do?
Che cosa devo fare?
kē kō'sä de'vō fä're

I *have (haven't)* **had a** *smallpox (cholera)* **vaccination.**
(Non sono) sono vaccinato contro *il vaiolo (il colera).*
(nōn sō'nō) sō'nō vätshēnä'tō kōn'trō ēl väyō'lō (ēl kōle'rä)

I'm traveling with the . . . group.
Faccio parte della comitiva di . . .
fä'tshō pär'te de'lä kōmētē'vä dē . . .

Can I get my visa here?
Posso avere qui il visto?
pō'sō äve're kōō·ē' ēl vē'stō?

The children are entered in my passport.
I figli sono registrati nel mio passaporto.
ē fē'lyē sō'nō rejēsträ'tē nel mē'ō päsäpōr'tō

May I please phone my consulate?
Posso telefonare al mio consolato?
pō'sō telefōnä're äl mē'ō kōnsōlä'tō

border	(la) frontiera	frōntye′rä
color of eyes	(il) colore degli occhi	kōlō′re de′lyē ō′kē
color of hair	(il) colore dei capelli	kōlō′re de′ē käpe′lē
date of birth	(la) data di nascita	dä′tä dē nä′shētä
departure	(la) partenza	pärten′tsä
distinguishing marks	(i) segni particolari	se′nyē pärtēkōlä′rē
driver's license	(la) patente	päten′te
entry	(l') entrata *f*	enträ′tä
entry visa	(il) visto d'entrata	vē′stō denträ′tä
exit visa	(il) visto d'uscita	vē′stō dōōshē′tä
extend	prolungare	prōlōōngä′re
height	(la) statura	stätōō′rä
identity card	(la) carta d'identità	kär′tä dēdentētä′
insurance certificate	(il) certificato d'assicurazione	tshertēfēkä′tō däsēkōōrätsyō′ne
international vaccination certificate	(il) certificato internazionale di vaccinazione	tshertēfēkä′tō ēnternätsyōnä′le dē vätshēnätsyō′ne
maiden name	(il) nome da ragazza	nō′me dä rägä′tsä
marital status	(lo) stato di famiglia	stä′tō dē fämē′lyä
- single	celibe/nubile	tshe′lēbe/nōō′bēle
- married	sposato/sposata	spōzä′tō/spōzä′tä
- widowed	vedovo/vedova	ve′dōvō/ve′dōvä
- divorced	divorziato/divorziata	dēvōrtsyä′tō/dēvōr-tsyä′tä
name	(il) nome	nō′me
- first name	(il) nome di battesimo	nō′me dē bäte′zēmō
- last name	(il) cognome	kōnyō′me
nationality	(la) nazionalità	nätsyōnälētä′
number	(il) numero	nōō′merō
occupation	(la) professione	prōfesyō′ne
passport	(il) passaporto	päsäpōr′tō
passport control	(il) controllo dei passaporti	kōntrō′lō de′ē päsäpōr′tē
place of birth	(il) luogo di nascita	lōō·ō′gō dē nä′shētä
place of residence	(la) residenza	resēden′tsä
renew	rinnovare	rēnōvä′re
signature	(la) firma	fēr′mä
valid	valido	vä′lēdō

Customs Control

*Do you have anything to declare?
Ha qualcosa da dichiarare?
ä kōō·älkō'sä dä dēkyärä're

I only have articles for my personal use.
Ho solo oggetti per uso personale.
ō sō'lō ōje'tē per ōō'zō persōnä'le

That's my suitcase.
Questa valigia è mia.
kōō·e'stä välē'jä e mē'ä

That isn't mine.
Questo non è mio.
kōō·e'stō nōn e mē'ō

*Please open ...
Per piacere, apra ...
per pyätshe're, ä'prä

This is a *present (souvenir).*
Questo è un *regalo (souvenir).*
kōō·e'stō e ōōn regä'lō (sōōvenēr)

I have ... *cigarettes (a bottle of perfume).*
Ho ... *sigarette (un flacone di profumo).*
ō ... sēgäre'te (ōōn fläkō'ne dē prōfōō'mō)

*What's in here?
Che cosa c'è dentro?
ke kō'sä tshe den'trō

That's all.
E' tutto.
e tōō'tō

*All right!
Va bene.
vä be'ne

How much can I bring in duty free?
Quanto è esente da tasse?
kōō·än'tō e ezen'te dä tä'se

What do I have to pay for it?
Quanto devo pagare per questo?
kōō·än'tō de'vō pägä're per kōō·e'stō

border	(la) frontiera	frōntye'rä
customs	(la) dogana	dōgä'nä
customs control	(il) controllo doganale .	kōntrō'lō dōgänä'le
customs declaration .	(la) dichiarazione	dēkyärätsyō'ne
customs office	(l') ufficio *m* doganale .	ōōfē'tshō dōgänä'le
customs officer	(l') impiegato *m*	ēmpyegä'tō
	doganale	dōgänä'le
duty	(la) tassa	tä'sä
– export duty	(la) tassa d'esporta-	tä'sä despōrtä-
	zione	tsyō'ne
– import duty	(la) tassa d'importa-	tä'sä dēmpōrtä-
	zione	tsyō'ne

ACCOMMODATIONS

Checking it out

Where is the ... *hotel (pension)?*
Dov'è *l'albergo (la pensione)* ...?
dōve' lälber'gō (lä pensyō'ne) ...

Can you recommend a good hotel?
Può raccomandarmi un buon albergo?
pōō·ō' räkōmändär'me ōōn bōō·ōn' älber'gō

Is (are) **there ...** *near here?*
C'è *(Ci sono)* qui vicino ...?
tshe (tshē sō'nō) kōō·ē' vētshē'nō ...

accommodations	un alloggio	ōōn älō'jō
apartments	degli appartamenti	de'lye äpärtämen'tē
a boarding house	una locanda	ōō'nä lōkän'dä
bungalows	dei bungalow	de'ē bōōn'gälō
a camping site	un campeggio	ōōn kämpe'jō
a hotel	un albergo	ōōn älber'gō
an inn	una locanda	ōō'nä lōkän'dä
a motel	un motel	ōōn mōtel'
a pension	una pensione	ōō'nä pensyō'ne
rooms in private homes	delle camere private ...	de'le kä'mere prē'vä'te
a youth hostel	un ostello per la gioventù	ōōn ōste'lō per lä jōventōō'

– near the beach.	**– in a quiet place (centrally located).**
vicino alla spiaggia.	in un posto *tranquillo (centrale).*
vētshē'nō ä'lä spyä'jä	ēn ōōn pō'stō tränkōō·e'lō (tshenträ'le)

How *are the prices (is the food)* **there?**
Come *sono i prezzi (è il vitto)* là?
kō'me sō'nō ē pre'tse (e ēl vē'tō) lä

Only the most modern European hotels have bathrooms attached to every room, and most rooming houses and pensions will require guests to share a bathroom with others.

Checking in

I reserved a room here.	**. . . six weeks ago.**
Ho prenotato una camera qui.	. . . sei settimane fa.
ō prenōtä′tō ōō′nä kä′merä kōō·ē′	. . . se′ē setēmä′ne fä

The . . . travel agency reserved a room for *me (us)*.
L' agenzia viaggi ha prenotato una camera per *me (noi)*.

läjentsē′ä vyä′jē ä prenōtä′tō ōō′nä kä′merä per me (nō′ē)

Have you got a *single (double)* room available?
C'è una camera *singola (doppia)* libera?

tshe ōō′nä kä′merä sēn′gōlä (dō′pyä) lē′berä

I'd like to have	Vorrei	vōre′ē . . .
– an apartment	un appartamento	ōon äpärtämen′tō
– double room	una doppia	ōō′nä dō′pyä
– a quiet room	una camera tranquilla	ōō′nä kä′merä tränkōo·ē′lä
– a room	una camera	ōō′nä kä′merä
– for . . . persons	per . . . persone	per . . . persō′ne
– on the third floor . .	al secondo (!) piano . .	äl sekōn′dō pyä′nō
– overlooking the sea	con vista sul mare	kōn vē′stä sōol mä′re
– with balcony	con balcone	kōn bälkō′ne
– with bath	con bagno	kōn bä′nyō
– with hot and cold running water	con acqua calda e fredda	kōn ä′kōo·ä käl′dä e fre′dä
– with shower	con doccia	kōn dō′tshä
– with terrace	con il terrazzo	kōn ēl terä′tsō
– with toilet	con i servizi	kōn ē sevē′tse

. . . for *one night (two nights, one week, four weeks)*.
. . . per *una notte (due notti, una settimana, quattro settimane)*.

. . . per ōō′nä nō′te (dōo′e nō′tē, ōō′nä setēmä′nä, kōō·ä′trō setēmä′ne

---

Careful! In order to find your room remember that all European countries use a different numbering system for the floors. The bottom floor is called the ground floor, or "pianterreno" and the second (American) floor is then called the first floor or "primo piano", also written "1° piano", the third floor the second ("2° piano"), and so on.

Can I have a look at the room?
Posso vedere la camera?
pō'sō vede're lä kä'merä

I like it.	**I'll (We'll) take it.**
Mi piace.	La *prendo (prendiamo)*.
nē pyä'tshe	lä pren'dō (prendyä'mō)

Could you show me another room?
Può farmi vedere un'altra camera?
pōō·ō' fär'mē vede're ōōnäl'trä kä'merä

Could you put in *an extra bed (a crib)*?
Può mettere un *altro letto (letto da bambino)*?
pōō·ō' me'tere ōōn äl'trō le'tō (le'tō dä bämbē'nō)

Price

How much is the room per *day (week)*?
Quanto costa la camera *al giorno (alla settimana)*?
ōō·än'tō kō'stä lä kä'merä äl jōr'nō (ä'lä setēmä'nä)

– with breakfast.	**– with two meals a day.**
– compresa la prima colazione.	– con due pasti al giorno.
– kōmpre'sä lä prē'mä kōlätsyō'ne	– kōn dōō'e päs'tē äl jōr'nō

– American plan.	**Is *everything (service)* included?**
– pensione completa.	E' compreso *tutto (il servizio)*?
– pensyō'ne kōmple'tä	e kōmpre'sō tōō'tō (ēl servē'tsyō)

What's the *single room surcharge (seasonal surcharge)*?
Quant'è *il supplemento per una singola (l'aumento stagionale)*?
ōō·änte' ēl sōōplemen'tō per ōō'nä sēn'gōlä (loumen'tō stäjōnä'le)

Are there reduced rates for children?
Ci sono riduzioni per i bambini?
shē sō'nō rēdōōtsyō'ne per ē bämbē'nē

In Italy it is the law that all accommodations must list their prices on the door of the room. Most listings are in a number of languages including English. Be sure that the price asked for the room agrees with the price listed on the door.

Registration, Luggage

Do you need our passports?
Vuole i nostri passaporti?
vōō·ō′le ē nō′strē päsäpōr′tē

When do you want back the registration form?
Quando Le devo dare il formulario compilato?
kōō·än′dō le de′vō dä′re ēl fōrmōōlär′yō kōmpēlä′tō

What do I have to fill out here?
Che cosa devo scrivere qui?
ke kō′sä de′vō skrē′vere kōō·ē′

*I just need your signature.
Basta la Sua firma.
bä′stä lä sōō′ä fēr′mä

Would you have my luggage picked up?
Può far ritirare il mio bagaglio?
pōō·ō′ fär rētērä′re ēl mē′ō bägä′lyō

It's still at the *station (airport)*.
E` ancora *alla stazione (all`aeroporto)*.
e änkō′rä ä′lä stätsyō′ne (älä·erōpōr′tō)

Here's the baggage check.
Ecco lo scontrino.
e′kō lō skōntrē′nō

Where's my luggage?
Dov`è il mio bagaglio?
dōve′ ēl mē′ō bägä′lyō

Is my baggage already up in the room?
E` già in camera il mio bagaglio?
e jä ēn kä′merä ēl mē′ō bägä′lyō

Can I leave my luggage here?
Posso lasciare il mio bagaglio qui?
pō′sō läshä′re ēl mē′ō bägä′lyō kōō·ē′

Would you put these valuables in the safe?
Può mettere questi oggetti di valore in cassaforte?
pōō·ō′ me′tere kōō·e′stē ōje′tē dē välō′re ēn käsäfōr′te

Do you have a *garage (parking lot)*?
C`è *un garage (un parcheggio)*?
tshe ōōn gärä′j (ōōn pärke′jō)

Reception, Desk Clerk

Where is room 308?
Dov'è la camera numero trecentotto?
dōve' lä kä'merä nōō'merō tretshentō'tō

The key, please.
La chiave, per favore.
lä kyä've, per fävō're

Number . . ., please.
Numero . . ., per favore.
nōō'merō . . . per fävō're

Has anyone asked for me?
Qualcuno ha chiesto di me?
kōō·älkōō'nō ä kye'stō dē me

Is there any mail for me?
C'è posta per me?
she pō'stä per me

What time does the mail come?
Quando arriva la posta?
kōō·än'dō ärrē'vä lä pō'stä

Do you have any *stamps (picture postcards)*?
Ha *dei francobolli (delle cartoline illustrate)*?
ä de'ē fränkōbō'lē (de'le kärtōlē'ne ēlōōsträ'te)

What's the postage on a *letter (postcard)* to the United States?
Quanto costa *una lettera (una cartolina)* per gli Stati Uniti?
kōō·än'tō kō'stä ōō'nä le'terä (ōō'nä kärtōlē'nä) per lyē stä'tē ōōnē'tē

Where can I *get (rent)* . . .?
Dove posso *avere (noleggiare)* . . .?
dō've pō'sō äve're (nōlejä're) . . .

Where do I sign up for the excursion to . . .?
Dove posso iscrivermi per l'escursione a . . .?
dō've pō'sō ēskrē'vermē per leskōōrsyō'ne ä . . .

Where can I *make a phone call (change some money)*?
Dove posso *telefonare (cambiare dei soldi)*?
dō've pō'sō telefōnä're (kämbyä're de'ē sōl'dē)

I'd like to place a long distance call to . . .
Vorrei avere una comunicazione interurbana con . . .
ōre'ē äve're ōō'nä kōmōōnēkätsyō'ne ēnterōōrbä'nä kōn . . .

I'm expecting a long distance call from the United States.
Aspetto una telefonata dagli Stati Uniti.
äspe'tō ōō'nä telefōnä'tä dä'lyē stätē ōōnē'tē

Where *is (are)* ...?
Dov'è (Dove sono) ...?
dōve′ (dō′ve sō′nō) ...

I'll be in the *lounge (bar)*.
Sono *nella sala di soggiorno (al bar)*.
sō′nō ne′lä sä′lä dē sōjōr′nō (äl bär)

Could you get me ...?
Può procurarmi ...?
pōō·ō′ prōkōōrär′mē ...

What's the voltage here?
Che voltaggio c'è qui?
ke vōltä′jō tshe kōō·ē′

---

*Most American appliances have 110 volts while most European have
220. Ask the desk clerk to be sure. Many hotels have small
transformers, "trasformatore". If your plug doesn't fit you will need
an adaptor plug, or "spina intermedia". The adaptor plug, however,
does not replace the transformer.*

I'll be back in *ten minutes (a couple of hours)*.
Sarò di ritorno fra *dieci minuti (due ore)*.
särō′ dē rētōr′nō frä dye′tshe mēnōō′tē (dōō′e ō′re)

We're going *down to the beach (into town)*.
Andiamo *alla spiaggia (in città)*.
ändyä′mō ä′lä spyä′jä (ēn tshētä′)

I *lost my key (left my key in the room)*.
Ho *perso la mia chiave (lasciato la chiave in camera)*.
ō per′sō lä mē′ä kyä′ve (läshä′tō lä kyä′ve ēn kä′merä)

What time are meals served?
A che ora si mangia?
ä ke ō′rä sē män′jä

Where's the dining room?
Dov'è la sala da pranzo?
dōve′ lä sä′lä dä prän′dzō

Can we have breakfast in the room?
Possiamo fare colazione in camera?
pōsyä′mō fä′re kōlätsyō′ne ēn kä′merä

Could we have breakfast at seven tomorrow morning, please?
Possiamo fare colazione domani già alle sette?
pōsyä′mō fä′re kōlätsyō′ne dōmä′nē jä ä′le se′te

I'd like a box lunch tomorrow morning, please.
Per favore, per domani mattina una colazione al sacco.
per fàvōre, per dōmä′nē mätē′nä ōō′nä kōlätsyō′ne äl sä′kō

Please wake me at 7:30 tomorrow.
Per favore, mi svegli domani alle sette e mezzo.
per fàvō′re, mē zve′lyē dōmä′nē ä′le se′te e me′dzō

Maid

Come in!
Avanti!
ävän′tē

Just a moment, please!
Un momento, per favore!
ōōn mōmen′tō, per fävō′re

Could you wait another *five (ten)* minutes?
Può aspettare ancora *cinque (dieci)* minuti?
pōō·ō′ äspetä′re änkō′rä tshēn′kōō·e (dye′tshē) mēnōō′tē

We'll be going out in another *quarter hour (half hour)*.
Andiamo fra *un quarto d'ora (mezz'ora)*.
ändyä′mō frä ōōn kōō·är′tō dō′rä (medzō′rä)

Please bring *me (us)* ...
Per favore, *mi (ci)* porti ...
per fävō′re, mē (tshē) pōr′tē ...

another blanket	ancora una coperta ...	änkō′rä ōō′nä kō-per′tä
another pillow	ancora un cuscino	änkō′rä ōōn kōōshē′nō
another towel	ancora un'asciugamano	änkō′rä ōōn äshōōgämä′nō
an ash tray	un portacenere	ōōn pōrtätshe′nere
a blanket	una coperta	ōō′nä kōper′tä
breakfast	la prima colazione	lä prē′mä kōläts-yō′ne
a cake of soap	una saponetta	ōō′nä säpōne′tä
a couple of clothes hangers	alcuni attaccapanni ...	älkōō′nē ätäkä-pä′nē

How does this thing work?
Come funziona questo?
kō′me fōōntsyō′nä kōō·e′stō

Is our room ready?
Ha già fatto la nostra camera?
ä jä fä′tō lä nō′strä kä′merä

Would you have these things laundered for me?
Può far lavare queste cose per me?
pōō·ō′ fär lävä′re kōō·e′ste kō′se per me

Thanks very much!
Tante grazie!
tän′te grä′tsye

This is for you.
Questo è per Lei.
kōō·e′stō e per le′ē

Complaints

I'd like to speak to the manager, please.
Vorrei parlare con il direttore, per favore.
vōre′ē pärlä′re kōn ēl dēretō′re, per fävō′re

There's no ...	**There are no ...**	**... doesn't work.**
Non c'è ...	Non ci sono ...	... non funziona
nōn tshe ...	nōn tshē sō′nō ...	... nōn foontsyō′nä

There's no light in my room.
Non c'è luce nella mia camera.
nōn tshe loo′tshe ne′lä mē′ä kä′merä

The fuse has blown.
E' saltato il fusibile.
e sältä′tō ēl foozē′bēle

The socket is broken.
La presa è rotta.
lä pre′sä e rō′tä

This bulb has burned out.
Questa lampadina è bruciata.
kooe′stä lämpädē′nä e brootshä′tä

The bell (heating) doesn't work.
Il campanello (riscaldamento) non funziona.
ēl kämpäne′lō (rēskäldämen′tō) nōn foontsyō′nä

The key doesn't fit.
La chiave non è giusta.
lä kyä′ve nōn e joo′stä

The rain comes in.
Piove dentro.
pyō′ve den′trō

This window won't shut properly (won't open).
Questa finestra non si chiude bene (non si apre).
kooe′stä fēne′strä nōn sē kyoo′de be′ne (nōn sē ä′pre)

There's no (hot) water.
Non c'è acqua (calda).
nōn tshe ä′koo·ä (käl′dä)

There's a leak in this pipe.
Il tubo perde.
ēl too′bō per′de

The toilet won't flush.
Lo scarico per la toletta non funziona.
lō skä′rēkō per lä tōle′tä nōn foontsyō′nä

The faucet drips.
Il rubinetto perde.
ēl roobēne′tō per′de

The drain is stopped up.
Il tubo di scarico è otturato.
ēl too′bō dē skä′rēkō e ōtoorä′tō

Checking out

I'll be leaving tomorrow.
Parto domani.
pär'tō dōmä'nē

We're continuing on tomorrow.
Ripartiamo domani.
rēpärtyä'mō dōmä'nē

Would you please make up my bill?
Prepari il conto, per favore.
prepä'rē ēl kōn'tō, per fävō're

Could I please have *my (our)* bill?
Potrei avere il *mio (nostro)* conto?
pōtre'ē äve're ēl mē'ō (nō'strō) kōn'tō

Please wake me tomorrow morning.
Per favore, mi svegli domani mattina.
per fävō're, mē zve'lyē dōmä'nē mätē'nä

Please order a taxi for me tomorrow morning at 8.
Per favore, mi faccia venire un tassì domani mattina alle otto.
per fävō're, mē fä'tshä venē're ōon täsē' dōmä'nē mätē'nä ä'le ō'tō

Would you have my luggage taken to the *station (airport)?*
Può far portare il mio bagaglio *alla stazione (all'aeroporto)?*
pŏŏ·ō' fär pōrtä're ēl mē'ō bägä'lyō ä'lä stätsyō'ne (älä·erōpōr'tō)

When does the *bus (train)* to ... leave?
Quando parte *l'autobus (il treno)* per ...?
kŏŏ·än'dō pär'te lou'tōbōos (ēl tre'nō) per ...

Please forward my mail.
Per favore, spedisca la posta al mio indirizzo.
per fävō're, spedēs'kä lä pō'stä äl mē'ō ēndērē'tsō

Thanks for everything!
Grazie mille di tutto!
grä'tsye mē'le dē tōo'tō

We had a very good *time (rest)* here.
E' stato molto bello qui da Voi *(ci siamo veramente riposati).*
e stä'tō mōl'tō be'lō kōo·ē' dä vō'ē (tshē syä'mō verämen'te rēpōsä'tē)

accommodations ..	(l') alloggio *m*	älō'jō
adapter plug	(la) spina intermedia ..	spē'nä ēnterme'dyä
air conditioning ...	(l') aria *f* condizionata .	är'yä kōndētsyōnä'tä

alternating current ..	(la) corrente alternata ·	kōren'te älternä'tä
American breakfast .	(la) colazione-buffet ···	kōlätsyō'ne-boofet'
American plan	(la) pensione completa ·	pensyō'ne kōmple'tä
armchair	(la) poltrona	pōltrō'nä
arrival	(l') arrivo *m*	ärē'vō
ash tray	(il) portacenere	pōrtätshe'nere
balcony	(il) balcone	bälkō'ne
basement	(il) seminterrato	semēnterä'tō
bathroom	(il) bagno	bä'nyō
bed	(il) letto	le'tō
– **bedspread**	(la) coperta	kōper'tä
– **blanket**	(la) coperta di lana	kōper'tä dē lä'nä
– **crib**	(il) lettino per bambini·	letē'nō per bämbē'nē
– **mattress**	(il) materasso	mäterä'sō
– **pillow**	(il) cuscino	kooshē'nō
bed and two meals ...	(la) mezza pensione ...	me'dzä pensyō'ne
bed linen	(la) biancheria da letto·	byänkerē'ä dä le'tō
– **pillowcase**	(la) federa	fe'derä
– **sheet**	(il) lenzuolo	lentsoo·ō'lō
bed rug	(il) scendiletto	shendēle'tō
bedside table	(il) comodino	kōmōdē'nō
bell	(il) campanello	kämpäne'lō
bill	(il) conto	kōn'tō
breakfast	(la) prima colazione ...	prē'mä kōlätsyō'ne
– **eat breakfast**	fare colazione	fä're kōlätsyō'ne
breakfast room	(la) sala per la prima colazione	sä'lä per lä prē'mä kōlätsyō'ne
bucket	(il) secchio	se'kyō
carpet	(il) tappeto	täpe'tō
category	(la) categoria	kätegōrē'ä
central heating	(il) riscaldamento centrale	rēskäldämen'tō tshenträ'le
chair	(la) sedia	se'dyä
check-in form	formulario di soggiorno	fōrmoolär'yō dē sōjōr'nō
chimney	(il) camino	kämē'nō
closet	(la) guardaroba	goo·ärdärō'bä
clothes hanger	(la) gruccia	groo'tshä
complaint	(il) reclamo	reklä'mō

concierge	(il) portinaio	pōrtēnä'yō
corridor	(il) corridoio	kōrēdō'yō
curtain	(la) tenda	ten'dä
day bed	(il) divano	dēvä'nō
deck chair	(lo) sdraio	zdrä'yō
departure	(la) partenza	pärten'tsä
deposit	(l') acconto m	äkōn'tō
dining room	(la) sala da pranzo	sä'lä dä prän'dzō
dinner	(il) pranzo	prän'dzō
door	(la) porta	pōr'tä
door handle	(la) maniglia della porta	mänē'lyä de'lä pōr'tä
drapery	(la) tenda	ten'dä
drawer	(il) cassetto	käse'tō
elevator	(l') ascensore m	äshensō're
entrance	(l') entrata f	enträ'tä
exit	(l') uscita f	ōoshē'tä
extension cord	(la) prolunga	prōlo͞on'gä
fan	(il) ventilatore	ventēlätō're
faucet	(il) rubinetto	ro͞obēne'tō
fireplace	(il) camino	kämē'nō
floor	(il) pavimento	pävēmen'tō
front door	(la) porta d'entrata	pōr'tä denträ'tä
fuse	(il) fusibile	fo͞ozē'bēle
garden umbrella	(l') ombrellone m	ōmbrelō'ne
grill room	(la) rosticceria	rōstētsherē'ä
guest house	(la) pensione	pensyō'ne
hall	(lo) hall m	äl
heating	(il) riscaldamento	rēskäldämen'tō
hotel	(l') hotel m	ōtel'
– beach hotel	(l') albergo m sulla spiaggia	älber'gō so͞o'lä spyä'jä
hotel restaurant	(il) ristorante dell'albergo	rēstōrän'te delälber'gō
house	(la) casa	kä'sä
house key	(la) chiave di casa	kyä've dē kä'sä
inquiry	(l') informazione f	ēnfōrmätsyō'ne
key	(la) chiave	kyä've
kitchen	(la) cucina	ko͞otshē'nä
kitchenette	(il) cucinotto	ko͞otshēnō'tō
lamp	(la) lampada	läm'pädä

laundry	(la) biancheria	byänkerē'ä
– do laundry	lavare	lävä're
– dry	asciugare	äshoōgä're
– iron	stirare	stērä're
light bulb	(la) lampadina	lämpädē'nä
lights	(le) luci	loō'tshē
lobby	(l') atrio *m*, (lo) hall	ä'tryō, äl
lock	(la) serratura	serätoō'rä
– lock up	chiudere a chiave	kyoō'dere ä kyä've
– unlock	aprire con chiave	äprē're kōn kyä've
lunch	(il) pranzo/	prän'dzō/
	(lo) spuntino	spoōntē'nō
maid	(la) cameriera	kämerye'rä
mirror	(lo) specchio	spe'kyō
move	trasferirsi	träsferēr'sē
move in	traslocare in	träzlōkä're ēn
move out	traslocare da	träzlōkä're dä
night's lodging	(l') alloggio *m* per una	älō'jō per oō'nä
	notte	nō'te
pail	(il) secchio	se'kyō
patio	(il) cortile interno	kōrtē'le ēnter'nō
pension	(la) pensione	pensyō'ne
plug	(la) spina	spē'nä
pot	(la) pentola	pen'tōlä
price	(il) prezzo	pre'tsō
private beach	(la) spiaggia privata	spyä'jä prēvä'tä
radiator	(il) radiatore	rädyätō're
reading lamp	(la) lampada da tavolo	läm'pädä dä tä'vōlō
refrigerator	(il) frigorifero	frēgōrē'ferō
rent *(noun)*	(l') affitto *m*	äfē'tō
rent *(verb)*	noleggiare	nōlejä're
rest room	(il) gabinetto	gäbēne'tō
– ladies' room	– signore	sēnyō're
– men's room	– signori	sēnyō'rē
room	(la) camera	kä'merä
– bedroom	(la) camera da letto	kä'merä dä le'tō
– living room	(il) salotto	sälō'tō
– nursery	(la) camera per i	kä'merä per ē
	bambini	bämbē'nē
season	(la) stagione	stäjō'ne

service	(il) servizio	servē'tsyō
service charge	(la) tassa di servizio	tä'sä dē servē'tsyō
shower	(la) doccia	dōtshä
sink	(il) lavandino	lävändē'nō
socket	(la) presa di corrente	pre'sä dē kōren'te
staircase	(la) scala	skä'lä
stairwell	(la) tromba delle scale	trōm'bä de'le skä'le
stove	(la) stufa	stoo'fä
swimming pool	(la) piscina	pēshē'nä
switch	(l') interruttore *m*	ēnteroōtō're
table	(il) tavolo	tä'vōlō
tablecloth	(la) tovaglia	tōvä'lyä
telephone	(il) telefono	tele'fōnō
terrace	(il) terrazzo	terä'tsō
toilet paper	(la) carta igienica	kär'tä ēje'nēkä
tour guide	(la) guida turistica	goo'ē·dä toorē'stēkä
travel agency	(l') agenzia *f* viaggi	äjentsē'ä vyä'jē
vacate the room	lasciare la camera	läshä're lä kä'merä
ventilation	(la) ventilazione	ventēlätsyō'ne
voltage	(il) voltaggio	vōltä'jō
wall	(la) parete	päre'te
water	(l') acqua *f*	ä'koo·ä
– cold water	l'acqua fredda	lä'koo·ä fre'dä
– hot water	l'acqua calda	lä'koo·ä käl'dä
water glass	(il) bicchiere da acqua	bēkye're dä ä'koo·ä
window	(la) finestra	fēne'strä
windowpane	(il) vetro	ve'trō

220 V ~

Camping, Youth Hostels

Is there a *camping site (youth hostel)* near here?
C'è qui un campeggio (un ostello per la gioventù)?
tshe kōō·ē' ōōn kämpe'jō (ōōn ōste'lō per lä jōventōō'

Can we camp here?
Possiamo campeggiare qui?
pōsyä'mō kämpejä're kōō·ē'

Is the site guarded at night?
Il campeggio è sorvegliato di notte?
ēl kämpe'jō e sōrvelyä'tō dē nō'te

Do you have room (for another tent)?
C'è ancora posto (per un'altra tenda)?
tshe änkō'rä pō'stō (per ōōnäl'trä ten'dä)

How much does it cost to stay overnight?
Qual'è il prezzo per una notte?
kōō·äle' ēl pre'tsō per ōō'nä nō'te

How much is it for the *car (trailer)*?
Quanto si paga per la macchina (la roulotte)?
kōō·än'tō sē pä'gä per lä mä'kēnä (lä rōōlōt')

I'l be staying ... *days (weeks)*.
Rimango ... giorni (settimane).
rēmän'gō ... jōr'nē (setēmä'ne)

Can we ... here?
Possiamo ... qui?
pōsyämō ... kōō·ē'

Is there a grocery store near here?
C'è vicino un negozio di generi alimentari?
tshe kōō·ē' vētshē'nō ōōn negō'tsyō dē je'nerē älēmentä're

Can I *rent bottled gas (exchange gas bottles)* here?
Dove si prendono (cambiano) bombole di gas?
dō've sē pren'dōnō (käm'byänō) bōm'bōle dē gäs

Where are the *rest rooms (wash rooms)*?
Dove sono i gabinetti (le docce)?
dō've sō'nō ē gäbēne'tē (le dō'tshe)

Where can I ...?
Dove posso ...?
dō've pō'sō ...

Are there any electric connections here?
Ci sono delle prese di corrente elettrica?
tshē sō'nō de'le pre'se dē kōren'te ele'trēkä

Can we drink the water?
L'acqua è potabile?
lä'kōō·ä e pōtä'bēle

Can I rent ...?
Posso prendere ... in prestito (affitto)?
pō'sō pren'dere ... ēn pre'stētō (äfē'tō)

camp bed	(il) lettino da campeggio	letē′nō dä kämpe′jō
camping	(il) campeggio	kämpe′jō
camping ID	(la) tessera di campeggio	te′serä dē kämpe′jō
camp out	campeggiare	kämpejä′re
camp site	(il) campeggio	kämpe′jō
check-in	registrare l'arrivo	rejēsträ′re lärē′vō
check-out	registrare la partenza	rejēsträ′re lä pärten′tsä
cook	cucinare	kōōtshēnä′re
cooking stove	(il) fornello	fōrne′lō
day room	(la) sala comune	sä′lä kōmōō′ne
dishes	(le) stoviglie	stōvē′lye
dormitory	(il) dormitorio	dōrmētōr′yō
drinking water	(l') acqua *f* potabile	ä′kōō·ä pōtä′bēle
get	ricevere	rētshe′vere
go swimming	andare a nuotare	ändä′re ä nōō·ōtä′re
hostel parents	(i) direttori dell'ostello	dēretō′rē delōste′lō
– hostel mother	(la) direttrice	dēretrē′tshe
– hostel father	(l') albergatore *m*	älbergätō′re
iron	(il) ferro da stiro	fe′rō dä stē′rō
membership card	(la) tessera	te′serä
park	parcheggiare	pärkejä′re
playground	(il) campo di giochi	käm′pō dē jō′kē
recreation room	(il) soggiorno	sōjōr′nō
rent	noleggiare	nōlejä′re
rental fee	(il) noleggio	nōle′jō
sleeping bag	(il) sacco a pelo	sä′kō ä pe′lō
take a bath	fare il bagno	fä′re ēl bä′nyō
tent	(la) tenda	ten′dä
trailer	(la) roulotte	rōōlōt′
usage fee	(la) tassa per l'uso	tä′sä per lōō′zō
wash	lavare	lävä′re
youth group	(il) gruppo di giovani	grōō′pō dē jō′väne
youth hostel	(l') ostello *m* per la gioventù	ōste′lō per lä jōventōō′
youth hostel card	(la) tessera per l'ostello	tese′rä per lōste′lō

FOOD AND DRINK

Ordering

Is there a *good (Chinese, seafood)* restaurant here?
C'è qui vicino un buon ristorante *(cinese, con specialità di pesce)*?
tshe kōō·ē′ vētshē′nō ōōn bōō·ōn′ rēstōrän′te (tshēne′se, kōn spetshälē-tä′ dē pe′she)

Would you please reserve a table for four at eight P.M.?
Per favore, ci riservi un tavolo per quattro per le otto?
per fävō′re, tshē rēser′vē ōōn tä′vōlō per kōō·ät′rō per le ō′tō

Is this *table (seat)* taken?
Questo *tavolo (posto)* è occupato?
kōō·e·stō′ tä′vōlō (pō′stō) e ōkōōpä′tō

Waiter!	**Waitress!**	**Is this your table?**
Cameriere!/Signore!	Signorina!	Lei serve qui?
kämerye′re/sēnyō′re	sēnyōrē′nä	le′ē ser′ve kōō·ē′

I'd like a meal.
Vorrei mangiare qualcosa.
vōre′ē mänjä′re kōō·älkō′sä

We'd like a drink.
Vorremmo bere qualcosa.
vōre′mō be′re kōō·älkō′sä

Could I see the *menu (wine list)*, please?
Posso avere la *lista (lista delle bevande)*, per favore?
pō′sō äve′re lä lē′stä (lē′stä de′le bevän′de), per fävō′re

What can we have right away?
Che cosa c'è di pronto?
ke kō′sä tshe dē prōn′tō

Do you have ...?
Ha ...?
ä ...

Do you have *vegetarian (diet)* food too?
Ci sono cibi *vegetariani (dietetici)*?
tshē sō′nō tshē′bē vejetäryä′nē (dyete′tētshē)

Please bring us *one portion (two portions)* of ...
Per favore, ci porti *una porzione (due porzioni)* di ...
per fävō′re, tshē pōr′tē ōō′nä pōrtsyō′ne (dōō′e pōrtsyō′nē) dē ...

A *cup (pot, glass, bottle)* of ..., please.
Per favore, *una tazza (un bricchetto, bicchiere, una bottiglia)* di ...
per fävō′re ōō′nä tä′tsä (ōōn brēke′tō, bēkye′re, ōō′nä bōtē′lyä) dē ...

Table Service

ash tray	(il) portacenere	pōrtätshe′nere
bottle	(la) bottiglia	bōtē′lyä
bottle opener	(l') apribottiglia *m*	äprēbōtē′lyä
bowl	(la) scodella	skōde′lä
bread basket	(il) cestino del pane	tshestē′nō del pä′ne
carafe	(la) caraffa	kärä′fä
corkscrew	(il) cavatappi	kävätä′pē
cruet stand	(l') oliera *f*	ōlye′rä
cup	(la) tazza	tä′tsä
- saucer	(il) piattino	pyätē′nō
cutlery	(le) posate	pōsä′te
decanter	(la) caraffa	kärä′fä
egg cup	(il) portauova	pōrtä·ōō·ō′vä
fork	(la) forchetta	fōrke′tä
glass	(il) bicchiere	bēkye′re
- water glass	– da acqua	dä′kōō·ä
- wine glass	– da vino	dävē′nō
knife	(il) coltello	kōlte′lō
mustard jar	(la) mostardiera	mōstärdye′rä
napkin	(il) tovagliolo	tōvälyō′lō
pepper mill	il macinino del pepe	mätshēnē′nō del pe′pe
pepper shaker	(il) portapepe	pōrtäpe′pe
plate	(il) piatto	pyä′tō
- bread plate	(il) piattino	pyätē′nō
- soup plate	(il) piatto fondo	pyä′tō fōn′dō
pot	(la) brocca	brō′kä
- coffee pot	(la) caffettiera	käfetye′rä
- tea pot	(la) teiera	teye′rä
salt shaker	(il) portasale	pōrtäsä′le
spoon	(il) cucchiaio	kōōkyä′yō
- soup spoon	– per la minestra	per lä mēne′strä
- teaspoon	(il) cucchiaino	kōōkyä·ē′nō
sugar bowl	(la) zuccheriera	tsōōkerye′rä
tablecloth	(la) tovaglia	tōvä′lyä
toothpick	(lo) stuzzicadente	stōōtsēkäde′nte
tray	(il) vassoio	väsō′yō

Breakfast

bread	(il) pane	pä'ne
– dark bread	(il) pane nero	pä'ne ne'rō
– rye bread	(il) pane di segale	pä'ne dē se'gäle
– whole wheat bread	(il) pane integrale	pä'ne ēntegrä'le
breakfast	(la) colazione	kōlätsyō'ne
– eat breakfast	fare colazione	fä're kōlätsyō'ne
butter	(il) burro	bōō'rō
cereal	(i) fiocchi di cereale	fyō'kē dē tshere·ä'le
coffee	(il) caffè	käfe'
– black	nero	ne'rō
– decaffeinated	decaffeinato	dekäfe·ēnä'tō
– with cream	con panna	kōn pä'nä
– with sugar	con zucchero	kōn tsōō'kerō
cold cuts	(l') affettato *m*	äfetä'tō
croissant	(la) brioche	brē·ōsh'
egg	(l') uovo *m*	ōō·ō'vō
– hard-boiled	sodo	sō'dō
– soft-boiled	alla coque	ä'lä kōk
– fried eggs	uova fritte	ōō·ō'vä frē'te
– scrambled eggs	uova strapazzate	ōō·ō'vä sträpätsä'te
fruit juice	(il) succo di frutta	sōō'kō dē frōō'tä
– grapefruit juice	succo di pompelmo	sōō'kō dē pōmpel'mō
– orange juice	succo d'arancia	sōō'kō därän'tshä
– tomato juice	succo di pomodoro	sōō'kō dē pōmōdō'rō
honey	(il) miele	mye'le
hot chocolate	(la) cioccolata	tshōkōlä'tä
jam	(la) marmellata	märmelä'tä
milk	(il) latte	lä'te
– condensed milk	(il) latte condensato	lä'te kōndensä'tō
roll	(il) panino	pänē'nō
sausage	(la) salsiccia	sälsēt'shä
slice	(la) fetta	fe'tä
sugar	(lo) zucchero	tsōō'kerō
tea	(il) tè	te
– with lemon	con limone	kōn lēmō'ne
– with milk	con latte	kōn lä'te

> On the European continent, breakfast is generally rather simple, consisting of coffee or tea, rolls, butter and jam. Persons wishing more than that should stipulate: "Una colazione grande con . . ." (see p. 98 for details).

Lunch and Dinner

I'd (We'd) like to have . . .
Desidero (desideriamo) . . .
dese'derō (desēderyä'mō) . . .

Would you bring us . . .?
Può portarci . . .?
pōō·ō' pōrtär'tshē . . .

Please pass . . .
Per favore mi passi . . .
per fävō're mē pä'sē . . .

What's the name of this dish?
Come si chiama questo piatto?
kō'me sē kyä'mä kōō·e'stō pyä'tō

*Would you like seconds on anything?
Desidera ancora qualcosa?
desē'derä änkō'rä kōō·älkō'sä

Yes, please.
Sì, grazie.
sē, grä'tsye

Yes, indeed!
Sì, volentieri!
sē, vōlentye're

Just a little.
Solo un poco.
sō'lō ōon pō'kō

Thanks, that's enough.
Grazie, basta così.
grä'tsye, bäs'tä kōse'

No, thanks.
No, grazie.
nō, grä'tsye

I've had enough.
Sono sazio.
sō'nō sä'tsyō

Nothing more, thanks.
Nient'altro, grazie.
nyentäl'trō, grä'tsye

*Did you like it?
Le è piaciuto?
le e pyätshōō'tō

Delicious!
Squisito!
skōō·ēzē'tō

*Empty your glass!
Finisca il Suo bicchiere!
fēnēs'kä ēl sōō'ō bēkye're

Cheers!
Alla salute!
ä'lä sälōō'te

This dish (The wine) is delicious!
Questo piatto (Il vino) è squisito!
kōō·e'stō pyä'tō (ēl vē'nō) e skōō·ēzē'tō

I'm not allowed to have any alcohol (I don't care for alcohol).
Non posso bere bevande alcooliche. (Rinuncio all`alcool).
nōn pō'sō be're bevän'de älkō·ō'lēke (rēnōōn'tshō äläl'kō·ōl)

Cooking

baked	cotto al forno	kō'tō äl fōr'nō
boiled	lessato, bollito	lesä'tō, bōlē'tō
braised	stufato	stoōfä'tō
cold	freddo	fre'dō
deep fried	fritto bene	frē'tō be'ne
fat	grasso	grä'sō
fresh	fresco	fre'skō
fried	fritto	frē'tō
grilled	alla griglia	ä'lä grē'lyä
hard	duro	doō'rō
hot	caldo	käl'dō
hot *(spicy)*	piccante	pēkän'te
juicy	sugoso	soōgō'sō
lean	magro	mä'grō
medium (done)	cotto a metà	kō'tō ä metä'
pickled	conservato in	kōnservä'tō ēn
	salamoia	sälämō'yä
rare	al sangue	äl sän'goo·e
raw	crudo	kroō'dō
roasted	arrostito	ärōstē'tō
salted	salato	sälä'tō
seasoned	condito	kōndē'tō
smoked	affumicato	äfoōmēkä'tō
soft	morbido	mōr'bēdō
steamed	cotto a vapore	kō'tō ä väpō're
stewed	cotto in umido	kō'tō ēn oō'mēdō
stuffed	farcito	färtshē'tō
stuffing	(il) ripieno	rēpye'nō
tender	tenero	te'nerō
tough	duro	doō'rō
well done	ben cotto	ben kō'tō

Ingredients

bacon	(il) lardo	lär'dō
basil	(il) basilico	bäzē'lēkō
butter	(il) burro	boō'rō
capers	(i) capperi	kä'perē
caraway	(il) comino *f*	kōmē'nō

hives	(l') erba cipollina *f*	er′ba tshēpolē′nä
innamon	(la) cannella	käne′lä
loves	(i) chiodi di garofano..	kyō′dē dē gärō′fänō
till	(l') aneto *m*	äne′tō
at	(il) grasso	grä′sō
garlic	(l') aglio *m*	ä′lyō
ginger	(il) zenzero	dzen′dzerō
herbs	(le) erbe.	er′be
horseradish	(il) rafano............	rä′fänō
elly *(aspic)*	(la) gelatina	jelätē′nä
elly *(fruit)*	(la) conserva di frutta .	kōnser′vä dē frōō′tä
ketchup	(il) ketchup...........	ket′shōp
emon	(il) limone............	lēmō′ne
mayonnaise	(la) maionese..........	mayōne′se
mayonnaise sauce .	(la) salsa di maionese	säl′sä dē mäyōne′se
mushrooms	(i) funghi	fōōn′gē
mustard	(la) senape	se′näpe
nutmeg	(la) noce moscata	nō′tshe mōskä′tä
oil	(l') olio *m*	ō′lyō
olives	(le) olive	ōlē′ve
onion	(la) cipolla	tshēpō′lä
paprika	(la) paprica	pä′prēkä
parsley	(il) prezzemolo........	pretse′mōlō
pepper	(il) pepe..............	pe′pe
pickles	(i) sottaceti	sōtätshe′tē
raisins	(l') uva *f* passa........	ōō′vä pä′sä
rosemary	(il) rosmarino	rōzmärē′nō
sage	(la) salvia	säl′vyä
salt	(il) sale	sä′le
sauce	(la) salsa	säl′sä
- cream sauce	(la) salsa alla crema ...	säl′sä ä′lä kre′mä
- gravy	(la) salsa forte	säl′sä fōr′te
seasoning, spices ..	(il) condimento	kōndēmen′tō
thyme	(il) timo..............	tē′mō
vanilla	(la) vaniglia	vänē′lyä
vinegar	(l') aceto *m*	ätshe′tō

THE MENU

Appetizers

acciughe	ätshoo'ge	anchovies
affettato misto	äfetä'tō mē'stō	cold cuts
alici piccanti	älē'tshē pēkän'tē	anchovies in a spicy sauce
anguilla affumicata	ängoo·ē'lä äfoomēkä'tä	smoked eel
antipasti, aperitivi	äntēpä'stē, äperētē'vē	hors d'oeuvres
bruschetta	brooske'tä	toasted bread
carciofini e funghetti sott'olio	kärtshōfē'nē e foonge'tē sōtō'lyō	artichokes and mush-rooms in oil
carpaccio	kär'pätshō	raw, sliced beef
caviale	kävyä'le	caviar
cocktail di gamberetti	kōktel' dē gämbere'tē	lobster cocktail
crostini di prosciutto	krōstē'nē dē prōshoo'tō	Italian bread, toasted with ham
gamberetti	gämbere'tē	shrimps
gamberi	gäm'berē	crab, crawfish
insalata di mare	ēnsälä'tä dē mä're	seafood salad
insalata di gamberi	ensälä'tä de gäm'berē	crab salad
lingua salmistrata	lēn'goo·ä sälmēsträ'tä	pickled tongue
lumache	loomä'ke	snails
melone e prosciutto	melō'ne e prōshoo'tō	melon with smoked ham
olive	olē've	olives
ostriche	ō'strēke	oysters
paté (pasticcio) di fegato d'oca	päte' (pästē'tshō) dē fe'gätō dō'kä	goose liver paté
peperoni in salsa	peperō'nē ēn säl'sä	green/red peppers in a sauce
prosciutto con fichi freschi	prōshoo'tō kōn fē'kē fres'kē	smoked ham with fresh figs
salmone affumicato	sälmō'ne äfoomēkä'tō	smoked salmon
sardine all'olio	särdē'ne älō'lyō	sardines in oil
succo di pomodoro	soo'kō dē pōmōdō'rō	tomato juice

Soups

brodetto (brodino leggero)	brōde'to (brōdē'nō leje'rō)	**clear soup**
brodo	brō'dō	**broth/consommé**
- con riso	kōn rē'sō	**with rice**
- con un uovo sbattuto	kōn ōon ōo·ō'vō zbätōo'tō	**with egg**
brodo di pollo	brō'dō dē pō'lō	**chicken broth**
brodo di tartaruga ..	brō'dō dē tärtärōo'gä	**turtle soup**
brodo di verdura	brō'dō dē verdōo'rä .	**leek soup**
crema di asparagi ...	kre'mä dē äspä'räjē .	**cream of asparagus soup**
crema di funghi	kre'mä dē fōon'gē ...	**cream of mushroom soup**
minestra	mēne'strä	**thick soup**
minestra di fagioli ...	mēne'strä dē fäjō'lē .	**bean soup**
minestrone	mēnestrō'ne	**vegetable soup**
pastina in brodo	pä'stē'nä ēn brō'dō ..	**noodle soup**
zuppa	tsōo'pä	**soup**
zuppa di cipolle	tsōo'pä dē tshēpō'le .	**onion soup**
zuppa di coda di bue	tsōo'pä dē kō'dä dē bōo'e	**oxtail soup**
zuppa alla pavese ...	tsōo'pä ä'lä päve'ze .	**bouillon with egg and toast dumplings**
zuppa alla marinara .	tsōo'pä ä'lä märe-nä'rä	**fish soup**
zuppa di pesce	tsōo'pä dē pe'she ...	**fish soup**
zuppa di pomodoro ..	tsōo'pä dē pōmōdō'rō	**tomato soup**

Eggs

frittata/omelette	frētä'tä/ōmlet'	**omelet**
omelette di verdura ..	ōmlet' dē verdōo'rä .	**filled vegetable omelet**
uova al tegame	ōo·ō'vä äl regä'me ..	**fried eggs**
uova alla coque	ōo·ō'vä ä'lä kōk	**soft-boiled eggs**
uova sode	ōo·ō'vä sō'de	**hard-boiled eggs**
uova strapazzate	ōo·ō'vä sträpätsä'te .	**scrambled eggs**

Rice and Noodle dishes

agnoletti	änyōle′tē	chopped spicy meat wrapped in noodle dough
gnocchi	nyō′kē	tiny dumplings
lasagne verdi	läzän′ye ver′dē	lasagne (with spinach)
maccheroni	mäkerō′nē	macaroni
pasta asciutta	pä′stä äshoo′tä	noodles, pasta
– al burro	äl boo′rō	– with butter
– al pomodoro	äl pōmōdō′rō	– with tomato sauce
– alle vongole	ä′le vōn′gōle	– with clams
– al sugo	äl soo′gō	– with tomato and meat sauce
con parmigiano	kōn pärmējä′no	– with cheese
polenta	pōlen′tä	corn meal mush
risotto alla	rēsō′tō ä′lä	
milanese	mēläne′se	rice in saffron sauce
– con funghi	kōn foon′gē	rice in mushroom sauce
– alla marinara	ä′lä märēnä′rä	rice with seafood
spaghetti alla	späge′tē ä′lä	spaghetti in a cream
carbonara	kärbōnä′rä	sauce with egg and ham
quadrettini	koo·ädretē′nē	small square noodles for soup
tagliatelle/fettucine	tälyäte′le/fetootshē′ne	wide noodles

Fish

anguilla	ängoo·ē′lä	eel
aringa	ärēn′gä	herring
baccalà	bäkälä′	stockfish/dried cod
carpa	kär′pä	carp
fritto di pesce	frē′tō dē pe′she	dish of fried fish
ipoglosso	ēpōglō′sō	halibut
luccio	loo′tshō	pike
merluzzo	merloo′tsō	cod
pesce	pe′she	fish
pesce passera	pe′she pä′serä	plaice

pesce persico	pe'she per'sēkō	perch
rombo	rōm'bō	turbot
salmone	sälmō'ne	salmon
sgombro	zgōm'brō	mackerel
sogliola	sō'lyōlä	sole
storione	stōryō'ne	sturgeon
tonno	tō'nō	tuna fish
trota	trō'tä	trout

Sea Food

aragosta	ärägō'stä	*spiny (rock)* lobster
calamari	kälämä'rē	cuttlefish
calamaretto	kälämäre'to	little squid
cozze	kō'tse	mussels
crostacei	krōstä'tshe·ē	shellfish
frittura di pesce	frētōō'rä dē pe'she	dish of baked (shell-)fish
frutti di mare	frōō'tē dē mä're	sea food
gamberetti, granchiolini	gämbere'tē, gränkyōlē'nē	shrimps, prawns
gambero, granchio	gäm'berō, grän'kyō	crab
ostriche	ō'strēke	oysters
tartaruga	tärtärōō'gä	turtle
vongole	vōn'gōle	clams

Poultry

anitra	ä'nēträ	duck
anitra selvatica	ä'nēträ selvä'tēkä	wild duck
cappone	käpō'ne	capon
coscia di pollo	kō'shä dē pō'lō	chicken drumstick
fagiano	fäjä'nō	pheasant
faraona	färä·ō'nä	guinea hen
oca arrosto	o'kä ärō'stō	roast goose
petto di pollo	pe'tō dē pō'lō	chicken breast
piccione	pētshō'ne	squab
pollastro, pollo	pōlä'strō, pō'lō	chicken
pollo arrosto	pō'lō ärō'stō	broiler, fryer
– alla cacciatore	ä'lä kätshätō're	– broiled chicken in a sauce

– fritto	frē´tō	fried chicken
– alla griglia	ä´lä grēlyä	roast chicken
tacchino	täkē´nō	turkey
pollame	pōlä´me	poultry

Meat

abbacchio	äbä´kyo	roast lamb
agnello	änye´lō	lamb
arrosto	ärō´stō	roast
bistecca di filetto	bēste´kä dē fēle´tō	rump steak
bollito misto	bōlē´tō mē´stō	diverse boiled meats
braciola	brätshō´lä	chop (lamb or pork)
braciola ai ferri	brätshō´lä ī fe´rē	grilled cutlet
bue	boo´e	beef
capretto	käpre´tō	suckling kid
capriolo	käprē·ō´lō	venison
cinghiale	tshēngyä´le	wild boar
coniglio	kōnē´lyō	rabbit
cosciotto	kōshō´tō	leg
costoletta (cotoletto)	kōstōle´tä (kōtōle´tō)	cutlet
costoletta di vitello	kōstōle´tä dē vēte´lō	veal cutlet
costoletta alla milanese	kōstōle´tä älä mēläne´se	Wiener Schnitzel
fegato	fe´gätō	liver
filetto	fēle´tō	filet
filetto di carne	fēle´tō dē kär´ne	tenderloin
filetto di manzo	fēle´tō dē män´dzō	beef filet
fritto misto	frē´tō mē´stō	mixed fried meat
stinco di maiale	stēnkō dē mäyä´le	pork hock
stinco di vitello	stēnkō dē vēte´lō	veal knuckle
involtini di manzo	ēnvōltē´nē dē män´dzō	beef rolls with a filling
lepre	le´pre	hare
lingua	lēn´goo·ä	tongue
maiale	mäyä´le	pork
manzo	män´dzō	beef
ossobuco	ōsōboo´kō	sliced veal knuckle
piccata	pēkä´tä	small veal escalopes
polmone	pōlmō´ne	lung

polpette	pōlpe′te	meat balls
polpettone	pōlpetō′ne	meat loaf
prosciutto	prōshoo̅′tō	ham
– cotto	kō′tō	boiled ham
– crudo	kroo̅′dō	raw ham
punta di petto	poo̅n′tä dē pe′tō	brisket
rognoni	rōnyō′nē	kidneys
rosbif	rōz′bēf	roast beef
salsicce	sälsē′tshe	sausages
saltimbocca alla romana	sältēmbō′kä ä′lä rōmä′nä	veal cutlet with finely sliced smoked ham and sage
scaloppine	skälōpē′ne	escalopes
sella	se′lä	saddle
selvaggina	selväjē′nä	game
spalla	spä′lä	shoulder
spezzatino	spetsätē′nō	goulash
stufato	stoo̅fä′tō	ragout, delicate stew
trippa	trē′pa	tripe
vitello	vēte′lō	veal
affumicato	äfoo̅mēkä′tō	smoked
lesso, bollito	le′sō, bōlē′tō	boiled
arrosto	ärō′stō	roasted
fritto	frē′tō	(deep) fried
in salamoia	ēn sälämō′yä	pickled, marinated
stufato	stoo̅fä′tō	stewed

Vegetables

asparagi	äspä′räjē	asparagus
broccoli	brō′kōlē	broccoli
carciofi	kärtshō′fē	artichokes
carote	kärō′te	carrots
cavolfiore	kävōlfyō′re	cauliflower
cavolo	kä′vōlō	cabbage
cavolo riccio	kä′vōlō rē′tshō	kale
cavolo rosso	kä′vōlō rō′sō	red cabbage
cavolini di Bruxelles	kävōlē′nē dē broo̅ksel′	Brussels sprouts
cetriolo	tshetrē·ō′lō	cucumber

cicoria	tshekō′rya	chicory
cipolla	tshēpō′lä	onion
crauti	krou′tē	sauerkraut
fagiolini	fäjōlē′nē	green beans
fagioli	fäjō′lē	beans
finocchio	fēnō′kyō	fennel
funghi	foon′gē	mushrooms
indivia	ēndē′vyä	endive
lattuga	lätoo′gä	lettuce
lenticchie	lentē′kye	lentels
melanzane	meländzä′ne	eggplants
patate	pätä′te	potatoes
– arroste	ärō′ste	roast potatoes
– fritte	frē′te	frenchfries
– lesse	le′se	boiled potatoes
peperoni	peperō′nē	peppers
piselli	pēze′lē	peas
pomodori	pōmōdō′rē	tomatoes
radicchio	rädē′kyō	radicchio salad
rape	rä′pe	beets
scarola	skärō′lä	iceberg lettuce
sedano	se′dänō	celery
sottaceti	sotätshe′tē	pickle
spinaci	spēnä′tshē	spinach
zucchini	tsookē′nē	zucchini squash
verdura	verdoo′rä	vegetables
verza	ver′tsä	savoy cabbage

Cheese

Bel Paese	bel pä·e′ze	bel paese, a soft, buttery cheese
formaggio grattugiato	fōrmä′jō grätoojä′tō	grated cheese
gorgonzola	gōrgōndzō′lä	blue cheese
gruviera	groovye′rä	gruyère
mozzarella	mōtsäre′lä	mozzarella
parmigiano	pärmējä′nō	parmesan cheese
pecorino	pekōrē′nō	cottage (sheep's) cheese
ricotta	rēkō′tä	farmer cheese, ricotta
stracchino	sträke′nō	cream cheese

Desserts

babà al rum	bäbä' äl room'	small raisin cake with rum
budino	boodē'nō	pudding
cassata	käsä'tä	ice cream with candied fruits
crema al caramello	kre'mä äl käräme'lō	crème au caramel
frutta cotta	froo'tä kō'tä	stewed fruit
gelato	jelä'tō	ice cream
macedonia	mätshedō'nyä	fruit salad
semifreddo	semēfre'dō	frozen dessert
tirami sù	tērämēsoo'	tasty cream with coffee topping
torta di cioccolato	tōr'tä dē tshōkōlä'tō	black chocolate cake
torta di mele	tōr'tä dē me'le	apple cake
torta di ricotta	tōr'tä dē rēkō'tä	cheese cake
zabaione	dzäbäyō'ne	cream of beaten eggs with wine and brandy
zuppa romana	tsoo'pä rōmä'nä	biscuit soaked in rum with cream filling

Fruit

ananas	ä'nänäs	pineapple
albicocca	älbēkō'kä	apricot
arancia	ärän'tshä	orange
banana	bänä'nä	banana
castagne	kästä'nye	chestnuts
cedro	tshe'drō	limes
ciliege	tshēlye'je	cherries
cocomero/anguria	kōkō'merō/ängoor'yä	watermelon
datteri	dä'terē	dates
fichi	fē'kē	figs
fragole	frä'gōle	strawberries
frutto	froo'tō	fruit
lamponi	lämpō'nē	raspberries
limone	lē'mōne	lemon
mandarino	mändärē'nō	tangerine
mandorle	män'dōrle	almonds

mela	me′lä	**apple**
mela cotogna	me′lä kōtō′nyä	**quince**
melone	melō′ne	**honeydew melon**
mirtilli	mērtē′lē	**blueberries**
more	mō′re	**blackberries**
nespola	nes′pōlä	**medlar**
noce di cocco	nō′tshe dē kō′kō	**coconut**
noci	nō′tshē	**walnuts**
nocciole	nōtshō′le	**hazel nuts**
pera	pe′rä	**pear**
pesca	pes′kä	**peach**
pompelmo	pōmpel′mō	**grapefruit**
prugna	proo′nyä	**prune**
rabarbaro	räbär′bärō	**rhubarb**
ribes rosso/nero	rē′bes rō′sō/ne′rō	**red/black currants**
uva	oo′vä	**grapes**
uva spina	oo′vä spē′nä	**gooseberries**

BEVERAGE LIST

Wine

wine	(il) vino	vē′nō
cider	(il) sidro	sē′drō
dessert wine	(il) vino liquoroso	vē′nō lēkoo·ōrō′sō
local wine	(il) vino nostrano	vē′nō nōsträ′nō
mulled wine	(il) vin brulè	vēn broole′
Muscatel	(il) moscato	mōskä′tō
red wine	(il) vino rosso	vē′nō rō′sō
sherry	(lo) sherry	she′rē
sparkling wine	(lo) spumante	spoomän′te
vermouth	(il) vermut	ver′moot
vintage	(la) vendemmia	vendem′yä
white wine	(il) vino bianco	vē′nō byän′kō
wine	(il) vino	vē′nō
– dry wine	– secco	se′kō
– sweet wine	– dolce/amabile	dōl′tshe/ämä′bēle

Beer

beer	(la) birra	bē′rä
dark beer	(la) birra scura	bē′rä skoo′rä
a glass of beer	un bicchiere di	oon bēkye′re dē
	birra	bē′rä
draught/draft	(la) birra alla spina	bē′rä älä spē′nä
light beer	(la) birra chiara	bē′rä kyä′rä
malt liquor	(la) birra al malto	bē′rä äl mäl′tō

Other Alcoholic Beverages

alcoholic beverages	(gli) alcolici	älkō′lētshē
bitters	(l') amaro *m*	ämä′rō
brandy	(l') acquavite *f*	äkoo·ävē′te
cognac	(il) cognac	kō′nyäk
gin	(il) gin	jēn
grog	(il) grog	grōg
liqueur	(il) liquore	lēkoo·ō′re
– apricot brandy	– (il) brandy	brän′dē
– Benedictine	– (il) benedettino	benedetē′nō
– cherry brandy	– (il) maraschino	märäske′nō
punch	(il) punch	poontsh
rum	(il) rum	room
vodka	(la) vodka	vōd′kä
whiskey	(il) whisky	oo·ē′skē

In virtually all European countries, when you order a whiskey, you are ordering Scotch whisky. If you would prefer rye, bourbon, or some other beverage, you should say this when placing your order.

Non-Alcoholic Beverages

For coffee, tea, chocolate and milk, please see pp. 113–114.

fruit juice	(il) succo di frutta	sōō′kō dē frōō′tä
– apple juice	– (il) succo di mele	sōō′kō dē me′le
– black currant juice .	– (il) succo di ribes	sōō′kō dē rē′bes
– grapefruit juice	– (il) succo di pompelmo	sōō′kō dē pōmpel′mō
– orange juice	– (il) succo d'arancia ...	sōō′kō därän′tshä
– red grape juice	– (il) succo d'uva nera	sōō′kō dōō′vä ne′rä
– white grape juice ..	– (il) succo d'uva bianca	sōō′kō dōō′vä byän′kä
– lemon juice	– (il) succo di limone ..	sōō′kō dē lēmō′ne
juice	(il) succo	sōō′kō
lemonade	(la) limonata	lēmōnä′tä
milk shake	(il) frappè di latte	fräpe′ dē lä′te
orangeade	(l') aranciata *f*	äräntshä′tä
soda water	(il) seltz	sels
soft drink	(la) bevanda analcolica	bevän′dä änälkō′lēkä
tonic	(l') acqua tonica *f*	ā′kōō·ä tō′nēkä
water	(l') acqua *f*	ā′kōō·ä
– mineral water	(l') acqua minerale *f* ...	ä′kōō·ä mēnerä′le
– carbonated	– gassata	gäsä′tä
– non-carbonated	– naturale	nätōōrä′le

In the Café

Coffee time is a less formal occasion in the romanic countries than in the germanic countries but that in no way limits the wide variety of coffees, teas and other drinks and snacks which an Italian café can offer. Besides the strong, dark tiny "espresso" you can order a "cappuccino" – the dark roasted espresso filled up with steamed, whipped milk to form a little hood, or 'cappuccino'. Than there is an almost endless variety of espressos with a touch of brandy – "coretteo" and other liqueurs. For breakfast, the "caffellatte" is popular – a bowl of hot coffee topped with steamed, whipped milk.

'd like	*desidero (vorrei)*	desē'derō (vōre'ē)
a piece of cake	una fetta di	ōō'nä fe'tä dē
	torta	tōr'tä
a cup of coffee	*una tazza di*	ōō'nä tä'tsä dē
	caffè (un caffè)	käfe' (ōōn käfe')
a cup of tea	un tè	ōōn te'
a dish of ice cream . .	un gelato	ōōn jelä'tō
- with (without)		
whipped cream	– con (senza) panna . . .	kōn (sen'tsä) pä'nä
a glass of orange	un bicchiere di	ōōn bēkye're dē
juice	succo d'arancia	sōō'kō därän'tshä
cake	(la) torta	tōr'tä
candy	(il) dolciume	dōltshōō'me
chocolate	(la) cioccolata	tshōkōlä'tä
chocolate with ice	(la) cioccolata con	tshōkōlä'tä kōn
cream	gelato	jelä'tō
confectionery	(la) pasticceria	pästētsherē'ä
cookies	(i) biscotti	bēskō'tē
- chocolate cookies . .	(i) biscotti al	bēskō'tē äl
	cioccolato	tshōkōlä'tō
cream	(la) crema	kre'mä
ice cream	(il) gelato	jelä'tō
- chocolate ice	(il) gelato al	jelä'tō äl
cream	cioccolato	tshōkōlä'tō
- strawberry ice	(il) gelato alla	jelä'tō ä'lä
cream	fragola	frä'gōlä

– vanilla ice cream	(il) gelato alla vaniglia	jelä′tō ä′lä vänē′lyä
– assorted ice cream .	(il) gelato misto	jelä′tō mē′stō
ice cream parlor	(la) gelateria	jeläterē′ä
macaroon	(il) biscotto amaretto ..	bēskō′tō ämäre′tō
meringue	(la) meringa	merēn′gä
milk	(il) latte	lä′te
– cold (warm) milk ..	latte *freddo* *(caldo)*	lä′te fre′dō (käl′dō)
– evaporated milk ...	latte condensato	lä′te kōndensä′tō
milk bar	(il) bar bianco	bär byän′kō
peach melba	(il) gelato con pesca sciroppata	jelä′tō kōn pes′kä shērōpä′tä
sherbet	(il) sorbetto	sōrbe′tō
– lemon sherbet	(il) sorbetto di limone	sōrbe′tō dē lēmō′ne
– orange sherbet	(il) sorbetto d`arancia .	sōrbe′tō d′ärän′- tshä
– raspberry sherbet	(il) sorbetto di lamponi	sōrbe′tō dē lämpō′nē
sugar	(lo) zucchero	tsōō′kerō
– cube sugar	(lo) zucchero in cubetti	tsōō′kerō ēn kōōbe′tē
sundae	(la) coppa di gelato con frutta	kō′pä dē jelä′tō kōn frōō′tä
sweets	(i) dolci	dōl′tshē
tart, fruit tart	(la) torta di frutta	tōr′tä dē frōō′tä
tea *(see p. 98)*	(il) tè	te′
wafers	(i) wafer	ōō·ä′fer
whipped cream	(la) panna montata	pä′nä mōntä′tä

Of course no one will expect you to know all the names of the delicate pastries and sweets offered. Since the tempting wares are on display, all you have to do is walk up to the glass counter and point to the things you would like. You might add "uno di questo per favore" [ōō′nō dē kōō•e′stō per fävō′re] *(one of these, please).*

Complaints, Paying the Check

We need *another portion (set of silverware, glass).*
Manca ancora una porzione (una posata, un bicchiere).
män'kä änkō'rä oo'nä pōrtsyō'ne (oo'nä pōsä'tä, oon bēkye're)

This isn't what I ordered.	**I wanted . . .**
Non ho ordinato questo.	Volevo . . .
nōn ō ōrdēnä'tō koo·e'stō	vōle'vō . . .

This is . . .	**This isn't fresh any more.**
Questo è . . .	Questo non è fresco.
koo·e'stō e . . .	koo·e'stō nōn e fres'kō

too fatty	troppo grasso	. . . .	trō'pō grä'sō
too hard	troppo duro	. . . .	trō'pō doo'rō
too hot *(temperature)*	troppo caldo		trō'pō käl'dō
too hot *(spicy)*	troppo piccante	. . . .	trō'pō pēkän'te
too cold	troppo freddo	. . . .	trō'pō fre'dō
too salty	troppo salato	. . . .	trō'pō sälä'tō
too sour	troppo acido	. . . .	trō'pō ä'tshēdō
too tough	troppo duro/		trō'pō doo'rō/
	legnoso	. . . .	lenyō'sō

I'd like to pay.	**The check, please!**
Vorrei pagare.	Il conto, per favore!
ōre'ē pägä're	ēl kōn'tō, per fävō're

All together, please.	**Separate checks, please.**
Tutto insieme, per favore.	Paghiamo separatamente.
oo'tō ēnsye'me, per fävō're	pägyä'mō sepärätämen'te

I don't think this is correct.	**Thanks very much.**
Mi sembra che ci sia un errore.	Tante grazie.
mē sem'brä ke tshē sē'ä oon erō're	tän'te grä'tsye

We didn't have that.	**Keep the change.**
Questo non l'abbiamo preso.	Tenga il resto.
koo·e'stō nōn läbyä'mō pre'sō	ten'gä ēl re'stō

DOWNTOWN

On the Street

Where is ...?	Dov'è ...?	dōve' ...
the bank	la banca	la bän'kä
the bus stop	la fermata dell'autobus	lä fermä'tä delou'tobōos
the Catholic church	la chiesa cattolica	lä kye'zä kätō'lēkä
city hall	il Municipio	ēl mōonētshē'pyō
the harbor	il porto	ēl pōr'tō
the ... Hotel	l'albergo	lälber'gō ...
the museum	il museo	ēl mōoze'ō
the police station	il commissariato di Pubblica Sicurezza	ēl kōmēsäryä'tō dē pōo'blēkä sēkōore'tsä
the post office	l'ufficio postale	lōofētshō pōstä'le
the Protestant church	la chiesa protestante	lä kye'zä prōtestän'te
... Square	la piazza	lä pyä'tsä ...
... Street	la strada (via)	lä strä'dä (vē'ä) ...
the station	la stazione	lä stätsyō'ne
the synagogue	la sinagoga	lä sēnägō'gä
the theatre	il teatro	te·ä'trō
a taxi stand	il posteggio dei tassi	ēl pōste'jō de·ē täse'
the tourist information	l'ufficio del turismo	lōofēt'sho del tōorēz'mo

Is it far from here?
E' lontano?
e lōntä'nō

How far is it to the ...?
Quanto tempo ci vuole per andare al (alla) ...?
kōo·än'tō tem'pō tshē vōo·ō'le per andä're ä (ä'lä) ...

How many minutes by foot?
Quanti minuti a piedi?
kōo·an'tē mēnōo'tē ä pye'dē

A good distance (Not far).
Abbastanza (non molto) lontano.
äbästän'tsä (nōn mōl'tō) lōntä'nō

Which direction is ...?
In che direzione è ...?
ēn ke dēretsyō'ne e ...

What street is ... on?
In che strada si trova ...?
ēn ke strä'dä sē trō'vä ...

There.	Straight ahead.	To the right.	To the left.
Là.	Diritto.	A destra.	A sinistra.
lä	dērē′tō	ä de′strä	ä sēnē′strä

Bus, Taxi

Can I get there by bus?
Si può andare in autobus?
sē pōō·ō′ ändä′re ēn ou′tōbōōs

Which bus goes to (the) ...?
Che autobus va a *(al, alla)* ...?
ke ou′tōbōōs vä ä (äl, ä′lä) ...

How many stops is it from here?
Quante fermate ci sono da qui?
kōō·än′te fermä′te tshē sō′nō dä kōō·ē′

Do I have to change?
Devo cambiare?
de′vō kämbyä′re

Where do I have to *get out (change)*?
Dove devo *scendere (cambiare)*?
dō′ve de′vō shen′dere (kämbyä′re)

Would you please tell me when we get there?
Mi può dire quando arriviamo lì?
mē pōō·ō′ dē′re kōō·än′dō ärēvyä′mō lē

A *one-way (transfer)* ticket to ...
Un biglietto (di coincidenza) per ...
ōon bēlye′tō (dē kō·ēntshēden′tsä) per ...

Where can I get a taxi?
Dove ci sono dei tassi?
dō′ve tshē sō′nō de′ē täsē′

Take me to ...
Mi porti *a (al, alla)* ...
mē pōr′tē ä (äl, ä′lä) ...

To the station, please.
Alla stazione, per favore.
ä′lä stätsyō′ne, per fàvō′re

How much is the fare to ...?
Quanto costa andare *a (al, alla)* ...?
kōō·än′tō kō′stä ändä′re ä (äl, ä′lä) ...

Could you show us some of the sights?
Può farci vedere alcune cose interessanti?
pōō·ō′ fär′tshē vede′re älkōō′ne kō′se ēnteresän′tē

Please *wait (stop)* here for a minute.
Aspetti *(Si fermi)* qui un momento, per favore.
äspe′tē (sē fer′mē) kōō·ē′ ōon mōmen′tō, per fàvō′re

Sight-seeing and Excursions

Two tickets to ... for tomorrow, please.
Vorrei due posti per domani per ...
vōre′ē dōō′e pō′stē per dōmä′nē per ...

Is lunch included?
Il pranzo è compreso nel prezzo?
ēl prän′dzō e kōmpre′sō nel pre′tsō

When (Where) do we meet?
Quando (dove) ci incontriamo?
kōō·än′dō (dōve) tshē ēnkōntrē·ä′mō

We'll be meeting ...
Ci troviamo ...
tshē trōvyä′mō ...

When do we get going?
A che ora si parte?
ä ke ō′rä sē pär′te

Will we be seeing the ... too?
Visiteremo anche ...?
vēzētere′mō än′ke ...

Will we have some free time?
Abbiamo tempo a nostra disposizione?
äbyä′mō tem′pō ä nō′strä dēspōzētsyō′ne

How much?
Quanto?
kōō·än′tō

Will we be able to do some shopping?
Possiamo fare degli acquisti?
pōsyä′mō fä′re de′lyē äkōō·ē′stē

When do we get back?
Quando torniamo?
kōō·än′dō tōrnyä′mō

How long will we stay in ...?
Quanto ci fermiamo a ...?
kōō·än′tō tshē fermyä′mō ä ...

Will we be going to ... too?
Passiamo anche per ...?
päsyä′mō än′ke per ...

What's worth seeing in ...?
Che cosa c'è da vedere a ...?
ke kō′sä tshe dä vede′re ä ...

When will we return?
A che ora torniamo?
ä ke ō′rä tōrnyä′mō

When does ... *open (close)* ...?
Quando apre *(chiude)* ...?
kōō·än′dō ä′pre (kyōō′de) ...

How much does the *admission (guided tour)* cost?
Quanto costa *l'ingresso (la visita guidata)*?
kōō·än′tō kō′stä lēngre′sō (lä vē′zētä gōō·ēdä′tä)

Is there an English speaking guide?
C'è una guida che parla inglese?
tshe ōō′nä gōō·ē′dä ke pär′lä ēn·gle′se

I'd like to see the . . .		**Can we take a look at . . . today?**
Desidero (vorrei) vedere . . .		Si può visitare oggi . . .?
desē'dērō (vōre'ē) vede're . . .		sē poō·ō' vēzētä're ō'jē . . .

the castle	il castello	ēl käste'lō
the cathedral	il duomo	ēl doō·ō'mō
the church	la chiesa	lä kye'zä
the fortress	la fortezza	lä fōrtet'sä
the exhibition	la mostra	lä mō'strä
the gallery	la galleria	lä gälerē'ä
the memorial	il monumento	ēl mōnoōmen'tō
	commemorativo	kōmemōrätē'vō
the museum	il museo	ēl moōze'ō
the palace	il palazzo	ēl pälä'tsō
the zoo	lo zoo	lō dzō'ō

When does the tour start?

Quando comincia la visita guidata?
koō·än'dō kōmēn'tshä lä vē'zētä
goō·ēdä'tä

Can we take pictures?

E permesso fotografare?
e perme'sō fōtōgräfä're

What is that *building (monument)*?

Che *edificio (monumento)* è questo?
ke edēfē'tshō (mōnoōmen'tō) e koō·e'stō

Who *painted this picture (sculpted this statue)*?

Di che è *questo quadro (questa statua)*?
dē kē e koō·e'stō koō·ä'drō (koō·e'stä stä'toō·ä)

What period does this . . . date from?

Di che periodo è questo . . .?
dē ke perē'ōdō e koō·e'stō . . .

When was . . . built?

Quando è stato costruito . . .?
koō·än'dō e stä'tō kōstroō·e'tō . . .

Who built . . .?

Chi ha costruito . . .?
kē ä kōstroō·e'tō . . .

Where can I find . . .?

Dove si trova . . .?
dō've sē trō'vä . . .

Is this . . .?

E' questo . . .?
e koō·e'stō . . .

*This is where . . . *lived (was born, died).*

Qui *viveva (nacque, morì)* . . .
koō·ē' vēve'vä (nä'koō·e, mōrē') . . .

Vocabulary

airport	(l') aeroporto *m*	ä·erōpōr'tō
alley	(il) viale	vyä'le
area	(la) zona, regione	dzō'nä, rejō'ne
avenue	(la) strada	strä'dä
boat trip	(la) gita in barca	jē'tä ēn bär'kä
botanical gardens	(il) giardino botanico	järdē'nō bōtä'nēkō
bridge	(il) ponte	pōn'te
building	(l') edificio *m*	edēfē'tshō
bus	(l') autobus *m*	ou'tōbōōs
capital	(la) capitale	käpētä'le
castle	(il) castello	käste'lō
cathedral	(il) duomo	dōō·ō'mō
cave	(la) caverna	käver'nä
cemetery	(il) cimitero	tshēmēte'rō
church	(la) chiesa	kye'zä
churchyard	(il) cimitero	tshēmēte'rō
city	(la) città	tshētä'
city hall	(il) municipio	mōōnētshē'pyō

In most Italian villages and towns the winemakers have cellars, some even with gardens where wine tasting can be done. Wine in large or small quantities can be bought here but one must generally bring an empty bottle to be filled if one wishes to take the wine away. However, an unforgettable afternoon or evening can be spent in these little wineries called "cantina" (käntē'nä). Small snacks of olives, pickled peppers, and artichokes with bread can be bought quite cheaply. Most "cantine" (käntē'ne) even allow you to bring along your own picnic as long as you buy your drinks there. This is certainly an interesting way to observe Italian families on an outing and talk to local people.

consulate	(il) consolato	kōnsōlä'tō
countryside	(il) paesaggio	pä·ezäd'jō
courthouse	(il) palazzo di giustizia	pälä'tsō dē jōōstē'tsyä
covered market	(il) mercato coperto	merkä'tō kōper'tō
dead-end street	(il) vicolo cieco	vē'kōlō tshe'kō
district	(il) quartiere	kōō·ärtye're

downtown area	(il) sobborgo	sōbōr'gō
embassy	(l') ambasciata *f*	ämbäshä'tä
environs	(i) dintorni	dēntōr'nē
excavations	(gli) scavi	skä'vē
excursion	(l') escursione *f/*	eskōōrsyō'ne/
	(la) gita	jē'tä
exhibition	(l') esposizione *f/*	espōzētsyō'ne/
	(la) mostra	mōsträ
farmhouse	(la) cascina	käshē'nä
fire department	(i) vigili del fuoco	vē'jēlē del fōō·ō'kō
first-aid station	(il) pronto soccorso	prōn'tō sōkōr'sō
fountain	(la) fontana	fōntä'nä
gallery	(la) galleria	gälerē'ä
garden	(il) giardino	järdē'nō
gate	(il) portone	pōrtō'ne
government office	(l') ufficio *m*	ōōfē'tshō
	governativo	gōvernätē'vō
grave	(la) tomba	tōm'bä
guide	(la) guida	gōō·ē'dä
harbor	(il) porto	pōr'tō
high-rise building	(il) grattacielo	grätätshe'lō
hiking path	(il) sentiero	sentye'rō
hill	(la) collina	kōlē'nä
hospital	(l') ospedale *m*	ōspedä'le
house	(la) casa	kä'sä
house number	(il) numero di casa	nōō'merō dē kä'sä
landscape	(il) paesaggio	pä·ezä'jō
lane	(la) stradina	strädē'nä
last stop	(il) capolinea	käpōlē'ne·ä
library	(la) biblioteca	bēblē·ōte'kä
lost and found	(l') ufficio *m* oggetti	ōōfē'tshō ōje'tē
office	smarriti	zmärē'tē
main street	(la) strada	strä'dä
	principale	prēntshēpä'le
memorial	(il) monumento	mōnōōmen'tō
	commemorativo	kōmemōrätē'vō
ministry	(il) ministero	mēnēste'rō
moat	(il) fosso	fō'sō
monument	(il) monumento	mōnōōmen'tō
mountain	(la) montagna	mōntän'yä
mountain range	(le) montagne	mōntän'ye

motion picture theatre	(la) sala cinematografica	sä'lä tshēnemätōgrä'fēkä
museum	(il) museo	mōoze'ō
national park	(il) parco nazionale	pär'kō nätsyōnä'le
observatory	(l') osservatorio m	ōservätōr'yō
old town	(il) centro storico	tshen'trō stō'rēkō
open market	(il) mercato	merkä'tō
palace	(il) palazzo	pälä'tsō
park	(il) parco	pär'kō
part of town	(il) quartiere	kōo·ärtye're
path	(il) cammino	kämē'nō
pedestrian	(il) pedone	pedō'ne
– pedestrian crossing	(il) passaggio pedonale	päsä'jō pedōnä'le
police	(la) polizia	pōlētsē'ä
police station	(la) questura	kōo·estōo'rä
policeman	(il) poliziotto	pōlētsyō'tō
port	(il) porto	pōr'tō
post office	(l') ufficio m postale	ōofē'tshō pōstä'le
public garden	(il) giardino pubblico	järde'nō pōo'blēkō
public rest room	(i) gabinetti pubblici	gäbēne'tē pōo'blētshē
river	(il) fiume	fyōo'me
road	(la) strada	strä'dä
ruin	(le) rovine	rōvē'ne
shop	(il) negozio	negō'tsyō
shopping mall	(il) centro d'acquisti	tshen'trō däkōo·ē'stē
side road	(la) strada laterale	strä'dä läterä'le
sidewalk	(il) marciapiede	märtshäpye'de
sightseeing	(il) giro turistico	jē'rō tōorēs'tēkō
square	(la) piazza	pyä'tsä
stadium	(lo) stadio	stä'dyō
station	(la) stazione	stätsyō'ne
stop	(la) fermata	fermä'tä
store	(il) magazzino	mägädzē'nō
street	(la) strada	strä'dä
suburb	(il) sobborgo	sōbōr'gō
suburban express train	(la) ferrovia urbana	ferōvē'ä ōorbä'nä
subway	(la) metropolitana	metrōpōlētä'nä

surroundings	(i) dintorni	dēntōr′nē
swimming area	(la) piscina	pēshē′nä
taxi	(il) tassì	täsē′
taxi stand	(il) posteggio-tassì	pōste′jō täsē
temple	(il) tempio	tem′pyō
throughway	(il) passaggio	päsä′jō
tomb	(la) tomba	tōm′bä
tower	(la) torre	tō′re
town	(la) città	tshētä′
traffic	(il) traffico	trä′fēkō
traffic light	(il) semaforo	semä′fōrō
travel agency	(l') agenzia *f* viaggi	äjentsē′ä vyä′jē
university	(l') università *f*	ōōnēversētä′
valley	(la) valle	vä′le
village	(il) *villaggio (paese)*	vēlä′jō, pä·e′ze
wall	(il) muro	mōō′rō
waterfall	(la) cascata	käskä′tä
zebra crossing	(le) strisce pedonali	strē′she pedōnä′lē
zoo	(lo) zoo	dzō′ō

Religion, Churches

Where is the Catholic church?
Dov'è la chiesa cattolica?
dōve′ lä kye′zä kätō′lēkä

... St. Mary's (St. George's) Church?
... di *Santa Maria (San Giorgio)*?
... dē sän′tä märē′ä (sän jōr′jō)

What time *are services (is high mass)*?
Quando si celebra *la messa (la messa solenne)*?
kōō·än′dō sē tshe′lebrä lä me′sä (lä me′sä sōle′ne)

Is there a *wedding (christening)* today?
C'è un *matrimonio (battesimo)* oggi?
tshe ōōn mätrēmō′nyō (bäte′zēmō) ō′jē

Who's preaching the sermon?
Chi sta facendo la predica?
kē stä fätshen′dō lä pre′dēkä

Do they have church concerts?
Ci sono concerti in chiesa?
tshē sō′nō kōntsher′tē ēn kye′zä

Please call a *clergyman (priest)*!
Per favore, chiami un *sacerdote (un prete)*!
per fävō′re, kyä′mē ōōn sätsherdō′te (ōōn pre′te)

I am a	Sono	sō′nō
Christian	cristiano	krēstyä′nō
Jew	ebreo	ebre′ō
Catholic	cattolico	kätō′lēkō
Methodist	metodista	metōdē′stä
Moslem	musulmano	mōosōōlmä′nō
Protestant	protestante	prōtestän′te

I don't belong to any religious denomination.
Non appartengo a nessuna religione.
nōn äpärten′gō ä nesōō′nä relējō′ne

abbey	(l') abbazia f	äbätsē′ä
altar	(l') altare m	ältä′re
arch	(la) volta	vōl′tä
baptism	(il) battesimo	bäte′zēmō
Baroque	barocco	bärō′kō
bell	(la) campana	kämpä′nä
candlestick	(il) candelabro	kändelä′brō
cathedral	(la) cattedrale	kätedrä′le
cemetery	(il) cimitero	tshēmēte′rō
chapel	(la) cappella	käpe′lä
choir	(il) coro	kō′rō
Christ	Cristo	krē′stō
church	(la) chiesa	kye′zä
churchyard	(il) cimitero	tshēmēte′rō
clergyman	(il) sacerdote	sätsherdō′te
communion	(la) comunione	kōmōōnyō′ne
confess	confessare	kōnfesä′re
confession	(la) confessione	kōnfesyō′ne
convent	(il) convento	kōnven′tō
cross	(la) croce	krō′tshe
crucifix	(il) crocefisso	krōtshefē′sō
crypt	(la) cripta	krēp′tä
cupola	(la) cupola	kōō′pōlä
denomination	(la) confessione	kōnfesyō′ne
dome	(la) cupola	kōō′pōlä
font	(il) fonte battesimale	fōn′te bätezēmä′le
fresco	(l') affresco m	äfres′kō
God	(il) Dio	dē′ō
Gospel	(il) Vangelo	vänje′lō

Gothic	gotico	gō'tēkō
grave	(la) tomba	tōm'bä
High Mass	(la) messa solenne	me'sä sōle'ne
Jewish	ebraico	ebrī'kō
mass	(la) messa	me'sä
monastery	(il) monastero	mōnäste'rō
mosaic	(il) mosaico	mōsī'kō
nave	(la) navata	nävä'tä
organ	(l') organo *m*	ōr'gänō
pillar	(la) colonna	kōlō'nä
portal	(il) portale	pōrtä'le
priest	(il) prete	pre'te
procession	(la) processione	prōtshesyō'ne
pulpit	(il) pulpito	pōōl'pētō
religion	(la) religione	relējō'ne
religious	religioso	relējō'sō
Romanesque	romanico	rōmä'nēkō
sacristan	(il) sagrestano	sägrestä'nō
sacristy	(la) sagrestia	sägreste'ä
sarcophagus	(il) sarcofago	särkō'fägō
sermon	(la) predica	pre'dēkä
service	(la) funzione	fōōntsyō'ne
	religiosa/(la) messa	relējō'sä/me'sä
Stations of the Cross	(la) Via Crucis	vē'ä krōō'tshēs
statue	(la) statua	stä'tōō·ä
synagogue	(la) sinagoga	sēnägō'gä
tomb	(la) tomba	tōm'bä
tower	(la) torre	tō're

GOING SHOPPING

Business hours: Food stores usually 8 am until 1:30 pm and 3 pm until 7:30 or 8 pm, closed Thursday afternoons in winter and Saturday afternoons in summer. Retail stores usually 9 am until 1 pm and 3:30 pm until 7:30 or 8 pm, closed Monday mornings. Banks are open from 8:30 am until 1:30 pm and closed Saturdays. Tourist exchanges are open at airport and train terminals. Different areas may vary slightly in their business hours and restaurants are usually closed one day a week on a posted day of the owner's choice.

General Words and Phrases

Where can I *get (buy)* ...?
Dove posso comprare ...?
dō've pō'sō kōmprä're ...

Is there a *leather (china)* shop here?
C'è qui un negozio di *pelle (porcellana)*?
tshe kōō·ē' ōōn negō'tsyō dē pe'le (pōrtshelä'nä)

Have you got ...?
Ha ...?
ä ...

I'd (We'd) like ...
Vorrei (vorremmo) ...
vōre'ē (vōre'mō) ...

Please show me ...
Per favore, mi faccia vedere ...
per fävō're, mē fä'tshä vede're ...

I need ...
Ho bisogno di ...
ō bēzō'nyō dē ...

Please give me ...
Per favore, mi dia ...
per fävō're, mē dē'ä

a bag	una *borsa*	ōō'nä bōr'sä
	(busta di	(bōō'stä dē
	plastica)	plä'stēkä)
a bottle	una bottiglia	ōō'nä bōtē'lyä
a box	una scatola	ōō'nä skä'tōlä
a few	alcuni (-e)	älkōō'nē (alkōō'ne)
a jar	un vaso	ōōn vä'zō
a pound	mezzo chilo	me'dzō kē'lō
a kilogram	un chilo	ōōn kē'lō
a pack *(packet)*	un pacco *(pacchetto)* ..	ōōn pä'kō (päke'tō)
a pair	un paio	ōōn pä'yō
a piece	un pezzo	ōōn pe'tsō
a quart	un quarto	ōōn kōō·är'tō
a roll	un rotolo	ōōn rō'tōlō
a tube	un tubetto	ōōn tōōbe'tō
two pounds	un chilo	ōōn kē'lō
100 grams	un etto	ōōn e'tō

That's plenty.	**A little more.**	**Even more.**
E' abbastanza.	Ancora un po'.	Di più.
e äbästän'tsä	änkō'rä ōōn pō	dē pyōō

Can you order it for me?
Può ordinarlo per me?
pŏŏ·ô′ ôrdēnär′lō per me

When will you get it in?
Quando lo riceve?
kŏŏ·än′dō lō rētshe′ve

Can I exchange it?
Posso cambiarlo?
pô′sō kämbyär′lō

I don't like the *shape (color)*.
Non mi piace *la forma (il colore)*.
nōn mē pyä′tshe lä fôr′mä (ēl kōlō′re)

This is ...
Questo è ...
kŏŏ·e′stō e ...

Do you have my size?
Ha la mia misura?
ä lä mē′ä mēzŏŏ′rä

too big	troppo grande	trō′pō grän′de
too dark	troppo scuro	trō′pō skŏŏ′rō
too expensive	troppo caro	trō′pō kä′rō
too *light (pale)*	troppo chiaro	trō′pō kyä′rō
too narrow	troppo stretto	trō′pō stre′tō
too small	troppo piccolo	trō′pō pē′kōlō
too wide	troppo largo	trō′pō lär′gō
too much	troppo	trō′pō
not enough	troppo poco	trō′pō pō′kō

Have you got something a little *nicer (less expensive)*?
Ha qualcosa *di meglio (di meno costoso)*?
ä kŏŏ·älkō′zä dē me′lyō (dē me′nō kōstō′sō)

I like that.
Questo mi piace.
kŏŏ·e′stō mē pyä′tshe

I'll take *it (them)*.
Lo (la; li; le) prendo.
lō (lä, lē, le) pren′dō

How much is that?
Quanto costa?
kŏŏ·än′tō kō′stä

Thanks, that'll be all.
Grazie, basta così.
grä′tsye, bä′stä kōsē′

Can you send everything to the ... Hotel please?
Può mandarmi tutto in albergo ...?
pŏŏ·ô′ mändär′mē tŏŏ′tō ēn älber′gō ...

Do you take *credit cards (traveller's cheques)*?
Accetta *carte di credito (traveller's cheque)*?
ätshē′tä kär′te dē kre′dētō (trä′velers tshek)

Stores

antique shop	(l') antiquario *m*	äntēkoo·är'yō
art gallery	(la) galleria d'arte	gälerē'ä där'te
bakery	(il) panificio	pänēfē'tshō
barber shop	(il) barbiere	bärbye're
beauty parlor	(il) parrucchiere	pärookye're
bookshop	(la) libreria	lēbrerē'ä
butcher shop	(la) macelleria	mätshelerē'ä
candy store	(la) pasticceria	pästētsherē'ä
china shop	(il) negozio di porcellane	negō'tsyō dē pōrtshelä'ne
cigar store	(la) tabaccheria	täbäkerē'ä
cobbler shop	(il) calzolaio	kältsōlä'yō
cosmetic salon	(il) salone di bellezza ..	sälō'ne dē bele'tsä
dairy	(la) latteria	läterē'ä
department store	(il) grande magazzino .	grän'de mägädzē'nō
drug store (*cosmetics & sundries*)	(la) drogheria	drōgerē'ä
drug store (*prescription pharmacy*)	(la) farmacia	färmätshē'ä
dry cleaner's	(la) tintoria	tēntōrē'ä
electrical shop	(il) negozio di apparecchi elettrici	negō'tsyō dē äpäre'kē ele'trētshe
fashion boutique	(la) boutique '	bootēk'
fish market	(la) pescheria	peskerē'ä
flower shop	(il) fiorista	fyōrē'stä
fruit market	(il) mercato frutta-verdura	merkä'tō froo'tä verdoo'rä
furrier	(la) pellicceria	pelētsherē'ä
grocery store	(il) negozio di alimentari	negō'tsyō dē älēmentä'rē
haberdashery	(l') abbigliamento *m* maschile	abēlyämen'tō mäskē'le
hairdresser	(il) parrucchiere	pärookye're
hat shop	(il) negozio di cappello	negō'tsyō dē käpe'lō
jewelry store	(la) gioielleria	jōyelerē'ä
laundromat	(la) lavanderia a gettone	lävänderē'ä ä jetō'ne

laundry	(la) lavanderia	lävänderē'ä
leather goods store	(la) pelletteria	peleterē'ä
lingerie shop	(il) negozio di biancheria	negō'tsyō dē byänkerē'ä
liquor store	(il) negozio di liquori	negō'tsyō dē lēkoo-ō'rē
music store	(il) negozio di musica	negō'tsyō dē moo'zēkä
newsdealer	(il) giornalaio	jōrnälä'yō
optician	(l') ottico *m*	ō'tēkō
perfume shop	(la) profumeria	prōfoomerē'ä
pet shop	(il) negozio di animali domestici	negō'tsyō dē änēmä'lē dōme'stētshē
photo shop	(il) fotografo	fōtō'gräfō
photographer's studio	(lo) studio fotografico	stoo'dyō fōtōgrä'fēkō
real estate agency	(l') agenzia *f* immobiliare	äjentsē'ä ēmōbēlyä're
record store	(i) dischi	dē'skē
second-hand bookshop	(la) libreria d'antiquariato	lēbrerē'ä däntēkoo-ärē-ä'tō
self-service	(il) self-service	self-ser'vēs
shoemaker's shop	(il) calzolaio	kältsōlä'yō
shoe store	(la) calzoleria	kältsōlerē'ä
souvenir shop	(il) negozio di souvenir	negōtsyō dē soovenēr'
sporting goods store	(gli) articoli sportivi	ärtē'kōlē spōrtē've
stationery store	(la) cartoleria	kärtōlerē'ä
supermarket	(il) supermercato	soopermerkä'tō
tailor shop	(il) sarto	sär'tō
textile store	(l') abbigliamento *m*	äbēlyämen'tō
toy store	(i) giocattoli	jōkä'tōlē
travel agency	(l') agenzia *f* viaggio	äjentsē'ä vyä'jō
vegetable market	(il) mercato della verdura	merkä'tō de'lä verdoo'rä
watchmaker's shop	(l') orologiaio *m*	ōrōlōjä'yō
wine shop	(il) negozio di vini	negō'tsyō dē vē'nē

Flowers

bouquet	(il) mazzo di fiori	mä′tsō dē fyō′rē
flower pot	(la) pianta	pyän′tä
flowers	(i) fiori	fyō′rē
gladioli	(i) gladioli	glädyō′lē
lilacs	(i) lillà	lēlä′
orchids	(le) orchidee	ōrkēde′e
roses	(le) rose	rō′ze
tulips	(i) tulipani	tōōlēpä′nē
vase	(il) vaso	vä′zō
violets	(le) violette	vyōle′te

Bookshop

autobiography	(l') autobiografia *f*	outōbē·ōgräfē′ä
biography	(la) biografia	bē·ōgräfē′ä
book	(il) libro	lē′brō
catalogue	(il) catalogo	kätä′lōgō
children's book	(il) libro per bambini . .	lē′brō per bämbē′nē
city map	(la) pianta della città . .	pyän′tä de′lä tshētä′
detective novel	(il) giallo	jä′lō
dictionary	(il) dizionario	dētsyōnär′yō
guide book	(la) guida	gōō·ē′dä
map	(la) carta geografica . . .	kär′tä je·ōgrä′fēkä
novel	(il) romanzo	rōmän′dzō
paperback	(il) tascabile	täskä′bēle
phrase book	(il) libro di frasi idiomatiche	lē′brō dē frä′zē ēdyōmä′tēke
record	(il) disco	dē′skō
road map	(la) carta automobilistica	kär′tä outōmōbēlē′stēkä
street map	(la) carta stradale	kär′tä strädä′le
thriller	(il) giallo	jä′lō
translation	(la) traduzione	trädōōtsyō′ne
travel reading	(le) letture per il viaggio	letōō′re per ēl vyä′jō
volume	(il) volume	vōlōō′me

Photo Shop

Would you please develop this film?

Vorrei far sviluppare *questo rotolo (questa pellicola)*.
vōre'ē fär zvēloopä're koo·e'stō rō'tōlō (koo·e'stä pelē'kōlä)

One *print (enlargement)* of each negative, please.

Una foto (un ingrandimento) per ogni negativa.
oo'nä fō'tō (oon ēngrändēmen'tō) per ō'nyē negätē'vä

– three by four (inches).

– sette per dieci.
– se'te per dye'tshē

**– three and a half by three and
a half (inches).**

– nove per nove.
– nō've per nō've

– three and a half by five (inches).

– nove per tredici.
– nō've per tre'dētshē

I'd like . . .

Vorrei . . .
vōre'ē . . .

– a cartridge film.

– una pellicola a caricatore.
– oo'nä pelē'kōlä ä kärēkätō're

– a super eight color film.

– una pellicola a colori super
otto.
– oo'nä pelē'kōlä a kōlō're
soo'per ō'tō

– a sixteen millimeter color film.

– una pellicola a colori da sedici
millimetri.
– oo'nä pelē'kōlä ä kōlō'rē dä
se'dētshē mēlē'metrē

– a black and white eight millimeter film.

– una pellicola in bianco e nero da otto millimetri.
– oo'nä pelē'kōlä ēn byän'kō e ne'rō dä ō'tō mēlē'metrē

– a film for color slides.

– una pellicola a colori per diapositive.
– oo'nä pelē'kōlä ä kōlō'rē per dē·äpōzētē've

– a *twenty (thirty-six)* exposure film.

– una pellicola da *venti (trentasei)* foto.
– oo'nä pelē'kōlä dä ven'tē (trentäse'ē) fō'tō

Would you please put the film in the camera for me?

Può caricarmi la macchina, per favore?
poo·ō' kärēkär'mē lä mä'kēnä, per fävō're

camera	(la) macchina	mä′kēnä
	fotografica	fōtōgrä′fēkä
color film	(la) pellicola a colori ..	pelē′kōlä ä kōlō′rē
color negative	(il) rotolo di foto	rō′tōlō dē fō′tō
film	a colori	ä kōlō′rē
daylight color	(il) rotolo a colori	rō′tōlō ä kōlō′rē
film	per diapositive	per dē-äpōzētē′ve
develop	sviluppare	zvēlo͞opä′re
diaphragm	(il) diaframma	dyäfrä′mä
8-mm film	(la) pellicola da	pelē′kōlä dä
	otto millimetri	ō′tō mēlē′metrē
enlargement	(l′) ingrandimento *m* ..	ēngrändēmen′tō
exposure	(la) posa	pō′zä
exposure meter	(l′) esposimetro *m*	espōzē′metrō
film *(verb)*	(la) pellicola	pelē′kōlä
film *(verb)*	filmare	fēlmä′re
flash bulb	(la) lampadina-flash ...	lämpädē′nä-fläsh
flash cube	(il) cubo-flash	ko͞o′bō-fläsh
lens	(l′) obiettivo *m*	ōbyetē′vō
movie camera	(la) cinepresa	tshēnepre′sä
negative	(la) negativa	negätē′vä
paper	(la) carta	kär′tä
– glossy	lucida	lo͞o′tshēdä
– matte	opaca	ōpä′kä
photo	(la) foto	fō′tō
photo *(verb)*	fotografare	fōtōgräfä′re
picture	(la) fotografia	fōtōgräfē′ä
picture size	(il) formato	fōrmä′tō
print	(la) copia	kō′pyä
– color print	a colori	ä kōlō′rē
reversal film	(la) pellicola	pelē′kōlä
	invertibile	ēnvertē′bēle
roll film	(la) pellicola in	pelē′kōlä ēn
	rotolo	rō′tōlō
shutter	(l′) otturatore *m*	ōto͞orätō′re
shutter (release)	(lo) scatto	skä′tō
slide	(la) diapositiva	dē-äpōzētē′vä
take a picture	fare una foto	fä′re o͞o′nä fō′tō
viewfinder	(il) mirino	mērē′nō
yellow filter	(il) filtro giallo	fēl′trō jä′lō

Jeweler

amber	(l') ambra *f*	äm'brä
bracelet	(il) braccialetto	brätshäle'tō
brooch	(la) spilla	spē'lä
costume jewelry	(la) bigiotteria	bējōterē'ä
cufflinks	(i) gemelli da camicia	jeme'lē dä kämē'tshä
diamond	(il) diamante	dē·ämän'te
ear clips	(gli) orecchini a clips	ōrekē'nē ä klēps
earrings	(gli) orecchini	ōrekē'nē
emerald	(lo) smeraldo	zmeräl'dō
gold	(l') oro *m*	ō'rō
gold plated	dorato	dōrä'tō
jewelry	(i) gioielli	jōye'lē
necklace	(la) collana	kōlä'nä
pearls	(le) perle	per'le
pendant	(il) ciondolo	tshōn'dōlō
ring	(l') anello *m*	äne'lō
ruby	(il) rubino	rōōbē'nō
sapphire	(lo) zaffiro	dzäfē'rō
silver	(l') argento *m*	ärjen'tō
silver plated	argentato	ärjentä'tō
wedding ring	(la) fede	fe'de

Clothing

May I try it on?	**I take a size ...**	**This is ...**
Posso provarlo?	Porto la taglia ...	E' ...
pō'sō prōvär'lō	pōr'tō lä tä'lyä ...	e ...

too long	troppo lungo	trō'pō lōōn'gō
too short	troppo corto	trō'pō kōr'tō
too tight	troppo stretto	trō'pō stre'tō
too wide	troppo largo	trō'pō lär'gō

Can it be altered? ... *fits just fine (doesn't fit)*.
Si può modificare un po'? ... *va bene (non va bene)*.
sē pōō·ō' mōdēfēkä're ōōn pō ... vä be'ne (nōn vä be'ne)

bathing cap	(la) cuffia da bagno . . .	koo′fyä dä bä′nyō
bathing suit	(il) costume da bagno .	kostoo′me dä bä′nyō
bathing trunks	(i) pantaloncini da bagno	päntälōntshē′nē dä bä′nyō
bathrobe	(l') accappatoio *m*	äkäpätō′yō
belt	(la) cintura	tshēntoo′rä
blouse	(la) camicetta	kämētshe′tä
blue jeans	(i) blue jeans	bloo jēns
bra, brassière	(il) reggiseno	rejēse′nō
cap	(il) berretto	bere′tō
cardigan	(il) golf	gōlf
coat	(il) cappotto	käpō′tō
corset	(il) busto	boo′stō
dress	(il) vestito, (l') abito *m* .	vestē′tō, ä′bētō
dressing gown	(la) vestaglia	vestä′lyä
fur coat	(la) pelliccia	pelē′tshä
fur jacket	(la) giacchetta di pelliccia	jäke′tä dē pelē′tshä
garter belt	(il) reggicalze	rejēkäl′tse
gloves	(i) guanti	goo·än′tē
handkerchief	(il) fazzoletto	fätsōle′tō
hat	(il) cappello	käpe′lō
– straw hat	(il) cappello di paglia . .	käpe′lō dē pä′lyä
jacket *(lady's)*	(la) giacchetta	jäke′tä
jacket *(man's)*	(la) giacca	jä′kä
knee socks	(i) calzettoni	kältsetō′nē
leather coat	(il) cappotto di pelle . .	käpō′tō dē pe′le
leather jacket	(la) giacchetta di pelle .	jäke′tä dē pe′le
lingerie	(la) biancheria	byänkerē′ä
nightshirt, nightie	(la) camicia da notte . .	kämē′tshä dä nō′te
pajamas	(il) pigiama	pējä′mä
panties	(i) calzoncini da donna	kältsōntshē′nē dä dō′nä
pants (trousers)	(i) pantaloni	päntälō′nē
pants suit	(il) tailleur pantalone . .	täyer′ päntälō′ne
parka	(la) giacca a vento	jä′kä ä ven′tō
petticoat	(la) sottoveste	sōtōve′ste
raincoat	(l') impermeabile *m* . .	ēmperme·ä′bēle
scarf	(la) sciarpa	shär′pä
shirt	(la) camicia	kämē′tshä

– drip-dry	– che non si deve stirare	ke nōn sē de′ve stě-rä′re
– short-sleeved	– a maniche corte	ä mä′nēke kōr′te
shorts	(gli) shorts	shōrts
ski pants	(i) pantaloni da sci	päntälō′ne dä shē
skirt	(la) gonna	gō′nä
slacks	(i) calzoni sportivi	kältsō′ne spōrtē′vē
slip	(lo) slip	slēp
socks	(i) calzini	kältsē′nē
sport shirt	(la) camicia sportiva	kämē′tshä spōr-tē′vä
sportswear	(i) vestiti sportivi	vestē′tē spōrtē′vē
stockings	(le) calze	kält′se
– panty hose	(il) collant	kōlän′
stole	(la) stola	stō′lä
suède coat	(il) soprabito in pelle scamosciata	sōprä′bētōēn pe′le skämōshä′tä
suède jacket	(la) giacca in pelle scamosciata	jä′kä ēn pe′le skämōshä′tä
suit *(lady's)*	(il) tailleur	täyer′
suit *(man's)*	(il) completo	kōmple′tō
summer dress	(il) vestito estivo	vestē′tō estē′vō
suspenders	(le) bretelle	brete′le
sweatshirt	(il) pullover cottone	pōōlō′ver kōtō′ne
sweater	(il) pullover	pōōlō′ver
swimsuit	(il) costume da bagno	kōstōō′me dä bä′nyō
tie	(la) cravatta	krävä′tä
tights	(il) collant	kōlän′
track suit	(la) tuta sportiva	tōō′tä spōrtē′vä
trousers	(i) pantaloni	päntälō′nē
two-piece	(i) due pezzi	dōō′e pe′tsē
underpants	(le) mutande	mōōtän′de
undershirt	(la) canottiera	känōtye′rä
underwear	(la) biancheria intima	byänkerē′ä ēn′tēmä
vest	(il) panciotto	päntshō′tō
windbreaker	(la) giacca a vento	jä′kä ä ven′tō

Dry Goods

accessories	(gli) accessori	ätshesō′rē
belt	(la) cintura	tshēntoō′rä
buckle	(la) fibbia	fē′byä
button	(il) bottone	bōtō′ne
darning cotton	(il) filo da rammendo··	fē′lō dä rämen′dō
dress-shield	(le) sottascelle	sōtäshe′le
dry goods	(le) mercerie	mertsherē′e
elastic	(l') elastico *m*	elä′stēkō
garters	(le) giarrettiere	järetye′re
hooks and eyes	(i) ganci e (gli) occhielli	gän′tshē e (lyē) ōkye′lē
lining	(la) fodera	fō′derä
needle	(l') ago *m*	ä′gō
– sewing needle	(l') ago da cucire	ä′gō dä koōtshē′re
pin	(lo) spillo	spē′lō
ribbon	(il) nastro	nä′strō
safety pin	(la) spilla di sicurezza	spē′lä dē sēkoōre′tsä
scissors	(le) forbici	fōr′bētshē
silk thread	(la) seta da cucire	se′tä dä koōtshē′re
snap	(il) bottone automatico	bōtō′ne outōmä′tēkō
suspenders	(le) bretelle	brete′le
tape	(la) fettuccia	fetoō′tshä
tape measure	(il) metro a nastro	me′trō ä nä′strō
thimble	(il) ditale	dētä′le
thread	(il) filo	fē′lō
wool	(la) lana	lä′nä
zipper	(la) cerniera lampo	tshernye′rä läm′pō

Fabrics

cloth	(la) stoffa	stō′fä
corduroy	(il) velluto a coste	veloō′tō ä kō′ste
cotton	(il) cotone	kōtō′ne
fabric	(il) tessuto	tesoō′tō
– checked	*– a quadretti (scozzese)*	ä koō·ädre′tē (skōtse′se)

– patterned	– a fantasia	ä fäntäzē′ä
– printed	– variopinto	väryōpēn′tō
– solid color	– a tinta unita	ä tēn′tä ōonē′tä
– striped	– a strisce	ä strē′she
flannel	(la) flanella	fläne′lä
jersey	(il) jersey	jer′sē
linen	(il) lino	lē′nō
material	(il) materiale	mäteryä′le
nylon	(il) nylon	nē′lōn
silk	(la) seta	se′tä
– artificial silk	(la) seta artificiale	se′tä ärtēfētshä′le
synthetic fibre	(la) fibra sintetica	fē′brä sēnte′tēkä
velvet	(il) velluto	velōo′tō
wool	(la) lana	lä′nä
– pure wool	(la) lana pura	lä′nä pōo′rä
– pure virgin wool ...	(la) lana pura vergine	lä′nä pōo′rä ver′jēne
worsted	lana pettinata	lä′nä petēnä′tä

Cleaning, Alterations, Repairs

I'd like to have this *dress (suit)* cleaned.
Vorrei far pulire questo *abito (vestito)*.
vōrre′ē fär pōolē′re kōo·e′stō ä′bētō (vestē′tō)

I'd like to have these things laundered.
Vorrei far lavare *questa biancheria (questo)*.
vōre′ē fär lävä′re kōo·e′stä byänkerē′ä (kōo·e′stō)

Would you please *press this (take out this stain)*?
Potrebbe far *stirare questo (levare questa macchia)*?
pōtre′be fär stērä′re kōo·e′stō (levä′re kōo·e′stä mä′kyä)

Could you *darn this (sew on this button)*?
Può *rammendare questo (attaccare questo bottone)*?
pōo·ō′ rämendä′re kōo·e′stō (ätäkä′re kōo·e′stō bōtō′ne)

Could you *lengthen (shorten)* this?
Può *allungare (accorciare)* questo?
pōo·ō′ älōongä′re (äkōrtshä′re) kōo·e′stō

Optician

Can you fix these glasses?
Può riparare questi occhiali?
poo·o′ rēpärä′re koo·e′stē ōkyä′lē

Can you replace these lenses?
Può sostituire queste lenti?
poo·o′ sōstētoo·ē′re koo·e′ste len′tē

I'm *near-sighted (far-sighted)*.
Sono *miope (presbite)*.
sō′nō mē′ope (pres′bēte)

binoculars	(il) binocolo	bēnō′kōlō
compass	(la) bussola	boo′sōlä
contact lenses	(le) lenti a contatto	len′tē ä kōntä′tō
eyeglass case	(l') astuccio *m* da occhiali	ästoo′tshō dä ōkyä′lē
frame	(la) montatura	mōntätoo′rä
glasses	(gli) occhiali	ōkyä′lē
spectacles	(gli) occhiali	ōkyä′lē
sunglasses	(gli) occhiali da sole ...	ōkyä′lē dä sō′le

Stationery

ball point pen	(la) biro	bē′rō
– ball point cartridge	(la) mina	mē′nä
crayons	(le) matite colorate	mätē′te kōlōrä′te
envelope	(la) busta	boo′stä
eraser	(la) gomma	gō′mä
fountain pen	(la) penna stilografica .	pe′nä stēlōgrä′fēkä
glue	(la) colla	kō′lä
ink	(l') inchiostro *m*	ēnkyō′strō
notebook	(il) quaderno	koo·äder′nō
pad	(il) blocco	blō′kō
– scratch pad	blocco per appunti	blō′kō per äpoon′tē
– sketch pad	blocco da disegno	blō′kō dä dēse′nyō
paper	(la) carta	kär′tä
– typewriter paper ...	(la) carta per scrivere a macchina	kär′tä per skrē′vere ä mä′kēnä
– wrapping paper	– da impacco	dä ēmpä′kō
– writing paper	– da lettere	dä le′tere
pencil	(la) matita	mätē′tä
photocopies	(le) fotocopie	fōtōkō′pye

Shoes

I'd like a pair of . . .		I take a size . . .
Vorrei un paio di . . .		Ho il numero . . .
vōre′ē ōon pä′yō dē . . .		ō ēl nōo′merō . . .

beach sandals	sandali da spiaggia	sän′dälē dä spyä′jä
bedroom slippers	pantofole	päntō′fōle
boots	stivali	stēvä′lē
ladies' shoes	scarpe da donna	skär′pe dä dō′nä
loafers	mocassini	mōkäsē′nē
rubber boots	stivali di gomma	stēvä′lē dē gō′mä
sandals	sandali	sän′dälē
sneakers,	scarpe da ginnastica	skär′pe dä
gym shoes		jēnä′stēkä
walking shoes	scarpe basse	skär′pe bä′se

They're too *tight (wide)*.		**They pinch here.**
Sono troppo *strette (larghe)*.		Mi fanno male qui.
sō′nō trō′pō stre′te (lär′ge)		mē fä′nō mä′le kōo·ē′

Could you fix these shoes for me?
Può ripararmi queste scarpe?
pōo·ō′ rēpärär′mē kōo·e′ste skär′pe

crêpe sole	(la) suola di gomma	sōo·ō′lä dē gō′mä
	crespata	krespä′tä
heel	(il) tacco	tä′kō
– flat	– basso	bä′sō
– high	– alto	äl′tō
in-sole	(la) soletta	sōle′tä
leather	(la) pelle//(il) cuoio	pe′le/kōo·ō′yō
leather sole	(la) suola di cuoio	sōo·ō′lä dē kōo·ō′yō
rubber sole	(la) suola di gomma	sōo·ō′lä dē gō′mä
shoe horn	(il) corno per le	kōr′nō per le
	scarpe	skär′pe
shoe laces	(i) lacci per le	lä′tshē per le
	scarpe	skär′pe
shoe polish	(il) lucido da scarpe	lōo′tshēdō dä skär′pe
sole *(noun)*	(la) suola	sōo·ō′lä
sole *(verb)*	risuolare	rēsōo·ōlä′re
suede	(la) pelle scamosciata	pe′le skämōshä′tä

Cigar Store

A pack of ... *cigarettes (tobacco)*, please.
Un pacchetto di *sigarette (tabacco)* ..., per favore.
ōōn päke'tō dē sēgäre'te (täbä'kō) ..., per fàvō're

Do you have American cigarettes?
Ha sigarette americane?
ä sēgäre'te ämerēkä'ne

A dozen cigars, please.
Dodici sigari, per favore.
dō'dētshē sē'gäre, per fàvō're

Would you please refill my lighter?
Mi carica l'accendino, per favore?
mē kä'rēkä lätshendē'nō, per fàvō're

A box of matches, please.
Una scatola di fiammiferi, per favore.
ōō'nä skä'tōlä dē fyämē'ferē, per fàvō're

cigar	(il) sigaro	sē'gärō
cigarette	(la) sigaretta	sēgäre'tä
– filtered	– con filtro	kōn fēl'trō
– unfiltered	– senza filtro	sen'tsä fēl'trō
cigarillo	(il) sigarillo	sēgärē'lō
flint	(la) pietrina per accendisigari	pyetrē'nä per ätshendēsē'gärē
lighter	(l') accendino *m*	ätshendē'nō
– gas lighter	– a gas	ä gäs
lighter fluid	(la) benzina per l' accendino	bendzē'nä per lätshendē'nō
matches	(i) fiammiferi	fyämē'ferē
pipe	(la) pipa	pē'pä
pipe cleaner	(il) nettapipe	netäpē'pe
tobacco	(il) tabacco	täbä'kō

Toiletries

after shave	(il) dopobarba	dōpōbär'bä
bath salts	(i) sali da bagno	sä'lē dä bä'nyō
bobby pins	(le) forcine	fōrtshē'ne
brush	(la) spazzola	spä'tsōlä
comb	(il) pettine	pe'tēne
compact	(il) portacipria	pōrtätshē'prē·ä

cream	(la) crema	kre'mä
curler	(il) bigodino	bēgōdē'nō
deodorant	(il) deodorante	de·ōdōrän'te
dye	(la) tintura	tēntōō'rä
eyeliner	(l') eye liner *m*	ä·yelē'ner
eye shadow	(l') ombretto	ōmbre'tō
eyebrow pencil	(la) matita per le soprac-ciglia	mätē'tä per le sō-prätshēl'yä
face cream	(la) crema per il viso	kre'mä per ēl vē'zō
hair conditioner	(la) sciacquatura cura	shäkōō·ätōō'rä kōō'rä
hair net	(la) retina	retē'nä
hair setting lotion	(il) fissatore	fēsätō're
hair spray	(la) lacca	lä'kä
hair tonic	(la) frizione	frētsyō'ne
hairbrush	(la) spazzola per i capelli	spä'tsōlä per ē käpe'lē
hairpins	(i) fermagli	fermä'lyē
lipstick	(il) rossetto	rōse'tō
mascara	(il) mascara	mäskä'rä
mirror	(lo) specchio	spe'kyō
mouthwash	(il) colluttorio	kōlōōtōr'yō
nail file	(la) lima per le unghie	lē'mä per le ōōn'gye
nail polish	(lo) smalto	zmäl'tō
nail polish remover	(il) dissolvente per lo smalto	dēsōlve'nte per lō zmä'ltō
nail scissors	(le) forbicine per le unghie	fōrbētshē'ne per le ōōn'gye
perfume	(il) profumo	prōfōō'mō
powder	(la) cipria	tshē'prē·ä
prophylactics	(i) profilattici	prōfēlä'tētshē
razor	(il) rasoio	räzō'yō
– electric shaver	(il) rasoio elettrico	räzō'yō ele'trēkō
– safety razor	(il) rasoio di sicurezza	räzō'yō dē sēkōōre'tsä
razor blades	(le) lamette	läme'te
rouge	(il) rossetto	rōse'tō
sanitary napkins	(gli) assorbenti igienici	äsōrben'tē ēje'nētshē

scissors	(le) forbici	fōr'bētshē
shampoo	(lo) shampoo	shäm'pōō
shaving brush	(il) pennello per la barba	pene'lō per lä bär'bä
shaving cream	(la) crema da barba	kre'mä dä bär'bä
shaving foam	(la) schiuma da barba	skyōō'mä dä bär'bä
shaving soap	(il) sapone da barba	säpō'ne dä bär'bä
soap	(il) sapone	säpō'ne
sponge	(la) spugna	spōō'nyä
sun tan cream	(la) crema solare	kre'mä sōlä're
– sun tan lotion	(la) lozione solare	lōtsyō'ne sōlä're
– sun tan oil	(l') olio *m* solare	ō'lyō sōlä're
tampons	(i) tamponi	tämpō'nē
tissues	(i) fazzoletti di carta	fätsōle'tē dē kär'tä
toilet articles, toiletries	(gli) accessori da toletta	ätsheso'rē dä tōle'tä
toilet kit	(il) beauty-case	byōōtē käs
toilet paper	(la) carta igienica	kär'tä ēje'nēkä
tooth brush	(lo) spazzolino per i denti	spätsōlē'nō per ē den'tē
tooth paste	(il) dentifricio	dentēfrē'tshō
tooth powder	(il) dentifricio in polvere	dentēfrē'tshō ēn pōl've re
towel	(l') asciugamano *m*	äshōōgämä'nō
– bath towel	(l') asciugamano da bagno *m*	äshōōgämä'nō dä bän'yō
tweezers	(le) pinzette	pēntse'te
wash cloth	(il) guanto spugna	gōō·än'tō spōō'nyä

Watchmaker

Can you fix this *watch (clock)*?
Può riparare quest'orologio?
pōō·ō' rēpärä're kōō·estōrōlō'jō

It's running *fast (slow)*.
Va *avanti (indietro)*.
vä ävän'tē (ēndye'trō)

How much will the repair cost?
Quanto costa la riparazione?
kōō·än'tō kō'stä lä rēpärätsyō'ne

alarm clock	(la) sveglia	zve'lyä
crystal	(il) vetro	ve'trō
clock	(l') orologio *m*	ōrōlō'jō
face	(il) quadrante	kōō·ädrän'te
hand	(la) lancetta	läntshe'tä
pocket watch	(l') orologio *m* da tasca	ōrōlō'jō dä täs'kä
spring	(la) molla	mō'lä
stop watch	(il) cronometro	krōnō'metrō
watch	(l') orologio *m*	ōrōlō'jō
watch band	(il) cinturino	tshēntōōrē'nō
wrist watch	(l') orologio da polso	ōrōlō'jō dä pōl'sō

Sundries

ash tray	(il) portacenere	pōrtätshe'nere
bag	(la) busta, borsetta	bōō'stä, bōrse'tä
ball	(la) palla	pä'lä
basket	(il) cesto	tshe'stō
battery	(la) batteria	bäterē'ä
beach bag	(la) borsa per la spiaggia	bōr'sä per lä spyä'jä
bottle opener	(l') apribottiglie *m*	äprēbōtē'lye
briefcase	(la) cartella	kärte'lä
camp stove	(il) fornello	fōrne'lō
can opener	(l') apriscatole *m*	äprēskä'tōle
candle	(la) candela	kände'lä
– beeswax	(la) cera d'api	tshe'rä dä'pē
candlestick	(il) portacandela	pōrtäkände'lä
candy	(i) dolci	dōl'tshē
canned goods	(le) conserve alimentari	kōnser've älēmentä'rē
cassette	(la) cassetta	käse'tä
ceramics	(la) ceramica	tsherä'mēkä
china	(la) porcellana	pōrtshelä'nä
corkscrew	(il) cavatappi	kävätä'pē
detergent	(il) detersivo	detersē'vō
– dishwashing detergent	(il) detersivo per piatti	detersē'vō per pyä'tē
doll	(la) bambola	bäm'bōlä
flashlight	(la) pila	pē'lä

flight bag	(la) borsa da viaggio	bōr'sä dä vyä'jō
	(per il volo)	(per ēl vō'lō)
hammock	(l') amaca *f*	ämä'kä
handbag	(la) borsetta	bōrse'tä
handicrafts	(i) lavori d'ago	lävō'rē dä'gō
handkerchief	(il) fazzoletto	fätsōle'tō
jackknife	(il) coltello a	kōlte'lō ä
	serramanico	serämä'nēkō
leash	(il) guinzaglio	gōō-ēntsä'lyō
mat	(il) piattino	pyätē'nō
paper napkins	(i) tovaglioli di	tōvälyō'lē dē
	carta	kär'tä
phonograph record . .	(il) disco	dē'skō
picture	(la) foto	fō'tō
plastic bag	(la) borsetta di	bōrse'tä dē
	plastica	plä'stēkä
playing cards	(le) carte da gioco	kär'te dä jō'kō
pocket knife	(il) coltellino	kōltelē'nō
purse	(il) borsellino	bōrselē'nō
recording tape	(il) nastro (magnetico) .	nä'strō (män-
		ye'tēkō)
rucksack	(lo) zaino	tsī'nō
Scotch tape	(lo) scotch	skōtsh
sled	(la) slitta	zlē'tä
spot remover	(lo) smacchiatore	zmäkyätō're
string	(lo) spago	spä'gō
stuffed animal	(l') animale *m* di	änēmä'le dē
	stoffa	stō'fä
suitcase	(la) valigia	väle'jä
tape recorder	(il) registratore	rejēsträtō're
thermometer	(il) termometro	termō'metrō
thermos bottle	(il) termos	ter'mōs
toy	(il) giocattolo	jōkä'tōlō
umbrella	(l') ombrello *m*	ōmbre'lō
vase	(il) vaso	vä'zō
video cassette	(la) videocassetta	vēde·ōkäse'tä
wallet	(il) portafoglio	pōrtäfō'lyō
wood carving	(la) scultura in	skōōltōō'rä ēn
	legno	le'nyō

AT THE POST OFFICE

The activities of European post offices are far broader in scope than they are in the United States. In addition to all the usual mail services, the post office is also the telegraph and telephone company, and provides full banking services, including checking and savings accounts, as well as exchange of foreign currency. They will also hold mail for travelers. Simply tell your correspondents to write you "Fermo in posta" (fer'mō ēn pō'stä) in the city of your destination.

Post Office

Where is the post office?	**Where is there a mail box?**
Dov'è l'ufficio postale?	Dov'è una cassetta per le lettere?
dōve' loofē'tshō pōstä'le	dōve' oo'nä käse'tä per le le'tere

How much does this *letter (card)* cost?	**– to Canada.**
Quanto costa questa *lettera (cartolina)*?	– per il Canadà.
koo·än'tō kō'stä koo·e'stä le'terä (kärtōlē'nä)	– per ēl känädä'

– to the United States.	**What's the postage on** ...
– per gli Stati Uniti.	Qual'è la tariffa postale per ...
– per lyē stä'tē oonē'tē	koo·äle' lä tärē'fä pōstä'le per ...

this air mail letter	questa lettera via aerea	koo·e'stä le'terä vē'ä ä·e're·ä
this letter abroad	questa lettera per l'estero	koo·e'stä le'terä per le'sterō
this local letter	questa lettera per l'interno	koo·e'stä le'terä per lēnter'nō
this parcel	questo pacco	koo·e'stō pä'kō
this post card	questa cartolina postale	koo·e'stäkärtōlē'nä pōstä'le
this printed matter ..	queste stampe	koo·e'ste stäm'pe
this registered letter .	questa raccomandata ..	koo·e'stä räkōmän-dä'tä
this small parcel	questo pacchetto	koo·e'stō päke'tō
this special delivery letter	questa lettera espresso	koo·e'stä le'terä espre'sō

Five ... Lire stamps please.
Per favore, cinque francobolli da ... Lire.
per fävō're, tshēn'koo·e fränkōbō'lē dä ... lē're

Do you have any special issues?
Ci sono francobolli di emissione
speciale?
tshē sō'nō fränkōbō'lē dē emēsyō'ne spetshä'le

Two of each, please.
Due di ogni serie, per favore.
dōō'e dē ō'nyē se'rē·e, per fävō're

I'd like to send this letter *by registered mail (special delivery)*.
Vorrei mandare questa lettera *per raccomandata (espresso)*.
vōrē'ē mändä're kōō·e'stä le'terä per räkōmändä'tä (espre'sō)

A postal transfer (money order), please.
Un vaglia postale (un versamento), per favore.
ōōn vä'lyä pōstä'le (ōōn versämen'tō) per fävō're

How long does it take for a *letter (package)* to get to ...?
Quanto tempo ci mette *la lettera (il pacco)* per arrivare a ...?
kōō·än'tō tem'pō tshē me'te lä le'terä (ēl pä'ko) per ärēvä're ä ...

Is there any mail here for me?
C'è della posta per me?
tshe de'lä pō'stä per me

My name is ...
Mi chiamo ...
mē kyä'mō ...

Do I need a customs declaration?
C'è bisogno di una dichiarazione doganale?
tshe bēzō'nyō dē ōō'nä dēkyärätsyō'ne dōgänä'le

I'd like to have my mail forwarded.
Per favore, faccia seguire la mia corrispondenza.
per fävō're, fä'tshä segōō·e're lä mē'ä kōrēspōnden'tsä

This is my new address.
Ecco il mio nuovo indirizzo.
e'kō ēl mē'ō nōō·ō'vō ēndērē'tsō

*Sign here, please.
Per favore, firmi qui.
per fävō're, fēr'mē kōō·ē'

---

*Even without a postal bank account, you can pay bills at the post
office, simply by transferring the money to your creditor's postal
account or having a money order delivered to him by mail. This is a
good way of taking care of possible medical bills which might come up
along the way. Of course, the Italian Post Offices can help you send
money to the United States, or almost any other country in the world.
Inquire at the* "Sportello bancario" *or* "bank counter".

Telegrams

A telegram form, please.
Un modulo per telegrammi, per favore.
o͞on mō′do͞olō per telegrä′mē, per fàvō′re

I'd like to send ...
Vorrei spedire ...
vōre′ē spedē′re ...

a telegram	un telegramma	o͞on telegrä′mä
an urgent telegram	un telegramma urgente	o͞on telegrä′mä o͞orjen′te
a night letter	un telegramma lettera	o͞on telegrä′mä le′terä

How much do ten words to ... cost?
Quanto costano dieci parole per ...?
ko͞o·än′tō kō′stänō dye′tshē pärō′le per ...

When will it arrive at ...?
Quando arriverà a ...?
ko͞o·än′dō ärēverä′ ä ...

Telephone

In most European countries it is wise to place long distance calls at the post office, as many hotels make sizable surcharges for use of the phone. Besides the post office there is another official office especially for telephone calls. It is called "SIP" (pronounced like sip). It is an office full of telephone booths for calls anywhere in Italy and around the world.

Where is the nearest phone booth?
Dov'è la cabina telefonica più vicina?
dōve′ lä käbē′nä telefō′nēkä pyo͞o vētshē′nä

May I use your phone?
Posso telefonare da qui?
pō′sō telefonä′re dä ko͞o·ē′

Where can I make a phone call?
Dove posso telefonare?
dō′ve pō′sō telefonä′re

The phone book, please.
L'elenco telefonico, per favore.
lelen′kō telefō′nēkō, per fàvō′re

What's the area code for ...?
Qual è il prefisso di ...?
ko͞o·äle′ ēl prefē′sō dē ...

Can I direct dial to ...?
Si può chiamare in teleselezione ...?
sē po͞o·ō′ kyämä′re ēn teleseletsyō′ne ...

You can direct dial the United States from almost any telephone in Europe. The country code for the U.S. and Canada is 001, followed, of course by the area code and the subscriber's number. You will need operator assistance for person-to-person or collect calls.

A long distance call to . . . please.
Un'interurbana per . . . per favore.
ōōnēnterōōrbä'nä per . . . per fàvō're

How long will that take?
Quanto tempo ci vuole?
kōō·än'tō tem'pō tshē vōō·ō'le

Can I have some coins for the pay phone?
Vorrei alcuni gettoni per il telefono.
vōre'ē älkōō'nē jetō'nē per ēl tele'fōnō

Most public telephones require special coins called "gettoni", they are brass and have a small groove on one side. They can usually be bought in cafés which have telephones or at the SIP office. A number of public telephones, especially those along the "autostrada" take normal coins, or gettoni or the new magnetic cards or "carta magnetica" which also can be bought at SIP or in cafés which have such phone booths. They are bought for a fixed fee and give you this amount in telephone services by placing it into the proper slot of the phone.

How much does a *local call (call to . . .)* cost?
Quanto costa una *telefonata urbana (telefonata per . . .)*?
kōō·än'tō kō'stä ōō'nä telefōnä'tä ōōrbä'nä (telefōnä'tä per . . .)

*Your call is ready in booth four.
La Sua comunicazione è in cabina quattro.
lä sōō'ä kōmōōnēkätsyō'ne e ēn käbē'nä kōō·ä'trō

*What's your number?
Che numero ha?
ke nōō'merō ä

Please connect me with . . .
Per favore, mi metta in comunicazione con . . .
per fàvō're, mē me'ta ēn kōmōōnēkätsyō'ne kōn . . .

Speaking!
Pronto!
prōn'tō

The line is *busy (out of order)*.
La linea è *occupata (disturbata)*.
lä lē'ne·ä e ōkōōpä'tä (dēstōōrbä'tä)

Please hold the line.
Per favore, rimanga in linea.
per fàvō're, rēmän'gä ēn lē'ne·ä

There's no answer at that number.
Non risponde a questo numero.
nōn rēspon'de ä kōō·e'stō nōō'merō

Would you please cancel that call.
Annulli la comunicazione, per favore.
änōō'lē lä kōmōōnēkätsyō'ne, per fàvō're

Code Alphabet

A	come Ancona	änkō'nä	N	come Napoli	nä'pōlē
B	come Bologna	bōlō'nyä	O	come Otranto	ōträn'tō
C	come Como	kō'mō	P	come Pisa	pē'zä
D	come Domodos-		Q	come Quattro	kōō·ä'trō
	sola	dōmōdō'sōlä	R	come Roma	rō'mä
E	come Empoli	em'pōlē	S	come Salerno	säler'nō
F	come Forlì	fōrlē'	T	come Torino	tōrē'nō
G	come Genova	je'nōvä	U	come Udine	ōō'dēne
H	come Hotel	ōtel'	V	come Venezia	vene'tsyä
I	come Imola	ē'mōlä	W	come	ōō·ä'sh-
J	come Jolanda	jōlän'dä		Washington	ingtōn
K	come cappa	kä'pä	X	come ics	ēks
L	come Livorno	lēvōr'nō	Y	come ypsilon	ēp'sēlōn
M	come Milano	mēlä'nō	Z	come zeta	dze'tä

address	(l') indirizzo *m*	ēndērē'tsō
addressee	(il) destinatario	destēnätär'yō
air mail	(la) posta aerea	pō'stä ä·e're·ä
area code	(il) prefisso	prefē'sō
c.o.d.	(il) contrassegno	kōnträse'nyō
coin changer	(il) distributore-monete	dēstrēbōōtō're-mōne'te
counter	(lo) sportello	spōrte'lō
customs	(la) dichiarazione	dēkyärätsyō'ne
declaration	doganale	dōgänä'le
destination	(la) destinazione	destēnätsyō'ne
dial	fare il numero	fä're ēl nōō'merō
direct dialing	(la) teleselezione	teleseletsyō'ne
information	(l') informazione *f*	ēnfōrmätsyō'ne
letter	(la) lettera	le'terä
local call	(la) chiamata urbana	kyämä'tä ōōrbä'nä
long distance call	(l') interurbana *f*	ēnterōōrbä'nä
mail box	(la) buca delle lettere	bōō'kä de'le le'tere
operator	(il/la) telefonista	telefōnē'stä
package	(il) pacco	pä'kō
package card	(la) bolletta di spedizione	bōle'tä dē spedētsyō'ne

picture post card	(la) cartolina illustrata	kärtōlē'nä ēlōōsträ'tä
post card	(la) cartolina postale ..	kärtōlē'nä pōstä'le
post office box	(la) casella postale	käze'lä pōstä'le
postage	(l') affrancatura *f*	äfränkätōō'rä
postal clerk	(l') impiegato *m* postale	ēmpyegä'tō pōstä'le
postal savings book ..	(il) libretto postale di risparmio	lēbre'tō pōstä'le dē rēspär'myō
poste restante	fermo in posta	fer'mō ēn pō'stä
postman	(il) postino	pōstē'nō
printed matter	(le) stampe	stäm'pe
receipt	(la) ricevuta	rētshevōō'tä
register	fare una raccomandata	fä're ōō'nä räkōmändä'tä
registered letter	(la) raccomandata	räkōmändä'tä
registered parcel with declared value	(il) pacco raccomandato con valore dichiarato ..	pä'kō räkōmändä'tō kōn välo're dēkyärä'tō
sender	(il) mittente	mēten'te
small parcel	(il) pacchetto	päke'tō

There is a special cheap postage rate for packages weighing less than two kilograms (domestically) and less than one kilogram (abroad).

---

special delivery	(l') espresso *m*	espre'sō
special delivery letter	(la) lettera per espresso	le'terä per espre'sō
special issue stamp ..	(il) francobollo emissione speciale	fränkōbō'lō emēsyō'ne spetshä'le
stamp *(noun)*	(il) francobollo	fränkōbō'lō
stamp *(verb)*	affrancare	äfränkä're
stamp machine	(il) distributore francobolli	dēstrēbōōtō're fränkōbō'lē
telegram	(il) telegramma	telegrä'mä
telephone	(il) telefono	tele'fōnō
unstamped	non affrancato	nōn äfränkä'tō
value declaration	(la) dichiarazione del valore	dēkyärätsyō'ne del välo're

BANK, CURRENCY EXCHANGE

> *The basic monitary unit in Italy is the* "lira" Lire italiane (L.it.). –
> *There are coins for 10, 50, 100, 200 and 500 lire. (coin =* "moneta").
> *There is also paper money for 500, 1000, 5000, 50 000, and 100 000
> lire. (paper money =* "biglietto").

Where can I change some money?
Dove posso cambiare del denaro?
dō've pō'sō kämbyä're del denä'rō

Where is the bank?
Dov'è la banca?
dōve' lä bän'kä⁀

I need a hundred dollars in Lire.
Vorrei cambiare cento dollari in Lire.
vōre'ē kämbyä're tshen'tō dō'lärē ēn lē're

How much will I get for ...?
Quanto ricevo per ...?
koo⸳än'tō rētshe'vō per ...

What's the rate of exchange?
Com'è il cambio?
kōme' ēl käm'byō

Can you change ... into Lire for me?
Può cambiarmi ... in Lire?
poo⸳ō' kämbyär'mē ... ēn lē're

Could I have some change please?
Può darmi degli spiccioli, per favore?
poo⸳ō' där'mē de'lye spē'tshōlē, per fävō're

Can you change this?
Può cambiare?
poo⸳ō' kämbyä're

I'd like to cash this *check (traveller's cheque).*
Vorrei riscuotere *questo assegno (traveller's cheque).*
vō're'ē rēskoo⸳ō'tere koo⸳e'stō äse'nyō (trä'velers tshek)

Has any money arrived for me?
E' arrivato del denaro per me?
e ärēvä'tō del denä'rō per me

amount	....	(l') importo *m*	....	ēmpōr'tō
bank	....	(la) banca	....	bän'kä
bank account	....	(il) conto corrente	.....	kōn'tō kōren'te
bank note	....	(la) banconota	....	bänkōnō'tä
bank transfer	....	(la) rimessa bancaria	..	rēme'sä bänkär'yä
bill	....	(il) biglietto	....	bēlye'tō
cash *(adj.)*	....	in contanti	....	ēn kōntän'tē
cash *(noun)*	....	(i) contanti	....	kōntän'tē

check	(l') assegno *m*	äsen'yō
coin	(la) moneta	mōne'tä
credit	(il) credito	kre'dētō
– take out a loan	prendere un	pren'dere ōōn
	prestito	pres'tētō
credit card	(la) carta di credito	kär'tä dē kre'dētō
currency	(la) valuta	välōō'tä
daily rate	(il) corso del giorno	kōr'sō del jōr'nō
deposit	versare	versä're
foreign currency	(la) valuta straniera	välōō'tä stränye'rä
form	(il) modulo	mo'dōōlō
letter of credit	(la) lettera di	le'terä dē
	credito	kre'dētō
money	(il) denaro	denä'rō
Austrian Schillings	scellini	shelē'nē
	austriaci	oustrē'ätshe
Canadian dollars	dollari	dō'lärē
	canadesi	känäde'sē
Swiss Francs	franchi	frän'kē
	svizzeri	zvē'tsere
American dollars	dollari	do'lärē
	americani	ämerēkä'nē
money exchange	(il) cambio	käm'byō
pay out	pagare	pägä're
payment	(il) pagamento	pägämen'tō
rate of exchange	(il) corso del cambio	kōr'sō del käm'byō
receipt	(la) ricevuta	rētshevōō'tä
savings bank	(la) Cassa di	kä'sä dē
	Risparmio	rēspär'myō
savings book	(il) libretto di	lēbre'tō dē
	risparmio	rēspär'myō
security	(il) titolo	tē'tōlō
share of stock	(l') azione *f*	ätsyō'ne
signature	(la) firma	fēr'mä
stock	(i) titoli	tē'tōlē
telegraphic	telegrafico	telegrä'fēkō
teller	(il) cassiere	käsye're
transfer	(la) rimessa	rēme'sä
traveler's cheque	(il) traveller's cheque	trä'velers tshek
withdraw	ritirare	rētērä're

AT THE POLICE STATION

Reporting

STOP

POLICE

I'd like to report ...
Vorrei denunciare ...
vōre'ē denōontshä're ...

an accident	un incidente	ōon ēntshēden'te
a blackmail attempt	un ricatto	ōon rēkä'tō
a hold up	una rapina	ōo'nä räpē'nä
a kidnapping	un sequestro	ōon sekōo·e'strō
a loss	uno smarrimento	ōo'nō zmärēmen'tō
a murder	un omicidio	ōon ōmētshē'dyō
a theft	un furto	ōon fōor'tō

My ... has been stolen.	**I lost my ...**
Mi hanno rubato ...	Ho perso ...
mē ä'nō rōobä'tō ...	ō per'sō ...

bag	la borsa	lä bōr'sä
billfold	il portafoglio	ēl pōrtäfō'lyō
	il borsellino	ēl bōrselē'nō
bracelet	il braccialetto	ēl brätshäle'tō
briefcase	cartella	kärte'lä
camera	la macchina	lä mä'kēnä
	fotografica	fōtōgrä'fēkä
car key	la chiava della	lä kyä've de'lä
	macchina	mä'kēnä
handbag	la borsetta	lä bōrse'tä
jewelry	i gioielli	ē jōye'lē
key	la chiave	lä kyä've
money	i soldi	ē sōl'dē
necklace	la collana	lä kōlä'nä
purse	il borsellino	ēl bōrselē'nō
	la borsetta	lä bōrse'tä
ring	l'anello	läne'lō
suitcase	la valigia	lä välē'jä
umbrella	l'ombrello	lōmbre'lō
wallet	il portafoglio	ēl pōrtäfō'lyō
watch	l'orologio	lōrōlō'jō
– wrist watch	l'orologio da polso	lōrōlō'jō dä pōl'sō

I have nothing to do with *it (this business)*.
Io non ho niente a che fare con *questo (questa faccenda)*.
ē'ō nōn ō nyen'te ä ke fà're kōn kōō·e'stō (kōō·e'stä fätshen'dä)

I'm innocent.	**I didn't do it.**
Sono innocente.	Io non ho fatto questo.
sō'nō ēnōtshen'te	ē'ō nōn ō fä'tō kōō·e'stō

How long do I have to stay here?
Per quanto devo restare qui?
per kōō·än'tō de'vō restä're kōō·ē'

This man is *bothering (following)* me.
Questo uomo mi *molesta (perseguita)*.
kōō·e'stō ōō·ō'mō mē mōle'stä (perse'gōō·ētä)

arrest	arrestare	ärestä're
attorney	(l') avvocato *m*	ävōkä'tō
confiscate	confiscare	kōnfēskä're
court	(il) tribunale	trēbōōnä'le
crime	(il) delitto	delē'tō
criminal	(il) reato	re·ä'tō
criminal investiga- tion division	(la) divisione investiga- tiva crimini	dēvēsyō'ne ēnves- tēgätē'vä krē'mēnē
custody	(la) detenzione	detentsyō'ne
– pre-trial custody	(la) detenzione preventiva	detentsyō'ne preventē'vä
drugs	(le) droghe	drō'ge
guilt	(la) colpa	kōl'pä
hold-up	(la) rapina	räpē'nä
judge	(il) giudice	jōō'dētshe
lawyer	(l') avvocato *m*	ävōkä'tō
narcotics	(i) narcotici	närkō'tētshē
police	(la) polizia	pōlētsē'ä
police car	(la) macchina della polizia	mä'kēnä de'lä pōlētsē'ä
police station	(il) commissariato di Pubblica sicurezza	kōmēsäryä'tō dē pōō'blēkä sēkōōre'tsä
prison	(la) prigione	prējō'ne
smuggling	(il) contrabbando	kōnträbän'dō
thief	(il) ladro	lä'drō
verdict	(la) sentenza	senten'tsä

BEAUTY SHOP / BARBER SHOP

At the Beauty Shop

May I make an appointment for Saturday?
Posso prenotarmi per sabato?
pō′sō prenōtär′mē per sä′bätō

Would you put me down for a permanent wave?
Potrebbe prenotarmi per la permanente?
pōtre′be prenōtär′mē per lä permänen′te

For tomorrow?
Per domani?
per dōmä′nē

Will I have to wait?
Devo aspettare?
de′vō äspetä′re

Will it take long?
Quanto ci vorrà?
kōō·än′tō tshē vōrä′

Wash and set, please.
Lavare e messa in piega, per favore.
lävä′re e me′sä ēn pye′gä, per fävō′re

I'd like a *permanent (set)*, please.
Vorrei *una permanente (la messa in piega)*.
vōre′ē ōō′nä permänen′te (lä me′sä ēn pye′gä)

Please set my hair for the evening.
Vorrei una pettinatura per la sera.
vōre′ē ōō′nä petēnätōō′rä per lä se′rä

Please *dye (rinse)* my hair ...
Per favore mi tinga i capelli ...
per fävō′re, mē tēn′gä ē käpe′lē ...

Please cut my hair a little shorter.
Mi accorci un po' i capelli, per favore.
mē äkōr′tshē ōōn pō ē käpe′lē, per fävō′re

Just trim it, please.
Solo una spuntatina, per favore.
sō′lō ōō′nä spōōntätē′nä, per fävō′re

Please cut it wet.
Me li tagli bagnati.
me lē tä′lye bänyä′tē

Please pin it up.
Per favore, me li raccolga su.
per fävō′re, me lē räkōl′gä sōō

Please tease it a little on the *top (sides)*.
Per favore, me li cotoni un po' *in alto (ai lati)*.
per fàvō're, me lē kōtō'nē ōōn pō ēn äl'tō (ī lä'tē)

It's a little too hot under the drier.
E' troppo caldo sotto il casco.
e trō'pō käl'dō sō'tō ēl käs'kō

No *setting lotion (hair spray)*, please.
Non metta *il fissatore (la lacca)*, per favore.
nōn me'tä ēl fēsätō're (lä lä'kä), per fàvō're

Could you give me a *manicure (pedicure)*?
Può farmi *la manicure (pedicure)*?
pōō·ō' fär'mē lä mänēkōō're (pedēkōō're)

Please file my nails *round (to a point)*.
Per favore limi le unghie *rotonde (a punta)*.
per fàvō're lē'mē le ōōn'gye rōtōn'de (ä pōōn'tä)

Just polish them, please.   **With (without) nail polish.**
Solo lo smalto incolore.   *Con lo (senza)* smalto.
sō'lō lō zmäl'tō ēnkōlō're   kōn lō (sen'tsä) zmäl'tō

Please *tweeze (shave)* my eyebrows.
Mi *ritocchi (rada)* le sopracciglia, per favore.
mē rētō'kē (rä'dä) le sōprätshēl'yä, per fàvō're

A *facial mask (face massage)*, please.
Una *maschera per il viso (un massaggio al viso)*, per favore.
ōō'nä mä'skerä per ēl vē'zō (ōōn mäsä'jō äl vē'zō), per fàvō're

Would you please put this *hairpiece (wig)* on for me?
Per favore, mi metta *questo posticcio (questa parrucca)*.
per fàvō're, mē me'tä kōō·e'stō pōstē'tshō (kōō·e'stä pärōō'kä)

Yes, thank you, that's just fine.   **Very nice!**
Sì, grazie, così va bene.   Molto bene!
sē, grä'tsye, kōsē' vä be'ne   mōl'tō be'ne

At the Barber Shop

(Shave and) A haircut, please.
Capelli (e barba), per favore.
käpe´lē (e bär´bä), per fävo´re

Not too short, please.
Non troppo corti, per favore.
nōn trō´pō kōr´tē, per fävō´re

(Very) short, please.
(Molto) corti, per favore.
(mōl´tō) kōr´tē, per fävō´re

– at the back.
– di dietro.
– dē dye´trō

– on top.
– sopra.
– sō´prä

– in front.
– davanti.
– dävän´tē

– on the sides.
– ai lati.
– ī lä´tē

A razor cut, please.
Per favore, un taglio al rasoio.
per fävo´re, ōōn tä´lyō äl räzō´yō

With (Without) part, please.
Con (senza) la riga, per favore.
kōn (sen´tsä) lä rē´gä, per fävō´re

Part on the *left (right)*, please.
Faccia la riga *a sinistra (a destra)*, per favore.
fä´tshä lä rē´gä ä sēnē´strä (ä de´strä), per fävō´re

A shampoo too, please!
Mi lavi anche i capelli, per favore.
mē lä´vē än´ke ē käpe´lē, per fävō´re

Scalp massage, please.
Una frizione, per favore.
ōō´nä frētsyō´ne, per fävō´re

Would you trim my *beard (moustache)*, please?
Mi spunti un po' *la barba (i baffi)*, per favore.
mē spōōn´tē ōōn pō´ lä bär´bä (ē bä´fē), per fävō´re

Just a shave, please.
Soltanto la barba.
sōltän´tō lä bär´bä

Please don't shave against the grain.
Non mi rada contropelo, per favore.
nōn mē rä´dä kōntrōpe´lō, per fävō´re

Some hair tonic (*A little brilliantine*), please.
Con *lozione (un po' di brillantina)*, prego.
kōn lōtsyō´ne (ōōn pō´ dē brēläntē´nä), pre´gō

Please leave it dry.
Li lasci secchi, prego.
lē lä´shē se´kē, pre´gō

Yes, thank you, that's just great.
Sì, grazie. Così va bene.
sē, grä´tsye kōsē´ vä be´ne

barber	(il) barbiere	bärbye′re
beard	(la) barba	bär′bä
beauty parlor	(il) salone di bellezza	sälö′ne dē bele′tsä
brilliantine	(la) brillantina	brēläntē′nä
cold wave	(la) permanente a freddo	permänen′te ä fre′dō
comb (*noun*)	(il) pettine	pe′tēne
comb (*verb*)	pettinare	petēnä′re
curls	(i) riccioli	rē′tshōlē
cut	tagliare	tälyä′re
dandruff	(la) forfora	fōr′fōrä
do someone's hair	fare i capelli	fä′re ē käpe′lē
dye	tingere	tēn′jere
hair	(i) capelli	käpe′lē
– **dry hair**	capelli secchi	käpe′lē se′kē
– **greasy hair**	capelli grassi	käpe′lē grä′sē
haircut	(il) taglio dei capelli	tä′lyō de′ē käpe′lē
hair-do	(la) pettinatura	petēnätōō′rä
hairdresser	(il) parrucchiere	pärōōkye′re
hair drier	(il) casco	käs′kō
hair loss	(la) caduta dei capelli	kädōō′tä de′ē käpe′lē
hair style	(la) pettinatura	petēnätōō′rä
hairpiece	(il) parrucchino	pärōōkē′nō
manicure	(la) manicure	mänekōō′re
moustache	(i) baffi	bä′fē
part	(la) riga	rē′gä
pedicure	(la) pedicure	pedēkōō′re
permanent wave	(la) permanente	permänen′te
scalp massage	(la) frizione	frētsyō′ne
set	(la) messa in piega	me′sä ēn pye′gä
shave	(la) barba	bär′bä
sideburns	(le) basette	bäze′te
strand	(la) frangetta	fränje′tä
tease	cotonare	kōtōnä′re
tint	tingere	tēn′jere
toupé	(il) tuppè	tōōpe′
wash	lavare	lävä′re
wig	(la) parrucca	pärōō′kä
wisp	(la) ciocca di capelli	tshō′kä dē käpe′lē

HEALTH

Pharmacy

Where is the next pharmacy?
Dov'è la farmacia più vicina?
Dōve' lä färmätshē'ä pyoō vētshē'nä

Which pharmacy has night duty?
Quale farmacia fa servizio notturno?
koō·ä'le färmätshē'ä fä serve'tsyō nōtoōr'nō

I'd like this medicine, please.
Vorrei questa medicina, per favore.
vōre'ē koō·e'stä medētshē'nä, per fävō're

Please give me something for . . .
Per favore, mi dia qualcosa contro . . .
per fävō're mē dē'ä koō·älkō'zä kōn'trō . . .

I'd like . . .
Vorrei . . .
vōre'ē . . .

Do I need a prescription for this medicine?
Ci vuole una ricetta per questa medicina?
shē voō·ō'le oō'nä rētshe'tä per koō·e'stä medētshē'nä

Can you order this medicine for me?
Mi può procurare questa medicina?
mē poō·ō' prōkoōrä're koō·e'stä medētshē'nä

Where can I pick it up?
Quando sarà qui?
koō·än'dō särä' koō·ē'

Can I wait for it?
Posso aspettare?
pō'sō äspetä're

for external use . . .	per uso esterno	per oō'zō ester'nō
for internal use	per uso interno	per oō'zō ēnter'nō
before meals	prima dei pasti	prē'mä de'ē pä'stē
after meals	dopo i pasti	dō'pō ē pä'stē
three times a day . .	tre volte al giorno .	tre vōl'te äl jōr'nō
as prescribed	come da prescri-zione medica	kō'me dä preskrēt-syō'ne me'dēkä
on an empty stomach	a stomaco vuoto . .	ä stō'mäkō voō·ō'tō

Medication and Bandages

absorbent cotton	(l') ovatta *f*	ōvä′tä
ace bandage	(la) benda elastica	ben′dä elä′stēkä
adhesive bandage	(il) cerotto	tsherō′tō
alcohol	(l') alcool *m*	äl′kō-ōl
aspirin	(l') aspirina *f*	äspērē′nä
bicarbonate of soda ..	(il) bicarbonato di sodio	bēkärbōnä′tō dē sō′dyō
boric acid ointment ..	(la) pomata all'acido borico	pōmä′tä älä′tshēdō bō′rēkō
burn ointment	(l') unguento *m* per le scottature	ōōngōō·en′tō per le skōtätōō′re
camomile tea	(la) camomilla	kämōmē′lä
cardiovascular drug .	(il) rimedio circolatorio	rēme′dyō tshērkōlä tōr′yō
castor oil	(l') olio *m* di ricino	ō′lyō dē rē′tshēnō
charcoal pills	(le) pastiglie di carbone	pästē′lye dē kärbō′ne
contraceptive pills ...	(le) pillole anticonce-zionali	pē′lōle äntē-kōntshetsyōnä′le
corn plaster	(il) callifugo	kälē′fōōgō
cotton swabs	(le) bacchette di ovatta	bäke′te dē ōvä′tä
cough syrup	(lo) sciroppo per la tosse	shērō′pō per lä tō′se
diaphoretic	(il) sudorifero	sōōdōrē′ferō
digestive tonic	(il) tonico digestivo ...	tō′nēkō dējestē′vō
disinfectant	(il) disinfettante	dēsēnfetän′te
diuretic	(il) diuretico	dyōōre′tēkō
drops	(le) gocce	gō′tshe
ear drops	(le) gocce per l'orecchio	gō′tshe per lōre′kyō
elastic stocking	(la) calza elastica	käl′tsä elä′stēkä
emetic	(l') emetico *m*	eme′tēkō
eye drops	(le) gocce per gli occhi .	gō′tshe per lyē ō′k
eye ointment	(la) pomata per gli occhi	pōmä′tä per lyē ō′kē
fever cure	(il) preparato contro la febbre	prepärä′tō kōn′trō lä fe′bre

first-aid kit	(la) cassetta pronto soccorso	käse'tä prōn'tō sōkōr'sō
gargle	(il) liquido per i gargarismi	lē'kōō·ēdō per ē gärgärē'zmē
gauze bandage	(la) garza	gär'tsä
glycerine	(la) glicerina	glētsherē'nä
hydrogen peroxide ...	(l') acqua f ossigenata .	ä'kōō·ä ōsējenä'tä
insect repellent	(l') insetticida f	ēnsetētshē'dä
iodine	(lo) iodio	yō'dyō
laxative	(il) lassativo	läsätē'vō
liniment	(il) linimento	lēnēmen'tō
medicine	(la) medicina	medētshē'nä
mouthwash	(il) colluttorio	kōlōōtōr'yō
ointment	(la) pomata	pōmä'tä
pain pills	(le) compresse contro il dolore	kōmpre'se kōn'trō ēl dōlō're
peppermint	(la) menta	men'tä
pill	(la) pastiglia	pästē'lyä
powder	(la) polverina	pōlverē'nä
prophylactics	(i) profilattici	prōfēlä'tētshē
quinine	(il) chinino	kēnē'nō
remedy	(il) rimedio	rēme'dyō
salve	(l') unguento m	ōōngōō·en'tō
sanitary napkins	(gli) assorbenti igienici	äsōrben'tē ēje'nētshē
sleeping pills	(il) sonnifero in pastiglie	sōnē'ferō ēn pästē'lye
styptic pencil	(l') antiemorragico m ..	äntē·emōrä'jēkō
suppository	(le) supposte	sōōpō'ste
tablet	(la) compressa	kōmpre'sä
talcum powder	(il) borotalco	bōrōtäl'kō
thermometer	(il) termometro	termō'metrō
tincture	(la) tintura	tēntōō'rä
tonic	(il) tonico	tō'nēkō
tranquilizer	(il) tranquillante	tränkōō·elän'te
valerian drops	(le) gocce di valeriana .	gō'tshe dē väleryä'nä
vaseline	(la) vaselina	väzelē'nä
wound salve	(la) pomata per una ferita	pōmä'tä per ōō'nä ferē'tä

The doctor is in

Quick, call a doctor!
Chiami subito il dottore, per favore!
kyä′mē sōō′bētō ēl dōtō′re, per fävō′re

Is there a doctor in the house?
C'è un medico qui (in albergo)?
tshe ōōn me′dēkō kōō·ē (ēn älber′gō)

Please get a doctor!
Faccia venire un medico!
fä′tshä venē′re ōōn me′dēkō

Where is there a doctor?
Dov'è un dottore?
dōve′ ōōn dōtō′re

Can he come here?
Può venire qui?
pōō·ō′ venē′re kōō·ē′

Where is there a hospital?
Dov'è un ospedale?
dōve′ ōōn ōspedä′le

Would you please come to the ...
Per favore, venga al (alla) ...
per fävō′re, ven′gä äl (ä′lä) ...

When does the doctor have office hours?
Quando riceve il dottore?
kōō·än′dō rētshe′ve ēl dōtō′re

I'm sick.
Sono malato (malata).
sō′nō mälä′tō (mälä′tä)

My husband (My wife, Our child) is sick.
Mio marito *(mia moglie, nostro figlio, no-*
stra figlia) è malato *(-a).*
mē′ō märē′tō (mē′ä mō′lye, nō′strō
fē′lyō, nō′strä fē′lyä) e mälä′tō (-ä)

doctor	(il) *dottore (medico)* ...	dōtō′re (me′dēkō)
dermatologist	(il) dermatologo	dermätō′lōgō
ear, nose and throat specialist	(l') otorinolaringo- iatra *m*	ōtōrēnōlärēn- gōyä′trä
eye doctor	(l') oculista *m*	ōkōōlē′stä
general practitioner .	(il) medico generico ...	me′dēkō jene′rēkō
gynecologist	(il) ginecologo	jēnekō′lōgō
internist	(l') internista *m*	ēnternē′stä
neurologist	(il) neurologo	ne·ōōrō′lōgō
orthopedist	(l') ortopedico *m*	ōrtōpe′dēkō
pediatrician	(il) pediatra	pedyä′trä
psychiatrist	(il) psichiatra	psēkyä′trä
psychologist	(il) psicologo	psēkō′lōgō
specialist	(lo) specialista	spetshälē′stä

surgeon	(il) chirurgo	kēroor'gō
– plastic surgery	chirurgia plastica	kēroorjē'ä plä'stēkä
urologist	(l') urologo *m*	ōorō'lōgō
doctor's office	(l') ambulatorio *m*	ämboolätōr'yō
office hours	(l') orario *m* di visita ..	ōrär'yō dē vē'zētä
waiting room	(la) sala d'aspetto	sä'lä däspe'tō

I haven't felt well the last few days.

Da alcuni giorni non mi sento bene.

dä älkoo'nē jōr'nē nōn mē sen'tō be'ne

My *head (throat, stomach)* hurts.

Mi fa male *la testa (la gola, lo stomaco)*.

mē fä mä'le lä te'stä (lä gō'lä, lō stō'mäkō)

It hurts here.

Mi fa male qui.

mē fä mä'le koo·ē'

I've got a *(severe, sharp, dull)* pain here.

Ho dei dolori *(forti, pungenti, sordi)* qui.

ō de'ē dōlō're (fōr'tē, poonjen'tē, sōr'dē) koo·ē'

I've got a (high) fever.

Ho la febbre (alta).

ō lä fe'bre (äl'tä)

I've caught a cold.

Mi sono *raffreddato (-a)*.

mē sō'nō räfredä'tō (-ä)

I can't handle the *heat (food)* here.

Non sopporto il caldo (Non riesco a mangiare).

nōn sōpōr'tō ēl käl'dō (nōn rē·es'kō ä mänjä're)

I must have done something to my stomach.

Ho fatto un'indigestione.

ō fä'tō oonēndējestyō'ne

I ate...

Ho mangiato ...

ō mänjä'tō ...

I threw up.

Ho rimesso.

ō rēme'sō

I feel sick.

Mi sento male.

mē sen'tō mä'le

I have *no appetite (diarrhea)*.

Non ho appetito (Ho la diarrea).

nōn ō äpetē'tō (ō lä dyäre'ä)

I'm constipated.

Sono costipato.

sō'nō kōstēpä'tō

My eyes hurt.
Mi fanno male gli occhi.
mē fä′nō mä′le lyē ō′kē

I have an earache.
Ho un dolore alle orecchie.
ō ōon dōlō′re ä′le ōrek′ye

I can't sleep.
Non riesco a dormire.
nōn rē·es′kō ä dōrmē′re

I feel nauseated.
Mi sento male, nauseato.
mē sen′tō mä′le, nouze·ä′tō

I've got chills.
Ho dei brividi.
ō de′ē brē′vēdē

I can't move. . .
Non posso muovere . . .
nōn pō′sō moo·ō′vere . . .

I'm diabetic.
Sono diabetico.
sō′nō dyäbe′tēkō

I'm expecting a baby.
Sono incinta.
sō′nō ēnshēn′tä

I fell.
Sono *caduto (-a)*.
sō′nō kädoo′tō (-ä)

I sprained my ankle.
Mi sono slogato il piede.
mē sō′nō zlōgä′tō ēl pye′de

. . . is (are) swollen.
. . . è gonfio (sono gonfi).
. . . e gōn′fyō (sō′nō gōn′fē)

Is it serious?
E' grave?
e grä′ve

I'm feeling a little (much) better.
Mi sento un po' (molto) meglio.
mē sen′tō ōon pō (mōl′tō) me′lyō

Could you give me a prescription for . . .?
Mi può dare una ricetta per . . .?
mē poo·ō′ dä′re ōo′nä rētshe′tä per . . .

I'd like to be vaccinated against . . .
Vorrei farmi vaccinare contro . . .
vōre′ē fär′mē vätshēnä′re kōn′trō . . .

The doctor will tell you:

Take your clothes off, please.
Si spogli, per favore.
sē spō′lyē, per fävō′re

Breathe deeply!
Respiri profondamente!
respē′rē prōfōndämen′te

Does this hurt?
Le fa male qui?
le fä mä′le koo·ē′

Open your mouth.
Apra la bocca.
ä′prä lä bō′kä

Let me see your tongue.

Mi faccia vedere la lingua.
mē fä'tshä vede're lä lēn'goo·ä

Cough.

Tossisca.
tō'sēskä

What have you been eating?

Che cosa ha mangiato?
ke kō'sä ä mänjä'tō

How long have you been ill?

Da quando è *malato (-a)?*
dä koo·än'dō e mälä'tō (-ä)

We'll have to do a *blood test (urinalysis).*

Bisogna esaminare *il sangue (l'orina).*
bēzō'nyä ezämēnä're ēl sän'goo·e (lōrē'nä)

You're going to need an operation.

Deve sottoporsi a una operazione.
de've sōtōpōr'sē ä oo'nä ōperätsyō'ne

I'll have to refer you to . . .

La manderò da . . .
lä mänderō' dä . . .

You must stop *drinking (smoking)!*

Deve smettere di *bere (fumare)!*
de've zme'tere dē be're (foomä're)

You'll have to stay *in bed (on a strict diet).*

Lei deve stare *a letto (con una dieta severa).*
le'ē de've stä're ä le'tō (kōn oo'nä dye'tä seve'rä)

Spend the next few days in bed.

Stia alcuni giorni a letto.
stē'ä älkoo'nē jōr'nē ä le'tō

Take *two tablets (ten drops)* three times a day.

Ne prenda *due compresse (dieci gocce)* tre volte al giorno.
ne pren'dä doo'e kōmpre'se (dye'tshē gō'tshe) tre vōl'te äl jōr'nō

It's nothing serious.

Non è niente di grave.
nōn e nyen'te dē grä've

Come back and see me a week from now.

Ritorni fra una settimana.
rētōr'nē frä oo'nä setēmä'nä

Parts of the Body and their Functions

abdomen	(l') addome *m*	ädō′me
ankle	(la) caviglia	kävē′lyä
appendix	(l') appendice *m*	äpen′dētshe
arm	(il) braccio	brä′tshō
armpit	(l') ascella *f*	äshe′lä
artery	(l') arteria *f*	ärter′yä
back	(la) schiena	skye′nä
bile	(la) bile	bē′le
bladder	(la) vescica	veshē′kä
blood	(il) sangue	sän′gōō·e
blood pressure	(la) pressione sanguigna	presyō′ne sängōō·ē′nyä
body	(il) corpo	kōr′pō
bone	(l') osso *m*	ō′sō
bowel movement	(il) movimento intestinale	mōvēmen′tō ēntestēnä′le
brain	(il) cervello	tsherve′lō
breast	(il) petto	pe′tō
breathing	(il) respiro	respē′rō
buttocks	(le) natiche	nä′tēke
calf	(il) polpaccio	pōlpä′tshō
cheek	(la) guancia	gōō·än′tshä
chest	(il) torace	tōrä′tshe
chin	(il) mento	men′tō
circulation	(la) circolazione	tshērkōlätsyō′ne
collarbone	(la) clavicola	klävē′kōlä
digestion	(la) digestione	dējestyō′ne
disc	(il) disco intervertebrale	dē′skō ēntervertebrä′le
ear	(l') orecchio *m*	ōre′kyō
eardrum	(il) timpano	tēm′pänō
elbow	(il) gomito	gō′mētō
eye	(l') occhio *m*	ō′kyō
– eyeball	(il) globo oculare	glō′bō ōkōōlä′re
– eyelid	la palpebra	lä päl′pebrä
face	(il) viso	vē′zō
finger	(il) dito	dē′tō
– thumb	(il) pollice	pō′lētshe

– index finger	(l') indice *m*	ēn'dētshe
– middle finger	(il) medio	me'dyō
– ring finger	(l') anulare *m*	änōōlä're
– pinkie	(il) mignolo	mē'nyōlō
foot	(il) piede	pye'de
forehead	(la) fronte	frōn'te
frontal sinus	(il) seno frontale	se'nō frōntä'le
gall bladder	(la) cistifellea	tshēstēfe'le·ä
genital organs	(gli) organi genitali	ōr'gäne jenētä'lē
gland	(la) ghiandola	gyän'dōlä
hair	(i) capelli	käpe'lē
hand	(la) mano	mä'nō
head	(la) testa	te'stä
heart	(il) cuore	kōō·ō're
heel	(il) calcagno	kälka'nyō
hip	(l') anca *f*	än'kä
instep	(il) collo del piede ...	kō'lō del pye'de
intestine	(l') intestino *m*	ēntestē'nō
– large intestine	l'intestino crasso	lēntestē'nō krä'sō
– small intestine	l'intestino tenue	lēntestē'nō te'nōō·e
jaw	(la) mascella	mäshe'lä
– upper jaw	la mascella superiore ..	lä mäshe'lä sōōperyō're
– lower jaw	la mascella inferiore ...	lä mäshe'lä ēnferyō're
joint	(la) giuntura	jōōntōō'rä
kidney	(il) rene	re'ne
knee	(il) ginocchio	jēnō'kyō
kneecap	(la) rotula	rō'tōōlä
larynx	(la) laringe	lärēn'je
leg	(la) gamba	gäm'bä
– thigh	il femore	femō're
– lower leg	il polpaccio	pōlpä'tshō
limbs	(gli) arti	är'tē
lip	(il) labbro	lä'brō
liver	(il) fegato	fe'gätō
lung	(il) polmone	pōlmō'ne
male organ	(l') organo maschile *m* .	ōr'gänō mäskē'le
maxillary sinus	(la) cavità mascellare ..	kävētä' mäshelä're
menstruation	(la) mestruazione	mestrōō·ätsyō'ne
metabolism	(il) metabolismo	metäbōlē'zmō

mouth	(la) bocca	bō´kä
mucous membrane	(la) mucosa	mōōkō´sä
muscle	(il) muscolo	mōōs´kōlō
nail	(l') unghia *f*	ōōn´gyä
neck	(il) collo	kō´lō
– back of the neck	(la) nuca	nōō´kä
– nape of the neck	(la) nuca	nōō´kä
nerve	(il) nervo	ner´vō
nerves	(i) nervi	ner´vē
nose	(il) naso	nä´sō
palate	(il) palato	pä´lätō
pancreas	(il) pancreas	pän´kre·äs
pelvis	(il) bacino	bätshē´nō
penis	(il) pene	pe´ne
pregnancy	(la) gravidanza	grävēdän´tsä
respiration	(la) respirazione	respĕrätsyō´ne
rib	(la) costola	kō´stōlä
shin	(lo) stinco	stēn´kō
shoulder	(la) spalla	spä´lä
sinew	(il) tendine	ten´dēne
skin	(la) pelle	pe´le
skull	(il) cranio	krä´nyō
sole	(la) pianta	pyän´tä
spinal cord	(il) midollo spinale	mēdō´lō spēnä´le
spine	(la) spina dorsale	spē´nä dōrsä´le
spleen	(la) milza	mēl´tsä
stomach	(lo) stomaco	stō´mäkō
temple	(la) tempia	tem´pyä
tendon	(il) tendine	ten´dēne
thorax	(il) torace	tōrä´tshe
throat	(la) trachea	träke´ä
toe	(il) dito del piede	dē´tō del pye´de
tongue	(la) lingua	lēn´gōō·ä
tonsils	(le) tonsille	tōnsē´le
tooth	(il) dente	den´te
urine	(l') urina *f*	ōōrē´nä
uterus	(l') utero *m*	ōō´terō
vagina	(la) vagina	väjē´nä
vein	(la) vena	ve´nä
wrist	(il) polso	pōl´sō

What's wrong?

abscess	(l') ascesso *m*	äshe'sō
airsickness	(il) mal d'aria	mäl där'yä
allergy	(l') allergia *f*	älerjē'ä
anemia	(l') anemia *f*	änemē'ä
appendicitis	(l') appendicite *f*	äpendētshē'te
arthritis	(l') artrite *f*	ärtrē'te
asthma	(l') asma *f*	äz'mä
attack	(l') attacco *m*	ätä'kō
backache	(il) mal die schiena	mäl dē skye'nä
bleeding	(l') emorragia *f*	emōräjē'ä
blood poisoning	(la) setticemia	setētshemē'ä
blood pressure	(la) pressione del sangue	presyō'ne del sän'gŏō·e
– high	– alta	äl'tä
– low	– bassa	bä'sä
boil	(il) foruncolo	fōrŏōn'kōlō
breathing problem	(i) problemi respiratori	prōble'mē respērätō'rē
bronchitis	(la) bronchite	brōnkē'te
bruise	(la) contusione	kōntŏōsyō'ne
burn	(la) scottatura	skōtätŏō'rä
cancer	(il) cancro	kän'krō
cardiac infarction	(l') infarto *m* cardiaco	ēnfär'tō kärdē'äkō
chicken pox	(la) varicella	värētshe'lä
chills	(i) brividi	brē'vēdē
cholera	(il) colera	kōle'rä
circulatory problem	(il) problema di circolazione	prōble'mä dē tshērkōlätsyō'ne
cold	(il) raffreddore	räfredō're
colic	(la) colica	kō'lēkä
concussion	(la) commozione cerebrale	kōmōtsyō'ne tsherebrä'le
conjunctivitis	(la) congiuntivite	kōnjŏōntēvē'te
constipation	(la) costipazione	kōstēpätsyō'ne
cough	(la) tosse	tō'se
cramp	(il) crampo	kräm'pō
cut	(la) ferita da taglio	ferē'tä dä tä'lyō
diabetes	(il) diabete	dyäbe'te
diarrhea	(la) diarrea	dyäre'ä

diphtheria	(la) difterite	dēfterē′te
disease	(la) malattia	mälätē′ä
– contagious disease	– infettiva	– ēnfetē′vä
dislocation	(la) lussazione	lo͞osätsyō′ne
dizziness	(il) capogiro	käpōjē′rō
dysentery	(la) dissenteria	dēsenterē′ä
eye inflammation	(l') infiammazione *f* all'occhio	ēnfyämätsyō′ne älō′kyō
fever	(la) febbre	fe′bre
fit	(l') attacco *m*	ätä′kō
flatulence	(la) flatulenza	fläto͞olen′tsä
flu	(l') influenza *f*	ēnflo͞o·en′tsä
food poisoning	(l') avvelenamento *m* da cibo	ävelenämen′tō dä tshē′bō
fracture	(la) frattura	fräto͞o′rä
frostbite	(il) congelamento	kōnjelämen′tō
gall stones	(i) calcoli biliari	käl′kōlē bēlyä′rē
German measles	(la) rosolia	rōzōlē′ä
hay fever	(la) febbre da fieno	fe′bre dä fye′nō
heart attack	(l') attacco *m* cardiaco	ätä′kō kärdē′äkō
heart problems	(i) problemi di cuore	prōble′mē dē ko͞o·ō′re
heartburn	(il) bruciore di stomaco	bro͞otshō′re dē stō′mäkō
hemorrhage	(l') emorragia *f*	emōräjē′ä
hemorrhoids	(le) emorroidi	emōrō′ēdē
hoarseness	(la) raucedine	routshe′dēne
hypertension	(l') ipertensione *f*	ēpertensyō′ne
illness	(l') indisposizione *f*	ēndēspōzētsyō′ne
indigestion	(l') indigestione *f*	ēndējestyō′ne
inflammation	(l') infiammazione *f*	ēnfyämätsyō′ne
influenza	(l') influenza *f*	ēnflo͞o·en′tsä
injury	(la) ferita	ferē′tä
insomnia	(l') insonnia *f*	ēnsō′nyä
intestinal catarrh	(il) catarro intestinale	kätä′rō ēntestēnä′le
jaundice	(l') itterizia *f*	ēterē′tsyä
kidney stones	(i) calcoli renali	käl′kōlē renä′lē
leukemia	(la) leucemia	le·o͞otshemē′ä
liver problem	(i) problemi di fegato	prōble′mē dē fe′gätō
lumbago	(la) lombaggine	lōmbä′jēne
measles	(il) morbillo	mōrbē′lō

middle ear inflammation	(l') infiammazione *f* dell'orecchio medio	ēnfyämätsyō'ne delōre'kyō me'dyō
mumps	(gli) orecchioni	ōrekyō'nē
nausea	(la) nausea	nou'ze·ä
nephritis	(la) nefrite	nefrē'te
neuralgia	(la) nevralgia	nevräljē'ä
nosebleed	(l') emorragia *f* nasale	emōräjē'ä näzä'le
pain	(il) dolore	dōlō're
paralysis	(la) paralisi	pärä'lēzē
passing out	(lo) svenimento	zvenēmen'tō
peptic ulcer	(l') ulcera *f* gastrica	ōōl'tsherä gä'strēkä
piles	(le) emorroidi	emōrō'ēdē
pleurisy	(la) pleurite	ple·ōōrē'te
pneumonia	(la) polmonite	pōlmōnē'te
poisoning	(l') avvelenamento *m*	ävelenämen'tō
pulled tendon	(lo) stiramento	stērämen'tō
rash	(l') esantema *m*	ezänte'mä
rheumatism	(il) reumatismo	re·ōōmätē'zmō
scarlet fever	(la) scarlattina	skärlätē'nä
sciatica	(la) sciatica	shä'tēkä
seasickness	(il) mal di mare	mäl dē mä're
shock	(lo) shock	shōk
skin disease	(la) dermatosi	dermätō'zē
skin lesion	(l') escoriazione *f*	eskōryätsyō'ne
smallpox	(il) vaiolo	väyō'lō
sore throat	(la) faringite	färēnjē'te
sprain	(lo) strappo muscoloso	strä'pō mōōskōlō'sō
stitch in the side	(la) fitta al fianco	fē'tä äl fyän'kō
stomach pains	(i) dolori di stomaco	dōlō'rē dē stō'mäkō
stroke	(l') apoplessia *f*	äpōplesē'ä
sunburn	(la) scottatura solare	skōtätōō'rä sōlä're
sunstroke	(l') insolazione *f*	ēnsōlätsyō'ne
suppuration	(la) suppurazione	sōōpōōrätsyō'ne
swelling	(il) gonfiore	gōnfyō're
tetanus	(il) tetano	te'tänō
tonsillitis	(la) tonsillite	tōnsēlē'te
tumor	(il) tumore	tōōmō're
typhoid fever	(il) tifo	tē'fō
ulcer	(l') ulcera *f*	ōōl'tsherä
vomiting	(il) vomito	vō'mētō
wound	(la) ferita	ferē'tä

In the Hospital

anesthetic	(la) narcosi	närkō´zē
bed	(il) letto	le´tō
blood count	(il) quadro ematologico	kōō·ä´drō emätō-lō´jēkō
blood test	(il) prelievo del sangue	prelye´vō del sän´gōō·e
blood transfusion	(la) trasfusione del sangue	träsfōōzyō´ne del sän´gōō·e
diagnosis	(la) diagnosi	dē·ä´nyōzē
discharge	(il) dimettere dall'ospedale	dēme´tere dälōspedä´le
doctor	(il) dottore	dōtō´re
examination	(l') analisi f	änä´lēzē
examine	visitare	vēzētä´re
head nurse	(l') infermiera-capo f	ēnfermye´rä-kä´pō
hospital	(l') ospedale m	ōspedä´le
infusion	(l') infuso m	ēnfōō´zō
injection	(l') iniezione f	ēnyetsyō´ne
intensive care unit	(il) reparto di cure intensive	repär´tō dē kōō´re ēntense´ve
medical director	(il) direttore medico	dēretō´re me´dēkō
night nurse	(l') infermiera f di notte	ēnfermye´rä dē nō´te
nurse	(l') infermiera f	ēnfermye´rä
operate (verb)	operare	ōperä´re
operation	(l') operazione f	ōperätsyō´ne
patient	(il) paziente	pätsyen´te
surgeon	(il) chirurgo	kērōōr´gō
temperature chart	(il) diagramma della temperatura	dyägrä´mä de´lä temperätōō´rä
visiting hours	(l') orario m delle visite	ōrär´yō de´le vē´zēte
ward	(la) corsia d'ospedale	kōrsē´ä dōspedä´le
x-ray (verb)	fare una radiografia	fä´re ōō´nä rädyōgräfē´ä

Nurse, could you give me a *pain killer (sleeping pill)*.
Infermiera, mi può dare *delle compresse contro il dolore (un sonnifero)*.
nfermye'rä, mē poo·ō' dä're dele kōmpre'se kōn'trō ēl dōlō're (ōon ōnē'ferō)

When can I get out of bed?
Quando posso alzarmi da letto?
koo·än'dō pō'sō ältsär'mē dä le'tō

What's the diagnosis?
Qual è la diagnosi?
koo·äle' lä dē·ä'nyōzē

At the Dentist's

Where is there a dentist here?
Dove si trova un dentista?
dō've sē trō'vä oon dentē'stä

I'd like to make an appointment.
Vorrei fissare un appuntamento.
vōre'ē fēsä're oon äpoontämen'tō

This tooth hurts. — **up here.** — **down here.**
Questo dente mi fa male. — *qui sopra.* — *qui sotto*
koo·e·stō den'te mē fä mä'le — koo·ē' sō'prä — koo·ē' sō'tō

I've lost a filling.
Io perso un'otturazione.
ō per'sō oonōtoorätsyō'ne

This tooth is loose.
Questo dente si muove.
koo·e·stō de'nte sē moo·ō've

Does this tooth have to be pulled?
Bisogna estrarre il dente?
bēzō'nyä esträ're ēl de'nte

... broke off.
... si è rotto.
... sē e rō'tō

Can you do a temporary repair on this tooth?
Può curarmi questo dente temporaneamente?
poo·ō' koorär'mē koo·e·stō den'te temporäne·ämen'te

Can you fix these dentures?
Può riparare questa protesi?
poo·ō' rēpärä're koo·e·stä pro'tezē

I've got a toothache.
Ho mal di denti.
ō mäl dē den'tē

*Please don't *eat anything (smoke)* for two hours.
Non mangi niente (non fumi) per due ore!
nōn man'jē nyen'te (nōn foo'mē) per doo'e ō're

When do you want me to come back?
Quando devo tornare?
koo·än'dō de'vō tōrnä're

abscess	(l') ascesso *m*	äshe'sō
anesthesia	(l') anestesia *f*	änestezē'ä
- local	l'anestesia locale	länestezē'ä lōkä'le

bicuspid, molar	(il) molare	mōlä´re
braces	(il) fermaglio dentario .	fermä´lyō dentär´yō
bridge	(il) ponte	pōn´te
cavities	(le) cavità	kävētä´
crown	(la) corona	kōrō´nä
cuspid	(il) dente canino	den´te känē´nō
dental clinic	(la) clinica odontoia-trica	klē´nēkä ōdōn-tōyä´trēkä
dentist	(il) dentista	dentē´stä
denture	(la) dentiera	dentye´rä
extract	estrarre	esträ´re
false tooth	(la) protesi	prō´tesē
fill	otturare	ōto̅o̅rä´re
filling	(l') otturazione *f*	ōto̅o̅rätsyō´ne
gums	(le) gengive	jenjē´ve
incisor	(il) dente incisivo	den´te ēntshēzē´vō
injection	(l') iniezione *f*	ēnyetsyō´ne
jaw	(la) mascella	mäshe´lä
nerve	(il) nervo	ner´vō
oral surgeon	(il) medico dentista	me´dēkō dentē´stä
orthodontist	(l') ortodontista *m*	ōrtōdōntē´stä
plaster cast	(il) modello in gesso ...	mōde´lō ēn je´sō
root	(la) radice	rädē´tshe
root canal work	(il) trattamento della radice	trätämen´tō de´lä rädē´tshe
tartar	(il) tartaro	tär´tärō
temporary filling	(l') otturazione *f* provvisoria	ōto̅o̅rätsyō´ne prōvēzōr´yä
tooth	(il) dente	den´te
tooth cervix	(il) colletto del dente ...	kōle´tō del den´te
toothache	(il) mal di denti	mäl dē den´tē
wisdom tooth	(il) dente del giudizio ..	den´te del jo̅o̅dē´ts-yō

Taking a Cure

bath	(il) bagno	bä′nyō
convalescent home	(la) casa di convalescenza	kä′sä dē kōnväleshen′tsä
cure	(la) cura	kōō′rä
cure tax	(la) tassa di soggiorno	tä′sä dē sōjōr′nō
cure vacation	(il) soggiorno di cura	sōjōr′no dē kōō′rä
diet	(la) dieta	dye′tä
gymnastics	(la) ginnastica	jēnä′stēkä
health resort	(la) stazione termale	stätsyō′ne termä′le
hot spring	(la) fonte termale	fōn′te termä′le
inhale	inalare	ēnälä′re
massage (noun)	(il) massaggio	mäsä′jō
massage (verb)	massaggiare	mäsäjä′re
masseur	(il) massaggiatore	mäsäjätō′re
masseuse	(la) massaggiatrice	mäsäjätrē′tshe
mineral bath	(il) bagno minerale	bä′nyō mēnerä′le
mineral spring	(la) fonte minerale/termale	fōn′te mēnerä′le/termä′le
minerals	(le) acque minerali	ä′kōō-e mēnerä′lē
mud	(il) fango	fän′gō
mud bath	fare i fanghi	fä′re ē fän′gē
mud pack	mettere il fango/l'impacco	me′tere ēl fän′gō/lēmpä′kō
pump room	(il) chiosco delle acque	kyōs′kō de′le ä′kōō-e
radiation therapy	(la) terapia dei raggi	teräpē′ä de′ē rä′jē
rest cure	(la) cura di riposo	kōō′rä dē rēpō′sō
sanatorium	(il) sanatorio	sänätōr′yō
sauna	(la) sauna	sou′nä
sea water	(l') acqua f di mare	ä′kōō-ä dē mä′re
short wave	(le) onde corte	ōn′de kōr′te
spa	(la) stazione balneare	stätsyō′ne bälnea′re
steam bath	(il) bagno a vapore	bä′nyō ä väpō′re
sunlamp	(la) lampada a raggi ultravioletti	läm′pädä ä rä′jē ōōlträvyōle′tē
ultrasonics	(gli) ultrasuoni	ōōlträsōō-ō′nē

CONCERT, THEATER, MOVIES

> *Most European theaters are repertory theaters, featuring a permanent company performing a different play, opera or operetta each evening.*

At the Box Office

What's on tonight?

Che cosa c'è stasera in programma?
ke kō′sä tshe stäse′rä ēn prōgrä′mä

When does *the performance (the concert)* start?

Quando comincia *lo spettacolo (il concerto)*?
kōō·än′dō kōmēn′tshä lō spetä′kōlō (ēl kōntsher′tō)

Where can we get tickets?

Dove si possono comprare i biglietti?
dō′ve se pō′sōnō kōmprä′re ē bēlye′tē

Are there any discounts for ...?

Ci sono delle riduzioni per ...?
tshē sō′nō de′le rēdōōtsyō′nē per

> *Many European theaters and concert halls provide discount tickets for the disabled, for students and senior citizens.*

Are there still tickets available for *this (tomorrow)* evening?

Ci sono ancora dei biglietti per *stasera (domani sera)*?
tshē sō′no änkō′rä de′ē bēlye′tē per stäse′rä (dōmä′nē se′rä)

One ticket in the *third (tenth)* row, please.

Un biglietto in *terza (decima)* fila, per favore.
ōōn bēlye′tō ēn ter′tsä (de′tshēmä) fē′lä, per fävō′re

Two seats in the third row, first balcony, please.

Due posti in terza fila, in prima galleria, per favore.
dōō′e pō′stē ēn ter′tsä fēlä, ēn prē′mä gälerē′ä, per fävō′re

– in the middle.

– al centro.
– äl tshen′trō

– on the side.

– al lato.
– äl lä′tō

box	(il) palco
pit, parquet	(la) platea
seat, seats	(il) posto, (i) posti
circle, balcony	(la) galleria
dress circle, 1st balcony	(la) prima galleria
uper circle, 2nd balcony	(la) seconda galleria
gallery	(la) terza galleria
row	(la) fila
sold out	Esaurito!

Concert, Theatre

accompanist	(l') accompagnatore m .	äkōmpänyätō′re
act	(l') atto m	ä′tō
actor	(l') attore m	ätō′re
actress	(l') attrice f	ätrē′tshe
advance ticket sales	(la) prevendita-biglietti	preven′dētä-bēlye′tē
ballet	(il) balletto	bäle′tō
band	(la) banda	bän′dä
box office	(il) botteghino di teatro	bōtegē′nō dē te·ä′trō
chamber music	(la) musica da camera .	mōō′zēkä dä kä′merä
check room	(il) guardaroba	gōō·ärdärō′bä
chorus	(il) coro	kō′rō
coat check	(lo) scontrino del guardaroba	skontrē′nō del gōō·ärdärō′bä
comedy	(la) commedia	kōme′dyä
concert hall	(la) sala da concerto	sä′lä dä kōntsher′tō
conductor	(il) direttore d'orchestra	dēretō′re dōrke′strä
costumes	(i) costumi	kōstōō′mē
curtain	(il) sipario	sēpär′yō
curtain time	(l') inizio m	ēnē′tsyō
dancer	(il) ballerino	bälerē′nō
drama	(il) dramma	drä′mä
duet	(il) duetto	dōō·e′tō

final curtain	(la) fine	fē'ne
grand piano	(il) piano a coda	pyä'nō ä kō'dä
intermission	(l') intervallo *m*	ēntervä'lō
lobby	(il) ridotto	rēdō'tō
opera glasses	(il) binocolo da opera	bēnō'kōlō dä ō'perä
orchestra seats	(i) posti di platea	pō'stē dē pläte'ä
overture	(il) preludio	preloo'dyō
part/rôle	(la) parte	pär'te
– leading role	(la) parte principale	pär'te prēntshēpä'le
performance	(la) rappresentazione	räprezentätsyō'ne
piano recital	(il) recital di pianoforte	retshētäl' dē pyänōfōr'te
piece of music	(il) pezzo di musica	pe'tsō dē moo'zēkä
play	(l') opera *f* drammatica	ō'perä drämä'tēkä
producer	(il) produttore	prōdoootō're
production	(la) messa in scena	me'sä ēn she'nä
program	(il) programma	prōgrä'mä
scenery/settings	(lo) scenario	shenär'yō
singer	(il) cantante	käntän'te
singing	(il) canto	kän'tō
soloist	(il) solista	sōlē'stä
song	(la) canzone	käntsō'ne
– folk song	la canzone popolare	lä käntsō'ne pōpōlä're
song recital	(la) serata di canto	serä'tä dē kän'tō
stage	(il) palcoscenico	pälkōshe'nēkō
stage director	(il) regista	rejē'stä
symphony concert	(il) concerto sinfonico	kōntsher'tō sēnfō'nēkō
theater	(il) teatro	te·ä'trō
theater schedule	(il) programma	prōgrä'mä
ticket	(il) biglietto	bēlye'tō
ticket sales	(la) vendita dei biglietti	ven'dētä de'ē bēlye'tē
tragedy	(la) tragedia	träje'dyä
violin recital	(il) recital di violino	retshētäl' dē vyōlē'nō
work	(l') opera *f*	ō'perä

At the Movies

What's on tonight at the movies?
Che cosa danno al cinema stasera?
ke kō′sä dä′nō äl tshē′nemä stäse′rä

What time does *the box office open (the film start)*?
A che ora comincia *la vendita dei biglietti (il film)*?
ä ke ō′rä kōmēn′tshä lä ven′dētä de′ē bēlye′tē (ēl fēlm)

How long is the picture?
Quanto dura lo spettacolo?
kōō·än′tō dōō′rä lō spetä′kōlō

auditorium	(la) sala degli spettatori	sä′lä de′lyē spetätō′rē
cartoon	(i) cartoni animati	kärtō′nē änēmä′tē
cinema	(il) cinema	tshē′nemä
color film	(il) film a colori	fēlm ä kōlō′rē
documentary	(il) documentario	dōkōōmentär′yō
drive-in movie	(il) cinema all'aperto	tshē′nemä äläper′tō
dubbed	doppiato	dōpyä′tō
dubbing	(il) doppiaggio	dōpyä′jō
educational film	(il) film educativo	fēlm edōōkätē′vō
feature film	(il) lungometraggio	lōōngōmeträ′jō
film	(il) film	fēlm
film actor	(l') attore *m* cinematografico	ätō′re tshēnemätōgrä′fēkō
film festival	(il) festival cinematografico	festē′väl tshēnemätōgrä′fēkō
film screening	(la) proiezione	prōyetsyō′ne
motion picture theater	(la) sala cinematografica	sä′lä tshēnemätōgrä′fēkä
movie	(il) film (a soggetto)	fēlm (ä sōje′tō)
movie house	(il) cinema	tshē′nemä
preview	(la) rassegna dei film	räse′nyä de′ē fēlm
screen	(lo) schermo	sker′mō
screenplay	(il) copione	kōpyō′ne
short subject	(il) cortometraggio	kōrtōmeträ′jō
subtitled	con i sottotitoli	kōn ē sōtōtē′tōlē
thriller	(il) film giallo	fēlm jä′lō
usher	(la) maschera	mäs′kerä

PASTIMES

Fun and Games

Where is there ...?
Dove c'è qui ...?
dō've tshe kōō·ē' ...

a bar	un bar	ōon bär
a discotheque	una discoteca	ōō'nä dēskōte'kä
an ice skating rink .	una pista di pattinaggio su ghiaccio	ōō'nä pē'stä dē pätē-nä'jō sōō gyä'tshō
a miniature golf course	un campo di minigolf .	ōon käm'pō dē mē'nē-gōlf
a night club	un night club	ōon nīt klōob
a pool hall	una sala da biliardo	ōō'nä sä'lä dä bēlyär'dō
a riding stable	una scuderia	skōōderē'ä
a sailing school	una scuola di navigazione a vela	ōō'nä skōō·ō'lä dē nävēgätsyō'ne ä ve'lä
a tennis court	un campo di tennis....	ōon käm'pō dē te'nēs

I'd like to ...
Vorrei ...
vōre'ē ...

play badminton	giocare al volano	jōkä're äl vōlä'nō
play miniature golf	giocare al minigolf	jōkä're äl mē'nē-gōlf
play ping pong	giocare a ping-pong ...	jōkä're ä pēng-pōng
watch the fashion show	assistere alla sfilata di moda	äsē'stere ä'lä sfēlä'tä dē mō'dä

Do you have television?
C'è la televisione?
tshe lä televēzyō'ne

Can I listen to the radio here?
Qui si può ascoltare la radio?
kōō·ē' sē pōō·o' äskōltä're lä rä'dyō

What station is that?
Che stazione è?
ke stätsyō'ne e

What's on today?
Che cosa danno oggi?
ke kōs'ä dä'nō ō'jē

Do you play *chess (ping-pong)*?
Gioca *agli scacchi (al ping-pong)*?
jō′kä ä′lyē skä′kē (äl pēng-pōng)

amusement	(il) divertimento	dēvērtēmen′tō
beauty contest	(il) concorso di bellezza	kōnkōr′sō dē bele′tsä
bowling alley	(la) pista del bowling	pē′stä del bō′lēng
card game	(il) gioco delle carte	jō′kō de′le kär′te
– cut	– alzare	ältsä′re
– deal	– dare	dä′re
– shuffle	– mescolare	meskōlä′re
– ace	(l') asso *m*	ä′sō
– jack	(il) fante	fän′te
– queen	(la) regina	rejē′nä
– king	(il) re	re
– clubs	(i) fiori	fyō′rē
– diamonds	(i) quadri	kōō·ä′drē
– hearts	(i) cuori	kōō·ō′rē
– spades	(le) picche	pē′ke
– joker	(il) jolly	jō′lē
– trick	(la) bazza	bä′tsä
– trump	(la) briscola	brē′skōlä
checkers	(la) dama	dä′mä
chess	(gli) scacchi	lyē skä′kē
– board	(la) scacchiera	skäkye′rä
– chessman	(il) pezzo	pe′tsō
– square	(lo) scacco	skä′kō
– bishop	(l') alfiere *m*	älfye′re
– castle	(la) torre	tō′re
– king	(il) re	re
– knight	(il) cavaliere	kävälye′re
– pawn	(la) pedina	pedē′nä
– queen	(la) regina	rejē′nä
– rook	(la) torre	tō′re
chip	(il) gettone	jetō′ne
circus	(il) circo	tshēr′kō
club	(il) club	klōōb
country fair	(la) sagra popolare	sä′grä pōpōlä′re
dice	(il) dado	dä′dō
– shoot dice	giocare ai dadi	jōkä′re ī dä′dē

gambling casino	(il) casinò	käzēnō′
gambling game	(il) gioco d'azzardo	jō′kō dädzär′dō
– banker	(il) tenitore del	tenētō′re del
	banco	bän′kō
– bet	puntare	pōontä′re
– draw	muovere	mōō-ō′vere
– move	(la) mossa	mō′sä
– piece	(la) pedina	pedē′nä
– play	giocare	jōkä′re
– stake	(la) posta	pō′stä
magazine	(la) rivista	rēvē′stä
– fashion magazine . .	(la) rivista di moda	rēvē′stä dē mō′dä
– glossy	(la) rivista illustrata . . .	rēvē′stä ēlōōsträ′tä
newspaper	(il) giornale	jōrnä′le
party games	(i) giochi di società	jō′kē dē sōtshetä′
pastime	(il) passatempo	päsätem′pō
ping-pong	(il) ping-pong	pēng-pōng
radio	(la) radio	rä′dyō
– FM	(l') onda *f* ultracorta . . .	ōn′dä ōōlträkōr′tä
– long wave	(l') onda *f* lunga	ōn′dä lōōn′gä
– medium wave	(l') onda *f* media	ōn′dä me′dyä
– short wave	(l') onda *f* corta	ōn′dä kōr′tä
– radio play	(la) radiocommedia . . .	rädyōkōme′dyä
– news	(il) giornale radio	jōrnä′le rä′dyō
record	(il) disco	dē′skō
record player	(il) giradischi	jērädēs′kē
recording tape	(il) nastro magnetico . .	nä′strō mänye′tēkō
table tennis	(il) ping-pong	pēng-pōng
tape recorder	(il) magnetofono	mänyetō′fōnō
television	(la) televisione	televēzyō′ne
– announcer	(l') annunciatore *m*	änōōntshätō′re
– breakdown	(il) disturbo	dēstōōr′bō
– news	(il) telegiornale	telejōrnä′le
– program	(il) programma	prōgrä′mä
– program schedule . .	(l') orario *m* dei	ōrär′yō de′ē
	programmi	prōgrä′mē
– turn off	spegnere	spen′yere
– turn on	accendere	ätshen′dere
– television play	(il) dramma televisivo .	drä′mä televēzē′vō

Getting acquainted

Hope you don't mind if I talk to you.
Scusi, se Le rivolgo la parola.
skoo͞ze′, se le rēvōl′gō lä pärō′lä

Mind if I join you?
Posso sedermi vicino a Lei?
pô′sō seder′mē vētshē′nō ä le′ē

May I treat you to a *drink (coffee, tea)*?
Vogliamo bere *qualcosa* insieme *(un caffè, un tè)*?
vōlyä′mō be′re koo͞·älkō′sä ēnsye′me (oo͞n käfe′, oo͞n te)

You got something on for this evening?
Ha già un impegno per stasera?
ä jä oo͞n ēmpen′yō per stäse′rä

Shall we dance?   **Is there a *discotheque (a dance hall)* here?**
Vogliamo ballare?   C'è una *discoteca (sala da ballo)* qui?
vōlyä′mō bälä′re   tshe′ oo͞′nä dēskōte′kä (sä′lä dä bä′lō) koo͞·ē′

May I have the next dance?
Posso invitarLa per il prossimo ballo?
pô′sō ēnvētär′lä per ēl prô′sēmō bä′lō

We can chat undisturbed here.
Qui possiamo parlare indisturbati.
koo͞·ē′ pōsyä′mō pärlä′re ēndēstoo͞rbä′tē

May I invite you to a party?   **I'll be expecting you at ...**
Posso invitarLa ad un party?   La aspetto alle ...
pô′sō ēnvētär′lä äd oo͞n pär′tē   lä äspe′tō ä′le ...

You look good in that dress.
Questo vestito Le sta proprio bene.
koo͞·e′stō vestē′tō le stä prō′prē·ō be′ne

When can you come visit me?
Quando viene a trovarmi?
koo͞·än′dō vye′ne ä trōvär′mē

When can we meet again?   **Where do you live?**
Quando possiamo rivederci?   Dove abita?
koo͞·än′dō pōsyä′mō rēveder′tshē   dō′ve ä′bētä

May I give you a lift home?
Posso accompagnarLa a casa con la macchina?
pō'sō äkōmpänyär'lä ä kä'sä kōn lä mä'kēnä

Won't you come in for a minute?
Vuole entrare un attimo?
vōō·ō'le enträ're ōon ä'tēmō

May I walk part of the way with you?
Posso accompagnarLa ancora un po'?
pō'sō äkōmpänyär'lä änkō'rä ōon pō'

Thanks very much for the nice evening.
Grazie per la simpatica serata.
grä'tsye per lä sēmpä'tēkä serä'tä

accompany	accompagnare	äkōmpänyä're
dance *(noun)*	(il) ballo	bä'lō
dance *(verb)*	ballare	bälä're
dance hall	(la) sala da ballo	sä'lä dä bä'lō
discotheque	(la) discoteca	dēskōte'kä
enjoy oneself	divertirsi	dēvertēr'sē
expect *(somebody)* ..	aspettare	äspetä're
invite	invitare	ēnvētä're
kiss *(noun)*	(il) bacio	bä'tshō
kiss *(verb)*	baciare	bätshä're
live	abitare	äbētä're
love *(noun)*	(l') amore *m*	ämō're
love *(verb)*	amare; voler bene	ämä're, vōler'be'ne
make love	fare l'amore	fä're lämō're
meet	incontrarsi	ēnkōnträr'sē
meet again	rivedersi	rēveder'sē
take a walk	fare una passeggiata	fä're ōo'nä päsejä'tä
visit	*andare* (*venire*) a trovare	ändä're (venē're) ä trōvä're
visit *(chat)*	fare quattro chiacchiere	fä're kōo·ä'trō kyä'kyere

On the Beach

Where can we go swimming here?
Dove si può fare il bagno qui?
dō've sē pōō·ō' fä're ēl bä'nyō kōō·ē'

Can we go swimming here?
Si può fare il bagno qui?
sē pōō·ō' fä're ēl bä'nyō kōō·ē'

Two tickets (with cabaña), please.
Due biglietti (con cabina) per favore.
dōō'e bēlye'tē (kōn käbē'nä) per fävō're

Can we swim *topless (nude)* here?
Si può fare il bagno *con il topless (nudi)* qui?
sē pōō·ō' fä're ēl bä'nyō kōn ēl tōp'les (nōō'dē) kōō·ē'

How *deep (warm)* is the water?
Quant'è profonda (Che temperatura ha) l'acqua?
kōō·änte' prōfōn'dä (ke temperätōō'rä ä) lä'kōō·ä

Is it dangerous for children?
E' pericoloso per i bambini?
e perēkōlō'sō per ē bämbē'nē

*No swimming!
Vietato bagnarsi!
vyetä'tō bänyär'sē

How far out can we swim?
Fin dove si può nuotare?
fēn dō've sē pōō·ō' nōō·ōtä're

Where is the lifeguard?
Dov'è il bagnino?
dōve' ēl bänye'nō

Is there an undertow here?
Ci sono delle correnti qui?
tshē sō'nō de'le kōren'tē kōō·ē'

How much does . . . cost?
Quanto costa . . .?
kōō·än'tō kō'stä . . .

A *deck chair (umbrella)*, please.
Una sedia a sdraio (un ombrellone), per favore.
ōō'nä se'dyä ä zdrä'yō (ōōn ōmbrelō'ne), per fävō're

I'd like to rent a *cabaña (boat)*.
Vorrei noleggiare una *cabina (barca)*.
vōrre'ē nōlejä're ōō'nä käbē'nä (bär'kä)

Where *is (are)* . . .?
Dov'è (Dove sono) . . .?
dōve' (dō've sō'nō) . . .

I'd like to go water skiing.
Vorrei fare lo sci nautico.
vōre'ē fä're lō shē nou'tēkō

Where can I go fishing?
Dove si può pescare?
dō've sē pōō·ō' peskä're

Would you be good enough to keep an eye on my gear.
E' così gentile da dare un'occhiata alla mia roba, per favore.
e kōsē' jentē'le dä dä're ōōnōkyä'tä ä'lä mē'ä rō'bä, per fävō're

air mattress	(il) materassino	mäteräsē'nō
	pneumatico	pne·ōomä'tēkō
bathing cap	(la) cuffia da bagno . . .	kōo'fyä dä bä'nyō
bathing suit	(il) costume da bagno .	kōstōo'me dä bä'nyō
– trunks	(gli) slip da bagno	slēp dä bä'nyō
bathrobe	(l') accappatoio *m*	äkäpätō'yō
bay	(la) baia	bä'yä
boat	(la) barca	bär'kä
– motorboat	(il) motoscafo	mōtōskä'fō
– pedal boat	(la) barca a pedale	bär'kä ä pedä'le
– sailboat	(la) barca a vela	bär'kä ä ve'lä
cabaña	(la) cabina	käbē'nä
dive *(verb)*	tuffarsi	tōofär'sē
diving board	(il) trampolino	trämpōlē'nō
jellyfish	(la) medusa	medōo'zä
locker room	(lo) spogliatoio	spōlyätō'yō
non-swimmer	(il) non nuotatore	nōn nōo·ōtätō're
nude beach	(la) spiaggia per nudisti	spyä'jä per
		nōodē'stē
sandy beach	(la) spiaggia sabbiosa . .	spyä'jä säbyō'sä
scuba diving	nuotare sott'acqua	nōo·ōtä're sōtä'kōo·ä
scuba equipment . . .	(l') attrezzatura *f*	ätretsätōo'rä
	subacquea	sōobä'kōo·e·ä
shower	(la) doccia	dō'tshä
swim	nuotare	nōo·ōtä're
swimmer	(il) nuotatore	nōo·ōtätō're
swimming pier	(il) pontile	pōntēle
water	(l') acqua *f*	ä'kōo·ä
water temperature .	(la) temperatura	temperätōo'rä
	dell'acqua	delä'kōo·ä

Sports

What sports events do they have here?
Che manifestazioni sportive ci sono qui?
ke mänēfestätsyō'nē spōrtē've tshē sō'nō kōo·ē'

Where's the *stadium (soccer field)*?
Dov'è lo stadio (il campo di calcio)?
dōve' lō stä'dyō (ēl käm'pō dē käl'tshō)

*... is playing ... today.
Oggi *il (la)* ... gioca contro *il (la)* ...
ō'jē ēl (lä) ... jō'kä kōn'trō ēl (lä) ...

I'd love to see the *game (race, fight)*.
Vorrei vedere *la partita (la corsa/la gara, l'incontro)*.
vōre'ē vede're lä pärtē'tä (lä kōr'sä/lä gä'rä, lēnkōn'trō)

When (Where) is the soccer game?
Quando (Dove) ha luogo la partita di calcio?
kōō·än'dō (dō've) ä lōō·ō'gō lä pärtē'tä dē käl'tshō

Can you get us tickets for it?	**Goal!**
Potrebbe procurarci dei biglietti?	Goal!
pōtre'be prōkōōrär'tshē de'ē bēlye'tē	gōl

What's the score?   ***The score is three to two for...**
Come siamo?   Siamo tre a due per ...
kō'me syä'mō   syä'mō tre ä dōō'e per ...

Is there an *outdoor (indoor)* swimming pool here?
C'è una piscina *all'aperto (coperta)* qui?
tshe ōō'nä pēshē'nä äläper'tō (kōper'tä) kōō·ē'

What sports do you like to play?   **I'm ...**   **I play ...**
Che sport *fa Lei (fai tu)?*   Sono ...   Gioco ...
ke spōrt fä le'ē (fī tōō)   sō'nō ...   jō'kō ...

auto racing	(la) corsa auto-mobilistica	kōr'sä outō-mōbēlē'stēkä
– race	(la) gara, (la) corsa	gä'rä, kōr'sä
– racing car	(la) macchina da corsa	mä'kēnä dä kōr'sä
bicycling	(il) ciclismo	tshēklē'zmō
– bicycle	(la) bicicletta	bētshēkle'tä
– bicycle race	(la) corsa ciclistica ...	kōr'sä tshēklē'stēkä
– bicycle rider	(il) ciclista............	tshēklē'stä
– ride a bike	andare in bicicletta....	ändä're ēn bētshē-kle'tä
boat racing	(la) corsa nautica	kōr'sä nou'tēkä
bowling	(il) gioco dei birilli	jō'kō de'ē bērē'lē
boxing	(il) pugilato	pōōjēlä'tō
– box	(la) boxe.............	bōkse
– boxer	(il) pugile	pōō'jēle

competition	(la) gara	gä′rä
– **championship**	(il) campionato	kämpyōnä′tō
– **defeat**	(la) sconfitta	skōnfē′tä
– **draw**	(il) pareggio	päre′jō
– **free style**	(lo) stile libero	stē′le lē′berō
– **game**	(il) gioco	jō′kō
– **goal**	(il) goal	gōl
– **half time**	(il) primo (secondo) tempo	prē′mō (sekōn′dō) tem′pō
– **match**	(la) partita	pärtē′tä
– **play**	giocare	jōkä′re
– **point**	(il) punto	pōōn′tō
– **practice**	(l') allenamento m	älenämen′to
– **result**	(il) risultato	rēsōōltä′tō
– **start**	(la) partenza, (il) via	pärten′tsä, vē′ä
– **victory**	(la) vittoria	vētōr′yä
– **win**	vincere	vēn′tshere
dog races	(le) corse di cani	kōr′se dē kä′nē
fencing	(la) scherma	sker′mä
figure skating	(il) pattinaggio artistico su ghiaccio	pätēnä′jō ärtē′stēkō sōō gyä′tshō
– **skate**	pattinare	pätēnä′re
– **skates**	(i) pattini	pä′tēnē
– **skater**	(il) pattinatore	pätēnätōr′e
fishing	(la) pesca	pes′kä
– **fishing rod**	(la) canna da pesca	kä′nä dä pes′kä
– **go fishing**	andare a pescare	ändä′re ä peskä′re
– **fishing license**	(la) licenza di pesca	lētshen′tsä dē pes′kä
golf	(il) golf	gōlf
gymnastics	(la) ginnastica	jēnä′stēkä
– **gymnast**	(il) ginnasta	jēnä′stä
– **gymnastics with apparatus**	(la) ginnastica atletica agli attrezzi	jēnä′stēkä ätle′tēkä ä′lyē ätre′tsē
– **balance beam**	(la) sbarra	zbä′rä
– **horizontal bar**	(le) parallele	päräle′le
– **rings**	(le) anelle	äne′le
handball	(la) pallamano	pälämä′nō
hockey	(l') hockey m	ō′kē
hunting	(la) caccia	kä′tshä
– **hunting license**	(il) permesso di caccia	perme′sō dē kä′tshä

judo	(il) judo	joō′dō
marksmanship	(il) tiro	tē′rō
– clay pigeon shooting	(il) tiro al piattello	tē′rō äl pyäte′lō
– rifle range	(il) poligono di tiro	pōlē′gōnō dē tē′rō
– shoot	sparare, tirare	spärä′re, tērä′re
– target	(il) bersaglio	bersä′lyō
mountain climbing	(l') alpinismo *m*	älpēnē′zmō
– mountain climber	(l') alpinista *m*	älpēnē′stä
ninepins	(i) birilli	bērē′lē
player	(il) giocatore	jōkätō′re
referee	(l') arbitro *m*	ärbē′trō
riding	(l') equitazione *f*	ekoō·ētätsyō′ne
– horse	(il) cavallo	kävä′lō
– horse race	(la) corsa di cavalli	kōr′sä dē kävä′lē
– jumping	(il) saltare	sältä′re
– ride	cavalcare	kävälkä′re
– rider	(il) cavalcatore	kävälkätō′re
– trotting race	(la) corsa al trotto	kōr′sä äl trō′tō
rowing	(il) canottaggio	känōtä′jō
– scull	(la) barca a remi	bär′kä ä re′mē
– oarsman	(il) rematore	remätō′re
– coxwain	(il) timoniere	tēmōnye′re
sailing	(lo) sport della vela	spōrt de′lä ve′lä
– sail *(noun)*	(la) vela	ve′lä
– sail *(verb)*	veleggiare	velejä′re
– sailboat	(la) barca a vela	bär′kä ä ve′lä
skiing	(lo) sport sciistico	spōrt shē·ē′stēkō
– ski *(noun)*	(lo) sci	shē
– ski *(verb)*	sciare	shē·ä′re
– ski binding	(l') attacco *m*	ätä′kō
– ski jump	(il) trampolino	trämpōlē′nō
– ski lift	(la) sciovia	shē·ōvē′ä
– ski wax	(la) sciolina	shē·ōlē′nä
soccer	(il) calcio	käl′tshō
– ball	(il) pallone	pälō′ne
– corner	(il) calcio d'angolo	käl′tshō dän′gōlō
– forward	(l') attaccante *m*	ätäkän′te
– free kick	(il) calcio di punizione	käl′tshō dē poōnētsyō′ne
– fullback	(il) terzino	tertsē′nō

– **kick a goal**	tirare un goal	tērä′re ōon gōl
– **goal**	(il) goal	gōl
– **goalie**	(il) portiere	pōrtye′re
– **halfback**	(il) mediano	medyä′nō
– **off-side**	(il) fuorigioco	fōo-ōrējō′kō
– **penalty kick**	(il) calcio di rigore	käl′tshō dē rēgō′re
– **play soccer**	giocare a pallone	jōkä′re ä pälō′ne
– **player**	(il) giocatore	jōkätō′re
– **throw-in**	(la) rimessa in gioco	rēme′sä ēn jō′kō
sports	(gli) sport	spōrt
– **athletic club**	(il) circolo sportivo	tshēr′kōlō spōr-tē′vō
– **sports fan**	(il) fan sportivo	fän spōrtē′vō
swimming	(il) nuoto	nōo-ō′tō
– **dive**	(il) tuffo	tōof′ō
– **diving board**	(il) trampolino	trämpōlē′nō
– **swimmer**	(il) nuotatore	nōo-ōtätō′re
team	(la) squadra	skōo-ä′drä
tennis	(il) tennis	te′nēs
– **singles/doubles**	(il) singolare/	sēngōlä′re/
	(il) doppio	dō′pyō
– **play tennis**	giocare a tennis	jōkä′re ä te′nēs
– **tennis ball**	(la) palla da tennis	pä′lä dä te′nēs
– **tennis court**	(il) campo da tennis	käm′pō dä te′nēs
– **badminton**	(il) volano	vōlä′nō
– **ping pong**	(il) ping-pong	pēng-pōng
tobogganing	(lo) sport della slitta	spōrt de′lä zlē′tä
– **toboggan**	(la) slitta	zlē′tä
track and field	(l´) atletica *f* leggera	ätle′tēkä leje′rä
umpire	(l´) arbitro *m*	ärbē′trō
volleyball	(il) pallavolo	pälävō′lō
wrestling	(la) lotta libera	lō′tä lē′berä
– **wrestle**	lottare	lōtä′re
– **wrestler**	(il) lottatore	lōtätō′re

> *Baseball and American football are virtually unknown sports in Europe. Think of them as something nice to look forward to when you get home.*

APPENDIX

Signs

ANTINCENDIO	äntēntshen'dyō	fire extinguisher
ARRIVI	ärē'vē	arrivals
ATTENTI AL CANE .	äten'tē äl kä'ne	beware of the dog
ATTENZIONE!	ätentsyō'ne	caution!
ATTENZIONE AI TRENI	ätentsyō'ne ī tre'nē ..	look out for the train
CHIUSO	kyōō'zō	closed
AFFITTASI	äfē'täsē	to let
ENTRATA .... INGRESSO	enträ'tä	entrance
GRATUITO	ēngre'sō grätōō·ē'tō .	admission free
IN VENDITA	ēn ven'dētä	for sale
NON APRIRE	nōn äprē're	do not open
PERICOLO DI MORTE	perē'kōlō dē mōr'te .	mortal danger
POSTEGGIO TASSÌ ..	pōste'jō täsē'	taxi stand
PRIMO PIANO	prē'mō pyä'nō	first (= second) floor
SCALA MOBILE	skä'lä mō'bēle	escalator
SECONDO PIANO ...	sekōn'dō pyä'nō	second (= third) floor
SIGNORE	sēnyō're	ladies
SIGNORI	sēnyō'rē	gentlemen
SI PREGA DI NON TOCCARE	sē pre'gä dē nōn tōkä're	do not touch
SPINGERE	spēn'jere	push
STRADA PRIVATA ..	strä'dä prēvä'tä	private (road)
TIRARE	tērä're	pull
USCITA (D'EMERGENZA) ...	ōōshē'tä (demerjen'-tsä	(emergency) exit
VERNICE FRESCA ..	vernē'tshe fres'kä ...	wet paint
VIETATO BAGNARSI	vyetä'tō bänyär'sē ...	no swimming allowed
VIETATO FUMARE .	vyetä'tō fōōmä're ...	no smoking
VIETATO L'INGRESSO	vyetä'tō lēngre'sō ...	no admittance

Abbreviations

Acc	(treno) Accelerato	**local train**
ACI	Automobile Club d'Italia	**Italian automobile club**
C	Celsius	**Celsius** *(see conversion table page 26)*
ca	circa	**approximately, about**
CAP	codice di avviamento postale	**postal code**
CIT	Compagnia Italiana del Turismo	**tourist agency**
C.P.	casella postale	**post office box**
C.R.I.	Croce rossa italiana	**Italian Red Cross**
DD	direttissimo	**express/fast train**
dir.	diretto	**semi-fast train**
dott.	dottore	**doctor**
ENIT	Ente Nazionale Industrie Turistiche	**the official tourist office**
FF.SS.	Ferrovie dello Stato	**State-owned railway**
g	grammo	**gram**
h	(h)ora	**hour**
L.it.	Lire italiane	**Italian Lire**
L.st.	Lire sterlina	**Pound**
mc	metro cubo	**cubic meter**
mq	metro quadrato	**square meters**
km/h	chilometri all'ora	**kilometers per hour**
N.U. (ONU)	Nazioni Unite	**United Nations**
N.U.	nettezza urbana	**garbage collection**
p.c.	per conoscenza	**for your information**
PP.TT.	Poste e Telecomunicazioni	**post and telephone**
P.S.	pubblica sicurezza	**police**
P.za	Piazza	**square/place**
R.A.I.	Radio Audizioni Italiane	**Italian Broadcasting**
RAI-TV	Radio televisione Italiana	**Italian Television**
S.; SS.	santo; santi	**Saint; Saints**
S.P.	il Santo Padre	**the Holy Father**
S.p.A.	Società per Azioni	**(stock) corporation**
T.C.I.	Touring Club italiana	**Italian touring club**
V.; V.le	via; viale	**street; avenue**
V.U.	vigili urbani	**police**

Weights and Measures

millimeter	un millimetro (mm) (0.039 in.)	o͞on mēlē′metrō
centimeter	un centimetro (cm) (0.39 in.)	o͞on tshentē′metrō
decimeter	un decimetro (dm) (3.94 in.)	o͞on detshē′metrō
meter	un metro (m) (3.28 feet)	o͞on me′trō
kilometer	un chilometro (km) (0.6214 miles)	o͞on kēlō′metrō
inch	un pollice (2.54 cm)	o͞on pō′lētshe
foot	un piede (30.48 cm)	o͞on pye′de
yard	una iarda (0.914 m)	o͞o′nä yär′dä
(statute) mile	un miglio (1.609 km)	o͞on mē′lyō
nautical mile	un miglio marittimo (1.853 km)	o͞on mē′lyō märē′tēmō
liter	un litro (l) (2.113 pints)	o͞on lē′trō
pint	(una pinta) (0.473 l)	o͞o′nä pēn′tä
quart	(un quarto) (0.946 l)	o͞on ko͞o·är′tō
gallon	(un gallone) (3.785 l)	o͞on gälō′ne
ounce	un'oncia (28.349 g)	o͞onōn′tshä
pound	mezzo chilo (una libbra) (453.59 g)	me′dzō kē′lō (o͞o′nä lē′brä)
pounds	un chilo(grammo)	o͞on kē′lo(grä′mō)
00 grams	un etto (3.214 oz.)	o͞on e′tō

> *Remember: in Italy the metric system is used and one calculates only in gram (il grammo) and kilogram (il chilogrammo). For exemple in a store one would buy* "un etto" *(100 g) or* due etti *(200 g),* "mezzo chilo" *(500 g) or* "un chilo" *(1000 g).*

piece (of …)	un pezzo (di)	o͞on pe′tsō (dē)
pair (of …)	un paio (di)	o͞on pä′yō (dē)
dozen	una dozzina	o͞o′nä dōdzē′nä
pack(et) (of …)	un pacco (un pacchetto) (di)	o͞on pä′kō (o͞on pä-ke′tō) (dē)

Colors

beige	beige	be´zh
black	nero	ne´rō
blonde	biondo	byōn´dō
blue	blu	blo͞o
– light blue	azzurro	ädzo͞o´rō
– navy blue	blu marino	blo͞o märē´nō
brown	bruno	bro͞o´nō
– chestnut brown	marrone	märō´ne
color	(il) colore	kōlō´re
– colored	colorato	kōlōrä´tō
– colorful	variopinto	väryōpēn´to
– solid-colored	in tinta unita	ēn tēn´tä o͞onē´tä
gold	dorato	dōrä´tō
green	verde	ver´de
– dark green	verde scuro	ver´de sko͞o´rō
– light green	verde chiaro	ver´de kyä´rō
gray	grigio	grē´jō
– ash gray	grigio cenere	grē´jō tshe´nere
– dark gray	grigio scuro	grē´jō sko͞o´rō
– pale gray	grigio chiaro	grē´jō kyä´rō
lavender/mauve	color lavanda/malva	kōlōr´ lävän´dä/mäl´vä
orange	arancione	äräntshō´ne
pink	rosa	rō´zä
purple	color porpora	kōlōr´ pōr´pōrä
red	rosso	rō´sō
– bright red	rosso chiaro	rō´sō kyä´rō
– fire engine red	rosso vivo	rō´sō vē´vō
– dark red/maroon	rosso scuro	rō´sō sko͞o´rō
silver	argento	ärjen´tō
violet	violetto	vyōle´tō
white	bianco	byän´kō
yellow	giallo	jä´lō

BASIC ITALIAN GRAMMAR RULES

I. The Noun

The Italian noun is either masculine or feminine.

Most of the nouns ending in -*o* are masculine, e.g. *abito* [ä'bētō] dress; most of the nouns ending in -*a* are feminine, e.g. *posta* [pō'stä] post office. Nouns ending in -*e* may be either masculine or feminine: *calore m* [kälō're] heat, *chiave f* [kyä've] key.

II. The Article

1. Definite Articles:

a) The definite article for masculine nouns is *il* [ēl] with nouns beginning with a consonant, e.g. *il cappello* [ēl käpe'lō] the hat, and *lo* with nouns beginning with *z*, or with an *s* followed by a consonant, e.g. *lo zucchero* [lō tsoo'kerō] the sugar, *lo specchio* [lō spe'kyō] the mirror. Before vowels, *lo* is shortened to *l'*, e.g. *l'anno* [lä'nō] the year.

b) The definite article for feminine nouns is *la* [lä] with nouns beginning with a consonant, e.g. *la casa* [lä kä'sä] the house, and *l'* before vowels, e.g. *l'amica* [lämē'kä] the (girl)friend.

2. Indefinite Articles:

a) The indefinite article for masculine nouns is *un* with nouns beginning either with a vowel or with a consonant, e.g. *un libro* [oon lē'brō] a book, *un amico* [oonämē'kō] a (boy)friend, and *uno* with nouns beginning with *z*, or with an *s* followed by a consonant, e.g. *uno scolaro* [oo'nō skōlä'rō] a pupil, *uno zaino* [oo'nō dzī'nō] a knapsack.

b) The indefinite article for feminine nouns is *una* with nouns beginning with a consonant, e.g. *una matita* [oo'nä mätē'tä] a pencil, and *un'* with nouns beginning with a vowel, e.g. *un'ora* [oonō'rä] an hour.

III. The Adjective

The adjective agrees in number and gender with the noun it modifies.

a) Adjectives ending in -*o* change to -*a* when modifying a feminine noun: *vino bianco* [vē'nō byän'kō] white wine, *la razza bianca* [lä rä'tsä byän'kä] the white race.

b) Adjectives ending in -*e* do not change: *il cane fedele* [ēl kä'ne fede'le] the loyal dog, *la copia fedele (di una lettera)* [lä kō'pyä fede'le] the accurate copy (of a letter).

IV. Formation of Plurals

a)   The article *il*   becomes *i* in the plural.
     The article *lo (l')*   becomes *gli* in the plural.
     The article *la (l')*   becomes *le* in the plural.

b) Masculine nouns and adjectives ending in *-o* change the singular ending to *-i*, e.g. *il vestito corto* [ēl vestē'tō kōr'tō] the short dress, *i vestiti corti* [ē vestē'tē kōr'tē] the short dresses.

Feminine nouns and adjectives ending in *-a* change the singular ending to *-e*, e.g. *la giacca rossa* [lä jä'kä rō'sä] the red coat, *le giacche rosse* [le jä'ke rō'se] the red coats.

The masculine and feminine nouns and adjectives ending in *-e* change the singular ending to *-i*, e.g. *il signore gentile* [ēl sēnyō're jentē'le] the kind gentleman, *i signori gentili* [ē sēnyō'rē jentē'lē] the kind gentlemen, *la chiave inglese* [lä kyä've ēngle'se] the wrench, *le chiavi inglesi* [le kyä'vē ēngle'sē] the wrenches.

V. Prepositions

The preposition *di* (before a vowel *d'*) expresses the possessive case of the Italian noun.

The prepositions *di* = of and *a* = to are used with the definite articles in the following contracted forms:

di	+	*il*	=	*del*	[del]	*a*	+	*il*	=	*al*	[äl]
di	+	*lo*	=	*dello*	[de'lō]	*a*	+	*lo*	=	*allo*	[ä'lō]
di	+	*l'*	=	*dell'*	[del]	*a*	+	*l'*	=	*all'*	[äl]
di	+	*la*	=	*della*	[de'lä]	*a*	+	*la*	=	*alla*	[ä'lä]
di	+	*i*	=	*dei*	[de'ē]	*a*	+	*i*	=	*ai*	[ī]
di	+	*gli*	=	*degli*	[de'lyē]	*a*	+	*gli*	=	*agli*	[ä'lyē]
di	+	*le*	=	*delle*	[de'le]	*a*	+	*le*	=	*alle*	[ä'le]

VI. Comparison

1. The comparative of adjectives is formed by placing *più* [pyōō] before the adjective: e.g. *caro* [kä'rō] expensive, *più caro* [pyōō kä'rō] more expensive.

2. The superlative is formed by adding the definite article to the comparative: e.g. *il più caro* [ēl pyōō kä'rō] the most expensive.

3. *Than* in comparisons is translated by *di*: e.g. *questa stoffa è più bella dell'altra* [koo·e'stä stō'fä e pyoo be'lä deläl'trä] this material is more beautiful than the other one.

Che is used instead of *di* before prepositions: e.g. *Mario è più gentile con te che con me* [mär'yō e pyoo jentē'le kōn te ke kōn me] Mario is nicer to you than to me.

4. An emphatic superlative is formed either through *molto* [mōl'tō] very (as in English) or by dropping the final vowel of the adjective and adding *-issimo* [ē'sēmō]: e.g. *grande* [grän'de] big, *molto grande* [mōl'tō grän'de] or *grandissimo* [grändē'sēmō] very big.

VII. Pronouns

Personal Pronouns

A. Unstressed (= Pronouns used in Accusative and Dative)

	Singular			Plural
mi	[mē]	me, to me	*ci* [tshē]	us, to us
ti	[tē]	you, to you	*vi* [vē]	you, to you
lo	[lō]	him, to him	*li* [lē]	*loro* (lō'rō) them, to them *m*
gli	[lyē]			
le	[le]	*la* [lä] her, to her	*le* [le]	*loro* [lō'rō] them, to them *f*
Le	[le]	*La* [lä] you, to you	*Le* [le]	*Loro* [lō'rō] you, to you
si	[sē]	yourself, himself, herself, itself	*si* [sē]	yourselves, themselves

Position: The **unstressed form** of the personal pronoun precedes the verb or the auxiliary verb, e.g. *ci domanda* [tshē dōmän'dä] he asks us, except for *loro*, e.g. *piace loro* [pyä'tshe lō'rō] you like it. The unstressed pronouns follow and are joined to the infinitive, the participle, the gerund and the affirmative imperative: e.g. *siamo lieti di vederlo* [syä'mō lye'tē dē veder'lō] we're glad to see him/it; *vedutolo* [vedoo'tōlō] having seen him/it, *vedendolo* [veden'dōlō] seeing him/it, *vedilo!* [ve'dēlō] see him/it!

B. Stressed

	Singular				Plural	
io	[ē'ō] me [me]	I, me		*noi*	[nō'ē]	we, us
tu	[tōō] te [te]	you		*voi*	[vō'ē]	you
lui	[lōō'ē]	he, him		*loro*	[lō'rō]	they, them (*m*)
lei	[le'ē]	she, her		*loro*	[lō'rō]	they, them (*f*)
se	[se]	himself, herself, itself		*se*	[se]	themselves

Position: The **stressed forms** of the personal pronouns are used:

1. for emphasis, e.g. *vedo soltanto lui* [ve'dō sōltän'tō lōō'ē] I only see *him*.

2. in combination with prepositions, e.g. *con lei* [kōn le'ē] with her.

Address. Along with the familiar forms of direct address in the singular *(tu)* and plural *(voi)* there are also formal (polite) forms of address: *Lei* [le'ē] when speaking to one person, and *Loro* [lō'rō] when speaking to more than one: e.g. *Lei è molto gentile* [le'ē e mōl'tō jentē'le] You are very kind; *quando partono Loro?* [kōō·än'dō pär'tōnō lō'rō] When are you (*plural*) leaving?

Possessive Pronouns

	Singular			Plural	
mio	[mē'ō]	*miei*	[mye'ē]		my, mine
tuo	[tōō'ō]	*tuoi*	[tōō·ō'ē]		your, yours
suo	[sōō'ō]	*suoi*	[sōō·ō'ē]		his, her, hers
Suo	[sōō'ō]	*Suoi*	[sōō·ō'ē]		your, yours
nostro	[nō'strō]	*nostri*	[nō'strē]		our, ours
vostro	[vō'strō]	*vostri*	[vō'strē]		your, yours
loro	[lō'rō]	*loro*	[lō'rō]		their, theirs
Loro	[lō'rō]	*Loro*	[lō'rō]		your, yours (*polite form of address*)

The feminine form is regular and is, in the singular, *mia, tua,* etc. and in the plural, *mie, tue,* etc. *Loro* remains unchanged. In Italian, the possessive pronoun always **requires an article:** e.g. *il mio amico* [ēl mē'ō ämē'kō] my (boy)friend.

The pronouns *suo, sua, suoi, sue* refer to one person, *loro* refers to more than one person.

Demonstrative Pronouns

questo [kōo·e′stō] this (*m*) and *questa* [kōo·e′stä] this (*f*) refer to persons or things near the speaker, *quel (lo)* [kōo·el′, kōo·e′lō] that (*m*), *quella* [kōo·e′lä] that (*f*) to persons or things near the listener or far from both speaker and listener. The forms of *quello* preceding a noun correspond to those of the definite article: *quel libro*; *quello scolaro*; *quell'oggetto*; *quei libri*; *quegli scolari*; *quegli oggetti*.

Interrogative Pronouns

che? [ke] what?, which? *quale* [kōo·ä′le] what? which? *che* can be used as an adjective, *quale* as an adjective and as a noun; e.g. *che libro?* or *quale libro?* which book?, but: *quale dei tuoi amici?* which of your friends?

VIII. The Verb

A. The Auxiliary Verbs

avere [äve′re] to have   *essere* [e′sere] to be

Past Participle

avuto [ävōo′tō] had   *stato* [stä′tō] been

Gerund

avendo [även′dō] having   *essendo* [esen′dō] being

Present

ho*) [ō] I have	*sono* [sō′nō] I am
hai [ä′ē] you have	*sei* [se′ē] you are
ha [ä] he, she, it has	*è* [e] he, she, it is
abbiamo [äbyä′mō] we have	*siamo* [syä′mō] we are
avete [äve′te] you have *pl.*	*siete* [sye′te] you are *pl.*
hanno [ä′nō] they have	*sono* [sō′nō] they are

Imperfect

avevo [äve′vō] I had	*ero* [e′rō] I was
avevi [äve′vē] you had	*eri* [e′rē] you were
aveva [äve′vä] he, she, it had	*era* [e′rä] he, she, it was
avevamo [ävevä′mō] we had	*eravamo* [erävä′mō] we were
avevate [ävevä′te] you had *pl.*	*eravate* [erävä′te] you were
avevano [äve′vänō] they had	*erano* [e′ränō] they were

*) The subject pronoun (*io*, *tu*, etc.) is used only for clarity or emphasis.

Future

avrò [ävrō′] I will have	*sarò* [särō′] I will be
avrai [ävrä′ē] you will have	*sarai* [särä′ē] you will be
avrà [ävrä′] he, she, it will have	*sarà* [särä′] he, she, it will be
avremo [ävre′mō] we will have	*saremo* [säre′mō] we will be
avrete [ävre′te] you will have *pl.*	*sarete* [säre′te] you will be *pl.*
avranno [ävrä′nō] they will have	*saranno* [särä′nō] they will be

Imperative

abbi [ä′bē] have (you *sing.*)	*sii* [sē′ē] be (you *sing.*)
abbia [ä′byä] have (you *sing.* polite)	*sia* [sē′ä] be (you *sing.* polite)
abbiamo [äbyä′mō] let us have	*siamo* [syä′mō] let us be
abbiate [äbyä′te] have (you *plural*)	*siate* [syä′te] be (you *plural*)
abbiano [ä′byänō] have (you *pl.* polite)	*siano* [sē′änō] be (you *pl.* polite)

B. The Regular Verbs

Italian verbs are divided into three groups, which, in the infinitive, end in *-are*, *-ere* or *-ire*, and are conjugated as follows:

1.	2.	3.
amare [ämä′re]	*temere* [teme′re]	*sentire* [sentē′re]
to love	to fear	to feel

Past Participle

amato [ämä′tō]	*temuto* [temoo′tō]	*sentito* [sentē′tō]
loved	feared	felt

Gerund

amando [ämä′ndō]	*temendo* [teme′ndō]	*sentendo* [sente′ndō]
loving	fearing	feeling

Present

amo [ä′mō] I love
ami [ä′mē] you love
ama [ä′mä] he, she, it loves
amiamo [ämyä′mō] we love
amate [ämä′te] you love
amano [ä′mänō] they love

temo [te′mō]	*sento* [sen′tō]
temi [te′mē]	*senti* [sen′tē]
teme [te′me]	*sente* [sen′te]
temiamo [temyä′mō]	*sentiamo* [sentyä′mō]
temete [teme′te]	*sentite* [sentē′te]
temono [te′mōnō]	*sentono* [sen′tōnō]

Imperfect

amavo [ämä′vō] I loved
amavi [ämä′vē] you loved
amava [ämä′vä] he, she, it loved
amavamo [ämävä′mō] we loved
amavate [ämävä′te] you loved *pl.*
amavano [ämä′vänō] they loved

temevo [teme′vō]	*sentivo* [sentē′vo]
temevi [teme′vē]	*sentivi* [sentē′vē]
temeva [teme′vä]	*sentiva* [sentē′vä]
temevamo [temevä′mō]	*sentivamo* [sentēvä′mō]
temevate [temevä′te]	*sentivate* [sentēvä′te]
temevano [teme′vänō]	*sentivano* [sentē′vänō]

Future

amerò [ämerō′] I will love
amerai [ämerä′ē] you will love
amerà [ämerä′] he, she, it will love
ameremo [ämere′mō] we will love
amerete [ämere′te] you will love *pl.*
ameranno [ämerä′nō] they will love

temerò [temerō′]	*sentirò* [sentērō′]
temerai [temerä′ē]	*sentirai* [sentērä′ē]
temerà [temerä′]	*sentirà* [sentērä′]
temeremo [temere′mō]	*sentiremo* [sentēre′mō]
temerete [temere′te]	*sentirete* [sentēre′te]
temeranno [temerä′nō]	*sentiranno* [sentērä′nō]

Imperative

ama [ä'mä] love (you *sing.*)
ami [ä'mē] love (you *sing.* polite)
amiamo [ämyä'mō] let us love
amate [ämä'te] love (you *plural*)
amino [ä'mēnō] love (you *pl.* polite)

temi [te'mē]	*senti* [sen'tē]
tema [te'mä]	*senta* [sen'tä]
temiamo [temyä'mō]	*sentiamo* [sentyä'mō]
temete [teme'te]	*sentite* [sentē'te]
temano [te'mänō]	*sentano* [sen'täno]

Note: Most verbs ending in *-ire* add *-isc-* to the stem of the present indicative and imperative, e.g.

Infinitive: finire [fēnē're] to finish

Present Indicative: I finish, etc.

finisco [fēnē'skō]
finisci [fēnē'shē]
finisce [fēnē'she]

finiamo [fēnyä'mō]
finite [fēnē'te]
finiscono [fēnēs'kōnō]

Final Remark: Since the Past Definite, the Conditional and the Subjunctive are not essential at this stage, we have omitted them.

The translations are followed by phonetic transcriptions and page references, so that this dictionary serves as an index as well.

A

abbey abbazia f [äbätsē'ä] 124

abdomen addome m [ädō'me] 166

abscess ascesso m [äshe'sō] 169

absorbant cotton ovatta f [ōvä'tä] 160

accelerator acceleratore m [ätshelerätō're] 51

access road strada f d'accesso [strä'dä dätshe'sō] 42

accessories accessori m/pl. [ätshesō'rē] 136

accident incidente m [ēntshēden'te] 51

accomodations alloggio m [älō'jō] 81

accompanist accompagnatore m [äkōmpänyätō're] 177

accompany accompagnare [äkōmpänyä're] 184

ace asso m [ä'sō] 181

act atto m [ä'tō] 177

actor attore m [ätō're] 177

actress attrice f [ätrē'tshe] 177

adapter plug spina f intermedia [spē'nä ēnterme'dyä] 90

address indirizzo m [ēndērē'tsō] 48

addressee destinatario m [destēnätär'yō] 149

admission ingresso m [ēngre'sō] 118

advance ticket sales prevendita-biglietti f [preven'dētä-bēlye'tē] 177

afraid: I'm ~ mi dispiace [mē dēspyä'tshe] 16

after shave dopobarba m [dōpōbär'bä] 140

afternoon pomeriggio m [pōmerē'jō] 31; **Good ~!** Buon giorno! [bōō·ōnjōr'nō] 12; **in the ~** nel pomeriggio [nel pōmerē'jō] 31; **this ~** oggi pomeriggio [ō'jē pōmerē'jō] 31

against contro [kōn'trō] 164

age età f [etä'] 35; **under ~** minorenne [mēnōre'ne] 35

ago: a month ~ un mese fa [ōōn me'se fä] 32

air aria f [är'yä] 26; **~ conditioning** aria f condizionata [är'yä kōndētsyōnä'tä] 75; **~ filter** filtro m d'aria [fēl'trō där'yä] 51; **~ jet** diffusore m di aria fresca [dēfōōzō're dē är'yä fres'kä] 70; **~ mail** posta f aerea [pō'stä ä·e're·ä] 149; **~ mattress** materassino m [mäteräsē'nō] 186; **~ pump** pompa f dell'aria [pōm'pä delär'yä] 57; **~ sickness** mal m d'aria [mäl där'yä] 70

aircraft aereo m [ä·e're·ō] 70

airline compagnia f aerea [kōmpänyē'ä ä·e're·ä] 70

air passenger passeggero m [päseje'rō] 70

airport aeroporto m [ä·erōpōr'tō] 68; **~ service charge** tassa f d'imbarco [tä'sä dēmbär'kō] 70

alcohol alcool m [äl'kō·ōl] 160

all tutto [tōō'tō] 80

allergy allergia f [älerjē'ä] 169

alley viale m [vyä'le] 120

allow permettere [permet'ere] 20

almonds mandorle f [män'dōrle] 110

alone da solo [dä sō'lō] 14

already già [jä] 69

altar altare m [ältä're] 124

alter modificare [mōdēfēkä're] 133

amber ambra f [äm'brä] 133

ambulance autoambulanza *f* [outō·-ämbōōlän'tsä] 48

American dollars dollari *m/pl*. americani [dō'lärē ämerēkä'nē] 152

American plan pensione *f* completa [pensyō'ne komple'tä] 83

American studies americanistica *f* [ämerēkänē'stēkä] 39

amount importo *m* [ēmpōr'tō] 151

amusement passatempo *m* [päsätem'pō] 181

anchor ancora *f* [än'kōrä] 75

anchovies acciughe *f/pl* [ätshōō'ge] 102

anemia anemia *f* [änemē'ä] 169

anesthesia anestesia *f* [änestezē'ä] 173; **local ~** anestesia *f* locale [änestezē'ä lōkä'le] 173

anesthetic narcosi *f* [närkō'zē] 172

ankle caviglia *f* [kävē'lyä] 166

announcer annunciatore *m* [änōōntshätō're] 182

another altro [äl'trō] 83

anti-freeze anticongelante *m* [äntēkönjelän'te] 51

anyone qualcuno [kōō·älkōō'nō] 85

anything qualcosa [kōō·älkō'sä] 80

apartments appartamenti *m/pl* [äpärtämen'tē] 81

apologize scusarsi [skōōzär'sē] 22

appendicitis appendicite *f* [äpendētshē'te] 169

appendix appendice *m* [äpendē'tshe] 166

appetite appetito *m* [äpetē'tō] 163

apple mela *f* [me'lä] 110

appointment appuntamento *m* [äpōōntämen'tō] 173

apprentice apprendista *m/f* [äprendē'stä] 36

approach avvicinarsi [ävētshēnär'sē] 70

apricot albicocca *f* [älbēkō'kä] 109

April aprile *m* [äprē'le] 33

arch volta *f* [vōl'tä] 124

archaeology archeologia *f* [ärke·ō·lōjē'ä] 39

architecture architettura *f* [ärkētetōō'rä] 39

area zona *f*, regione *f* [dzō'nä, rejō'ne] 120; **~ code** prefisso *m* [prefē'sō] 149

arm braccio *m* [brä'tshō] 166

armchair poltrona *f* [pōltrō'na] 90

armpit ascella *f* [äshe'lä] 166

arrest arrestare [ärestä're] 154

arrival arrivo *m* [ärē'vō] 67

arrive arrivare [ärēvä're] 34

art history storia *f* dell'arte [stō'ryä delär'te] 39

art gallery galleria *f* d'arte [gälerē'ä där'te] 128

artery arteria *f* [ärter'yä] 166

arthritis artrite *f* [ärtrē'te] 169

artichokes carciofi *m/pl* [kärtshō'fē] 102

articles oggetti *m/pl* [ōje'tē] 80

artist artista *m/f* [ärtē'stä] 36

ash tray portacenere *m* [pōrtätshe'nere] 87

ashore; to go ~ sbarcare [zbärkä're] 72

asparagus asparagi *m/pl* [äspä'räjē] 107

aspirin aspirina *f* [äspērē'nä] 160

asthma asma *m* [äz'mä] 169

athletic club circolo *m* sportivo [tshēr'kōlō spōrtē'vō] 189

atmospheric pressure pressione *f* atmosferica [presyō'ne ätmōsfe'rēkä] 26

attack attacco *m* [ätä'kō] 169

attend university frequentare l'università [frekōō·entä're lōōnēversētä'] 38

attorney avvocato *m* [ävōkä'tō] 154

auditorium sala *f* degli spettatori [sä'lä de'lyē spetätō'rē] 179

August agosto *m* [ägō'stō] 33

aunt zia *f* [tsē'ä] 35

Austrian Schillings scellini *m/pl* austriaci [shelē'nē oustrē'ätshē] 152

auto racing corsa f automobilistica [kōr'sä outōmōbēlē'stēkä] 187

autobiography autobiografia f [outōbē·ōgräfē'ä] 130

automatic transmission cambio m automatico [käm'byō outōmä'tēkō] 51

avenue strada f [strä'dä] 120

axle asse f [ä'se] 51

B

back schiena f [skye'nä] 166; ~ **seat** sedile m posteriore [sedē'le pōsteryō're] 55; ~ **wheel** ruota f di dietro [rōō·ō'tä dē dye'trō] 47

backache mal m di schiena [mäl dē skye'nä] 169

backfire accensione f a vuoto [ätshensyō'ne ä vōō·ō'tō] 51

bacon lardo m [lär'dō] 100

bad: too ~ che peccato [ke pekä'tō] 22

badminton volano m [vōlä'nō] 180

bag borsa f [bōr'sä] 126; busta f, borsetta f [bōō'stä, bōrse'tä] 143; ~ **beach** ~ borsa f per la spiaggia [bōr'sä per lä spyä'jä] 143; **flight** ~ borsa f da viaggio (per il volo) [bōr'sä dä vyä'jō (per ēl vō'lō)] 144; **plastic** ~ borsetta f di plastica [bōrse'tä dē plä'stēkä] 144; **travelling** ~ borsa f [bōr'sä] 63

baggage bagaglio m [bägä'lyō] 63; ~ **car** bagagliaio m [bägälyä'yō] 67; ~ **check** scontrino m [skōntrē'nō] 84; ~ **check area** accettazione f bagagli [ätshetätsyō'ne bägä'lyē] 63; deposito m [depō'sētō] 64; ~ **claim area** consegna f bagagli [kōnse'nyä bägä'lyē] 63; ~ **deposit area** deposito m bagagli [depō'sētō bägä'lyē] 63

baked cotto al forno [kō'tō äl fōr'nō] 100

baker fornaio m [fōrnä'yō] 36

bakery panificio m [pänēfē'tshō] 128

balance beam sbarra f [zbä'rä] 188

balcony balcone m [bälkō'ne] 82; galleria f [gälerē'ä] 176

ball palla f [pä'lä] 143; pallone m [pälō'ne] 189; ~ **bearings** cuscinetti m a sfere [kōōshēne'tē ä sfe're] 51; ~ **point cartridge** mina f [mē'nä] 138

ballet balletto m [bäle'tō] 177

banana banana f [bänä'nä] 109

band banda f [bän'dä] 177

bandage: ace ~ benda f elastica [ben'dä elä'stēkä] 160; **adhesive** ~ cerotto m [tsherō'tō] 160

bandages garze f/pl [gär'tse] 48

bank banca f [bän'kä] 151; **savings** ~ cassa f di Risparmio [kä'sä dē rēspär'myō] 152; ~ **account** conto m corrente [kōn'tō kōren'te] 151; ~ **note** banconota f [bänkōnō'tä] 151; ~ **teller** cassiere m [käsye're] 36; ~ **transfer** rimessa f bancaria [rēme'sä bänkär'yä] 151

bank sponda f [spōn'dä] 75

banker tenitore m del banco [tenētō're dēl bän'kō] 181

baptism battesimo m [bäte'zēmō] 124

bar bar m [bär] 74

barber shop barbiere m [bärbye're] 74

barge scialuppa f [shälōō'pä] 75

barometer barometro m [bärō'metrō] 25

Baroque barocco m [bärō'kō] 124

basement seminterrato m [semēnterä'tō] 90

bath bagno m [bä'nyō] 82; **mineral** ~ bagno m minerale [bä'nyō menerä'le] 175; **steam** ~ bagno m a vapore [bä'nyō ä väpō're] 175; ~ **salts** sali m/pl da bagno [sä'lē dä bä'nyō] 140; **take a** ~ fare il bagno [fä're ēl bä'nyō] 95

bathing cap cuffia *f* da bagno [kōō'fyä dä bä'nyō] 134

bathing suit costume *m* da bagno [kōstōō'me dä bä'nyō] 134

bathing trunks pantaloncini *m/pl* da bagno [päntälōntshē'nē dä bä'nyō] 134; **slip** *m/pl* da bagno [slēp dä bä'nyō] 186

bathrobe accappatoio *m* [äkäpätō'yō] 134

bathroom bagno *m* [bä'nyō] 90

battery batteria *f* [bäterē'ä] 51

bay baia *f* [bä'yä] 75

beach spiaggia *f* [spyä'jä] 81; **priva-te** ~ spiaggia *f* privata [spyä'jä prēvä'tä] 92; **sandy** ~ spiaggia *f* sabbiosa [spyä'jä säbyō'sä] 186

beans fagioli *m/pl.* [fäjō'lē] 107; **green** ~ fagiolini *m/pl.* [fäjōlē'nē] 107

beard barba *f* [bär'bä] 157; baffi *m/pl.* [bä'fē] 157

beauty contest concorso *m* di bellezza [kōnkōr'sō dē bele'tsä] 181

beauty parlor salone *m* di bellezza [sälō'ne dē bele'tsä] 158; parrucchiere *m* [pärōōkye're] 74

bed letto *m* [le'tō] 90; ~ **and two meals** mezza pensione *f* [me'dzä pensyō'ne] 90; ~ **linen** biancheria *f* da letto [byänkerē'ä dä le'tō] 90; ~ **rug** scendiletto *m* [shendēle'tō] 90; **day** ~ divano *m* [dēvä'nō] 91

bedroom camera *f* da letto [kä'merä dä le'tō] 93

bedside table comodino *m* [kōmōdē'nō] 90

bedspread coperta *f* [kōper'tä] 90

beef manzo *m* [män'dzō] 106

beer birra *f* [bē'rä] 111; **bock** ~ birra *f* di marzo [bē'rä dē mär'tsō] 111; **dark** ~ birra *f* scura [bē'rä skōō'rä] 111; **light** ~ birra *f* chiara [bē'rä kyä'rä] 111

beeswax cera *f* d'api [tshe'rä dä'pē] 143

beige beige [be'zh] 194

bell campana *f* [kämpä'nä] 124; campanello *m* [kämpäne'lō] 88

belt cintura *f* [tshēntōō'rä] 134

bet puntare [pōōntä're] 182

beverages: alcoholic ~ alcolic *m/pl.* [älkō'lētshē] 112

bicupid molare *m* [mōlä're] 174

bicycle bicicletta *f* [bētshēkle'tä] 41 **to go by** ~ andare in bicicletta [ändä're ēn bētshēkle'tä] 42; ~ **race** corsa *f* ciclistica [kōr'sä tshēklē'stēkä] 187; ~ **rider** ciclista *m* [tshēklē'stä] 187

bicycling ciclismo *m* [tshēklē'zmō] 187

big grande [grän'de] 127

bike: ride a ~ andare in bicicletta [ändä're ēn bētshēkle'tä] 187; ~ **lane** ciclopista *f* [tshēklōpē'stä] 42

bile bile *f* [bē'le] 166

bill biglietto *m* [bēlye'tō] 151; conto *m* [kōn'tō] 89

billfold portafoglio *m* [pōrtäfō'lyō] 153; borsellino *m* [bōrselē'nō] 153

binoculars binocolo *m* [bēnō'kōlō] 138

biography biografia *f* [bē·ōgräfē'ä] 130

biology biologia *f* [bē·ōlōjē'ä] 39

birthday compleanno *m* [kōmple·ä'nō] 22; **happy** ~ ! buon compleanno! [bōō·ōn' kōmple·ä'nō] 23

bishop alfiere *m* [älfye're] 181

bitters amaro *m* [ämä'rō] 112

black nero [ne'rō] 194; ~ **chocolate cake** torta *f* di cioccolato [tōr'tä dē tshōkōlä'tō] 109

blackberries more *f/pl.* [mō're] 110

blackmail attempt ricatto *m* [rēkä'tō] 153

bladder vescica *f* [veshē'kä] 166

blanket coperta *f* di lana [kōper'tä dē lä'nä] 75

bleeding emorragia *f* [emōräjē'ä] 169

blinker lampeggiatore *m* [lämpejä-tō're] 51

blizzard tormenta *f* [tōrmen'tä] 26

blonde biondo [byōn'dō] 194

blood sangue *m* [sän'gōo·e] 165; **~ count** quadro *m* ematologico [kōo·ä'drō emätōlō'jēkō] 172; **~ poisoning** setticemia *f* [setētshe-mē'ä] 169; **~ pressure** pressione *f* sanguigna [presyō'ne sängōo·ē'nyä] 166; **~ test** prelievo *m* del sangue [prelye'vō del sän'gōo·e] 172; **~ transfusion** trasfusione *f* del sangue [träsfōozyō'ne del sän'gōo·e] 172

blouse camicetta *f* [kämētshe'tä] 134

blow *(fuse)* saltare [sältä're] 55

blow-out foratura *f* [fōrätōo'rä] 47

blue blu [blōo] 194; **light ~** azzurro [ädzōo'rō] 194; **navy ~** blu marino [blōo märē'nō] 194; **~ jeans** blue jeans *m/pl.* [blōo jēns] 134

blueberries mirtilli *m/pl.* [mērtē'lē] 110

boar: **wild ~** cinghiale *m* [tshēn-gyä'le] 106

board bordo *m* [bōr'dō] 72; scacchiera *f* [skäkye'rä] 181

boarding house locanda *f* [lō-kän'dä] 81

boat barca *f* [bär'kä] 75; **pedal ~** barca *f* a pedale [bär'kä ä pedä'le] 186; **~ racing** corsa *f* nautica [kōr'sä nou'tēkä] 187; **~ trip** gita *f* in barca [jē'tä ēn bär'kä] 120

body corpo *m* [kōr'pō] 166; *(car)* carrozzeria *f* [kärōtserē'ä] 51; **~ and fender damage** danno *m* alla carrozzeria e al parafango [dä'nō ä'lä kärōtserē'ä e äl päräfän'gō] 49

boiled lessato, bollito [lesä'tō, bōlē'-tō] 100; lesso [le'sō] 107

bolt bullone *m* [bōolō'ne] 51; vite *f* [vē'te 57]; **~ nut** dado *m* [dä'dō] 51; madrevite *f* [mädrevē'te] 57

bone osso *m* [ō'sō] 166

book libro *m* [lē'brō] 130; **children's ~** libro per bambini [lē'brō per bämbē'nē] 130; **guide ~** guida *f* [gōo·ē'dä] 130; **phrase ~** libro *m* di frasi idiomatiche [lē'brō dē frä'-zē ēdyōmä'tēke] 130

bookkeeper contabile *m* [kōntä'-bēle] 36

bookseller libraio *m* [lēbrä'yō] 36

bookshop libreria *f* [lēbrerē'ä] 128; **second-hand ~** libreria *f* d'antiquariato [lēbrerē'ä däntēkōo·ä-rē·ä'tō] 129

booth cabina *f* [käbē'nä] 148

boots stivali *m/pl.* [stēvä'lē] 139

border frontiera *f* [frōntye'rä] 78

born nato [nä'tō] 34

botanical gardens giardino *m* botanico [järdē'nō bōtä'nēkō] 120

bother disturbare [dēstōorbä're] 16; molestare [mōlestä're] 154

bottle bottiglia *f* [bōtē'lyä] 96; **~ opener** apribottiglie *m* [äprēbō-tē'lye] 143

bouquet mazzo *m* di fiori [mä'tsō dē fyō're] 130

bowel movement movimento *m* intestinale [mōvēmen'tō ēntestēnä'-le] 166

bowl scodella *f* [skōde'lä] 97

bowling gioco *m* dei birilli [jō'kō de'ē bērē'lē] 187; **~ alley** pista *f* del bowling [pē'stä del bō'lēng] 181

box scatola *f* [skä'tōlä] 126; **~ lunch** colazione *f* al sacco [kōlätsyō'ne äl sä'kō] 86

box boxe *f* [bōks] 187

boxer pugile *m* [pōo'jēle] 187

boxing pugilato *m* [pōojēlä'tō] 187

boy ragazzo *m* [rägä'tsō] 35

bra, brassière reggiseno *m* [rejēse'-nō] 134

bracelet braccialetto *m* [brätshäle'tō] 133

braces fermaglio *m* dentario [fermäˈlyō dentärˈyō] 174

brain cervello *m* [tsherveˈlō] 166

brake *(verb)* frenare [frenäˈre] 43; *(noun)* freno *m* [freˈnō] 51; ~ **drum** tamburo *m* di freno [tämbōōˈrō dē freˈnō] 51; ~ **fluid** liquido *m* per i freni [lēˈkōō-ēdō per ē freˈnē] 45; ~ **lights** fanali *m* d'arresto [fänäˈlē däreˈstō] 51; ~ **lining** guarnizione *f* dei freni [gōō-ärnētsyōˈne deˈē freˈnē] 51; ~ **pedal** pedale *m* del freno [pedäˈle del freˈnō] 51

brandy acquavite *f* [äkōō-äveˈte] 112; **apricot** ~ brandy *m* [bränˈde] 112; **cherry** ~ maraschino [märäskēˈnō] 112

brassière reggiseno *m* [rejēseˈnō] 134

bread pane *m* [päˈne] 98; **dark** ~ pane *m* nero [päˈne neˈrō] 98; **whole wheat** ~ pane *m* integrale [päˈne ēntegräˈle] 98; ~ **basket** cestino *m* del pane [tshesteˈnō del päˈne] 97

breakdown guasto *m* [gōō-äˈstō] 48; disturbo *m* [dēstōōrˈbō] 182

breakfast (prima) colazione *f* [(prēˈmä) kōlätsyōˈne] 83; ~ **room** sala *f* per la prima colazione [säˈlä per lä prēˈmä kōlätsyōˈne] 90; **eat** ~ fare colazione [fäˈre kōlätsyōˈne] 90

breast petto *m* [peˈtō] 166

breathe respirare [respēräˈre] 164

breathing respiro *m* [respēˈrō] 166; ~ **problem** problemi *m/pl.* respiratori [prōbleˈme respērätōˈrē] 169

breeze brezza *f* [breˈdzä] 75

bricklayer muratore *m* [mōōrätōˈre] 36

bridge ponte *m* [pōnˈte] 42

briefcase cartella *f* [kärteˈlä] 143

brilliantine brillantina *f* [brēläntēˈnä] 157

bring portare [pōrtäˈre] 20; ~ **back** riportare [rēpōrtäˈre] 41

brisket punta *f* di petto [pōōnˈtä dē peˈtō] 107

broccoli broccoli *m/pl.* [brōˈkōlē] 107

broiler pollo *m* arrosto [pōˈlō ärōˈsto] 105

broken rotto [rōˈtō] 23

bronchitis bronchite *f* [brōnkēˈte] 169

brooch spilla *f* [spēˈlä] 133

broth brodo *m* [brōˈdō] 103; **chicken** ~ brodo *m* di pollo [brōˈdō dē pōˈlō] 103

brother fratello *m* [fräteˈlō] 35; ~ **-in-law** cognato *m* [kōnyäˈtō] 35

brown bruno [brōōˈnō] 194; **chestnut** ~ marrone [märōˈne] 194

bruise contusione *f* [kōntōōzyōˈne] 169

brush spazzola *f* [späˈtsōlä] 140

Brussels sprouts cavolini *m/pl.* di Bruxelles [kävōlēˈnē dē brōōkselˈ] 108

bucket secchio *m* [seˈkyō] 90

buckle fibbia *f* [fēˈbyä] 136

building edificio *m* [edēfēˈtshō] 119

bulb lampadina *f* [lämpädēˈnä] 51

bumper paraurti *m/inv.* [pärä-ōōrˈtē] 51

bungalow bungalow *m* [bōōnˈgälō] 81

buoy boa *f* [bōˈä] 75

burn *(noun)* scottatura *f* [skōtätōōˈrä] 169; *(verb)* scottare [skōtäˈre] 26; ~ **out** bruciare [brōōtshäˈre] 88

bus autobus *m* [ou'tōbōōs] 58; ~ **stop** fermata *f* dell'autobus [fermäˈtä delou'tōbōōs] 58; ~ **terminal** stazione *f* autocorriera [stätsyōˈne outōkōryeˈrä] 58

business administration amministrazione *f* contabile [ämēnēsträtsyōˈne kōntäˈbēle] 39

business school scuola f commerciale [skōō·ō'lä kōmer·tshä'le] 38
busy *(teleph.)* occupato [ōkōōpä'tō] 148
butcher macellaio m [mätshelä'yō] 36
butter burro m [bōō'rō] 98
buttocks natiche f/pl. [nä'tēke] 166
button bottone m [bōtō'ne] 136
buy comprare [kōmprä're] 126

C

cabaña cabina f [käbē'nä] 185
cabbage cavolo m [kä'vōlō] 107
cabin cabina f [käbē'nä] 73; **double ~** cabina f a due letti [käbē'nä ä dōō'e le'tē] 73; **inside ~** cabina f interna [käbē'nä ēnter'nä] 73; **outside ~** cabina f esterna [käbē'nä ester'nä] 73; **single ~** cabina f singola [käbē'nä sēn'gōlä] 73
cabinetmaker ebanista m [ebänē'stä] 36
cable cavo m [kä'vō] 51
cake torta f [tōr'tä] 113
calf polpaccio m [pōlpä'tshō] 166
call *(verb)* chiamare [kyämä're] 48; **~ (at port)** fare scalo m [fä're skä'lō] 75; **~ (noun)** telefonata f [telefōnä'tä] 148; **give s.o. a ~** telefonare a qu. [telefōnä're] 17; **long distance ~** interurbana f [ēnter-ōōrbä'nä] 148
camera macchina f fotografica [mä'kēnä fōtōgrä'fēkä] 132; **movie ~** cinepresa f [tshēnepre'sä] 132
camomile tea camomilla f [kämō-mē'lä] 160
camp (out) campeggiare [kampejä're] 94; **~ bed** lettino m da campeggio [letē'nō dä kämpe'jō] 95; **~ site** campeggio m [kämpe'jō] 95; **~ stove** fornello m [fōrne'lō] 143

camping (site) campeggio m [kämpe'jō] 81; **~ ID** tessera f di campeggio [te'serä dē kämpe'jō] 95; **~ trailer** roulotte f [rōōlōt'] 40
camshaft albero m a camme [äl'berō ä kä'me] 51
can *(verb)* potere [pōte're] 18
can opener apriscatole m [äprēskä'-tōle] 143
canal canale m [känä'le] 75
cancel annullare [änōōlä're] 69
cancellation annullamento m [änōō-lämen'tō] 69
cancer cancro m [kän'krō] 169
candle candela f [kände'lä] 143; **~ stick** portacandela m [pōrtäkände'lä] 143; candelabro m [kände-lä'brō] 124
candy dolci m/pl. [dōl'tshē] 143; dolciume m [dōltshōō'me] 113
canned goods conserve f/pl. alimentari [kōnser've älēmentä'rē] 143
cap berretto m [bere'tō] 134
capers capperi m/pl. [kä'perē] 100
capital capitale m [käpētä'le] 120
capon cappone m [käpō'ne] 105
captain capitano m [käpētä'nō] 74
captain's table tavola f di capitano [tä'vōlä dē käpētä'nō] 75
car macchina f [mä'kēnä] 40; **~ door** portiera f [pōrtye'rä] 52; **~ ferry** nave f traghetto [nä've träge'tō] 72; **~ keys** chiavi f/pl. della macchina [kyä'vē de'lä mä'kēnä] 52; **~ repair service** servizio m riparazioni auto [servē'tsyō rēpä-rätsyō'nē ou'tō] 45; **go by ~** andare in macchina [ändä're ēn mä'kē-nä] 42
carafe caraffa f [kärä'fä] 97
caraway comino m [kōmē'nō] 101
carburetor carburatore m [kärbōō-rätō're] 52; **~ jet** ugello m [ōōje'-lō] 52
card cartolina f [kärtōlē'nä] 145; **post ~** cartolina f postale [kärtō-

lē'nä pōstä'lle] 145; ~ game gioco m delle carte [jō'kō de'le kär'te] 181

cardiac infarction infarto m cardiaco [ēnfär'tō kärdē'äkō] 169

cardigan golf m [gōlf] 134

cardiovascular drug rimedio m circolatorio [rēme'dyō tshērkōlätōr'-yō] 160

carp carpa f [kär'pä] 104

carpenter carpentiere m [kärpentye're] 36

carpet tappeto m [täpe'tō] 90

carrots carote f/pl. [kärō'te] 107

cartoon cartoni m/pl. animati [kärtō'nē änēmä'tē] 179

cash contanti m/pl. [kōntän'tē] 151

cassette cassetta f [käse'tä] 143

castle castello m [käste'lō] 119; torre f [tō're] 181

castor oil olio m di ricino [ō'lyō dē rē'tshēnō] 160

catalogue catalogo m [kätä'lōgō] 130

category categoria f [kätegōrē'ä] 90

cathedral duomo m [dōō·ō'mō] 119; cattedrale f [kätedrä'le] 124

cauliflower cavolfiore m [kävōlfyō'-re] 107

cave caverna f [käver'nä] 120

caviar caviale m [kävyä'le] 102

cavities cavità f/pl. [kävētä'] 174

celery sedano m [se'dänō] 108

cemetery cimitero m [tshēmēte'rō] 120

center strip linea f di mezzo [lē'ne·ä dē med'zō] 42

centimeter centimetro m [tshentē'-metrō] 193

ceramics ceramica f [tsherä'mēkä] 143

cereal fiochi m/pl. di cereale [fyō'kē dē tshere·ä'le] 98

certainly certamente [tshertämen'-te] 20; ~ not in nessun caso [ēn nesōōn' kä'zō] 21

chain catena f [käte'nä] 52

chair sedia f [se'dyä] 90; **deck ~** sdraio m [zdrä'yō] 91

chamber music musica f da camera [mōō'zēkä dä kä'merä] 177

championship campionato m [kämpyōnä'tō] 188

change (noun) resto m [re'stō] 115; spiccioli m/pl [spē'tshōle] 151, (verb) cambiare [kämbyä're] 46; (wind) girare [jērä're] 26

chapel cappella f [käpe'lä] 124

charcoal pills pastiglie f/pl. di carbone [pästē'lye dē kärbō'ne] 160

charge (verb) caricarsi [kärēkär'sē] 52; (noun) tassa f d'imbarco [tä'sä dēmbär'kō] 70

charter plane charter m [tshär'ter] 70

chassis telaio m [telä'yō] 52

chat parlare [pärlä're] 183

chauffeur autista m [outē'stä] 41

check (noun) conto m [kōn'tō] 115; assegno m [äsen'yō] 152; (verb) controllare [kōntrōlä're] 45; mettere a punto [me'tere ä pōōn'tō] 56; ~ **room** guardaroba m [gōō·ärdärō'bä] 177

checked a quadretti (scozzese) [ä kōō·ädre'tē (skōtse'se)] 137

checkers dama f [dä'mä] 181

check-in registrare l'arrivo [rejē·strä're lärē'vō] 95

check-out registrare la partenza [rejēsträ're lä pärten'tsä] 95

cheek guancia f [gōō·än'tshä] 166

cheers! alla salute! [älä sälōō'te] 99

cheese: blue ~ gorgonzola m [gōr·gōndzō'lä] 108; **cottage (sheep's)** ~ pecorino m [pekōrē'nō] 109 **cream ~** stracchino m [sträkē'nō] 109; **farmer ~** ricotta f [rēkō'tä] 109; ~ **cake** torta f di ricotta [tōr'tä dē rēkō'tä] 109

chef cuoco m [kōō·ō'kō] 36

chemistry chimica f [kē'mēkä] 39

cheque: traveller's ~ traveller's cheque m [träv'elers tshek] 127

cherries ciliege *f/pl.* [tshēlye'je] 109

chess scacchi *m/pl.* [skä'kē] 181

chessman pezzo *m* [pe'tsō] 181

chest torace *m* [tōrä'tshe] 166

chicken pollastro *m* [pōlä'strō] 106; pollo *m* [pō'lō] 106; **broiled ~** pollo *m* alla cacciatore [pō'lō ä'lä kätshätō're] 106; **deep fried ~** pollo *m* fritto [pō'lō frē'tō] 106; **~ breast** petto *m* di pollo [pe'tō dē pō'lō] 105; **~ drumstick** coscia *f* di pollo [kō'shä de pō'lō] 105; **~ pox** varicella *f* [värētshe'lä] 169

child figlio *m*, figlia *f* [fē'lyō, fē'lyä] 162

children ragazzi *m/pl.* [rägä'tsē] 34; bambini *m/pl.* [bämbē'nē] 185; figli *m/pl.* [fē'lyē] 78

chills brividi *m/pl.* [brē'vēdē] 164

chimney camino *m* [kämē'nō] 91

chin mento *m* [men'tō] 166

china porcellana *f* [pōrtshelä'nä] 126

chip gettone *m* [jetō'ne] 181

chisel scalpello *m* [skälpe'lō] 57

chives erba *f* cipollina [er'ba tshēpōlē'nä] 101

chocolate cioccolata *f* [tshōkōlä'tä] 113

choir coro *m* [kō'rō] 124

cholera colera *m* [kōle'rä] 78

chop braciola *f* [brätshō'lä] 106

chorus coro *m* [kō'rō] 177

christening battesimo *m* [bäte'zēmo] 123

church chiesa *f* [kye'zä] 116; **Catholic ~** chiesa *f* cattolica [kye'zä kätō'lēkä] 116; **Protestant ~** chiesa *f* protestante [kye'zä prōtestän'te] 116

churchyard cimitero *m* [tshēmēte'rō] 120

cider sidro *m* [sē'drō] 111

cigar sigaro *m* [sē'gärō] 140

cigarette sigaretta *f* [sēgäre'tä] 140; **filtered ~** sigaretta *f* con filtro [sēgäre'tä kōn fēl'trō] 140; **unfiltered**

~ sigaretta *f* senza filtro [sēgäre'tä sen'tsa fēl'trō] 140

cigarillo sigarillo *m* [sēgärē'lō] 140

cinema cinema *m* [tshē'nemä] 179

cinnamon cannella *f* [käne'lä] 101

circulation circolazione *f* [tshērkōlätsyō'ne] 166

circulatory problem problema *m* di circolazione [prōble'mä dē tshērkōlätsyō'ne] 169

circus circo *m* [tshēr'kō] 182

city città *f* [tshētä'] 120; **~ hall** municipio *m* [mōōnētshē'pyō] 116

civil servant funzionario *m* statale [fōōntsyōnär'yō stätä'le] 36

claim *(luggage)* ritirare [rētērä're] 63; **~ check** scontrino *m* [skōntrē'nō] 63

clams vongole *f/pl.* [vōn'gōle] 105

class classe *f* [klä'se] 73; **first ~** prima classe *f* [prē'mä klä'se] 73; **tourist ~** classe *f* turistica [klä'se tōōrē'stēkä] 73

clay pigeon shooting tiro *m* al piattello [tē'rō äl pyäte'lō] 188

clean pulire [pōōlē're] 56

clear *(sky)* sereno [sere'nō] 26

clergyman sacerdote *m* [sätsherdō'te] 123

climate clima *m* [klē'mä] 26

climb alzarsi [ältsär'sē] 70

clock orologio *m* [ōrōlō'jō] 31; **alarm ~** sveglia *f* [zve'lyä] 143

close chiudere [kyōō'dere] 18

closet guardaroba *f* [gōō·ärdärō'bä] 91

cloth strofinaccio *m* [strōfēnä'tshō] 57; stoffa [stō'fä] 136

clothes hanger attaccapanni *m/inv.* [ätäkäpä'nē] 87; gruccia *m* [grōō'tshä] 91

cloud nuvola *f* [nōō'vōlä] 26; **~ cover** cielo *m* coperto/nuvoloso [tshe'lō kōper'tō/nōōvōlō'sō] 26

cloudburst temporale *m* [tempōrä'le] 26

cloudy nuvoloso [nōōvōlō'sō] 26

cloves chiodi *m/pl.* di garofano [kyō'dē dē gärō'fänō] 101

club club *m* [klōōb] 182

clubs *(cards)* fiori *m/pl.* [fyō'rē] 181

clutch frizione *f* [frētsyō'ne] 52; ~ **pedal** pedale *m* della frizione [pedä'le de'lä frētsyō'ne] 52

coast costa *f* [kō'stä] 75

coastal road strada *f* costiera [strä'dä kōstye'rä] 43

coat capotto *m* [käpō'tō] 134; ~ **check** scontrino *m* del guardaroba [skōntrē'nō del gōō·ärdärō'bä] 177

cobbler calzolaio *m* [kältsōlä'yō] 36

coconut noce *f* di coco [nō'tshe dē kō'kō] 110

cod (haddock) merluzzo *m* [merlōō'tsō] 105

c.o.d. contrassegno *m* [kōnträse'nyō] 149

code: area ~ prefisso *m* [prefē'sō] 147

coffee caffè *m* [käfe'] 98; **black** ~ caffè *m* nero [käfe' ne'rō] 98; **decaffeinated** ~ caffè *m* decaffeinato [käfe' dekäfe·ēnä'tō] 98; ~ **with cream** caffè *m* con panna [käfe' kōn pä'nä] 98; ~ **with sugar** caffè *m* con zucchero [käfe' kōn tsōō'ke'rō] 98

cognac cognac *m* [kō'nyäk] 112

coin moneta *f* [mōne'tä] 152; ~**s** *(teleph.)* gettoni *m/pl.* [jetō'nē] 148; ~ **changer** distributore-monete *m* [dēstrēbōōtō're-mōne'te] 149

cold *(noun)* raffreddore *m* [räfredō're] 169; *(adj.)* freddo [fre'dō] 25; ~ **cuts** affettato *m* (misto) [äfetä'tō (mē'stō)] 98, 102; ~ **wave** permanente *f* a freddo [permänen'te ä fre'dō] 158

colic colica *f* [kō'lēkä] 169

collarbone clavicola *f* [klävē'kōlä] 166

college scuola *f* [skōō·ō'lä] 38

color colore *m* [kōlō're] 127; ~ **of**

eyes colore *m* degli occhi [kōlō're de'lyē ō'kē] 79; ~ **of hair** colore *m* dei capelli [kōlō're de'ē käpe'lē] 79

colored colorato [kōlōrä'tō] 194

colorful variopinto [väryōpēn'tō] 194

comb *(noun)* pettine *m* [pe'tēne] 140; *(verb)* pettinare [petēnä're] 158

come venire [venē're] 16; ~ **in** *(trains etc.)* arrivare [ärēvä're] 61; ~ **in!** avanti! [ävän'tē] 16; si avvicini! [sē ävētshē'nē] 16

comedy commedia *f* [kōme'dyä] 177

communion comunione *f* [kōmōōnyō'ne] 124

compact portacipria *m* [pōrtätshē'prē·ä] 140

compartment scompartimento *m* [skōmpärtēmen'tō] 67

compass bussola *f* [bōō'sōlä] 138

competition gara *f* [gä'rä] 188

complaint reclamo *m* [reklä'mō] 91; **register, make a** ~ fare un reclamo [fä're ōōn reklä'mō] 23

compression compressione *f* [kōmpresyō'ne] 52

concert concerto *m* [kōntsher'tō] 123; ~ **hall** sala *f* da concerto [sä'lä dä kōntsher'tō] 177

concierge portinaio *m* [pōrtēnä'yō] 91

concussion commozione *f* cerebrale [kōmōtsyō'ne tsherebrä'le] 169

condenser condensatore *m* [kōndensätō're] 52

condolences condoglianze *f/pl.* [kōndōlyän'tse] 23

conductor bigliettaio *m* [bēlyetä'yō] 58; controllore *m* [kōntrōlō're] 67; *(music)* direttore *m* d'orchestra [dēretō're dōrke'strä] 177

confectionery pasticceria *f* [pästētsherē'ä] 113

confess confessare [kōnfesä're] 124

confession confessione f [kōnfes-yō'ne] 124

confiscate confiscare [kōnfēskä're] 154

congratulations! auguri! [ougōō'rē] 22

conjunctivitis congiuntivite f [kōn-jōōntēvē'te] 165

connect *(teleph.)* mettere in comunicazione [me'tere ēn kōmōōnēkätsyō'ne] 148

connecting rod biella f [bye'lä] 52; ~ **bearing** supporti m/pl. della biella [sōōpōr'tē de'lä bye'lä] 52

connection coincidenza f [kō-ēntshēden'tsä] 61

constipate costipare [kōstēpä're] 163

constipation costipazione f [kōstēpätsyō'ne] 169

consulate consolato m [kōnsōlä'tō] 78

contact contatto m [kōntä'tō] 52; ~ **lenses** lenti f/pl. a contatto [len'tē ä kōntä'tō] 138

contraceptive pills pillole f/pl. anticoncezionali [pē'lōle äntēkōntshetsyōnä'lē] 160

convalescent home casa f di convalescenza [kä'sä de kōnväleshen'tsä] 175

convent convento m [kōnven'tō] 124

cook cucinare [kōōtshēnä're] 95

cookies biscotti m/pl. [bēskō'tē] 113

cordial cordiale [kōrdyä'le] 12

cordially yours cordiali saluti m/pl. [kōrdyä'lē sälōō'tē] 13

corduroy velluto m a coste [velōō'tō ä kō'ste] 136

corkscrew cavatappi m [kävätä'pē] 143

corn plaster callifugo m [kälē'fōōgō] 160

corridor corridoio m [kōrēdō'yō] 91

corset busto m [bōō'stō] 134

cosmetic salon salone f di bellezza [sälō'ne dē bele'tsä] 128

cost costare [kōstä're] 18

costumes costumi m/pl. [kōstōō'mē] 177

cotton cotone m [kōtō'ne] 136; ~ **swabs** bacchette f/pl. di ovatta [bäke'te dē ōvä'tä] 160

couchette car, couchette sleeper carozza f cuccette [kärō'tsä kōōtshe'te] 60, 64

cough *(verb)* tossire [tōsē're] 165; *(noun)* tosse f [tō'se] 169; ~ **syrup** sciroppo m per la tosse [shērō'pō per lä tō'se] 160

counter sportello m [spōrte'lō] 149

country fair sagra f popolare [sä'grä pōpōlä're] 182

country road strada f di campagna [strä'dä dē kämpä'nyä] 43

countryside paesaggio m [pä·ezäd'jō] 120

course rotta f [rō'tä] 75; **of ~** naturalmente [nätōōrälmen'te] 21

court tribunale m [trēbōōnä'le] 154

courthouse palazzo m di giustizia [pälä'tsō dē jōōstē'tsyä] 120

cousin *(male)* cugino m [kōōjē'nō] 35; *(female)* cugina f [kōōjē'nä] 35

covered market mercato m coperto [merkä'to kōper'tō] 120

coxwain timoniere m [tēmōnye're] 189

crab gambero m [gäm'berō] 102; granchio m [grän'kyō] 105

cramp crampo m [kräm'pō] 169

cranberries mirtilli m/pl. [mērtē'lē] 110

crankshaft manopola f [mänō'pōlä] 52

crawfish gamberi m/pl. [gäm'berē] 102

crayons matite f/pl. colorate [mätē'te kōlōrä'te] 138

cream crema f [kre'mä] 113; **face ~** crema f per il viso [kre'mä per ēl

vē'zo] 141; **whipped** ~ panna f
montata [pä'nä mõntä'tä] 114

credit credito m [kre'dētõ] 152; ~
card carta f di credito [kär'tä dē
kre'dētõ] 127; **letter of** ~ lettera f
di credito [le'terä dē kre'dētõ]
152

crew equipaggio m [ekōō·ēpä'jõ] 70

crib letto m da bambino [le'tõ dä
bämbē'nõ] 83; lettino m per bambini [letē'nõ per bämbē'nē] 90

crime delitto m [delē'tõ] 154

criminal reato m [re·ä'tõ] 154; ~ **in-
vestigation division** divisione f in-
vestigativa crimini [dēvēzyõ'ne
ēnvestēgätē'vä krē'mēnē] 154

croissant brioche f [brē·ōsh'] 98

cross croce f [krõ'tshe] 124; ~ **road**
strada f trasversale [strä'dä träz-
versä'le] 43

crossing traversata f [träversä'tä] 72

crown corona f [kōrõ'nä] 174

crucifix crocefisso m [krõtshefē'sõ]
124

cruet stand oliera f [ōlye'rä] 97

cruise crociera f [krõtshe'rä] 75

crystal vetro m [ve'trõ] 143

cucumber cetriolo m [tshetrē·õ'lõ]
108

cufflinks gemelli m/pl. da camicia
[jeme'lē dä kämē'tshä] 133

cup tazza f [tä'tsä] 96

cure cura f [kōō'rä] 75; ~ **tax** tassa f
di soggiorno [tä'sä dē sõjõr'nõ]
175; ~ **vacation** soggiorno m di
cura [sõjõr'nõ dē kōō'rä] 175; **rest**
~ cura f di riposo [kōō'rä dē rē-
põ'sõ] 175

curler bigodino m [bēgōdē'nõ] 141

curls riccioli m/pl. [rē'tshōlē] 158

currency valuta f [välōō'tä] 152; **foreign** ~ valuta f straniera [välōō'tä
stränye'rä] 152

current: alternating ~ corrente f al-
ternata [kõren'te älternä'tä] 90

curtain tenda f [ten'dä] 91; sipario m
[sēpär'yõ] 177; ~ **time** inizio m

[ēnē'tsyõ] 177; **final** ~ fine f
[fē'ne] 178

curve curva f [kōōr'vä] 42

cuspid dente m canino [den'te kä-
nē'nõ] 174

custody detenzione f [detentsyõ'ne]
154; **pre-trial** ~ detenzione f pre-
ventiva [detentsyõ'ne preventē'-
vä] 154

customs dogana f [dõgä'nä] 80; ~
control controllo m doganale
[kõntrõ'lõ dõgänä'le] 80; ~ **declaration** dichiarazione f (doganale) [dēkyärätsyõ'ne (dõgänä'le)]
80, 146; ~ **office** ufficio m doganale [ōōfē'tshõ dõgänä'le] 80; ~
officer impiegato m doganale
[ēmpyegä'tõ dõgänä'le] 80

cut (verb) accorciare [äkõrtshä're]
155; tagliare [tälyä're] 158; (cards)
alzare [ältsä're] 181; (noun) ferita
f da taglio [ferē'tä dä tä'lyõ] 169

cutlery posate f/pl. [põsä'te] 97

cutlet costoletta f (cotoletto m) [kõ-
stõle'tä (kõtõle'tõ)] 106

cylinder cilindro m [tshēlēn'drõ] 52;
~ **head** testata f del cilindro
[testä'tä del tshēlēn'drõ] 52

Canadian dollars dollari m/pl. cana-
desi [dõ'lärē känäde'sē] 152

Catholic cattolico m [kätõ'lēkõ] 124

Christ cristo m [krē'stõ] 124

Christmas Natale m [nätä'le] 33;
Merry ~ Buon Natale! [bōō·õn'
nätä'le] 23

D

daily ogni giorno [õ'nye jõr'nõ] 31;
~ **rate** corso m del giorno [kõr'sõ
del jõr'nõ] 152

dairy latteria f [läterē'ä] 128

damage (verb) danneggiare [däne-
jä're] 49; (noun) danno m [dä'nõ]
49

dance *(verb)* ballare [bälä're] 183; *(noun)* ballo *m* [bäl'lō] 183; **~ hall** sala *f* da ballo [sä'lä dä bäl'lō] 183

dancer ballerino *m* [bälerē'nō] 177

dandruff forfora *f* [fōr'fōrä] 158

danger pericolo *m* [perē'kōlō'] 49

dangerous pericoloso [perēkōlō'sō] 185

dark scuro [skōō'rō] 127

darn rammendare [rämmendä're] 137

darning cotton filo *m* da rammendo [fē'lō dä rämen'dō] 136

date of birth data *f* di nascita [dä'tä dē nä'shētä] 79

daughter figlia *f* [fēl'yä] 14

daughter-in-law nuora *f* [nōō·ō'rä] 35

day giorno *m* [jōr'nō] 31; **New Year's ~** Primo *m* dell'anno [prē'mō delä'nō] 33; **~ room** sala *f* comune [sä'lä kōmōō'ne] 95

dead-end street vicolo *m* cieco [vē'kōlō tshe'kō] 120

deal dare [dä're] 181

dealership garage officina *f* concessionaria [ōfētshē'nä kōntshesyō-när'yä] 49

decanter caraffa *f* [kärä'fä] 97

December dicembre *m* [dētshem'-bre] 33

decimeter decimetro *m* [detshē'me-trō] 193

deck coperta *f* [kōper'tä] 75; **boat ~** ponte *m* delle scialuppe [pōn'te de'lle shälōō'pe] 75; **fore ~** ponte *m* di prua [pōn'te dē prōō·'ä] 76; **main ~** ponte *m* principale [pōn'te prēntshēpä'le] 76; **poop ~** ponte *m* di poppa [pōn'te dē pō'pä] 76; **promenade ~** ponte *m* di passeggio [pōn'te dē päse'jō] 76; **saloon ~** ponte *m* coperto [pō'nte kōper'tō] 76; **sun ~** solario *m* [sō-lär'yō] 76; **upper ~** ponte *m* superiore [pōn'te sōōperyō're] 76; **~ chair** sdraio *m* di coperta [zdrä'yō

dē kōper'tä] 76; sedia *f* a sdraio [se'dyä ä zdrä'yō] 185

declare dichiarare [dēkyärä're] 80

deep profondo [prōfōn'dō] 185

defeat sconfitta *f* [skōnfē'tä] 188

delicate stew stufato *m* [stōōfä'tō] 107

delicious squisito [skōō·ēzē'tō] 99

delighted: I'm ~ mi fa molto piacere [mē fä mōl'tō pyätshe're] 12

delivery truck furgoncino *m* [fōōr-gōntshē'nō] 40

denomination: religious ~ religione *f* [relējō'ne] 124

dental clinic clinica *f* odontoiatrica [klē'nēkä ōdōntōyä'trēkä] 174

dentist dentista *m* [dentē'stä] 173

dentistry odontologia *f* [ōdōntōlō-jē'ä] 39

denture protesi *f* [prō'tezē] 173

deodorant deodorante *m* [de·ōdō-rän'te] 141

depart partire [pärtē're] 67

departure partenza *f* [pärten'tsä] 67

deposit *(noun)* acconto *m* [äkōn'tō] 91; *(verb)* versare [versä're] 152; dare come cauzione [dä're kō'me koutsyō'ne] 41

dermatologist dermatologo *m* [der-mätō'lōgō] 162

destination destinazione *f* [destē-nätsyō'ne] 70

detergent detersivo *m* [detersē'vō] 143; **dishwashing ~** detersivo *m* per piatti [deterse'vō per pyä'tē] 143

detour deviazione *f* [devyätsyō'ne] 42

develop sviluppare [zvēlōōpä're] 131

dew rugiada *f* [rōōjä'dä] 26

diabetes diabete *m* [dyäbe'te] 170

diabetic diabetico [dyäbe'tēkō] 164

diagnosis diagnosi *f* [dē·a'nyōzē] 172

dial fare il numero [fä're ēl nōō'me-rō] 149

diamond diamante *m* [dē·ämän'te] 133

diamonds *(cards)* quadri *m/pl.* [kōō·ä'drē] 181

diaphoretic sudorifero *m* [sōōdōrē'ferō] 160

diaphragm diaframma *m* [dyäfrä'mä] 132

diarrhea diarrea *f* [dyäre'ä] 163

dice dado *m* [dä'dō] 182; **shoot ~** giocare ai dadi [jōkä're ä'ē dä'dē] 182

dictionary dizionario *m* [dētsyōnär'yō] 130

die morire [mōrē're] 119

diesel diesel *m* [dē'zel] 45; **~ motor** motore *m* a diesel [mōtō're ä dē'zel] 54; **~ nozzle** polverizzatore *m* [pōl'verēdzätō're] 52

diet dieta *f* [dye'tä] 165

differential differenziale *m* [deferentsyä'le] 52

digestion digestione *f* [dējestyō'ne] 166

digestive tonic tonico *m* digestivo [tō'nēkō dējestē'vō] 160

dill aneto *m* [äne'tō] 101

dining car vagone *m* ristorante [vägō'ne rēstōrän'te] 60

dining room sala *f* da pranzo [sä'lä dä prän'dzō] 74

dinner pranzo *m* [prän'dzō] 91

dip stick bacchetta *f* misura-olio [bäke'tä mēzōō'rä-ōl'yō] 52

diphtheria difterite *f* [dēfterē'te] 170

dimmed headlights luce *f* anabbagliante [lōō'tshe änäbälyän'te] 53

direct diretto [dēre'tō] 68; **~ dial** chiamare in teleselezione [kyämä're ēn teleseletsyō'ne] 147; **~ dialing** teleselezione *f* [teleseletsyō'ne] 149

direction direzione *f* [dēretsyō'ne] 58; **~ sign** indicatore *m* stradale [ēndēkätō're strädä'le] 42

disc disco *m* intervertebrale [dē'skō ēntervertebrä'le] 166; **~ brake**

freno *m* a disco [fre'nō ä dē'skō] 51

discharge dimettere *m* dall'ospedale [dēme'tere dälospedä'le] 172

discotheque discoteca *f* [dēskōte'kä] 180

discount riduzione *f* [rēdōōtsyō'ne] 176

disease malattia *f* [mälätē'ä] 170; **contagious ~** malattia *f* infettiva [mälätē'ä ēnfetē'vä] 170

disembark sbarcare [zbärkä're] 76

disengage separare [sepärä're] 53

dish piatto *m* [pyä'tō] 99

dishes stoviglie *f/pl.* [stōvē'lye] 95

disinfectant disinfettante *m* [dēsēnfetän'te] 160

dislocation lussazione *f* [lōōsätsyō'ne] 170

distilled water acqua *f* distillata [ä'kōō·ä dēstēlä'tä] 45

distributor spinterogeno *m* [spēnterō'jenō] 52

district quartiere *m* [kōō·ärtye're] 120

diuretic diuretico *m* [dyōōre'tēkō] 160

dive *(verb)* tuffarsi [tōōfär'sē] 186; *(noun)* tuffo *m* [tōō'fō] 190

diving board trampolino *m* [trämpōlē'nō] 186

divorced divorziato [dēvōrtsyä'tō] 79

dizziness capogiro *m* [käpōje'rō] 170

do fare [fä're] 18

dock approdare [äprōdä're] 76; far scalo [fär skä'lō] 72

doctor dottore *m* [dōtō're] 36; medico *m* [me'dēkō] 48; **~** *(in names)* Dottore [dōtō're] 13; Dottoressa [dōtōre'sä] 13

doctor's office ambulatorio *m* [ämbōōlätōr'yō] 163

documentary documentario *m* [dōkōōmentär'yō] 179

doll bambola *f* [bäm'bōlä] 143

dome cupola *f* [kōō'pōlä] 124

door porta *f* [pōr'tä] 91; **~ handle** maniglia *f* della porta [mänē'lyä de'lä pōr'tä] 91; **~ lock** serratura *f* della portiera [serätōō'rä de'lä pōrtye'rä] 52

dormitory dormitorio *m* [dōrmētōr'yō] 95

doubles *(tennis)* doppio *m* [dō'pyō] 190

downtown area sobborgo *m* [sōbōr'gō] 121

dozen dozzina *f* [dōdzē'nä] 193

drain tubo *m* di scarico [tōō'bō dē skä'rēkō] 88

drama dramma *m* [drä'mä] 177

drapery tenda *f* [ten'dä] 91

draw *(noun) (sports)* pareggio *m* [päre'jō] 188

drawer cassetto *m* [käse'tō] 91

dress vestito *m* [vestē'tō] 134; abito *m* [ä'bētō] 134

dressing gown vestaglia *f* [vestä'lyä] 134

dressmaker sarta *f* [sär'tä] 36

dress-shield sottascelle *f/pl.* [sōtäshe'le] 136

drier casco *m* [käs'kō] 156

drill trapano *m* [trä'pänō] 57

drink *(verb)* bere [be're] 165

drinking water acqua *f* potabile [ä'kōō·ä pōtä'bēle] 65

drip-dry che non si deve stirare [ke nōn sē de've stērä're] 135

drive andare [ändä're] 42; **~ shaft** albero *m* motore [äl'berō mōtō're] 52

drive-in movie cinema *m* all'aperto [tshē'nemä äläper'tō] 179

driver autista *m* [outē'stä] 36

driver's license patente *f* [päten'te] 42

driver's seat sedile *m* dell'autista [sedē'le deloutē'stä] 55

driveway entrata *f* [enträ'tä] 42

drop *(wind)* calmarsi [kälmär'sē] 26; **~ by** ritornare [rētōrnä're] 15

drops gocce *f/pl.* [gō'tshe] 160; **ear ~** gocce *f/pl.* per l'orecchio [gō'tshe per lōre'kyō] 160; **eye ~** gocce *f/pl.* per gli occhi [gō'tshe per lyē ō'kē] 160

druggist *(pharmacist)* farmacista *m* [färmätshē'stä], *(drugstore owner)* droghiere *m* [drōgē·e're] 36

drugs droghe *f/pl.* [drō'ge] 154

dry asciugare [äshōōgä're] 92; **~ cleaner's** tintoria *f* [tēntōrē'ä] 128; **~ goods** mercerie *f/pl.* [mertsherē'e] 136

dubbed doppiato [dōpyä'tō] 179

dubbing doppiaggio *m* [dōpyä'jō] 179

duck anitra *f* [ä'nēträ] 105; **wild ~** anitra *f* selvatica [ä'nēträ selvä'tēkä] 105

duet duetto *m* [dōō·e'tō] 177

dull sordo [sōr'dō] 163

dumpling: tiny ~s gnocchi *m/pl.* [nyō'kē] 104

during durante [dōōrän'te] 32

dusk crepuscolo *m* [krepōō'skōlō] 26

duty tassa *f* [tä'sä] 80; **~ -free** esente da tasse [ezen'te dä tä'se] 80; **~ -free shop** duty-shop *m* [dyōō'tēshōp] 69; **export ~** tassa *f* d'esportazione [tä'sä despōrtätsyō'ne] 80; **import ~** tassa *f* d'importazione [tä'sä dēmpōrtätsyō'ne] 80

dye *(verb)* tingere [tēn'jere] 155; *(noun)* tintura *f* [tēntōō'rä] 141

dynamo dinamo *m* [dē'nämō] 52

dysentery dissenteria *f* [dēsenterē'ä] 170

E

ear orecchio *m* [ōre'kyō] 166; **~ clips** orecchini *m/pl.* a clips [ōrekē'nē ä klēps] 133

earache dolore *m* agli orecchi [dōlō're ä'lyē ore'kē] 164

eardrum timpano *m* [tēm'pänō] 166
earlier prima [prē'mä] 32
early presto [pre'stō] 31
earrings orecchini *m/pl.* [ōrekē'nē] 133
Easter Pasqua *f* [päs'kōō·ä] 33
economics economia *f* [ekōnōmē'ä] 39
economy class classe *f* turistica [klä'se tōōrē'stēkä] 69
education pedagogia *f* [pedägōjē'ä] 39
eel anguilla *f* [ängōō·ē'lä] 104; **smoked** ~ anguilla *f* affumicata [ängōō·ē'lä äfōōmēkä'tä] 102
egg uovo *m* [ōō·ō'vō] 98; **hardboiled** ~ uovo *m* sodo [ōō·ō'vō sō'dō] 98; **soft-boiled** ~ uovo *m* alla coque [ōō·ō'vō ä'lä kōk] 98; **fried** ~s uova fritte [ōō·ō'vä frē'te] 98; **scrambled** ~s uova strapazzate [ōō·ō'vä sträpätsä'te] 98; ~ **cup** portauova *m* [pōrtä·ōō·ō'vä] 97
eight otto [ō'tō] 28
eighty ottanta [ōtän'tä] 28
elastic elastico *m* [elä'stēkō] 136; ~ **stocking** calza *f* elastica [käl'tsa elä'stēkä] 160
elbow gomito *m* [gō'mētō] 166
electric shaver rasoio *m* elettrico [räzō'yō ele'trēkō] 141
electrical connection presa *f* di corrente elettrica [pre'sä dē kōren'te ele'trēkä] 94
electrician elettricista *m* [eletrē-tshē'stä] 36
elevator ascensore *m* [äshensō're] 91
embassy ambasciata *f* [ämbäshä'tä] 121
emerald smeraldo *m* [zmeräl'dō] 133
emergency: ~ **brake** freno *m* d'allarme [frē'no dälär'me] 66; ~ **chute** scivolo *m* d'emergenza [shē'vōlō demerjen'tsä] 70; ~ **exit**

uscita *f* d'emergenza [ōōshē'tä demerjen'tsä] 70; ~ **landing** atterraggio *m* di fortuna [äterä'jō dē fōrtōō'nä] 70
emetic emetico *m* [eme'tēkō] 160
empty vuoto [vōō·ō'tō] 159
endive indivia *f* [ēndē'vyä] 107
engine macchina *f* [mä'kēnä] 71; ~ *(railroad)* locomotiva *f* [lōkōmō-tē'vä] 67
engineer *(scientific)* ingegnere *m* [ēnjenye're] 36; *(railroad)* macchinista *m* [mäkēnē'stä] 36
English inglese [ēn·gle'se] 24; ~ *(subject)* anglistica *f* [änglē'stēkä] 39
enjoy oneself divertirsi [dēvertēr'sē] 184
I enjoyed myself mi è piaciuto [mē e pyätshōō'tō] 17
enlargement ingrandimento *m* [ēn-grändēmen'tō] 131
enough: not ~ troppo poco [trō'pō pō'kō] 127
enter entrare [enträ're] 79; *(name)* registrare [rejēsträ're] 78
entrance entrata *f* [enträ'tä] 67
entry entrata *f* [enträ'tä] 79; ~ **visa** visto *m* d'entrata [vē'stō denträ'tä] 79
envelope busta *f* [bōō'stä] 138
environs dintorni *m/pl.* [dēntōr'nē] 121
eraser gomma *f* [gō'mä] 138
essential: the ~s riparazioni *f/pl.* più urgenti [rēpärätsyō'nē pyōō ōōrgen'tē] 50
Eve: New Year's ~ Capodanno *m* [käpōdä'nō] 33
evening serata *f* [serä'tä] 16; sera *f* [se'rä] 155; **good** ~! buonasera! [bōō·ōnäse'rä] 12; **in the** ~ di sera [dē se'rä] 31; **this** ~ stasera [stäse'rä] 31; questa sera [kōō·e'stä se'rä] 44
every ogni [ō'nye] 32; ~ **day** ogni giorno [ō'nye jōr'nō] 31

everything tutto [tōō'tō] 83

exact esatto [ezä'tō] 30; **~ly** in punto [ēn pōōn'tō] 30

examination analisi f [änä'lēzē] 172

examine visitare [vēzētä're] 172

excavations scavi m/pl. [skä've] 121

excess baggage sovrappeso m [sōvräpe'sō] 68; bagaglio m in eccedenza [bägä'lyō ēn etsheden'tsä] 71

exchange *(verb)* cambiare [kämbyä're] 127; *(noun):* **money ~** cambio m [käm'byō] 152; **rate of ~** corso m del cambio [kōr'sō del käm'byō] 152

excursion escursione f [eskōōrsyō'ne] 72; gita f [jē'tä] 121; **~ program** programma m d'escursione [prōgrä'mä deskōōrsyō'ne] 76; **land ~s** escursioni f/pl. a terra [eskōōrsyō'nē ä te'rä] 72

excuse ~ me (mi) scusi [(mē) skōō'zē] 20, 22

exhaust scappamento m [skäpämen'tō] 52

exhibition mostra f [mō'strä] 119; esposizione f [espōzētsyō'ne] 121

exit uscita f [ōōshē'tä] 42; **~ visa** visto m d'uscita [vē'stō dōōshē'tä] 79

expect aspettare [äspetä're] 85; **~ a baby** essere incinta [e'sere ēntshēn'tä] 164

expensive caro [kä'rō] 127

exposure posa f [pō'zä] 132; **~ meter** esposimetro m [espōzē'metrō] 132

express train direttissimo m [dēretē'sēmō] 60

extend prolungare [prōlōōngä're] 79

extension cord prolunga f [prōlōōn'gä] 91

external esterno [ester'nō] 159

extract estrarre [esträ're] 174

eye occhio m [ō'kyō] 166; **~ doctor** oculista m [ōkōōlē'stä] 162; **~ inflammation** infiammazione f all'

occhio [ēnfyämätsyō'ne älō'kyō] 170; **~ shadow** ombretto m [ōmbre'tō] 141

eyeball globo m oculare [glō'bō ōkōōlä're] 166

eyebrow sopracciglio m (pl. le -a) [sōprätshēl'yō] 156; **~ pencil** matita f per le sopracciglia [mätē'tä per le sōprätshēl'yä] 141

eyeglass case astuccio m da occhiali [ästōō'tshō dä ōkyä'lē] 138

eyelid palpebra f [päl'pebrä] 166

eyeliner eye-liner m [ä·yelē'ner] 141

F

fabric tessuto m [tesōō'tō] 136

face viso m [vē'zō] 156; *(clock)* quadrante m [kōō·ädrän'te] 143; **~ massage** massaggio m al viso [mäsä'jō äl vē'zō] 156

facial mask maschera f per il viso [mä'skerä per ēl vē'zō] 156

fall *(verb)* cadere [käde're] 164; *(barometer)* scendere [shen'dere] 25; *(noun) (season)* autunno m [outōō'nō] 33

falling rocks caduta f massi [kädōō'tä mä'sē] 42

false tooth protesi f [prō'tezē] 174

family famiglia f [fämē'lyä] 35

fan ventilatore m [ventēlätō're] 53; **~ belt** cinghia f [tshēn'gē·ä] 53

far lontano [lōntä'nō] 58; **as ~ as** fino a [fē'nō ä] 40; **how ~** che distanza [ke dēstän'tsä] 40

fare tariffa f [tärē'fä] 62; **~ discount** riduzione f [rēdōōtsyō'ne] 67; **excess ~** supplemento m [sōōplemen'tō] 66

farewell dinner pranzo m d'addio [prän'dzō dädē'ō] 76

farmer agricoltore m [ägrēkōltō're] 36

farmhouse cascina f [käshē'nä] 121

far-sighted presbite [prez'bēte] 138

fashion boutique boutique *f* [bōō-tēk'] 128

fashion show sfilata *f* di moda [sfē-lä'tä dē mō'dä] 180

fast veloce [velō'tshe] 42, ~ **train** diretto *m* [dēre'tō] 60

fasten allacciare [älätshä're] 70

fat, fatty grasso [grä'sō] 100, 115

father padre *m* [pä'dre] 35

father-in-law suocero *m* [sōō·ō'-tsherō] 35

faucet rubinetto *m* [rōōbēne'tō] 88

fault colpa *f* [kōl'pä] 49

February febbraio *m* [febrä'yō] 33

fee: rental ~ noleggio *m* [nōle'jō] 95; **usage** ~ tassa *f* per l'uso [tä'sä per lōō'zō] 95

feel sentire [sentē're] 12

fencing scherma *f* [sker'mä] 188

fender parafango *m* [päräfän'gō] 53

ferry traghetto *m* [träge'tō] 72; **car** ~ nave *f* traghetto [nä've träge'tō] 76; **train** ~ traghetto *m* ferroviario [träge'tō ferövyär'yō] 76

fetch andare a prendere [ändä're ä pren'dere] 20

fever febbre *f* [fe'bre] 170; ~ **cure** preparato *m* contro la febbre [prepärä'tō kōn'trō lä fe'bre] 160

fiancé fidanzato *m* [fēdäntsä'tō] 14

fiancée fidanzata *f* [fēdäntsä'tä] 14

fibre: synthetic ~ fibra *f* sintetica [fē'brä sēnte'tēkä] 137

fight (*sports*) gara *f* [gä'rä] 187

figs fichi *m/pl.* [fē'kē] 109

figure skating pattinaggio *m* artistico su ghiaccio [pätēnä'jō ärtē'stēkō sōō gyä'tshō] 88

file (*verb*) limare [lēmä're] 156; (*noun*) lima *f* [lē'mä] 57

filet filetto *m* [fēle'tō] 106

fill otturare [ōtōōrä're] 174; ~ **in, up** riempire [rē·empē're] 45

filling otturazione *f* [ōtōōrätsyō'ne] 173; **temporary** ~ otturazione *f* provvisoria [ōtōōrätsyō'ne prōvē-zōr'yä] 174

film (*noun*) pellicola *f* [pelē'kōlä] 131; rotolo *m* [rō'tōlō] 131; film *m* [fēlm] 179; (*verb*) filmare [fēlmä're] 132; **cartridge** ~ pellicola *f* a caricatore [pelē'kōlä ä kärēkätō're] 131; **color** ~ pellicola *f* a colori [pelē'kōlä ä kōlō'rē] 132; **color negative** ~ rotolo *m* di foto a colori [rō'tōlō dē fō'tō ä kōlō'rē] 132; **daylight color** ~ rotolo *m* a colori per diapositive [rō'tōlō ä kōlō'rē per dē·äpōzētē've] 132; **educational** ~ film *m* educativo [fēlm edōōkätē'vō] 179; **feature** ~ lungometraggio *m* [lōōngō-meträ'jō] 179; **reversal** ~ pellicola *f* invertibile [pelē'kōlä ēnvertē'bēle] 132; **roll** ~ pellicola *f* in rotolo [pelē'kōlä ēn rō'tōlō] 132; **sixteen millimeter color** ~ pellicola *f* a colori da sedici millimetri [pelē'kōlä ä kōlō'rē dä se'dētshē mēlē'me-trē] 131; **super eight color** ~ pellicola *f* a colori super otto [pelē'kōlä ä kōlō'rē sōō'per ō'tō] 131; **twenty exposure** ~ pellicola *f* da venti foto [pelē'kōlä dä ven'tē fō'tō] 131; ~ **actor** attore *m* cinematografico [ätō're tschēnemätō-grä'fēkō] 179; ~ **festival** festival *m* cinematografico [fe'stēväl tschē-nemätōgrä'fēkō] 179; ~ **screening** proiezione *f* [prōyetsyō'ne] 179

filter: yellow ~ filtro *m* giallo [fēl'trō jä'lō] 132

find trovare [trōvä're] 19

fine bene [be'ne] 12; ~ **weather** bel tempo *m* [bel tem'pō] 25

finger dito *m* [dē'tō] 166; **index** ~ indice *m* [ēn'dētshe] 167; **middle** ~ medio *m* [me'dyō] 167; **ring** ~ anulare *m* [änōōlä're] 167

fire: ~ **department** vigili *m/pl.* del fuoco [vē'jēlē del fōō·ō'kō] 49; ~ **extinguisher** estintore *m* [estēntō're] 53

replace camino m [kämē'nō] 91

rst primo [prē'mō] 29; ~ **class** (di) prima classe f [(dē) prē'mä clä'se] 62, 64

rst-aid kit cassetta f pronto soccorso [käse'tä prōn'tō sōkōr'sō] 161

rst-aid station (posto m di) pronto soccorso m [(pō'stō dē) prōn'tō sōkōr'sō] 49, 60

sh pesce m [pe'she] 105; ~ **market** pescheria f [peskerē'ä] 128

sherman pescatore m [peskätō're] 36

shing pesca f [pes'kä] 188; **go ~** andare a pescare [ändä're ä pes-kä're] 188; ~ **license** licenza f di pesca [lētshen'tsä dē pes'kä] 188; ~ **rod** canna f da pesca [kä'nä dä pes'kä] 188; ~ **trawler** barca f da pesca [bär'kä dä pes'kä] 75

t (verb) andare bene [ändä're be'ne] 133; (noun) attacco m [ätä'kō] 170

ve cinque [tshēn'kōō·e] 28

x riparare [rēpärä're] 50

annel flanella f [fläne'lä] 137

ash: ~ **bulb** lampadina-flash f [lämpädē'nä-fläsh] 132; ~ **cube** cubo-flash m [kōō'bō-fläsh] 132

ashlight pila f [pē'lä] 143

at basso [bä'sō] 139

atulence flatulenza f [flätōōlen'tsä] 170

ight volo m [vō'lō] 71; ~ **attendant** assistente m di volo [äsēsten'te dē vō'lō] 71

lint pietrina f per accendisigari [pyetrē'nä per ätshendēsē'gäre] 140

oor pavimento m [pävēmen'tō] 91; piano m [pyä'nō] 82; **third ~** secondo piano m [sekōn'dō pyä'nō] 82

lower fiore m [fyō're] 130; ~ **pot** pianta f [pyän'tä] 130

u influenza f [ēnflōō·en'tsä] 170

fly volare [vōlä're] 71

flying time tempo m di volo [tem'pō dē vō'lō] 71

FM onda f ultracorta [ōn'dä ōōlträ-kōr'tä] 182

fog nebbia f [ne'byä] 26

follow perseguire [persegōō·ē're] 154

font fonte m battesimale [fōn'te bä-tezēmä'le] 124

food vitto m [vē'tō] 81; **diet ~** cibi m/pl. dietetici [tshē'bē dyete'tētshē] 96; **vegetarian ~** cibi m/pl. vegetariani [tshē'bē vejetäryä'nē] 96; ~ **poisoning** avvelenamento m da cibo [ävelenämen'tō dä tshē'bō] 170

foot piede m [pye'de] 167; **by ~** a piedi [ä pye'dē] 116; ~ **brake** freno m a pedale [fre'nō ä pedä'le] 51

footpath sentiero m [sentye'rō] 42

for per [per] 20; (time) da [dä] 32

forehead fronte f [frōn'te] 167

forester guardia f forestale [gōō·är'-dyä fōrestä'le] 36

fork forchetta f [fōrke'tä] 97

form modulo m [mō'dōōlō] 78

fortress fortezza f [fōrtet'sä] 119

forward (noun) (sports) attaccante m [ätäkän'te] 189

fountain fontana f [fōntä'nä] 121

four quattro [kōō·ä'trō] 28

fracture frattura f [frätōō'rä] 170

frame (opt.) montatura f [mōntä-tōō'rä] 138

free libero [lē'berō] 44; ~ **kick** calcio m di punizione [käl'tshō dē pōōnētsyō'ne] 189; ~ **style** stile m libero [stē'le lē'berō] 188

freeze: it's freezing gela [je'lä] 27

freighter nave f mercantile [nä've merkäntē'le] 77

French francese [fräntshe'se] 24

fresco affresco m [äfres'kō] 124

fresh fresco [fre'skō] 100

Friday venerdì m [venerdē'] 33;

Good ~ Venerdì *m* Santo [vener-dēˈ sänˈtō] 33

fried fritto [frēˈtō] 100; **deep** ~ fritto bene [frēˈtō beˈne] 100

friend *(male)* amico *m* [ämēˈkō] 14; *(female)* amica *f* [ämēˈkä] 14

from da [dä] 64; ~ ...**to** da...a [dä...ä] 30

front *(train)* testa *f* [teˈstä] 66; **up** ~ in testa [ēn teˈstä] 65; ~ **door** porta *f* dˈentrata [pōrˈtä denträˈtä] 91; ~ **seat** sedile *m* anteriore [sedēˈle änteryōˈre] 55; ~ **passenger seat** sedile *m* del passeggero [sedēˈle del päseˈjerō] 55; ~ **wheel** ruota *f* davanti [rōō·ōˈtä dävänˈtē] 47

frontal sinus seno *m* frontale [seˈnō frōntäˈle] 167

frost gelo *m* [jeˈlō] 27

frostbite congelamento *m* [kōnje-lämenˈtō] 170

frozen dessert semifreddo *m* [se-mēfreˈdō] 109

fruit frutto *m* [frōōˈtō] 109; ~ **market** mercato *m* fruttaverdura [merkäˈtō frōōtäverdōōˈrä] 128; ~ **salad** macedonia *f* [mätshedōˈnyä] 109

fryer pollo *m* arrosto [pōˈlō ärōˈstō] 106

fuel: ~ **injector** iniettore-combustibile [ēnyetōˈre-kōmbōōstēˈbēle] 53; ~ **lines** conduttura *f* della benzina [kōndōōtōōˈrä deˈlä bendzēˈnä] 53; ~ **pump** pompa *f* della benzina [pōmˈpä deˈlä bendzēˈnä] 53

full coverage insurance assicurazione *f* integrale [äsēkōōrätsyōˈne ēntegräˈle] 41

fullback *(sports)* terzino *m* [tertsēˈnō] 189

fun divertimento *m* [dēvertēmenˈtō] 20

funnel imbuto *m* [ēmbōōˈtō] 57

fur coat pelliccia [pelēˈtshä] 134

fur jacket giacchetta *f* di pelliccia [jäkeˈtä dē pelēˈtshä] 134

furrier pellicceria *f* [pelētsherēˈ] 128

fuse fusibile *m* [fōōzēˈbēle] 53

G

gall bladder cistifellea *f* [tshēstēfe-leˈä] 167

gall stones calcoli *m/pl.* biliari [käˈkōlē bēlyäˈrē] 170

gallery galleria *f* [gälerēˈä] 119

gallon gallone *m* [gälōˈne] 193

gambling: ~ **casino** casinò *m* [ka-sēnō'] 182; ~ **game** giocco d'azzardo [jōˈkō dädzärˈdō] 182

game *(sports)* partita *f* [pärtēˈtä] 187; *(animals)* selvaggina *f* [selvä-jēˈnä] 107; **card** ~ gioco *m* delle carte [jōˈkō deˈle kärˈte] 181

gangway passerella *f* [päsereˈlä] 76

garage garage *m* [gäräjˈ] 44; autorimessa *f* [outōreˈmeˈsä] 44; officina *f* di riparazioni [ōfētshēˈnä dē rēpärätsyōˈnē] 50

garden giardino *m* [järdēˈnō] 121

gardener giardiniere *m* [jardēnyeˈre] 36

gargle liquido *m* per i gargarismi [lēˈkōō·ēdō per ē gärgärēˈzmē] 161

garlic aglio *m* [äˈlyō] 101

garter belt reggicalze *m* [rejēkälˈtse] 134

garters giarrettiere *f/pl.* [järetyeˈre] 136

gas benzina *f* [bendzēˈnä] 53; ~ **bottle** bombola *f* di gas [bōmˈbōlä dē gäs] 94; ~ **station** distributore *m* di benzina [dēstrēbōōtōˈre dē bendzēˈnä] 45

gasket guarnizione *f* [gōō·ärnē-tsyōˈne] 53

gasoline benzina *f* [bendzēˈnä] 41

gate portone *m* [pōrtōˈne] 121

gauze bandage garza *f* [gärˈtsä] 161

gear cose f/pl. [kō'se] 185; (car) marcia f [mär'tshä] 52; **put it in ~** innestare la marcia [ēnestär're lä mär'tshä] 53; **~ box** cambio m [käm'byō] 52; **~ lever** leva f del cambio [le'vä del käm'byō] 53; **~ oil** olio m per il cambio [ō'lyō per ēl käm'byō] 46; **~ shift** cambio m (delle marce) [käm'byō (de'le mär'tshe)] 52

general practitioner medico m generico [me'dēkō jene'rēkō] 162

genital organs organi m/pl. genitali [ōr'gänē jenētä'lē] 167

gentlemen signori m/pl. [sēnyō'rē] 65

geology geologia f [je·ōlōjē'ä] 39

German measles rosolia f [rōzōlē'ä] 170

get ricevere [rētshe'vere] 20; avere [äve're] 18; andare a prendere [ändä're ä pren'dere] 20; **~ aboard** salire [sälē're] 67; **~ in** salire [sälē're] 67; **~ off** scendere [shen'dere] 67; **~ out** uscire [ōōshē're] 43; scendere [shen'dere] 117

gin gin m [jēn] 112

ginger zenzero m [dzen'dzerō] 101

girl ragazza f [rägä'tsä] 35

give dare [dä're] 20

glad felice [felē'tshe] 12

gladioli gladioli m/pl. [glädyō'lē] 130

gland ghiandola f [gyän'dōlä] 167

glass bicchiere m [bēkye're] 96; **water ~** bicchiere m da acqua [bēkye're dä ä'kōō·ä] 97; **wine ~** bicchiere m da vino [bēkye're dä vē'nō] 97

glasses occhiali m/pl. [ōkyä'lē] 138

glazier vetraio m [veträ'yō] 36

glossy (adj.) lucido [lōō'tshēdō] 132; (noun) rivista f illustrata [rē-vē'stä ēlōōsträ'tä] 182

gloves guanti m/pl. [gōō·än'tē] 134

glue colla f [kō'lä] 138

glycerine glicerina f [glētsherē'nä] 161

go andare [ändä're] 15

goal goal m [gōl] 188; **kick a ~** tirare un goal [tērä're ōōn gōl] 190

goalie portiere m [pōrtye're] 190

God Dio m [dē'ō] 124

gold (noun) oro m [ō'rō] 133; (adj.) dorato [dōrä'tō] 194; **~ plated** dorato [dōrä'tō] 133

golf golf m [gōlf] 188

good-bye! arrivederci! [ärēveder'-tshē] 17; **say ~** congedarsi [kōnjedär'sē] 17

goods merci f/pl. [mer'tshē] 70

goose: roast ~ oca f arrosto [ō'kä ärō'stō] 105; **~ liver paté** paté (pasticcio) m di fegato d'oca [päte' (pästē'tshō) dē fe'gätō dō'kä] 102

gooseberries uva spina f [ōō'vä spē'nä] 110

Gospel Vangelo m [vänje'lō] 124

Gothic gotico [gō'tēkō] 124

goulash spezzatino m [spetsätē'nō] 107

government office ufficio m governativo [ōōfē'tshō gōvernätē'vō] 121

grain: against the ~ contropelo (adv.) [kōntrōpe'lō] 157

gram grammo m [grä'mō] 193

grammar school scuola f elementare [skōō·ō'lä elementä're] 38

grand piano piano m a coda [pyä'nō ä kō'dä] 178

grandchild nipote m/f [nēpō'te] 35

granddaughter nipote f [nēpō'te] 35

grandfather nonno m [nō'nō] 35

grandmother nonna f [nō'nä] 35

grandparents nonni m/pl. [nō'nē] 35

grandson nipote m [nēpō'te] 35

grapefruit pompelmo m [pōmpel'-mō] 110; **~ juice** succo m di pompelmo [sōō'kō dē pōmpel'mō] 98

grapes uva f [ōō'vä] 110

grave tomba f [tōm'bä] 121

gravy salsa f forte [säl'sä fōr'te] 101

gray grigio [grē'jō] 194; **ash ~** grigio cenere [grē'jō tshe'nere] 194; **dark ~** grigio scuro [grē'jō skōō'rō] 194; **pale ~** grigio chiaro [grē'jō kyä'rō] 194

greasy grasso [grä'sō] 158

great grande [grän'de] 22

green verde [ver'de] 194; **dark ~** verde scuro [ver'de skōō'rō] 194; **light ~** verde chiaro [ver'de kyä'rō] 194

grill room rosticceria f [rōstētsherē'ä] 91

grilled alla griglia [ä'lä grē'lyä] 100

grocery store negozio m di generi alimentari [negō'tsyō dē je'nere älēmentä'rē] 94

grog grog m [grōg] 112

group fare ticket biglietto per comitiva [bēlye'tō per kōmētē'vä] 62

grown up maggiorenne [mäjōre'ne] 35

guard custodire [kōōstōdē're] 44; sorvegliare [sōrvelyä're] 94

guest house pensione f [pensyō'ne] 91

guide guida f [gōō·ē'dä] 121

guilt colpa f [kōl'pä] 154

guinea hen faraona f [färä·ō'nä] 105

gums gengive f/pl. [jenjē've] 174

gym shoes scarpe f/pl. da ginnastica [skär'pe dä jēnä'stēkä] 139

gymnast ginnasta m [jēnä'stä] 188

gymnastics ginnastica f [jēnä'stēkä] 175; **~ with apparatus** ginnastica atletica agli attrezzi [jēnä'stēkä ätle'tēkä ä'lye ätre'tsē] 188

gynecologist ginecologo m [jēnekō'lōgō] 162

H

haberdashery merceria f [mertsherē'ä] 128

haddock merluzzo m [merlōō'tsō] 105

hail *(noun)* grandine f [grän'dēne] 27 *(verb)* grandinare [grändēnä're] 27

hair capelli m [käpe'lē] 155; **~ conditioner** sciacquatura cura f [skä kōō·ätōō'rä kōō'rä] 141; **~ drier** casco m [käs'kō] 158; **~ loss** caduta f dei capelli [kädōō'tä de' käpe'lē] 158; **~ net** retina f [retē'nä] 141; **~ spray** lacca f [lä'kä] 141; **~ style** pettinatura f [petēnä tōō'rä] 158; **~ tonic** frizione f [frētsyō'ne] 141; lozione f [lōtsyō'ne] 157

hairbrush spazzola f per i capelli [spä'tsōlä per ē käpe'lē] 141

haircut taglio m dei capelli [tä'lyō de'ē käpe'lē] 158

hair-do pettinatura f [petēnätōō'rä] 158

hairdresser parucchiere m [pärōō kye're] 158

hairpiece posticcio m [pōstē'tshō] 156; parrucchino m [pärōōkē'nō] 158

hairpins fermagli m/pl. [fermä'lye] 141

half mezzo [me'dzō] 30; **~ fare** biglietto m per ragazzi [bēlye'tō per rägät'sē] 62; **~ time** primo (secondo) tempo m [prēmō (sekōn dō) tem'pō] 188

halibut ipoglosso m [ēpōglō'sō] 104

hall hall m [äl] 91

ham prosciutto m [prōshōō'tō] 102

hammer martello m [märte'lō] 57

hammock amaca f [ämä'kä] 144

hand mano f [mä'nō] 167; *(clock)* lancetta f [läntshe'tä] 143; **~ brake** freno m a mano [fre'nō mä'nō] 51; **~ luggage** bagaglio m a mano [bägä'lyō ä mä'nō] 63

handbag borsetta f [bōrse'tä] 144

handball pallamano f [pälämä'nō] 188

handicrafts artigianato m [ärtējänä tō] 144

handkerchief fazzoletto *m* [fätsō-le'tō] 134

handle maniglia *f* [mänēl'yä] 53

happen succedere [sōōtshe'dere] 18

harbor porto *m* [pōr'tō] 72

hard duro [dōō'rō] 100

hare lepre *f* [le'pre] 106

hat cappello *m* [käpe'lō] 134; **straw ~** cappello *m* di paglia [käpe'lō dē pä'lyä] 134

have avere [äve're] 20; **~ to** dovere [dōve're] 17

hay fever febbre *f* da fieno [fe'bre dä fye'nō] 170

hazel nuts nocciole *f/pl.* [nōtshō'le] 110

head testa *f* [te'stä] 167; **~ conductor** capotreno *m* [käpōtre'nō] 67; **~ nurse** infermiera-capo *f* [ēnfermye'rä-kä'pō] 172

headlight faro *m* [fä'rō] 53

head-on collision scontro *m* frontale [skōn'trō frōntä'le] 49

health resort stazione *f* termale [stätsyō'ne termä'le] 175

heart cuore *m* [kōō·ō're] 167; **~ attack** attacco *m* cardiaco [ätä'kō kärdē'äkō] 170; **~ problems** problemi *m/pl.* di cuore [prōble'mē dē kōō·ō're] 170

heartburn bruciore *m* di stomaco [brōōtshō're dē stō'mäkō] 170

hearts *(cards)* cuori *m/pl.* [kōō·ō'rē] 181

heat calore [*m* kälō're] 27; caldo *m* [käl'dō] 163

heating (system) riscaldamento *m* [rēskäldämen'tō] 53; **central ~** riscaldamento *m* centrale [rēskäldämen'tō tshenträ'le] 90

heel tacco *m* [tä'kō] 139; calcagno *m* [kälkä'nyō] 167

height statura *f* [stätōō'rä] 79

helicopter elicottero *m* [elēkō'terō] 71

hello! salve! [säl've] 12; *(on answering phone)* pronto! [prōn'tō] 12

helm timone *m* [tēmō'ne] 76

helmsman timoniere *m* [tēmōnye're] 76

help *(noun)* aiuto *m* [äyōō'tō] 21; *(verb)* aiutare [äyōōtä're] 20

hemorrhage emorragia *f* [emōrä-jē'ä] 170

hemorrhoids emorroidi *f/pl.* [emōrō'ēdē] 170

herbs erbe *f/pl.* [er'be] 101

here qui [kōō·ē'] 14

herring aringa *f* [ärēn'gä] 104

hi! ciao! [tshou] 12

high alto [äl'tō] 139; **~ mass** messa *f* solenne [me'sä sōle'ne] 123; **~ pressure (system)** alta pressione *f* [äl'tä presyō'ne] 27; **~ school** scuola *f* superiore [skōō·ō'lä sōōperyō're] 38; liceo *m* [lētshe'ō] 38; ginnasio *m* [jēnä'zyō] 38; **~ test** super *m* [sōō'per] 45

high-rise building grattacielo *m* [grätätshe'lō] 121

highway autostrada *f* [outōsträ'dä] 42

hiking path sentiero *m* [sentye'rō] 121

hill collina *f* [kōlē'nä] 121

hip anca *f* [än'kä] 167

history storia *f* [stō'ryä] 39

hitch-hike fare l'autostop [fä're loutōstōp'] 43

hoarseness raucedine *f* [routshe'-dēne] 170

hockey hockey *m* [ō'kē] 188

hold up rapina *f* [räpē'nä] 153

home *(adv.)* in casa [ēn kä'sä] 15; a casa [ä kä'sa] 17

honey miele *m* [mye'le] 98

hood cofano *m* di motore [kō'fänō dē mōtō're] 53

hook and eyes ganci *m/pl.* e occhielli *m/pl.* [gän'tshē e ōkye'lē] 136

horizontal bar parallele *f/pl.* [pärä-le'le] 188

horn clacson *m* [kläk'sōn] 53

horse cavallo *m* [kävä'lō] 189; ~ **race** corsa *f* di cavalli [kōr'sä dē kävä'lē] 189

horseradish rafano *m* [rä'fänō] 101

hospital ospedale *m* [ōspedä'le] 49

hostel: ~ **father** albergatore *m* [älbergätō're] 95; ~ **mother** direttrice *f* [dēretrē'tshe] 95; ~ **parents** direttori *m/pl.* dell'ostello [dēretō'rē delōste'lō] 95

hot caldo [käl'dō 25; *(spicy)* piccante pēkän'te] 100; ~ **chocolate** cioccolata *f* [tshōkōlä'tä] 98; ~ **spring** fonte *f* termale [fōn'te termä'le] 175

hotel albergo *m* [älber'gō] 81; hotel *m* [ōtel'] 91; **beach** ~ albergo *m* sulla spiaggia [älber'gō sōō'lä spyä'jä] 91; ~ **restaurant** ristorante *m* dell'albergo [rēstōrän'te delälber'gō] 91

hour ora *f* [ō'rä] 31; **half** ~ mezz'ora *f* [medzō'rä] 87; **quarter** ~ quarto *m* d'ora [kōr'tō dō'rä] 87

hourly tutte le ore [tōō'te le ō're] 31

house casa *f* [kä'sä] 91; ~ **key** chiave *f* di casa [kyä've dē kä'sä] 91; ~ **number** numero *m* di casa [nōō'merō dē kä'sä] 121

how come [kō'me] 18; ~ **far is . . .** quant'è lontano . . . [kōō·äntē'lōntä'nō] 72

hub mozzo *m* di ruota [mō'tsō dē rōō·ō'tä] 53; ~ **cap** calotta *f* [kälō'tä] 53

hundred cento [tshen'tō] 28

hunting caccia *f* [kä'tshä] 188; ~ **license** permesso *m* di caccia [perme'sō dē kä'tshä] 188

hurt far male [fär mä'le] 163; ferire [ferē're] 49

husband marito *m* [marē'tō] 13

hydrogen peroxide acqua *f* ossigenata [ä'kōō·ä ōsējenä'tä] 161

hypertension ipertensione *f* [ēpertensyō'ne] 170

I

ice ghiaccio *m* [gyä'tshō] 27; gelo *m* [je'lō] 27

ice cream gelato *m* [jelä'tō] 109; ~ **parlor** gelateria *f* [jeläterē'ä] 114; **assorted** ~ gelato *m* misto [jelä'tō mē'stō] 114; **chocolate** ~ gelato *m* al cioccolato [jelä'tō äl tshōkōlä'tō] 113; **chocolate with** ~ cioccolata *f* con gelato [tshōkōlä'tä kōn jelä'tō] 113; **strawberry** ~ gelato *m* alla fragola [jelä'tō ä'lä frä'gōlä] 113; **vanilla** ~ gelato *m* alla vaniglia [jelä'tō ä'lä vänē'lyä] 114

ice skating rink pista *f* di pattinaggio su ghiaccio [pē'stä dē pätēnä'jō sōō gyä'tshō] 180

iceberg lettuce scarola *f* [skärō'lä] 108

icy road strada *f* ghiacciata [strä'dä gyätshä'tä] 27

identity card carta *f* d'identità [kär'tä dēdentē'tä] 79

ignition accensione *f* [ätshensyō'ne] 54; ~ **cable** cavo *m* d'accensione [kä'vō dätshensyō'ne] 54; ~ **key** chiavetta *f* d'accensione [kyä·ve'tä dätshensyō'ne] 54; ~ **lock** serratura *f* d'accensione [serätōō'rä dätshensyō'ne] 54; ~ **system** impianto *m* d'accensione [ēmpyän'tō dätshensyō'ne] 54

illness indisposizione *f* [ēndēspōzētsyō'ne] 170

impact urto *m* [ōōr'tō] 49

inch pollice *m* [pō'lētshe] 193

incisor dente *m* incisivo [den'te ēntshēzē'vō] 174

include comprendere [kōmpren'dere] 41

indicator light spia [spē'ä] 54

indigestion indigestione *f* [ēndējestyō'ne] 170

inflammation infiammazione *f* [ēnfyämätsyō'ne] 170

influenza influenza *f* [ēnflōō·enّtsä] 170

information informazioni *f/pl.* [ēnförmätsyō'nē] 65; **~ counter** ufficio *m* informazioni [ōōfē'tshō ēnförmätsyō'nē] 69; **~ office** informazioni *f/pl.* [ēnförmätsyō'nē] 60

infusion infuso *m* [ēnfōō'zō] 172

inhale inalare [ēnälä're] 175

injection iniezione *f* [ēnyetsyō'ne] 172

injured *(person)* ferito *m* [ferē'tō] 48

injury ferita *f* [ferē'tä] 49

ink inchiostro *m* [ēnkyō'strō] 138

inn locanda *f* [lōkän'dä] 81

inner tube camera *f* d'aria [kä'merä där'yä] 46

innocent innocente [ēnōtshen'te] 154

inquiry informazione *f* [ēnförmätsyō'ne] 92

insect repellent insetticida *f* [ēnsetētshē'dä] 161

in-sole soletta *f* [sōle'tä] 139

insomnia insonnia *f* [ēnsō'nyä] 170

inspection light lampada *f* di collaudo [läm'pädä dē kōlou'dō] 57

insulation isolante *f* [ēzōlän'te] 54

insurance assicurazione *f* [äsēkōōrätsyō'ne] 49; **~ certificate** certificato *m* d'assicurazione [tshertēfēkä'tō däsēkōōrätsyō'ne] 79

insure assicurare [äsēkōōrä're] 49

intensive care unit reparto *m* di cure intensive [repär'tō dē kōō're ēntensē've] 172

intermediate landing scalo *m* [skä'lō] 71

intermission intervallo *m* [ēntervä'lō] 177

internal interno [ēnter'nō] 159

internist internista *m* [ēnternē'stä] 162

interpreter interprete *m* [ēnter'prete] 36

interrupt interrompere [ēnterōm'pere] 61

interrupter interruttore *m* [ēnterōōtō're] 54

intersection incrocio *m* [ēnkrō'tshō] 42

intestinal catarrh catarro *m* intestinale [kätä'rō ēntestēnä'le] 170

intestine intestino *m* [ēntestē'nō] 167

invitation invito *m* [ēnvē'tō] 16

invite invitare [ēnvētä're] 183

iodine iodio *m* [yō'dyō] 161

iron *(noun)* ferro *m* da stiro [fe'rō dä stē'rō] 95; *(verb)* stirare [stērä're] 92

island isola [*f* ē'zōlä] 76

J

jack *(cards)* fante *m* [fän'te] 181; *(tool)* cric *m* [krēk] 47

jacket *(lady's)* giacchetta *f* [jäke'tä] 134; *(man's)* giacca *f* [jä'kä] 134

jackknife coltello *m* a serramanico [kōlte'lō ä serämä'nēkō] 144

jam marmellata *f* [märmelä'tä] 98

January gennaio *m* [jenä'yō] 33

jar vaso *m* [vä'zō] 126

jaundice itterizia *f* [ēterē'tsyä] 170

jaw mascella *f* [mäshe'lä] 167; **lower ~** mascella *f* inferiore [mäshe'lä ēnferyō're] 167; **upper ~** mascella *f* superiore [mäshe'lä sōōperyō're] 167

jelly *(aspic)* gelatina *f* [jelätē'nä] 101; *(fruit)* conserva *f* di frutta [kōnser'vä dē frōō'tä] 101

jersey jersey *m* [jer'sē] 137

jet *(plane)* jet *m* [jet] 71

jetty molo *m* [mō'lō] 76

Jew ebreo *m* [ebre'ō] 124

jewelry gioielli *m/pl.* [jōye'lē] 133; **costume ~** bigiotteria *f* [bējōterē'ä] 133

Jewish ebraico [ebrī'kō] 125

joint giuntura *f* [jōōntōō'rä] 167

joker *(cards)* jolly *m* [jō'lē] 181

journalism giornalismo *m* [jörnä-lēz'mō] 39

journalist giornalista *m* [jörnälē'stä] 36

journey gita *f* [jē'tä] 43; viaggio *m* [vyä'jō] 43

judge giudice *m* [jōō'dētshe] 36

judo judo *m* [jōō'dō] 189

juice succo *m* [sōō'kō] 112; **apple ~** succo *m* di mele [sōō'kō dē me'le] 112; **fruit ~** succo *m* di frutta [sōō'kō dē frōō'tä] 98; **grapefruit ~** succo *m* di pompelmo [sōō'kō dē pômpel'mō] 98; **orange ~** succo *m* d'arancia [sōō'kō därän'tshä] 98

juicy sugoso [sōōgō'sō] 100

July luglio *m* [lōō'lyō] 33

jumping saltare *m* [sältä're] 189

June giugno *m* [jōō'nyō] 33

K

kale cavolo *m* riccio [kä'vōlō rē'tshō] 107

keep tenere [tene're] 115

ketchup ketchup *m* [ket'shōp] 101

key chiave *f* [kyä've] 85

kidnapping sequestro *m* [sekōō·e'strō] 153

kidney (anat.) rene *m* [re'ne] 167; (cul.) rognone *m* [rōnyō'ne] 107; **~ stones** calcoli *m/pl.* renali [käl'kōlē renä'lē] 170

kilogram chilo(grammo) *m* [kē'lō (-grä'mō)] 193

kilometer chilometro *m* [kēlō'metrō] 40

kind: what ~ of... quale/quali [kōō·ä'le/kōō·ä'lē] 18

king re *m* [re] 181

kiss (noun) bacio *m* [bä'tshō] 184; (verb) baciare [bätshä're] 184

kitchen cucina *f* [kōōtshē'nä] 92

kitchenette cucinotto *m* [kōōtshē-nō'tō] 92

knee ginocchio *m* [jēnō'kyō] 167; **~ socks** calzettoni *m/pl.* [kältsetō'-nē] 134

kneecap rotula *f* [rō'tōōlä] 167

knife coltello *m* [kōlte'lō] 97; **pocket ~** coltellino *m* [kōltelē'nō] 144

knight cavaliere *m* [kävälye're] 181

knot nodo *m* [nō'dō] 76

L

ladies signore *f/pl.* [sēnyō're] 65; **~ room** (gabinetto *m* per) signore *f/pl.* [(gäbēne'tō per) sēnyō're] 92; **~ shoes** scarpe *f/pl.* da donna [skär'pe dä dō'nä] 139

lake lago *m* [lä'gō] 76

lamb agnello *m* [änye'lō] 106

lamp lampadina *f* [lämpädē'nä] 54; lampada *f* [läm'pädä] 92; **reading ~** lampada *f* da tavolo [läm'pädä dä tä'vōlō] 92

land (noun) terra *f* [te'rä] 72; (verb) far scalo [fär skä'lō] 72; approdare [äprōdä're] 76; (plane) atterrare [äterä're] 69

landing atterraggio *m* [äterä'jō] 71; **~ gear** carrello *m* d'atterraggio [käre'lō däterä'jō] 71; **~ stage** pontile *m* d'approdo [pontē'le däprō'dō] 76

landscape paesaggio *m* [pä·ezä'jō] 121

lane corsia *f* [kōrsē'ä] 42; stradina *f* [strädē'nä] 121

larynx laringe *f* [lärēn'je] 167

last ultimo [ōōl'tēmō] 58; **~ year** anno *m* scorso [ä'nō skōr'sō] 32; **~ stop** capolinea *m* [käpōlē'ne·ä] 58

late (adv.) tardi [tär'dē] 17; **to be ~** essere in ritardo [e'sere ēn rētär'dō] 61

later più tardi [pyōō tär'dē] 32

launch scialuppa *f* [shälōō'pä] 75

launder lavare [lävä're] 87

laundromat lavanderia *f* a gettone [lävänderēˈä ä jetōˈne] 129

laundry biancheria *f* [byänkerēˈä] 92; *(shop)* lavanderia *f* [lävänderēˈä] 129

lavender color *m* lavanda [kōlōrˈ lävänˈdä] 194

law legge *f* [leˈje] 39

lawyer avvocato *m* [ävōkäˈtō] 36

laxative lassativo *m* [läsätēˈvō] 161

lead *(road)* portare [pōrtäˈre] 19

lean magro [mäˈgrō] 100

leash guinzaglio *m* [gōō·ēntsäˈlyō] 144

leather pelle *f* [peˈlle] 126; cuoio *m* [kōō·ōˈyō] 139; ~ **coat** capotto *m* di pelle [käpōˈtō dē peˈlle] 134; ~ **jacket** giacchetta *f* di pelle [jäkeˈtä dē peˈlle] 134

leave *(let)* lasciare [läshäˈre] 44; *(for a trip)* partire [pärtēˈre] 34; ripartire [rēpärtēˈre] 44; ~ **for** partire per [pärtēˈre per] 72

lecture lezione *f* [letsyōˈne] 38

left a sinistra [ä sēnēˈsträ] 40

leg gamba *f* [gämˈbä] 167; *(cul.)* cosciotto *m* [kōshōˈtō] 106; **lower** ~ polpaccio *m* [pōlpäˈtshō] 167

lemon limone *m* [lēmōˈne] 101

lemonade limonata *f* [lēmōnäˈtä] 112

lend imprestare [ēmprestäˈre] 48

lengthen allungare [älōōngäˈre] 137

lens *(opt.)* lente *f* [lenˈte] 138; *(phot.)* obiettivo *m* [ōbyetēˈvō] 132

letter lettera *f* [leˈterä] 85; ~ **abroad** lettera *f* per l'estero [leˈterä per leˈsterō] 145; **local** ~ lettera *f* per l'interno [leˈterä per lēnterˈnō] 145; **night** ~ telegramma *m* lettera [telegräˈmä leˈterä] 147; **registered** ~ raccomandata *f* [räkōmändäˈtä] 145; **special delivery** ~ lettera *f* espresso [leˈterä espreˈsō] 145

leukemia leucemia *f* [le·ōōtshemēˈä] 170

librarian bibliotecario *m* [bēblē·ōtekärˈyō] 36

library biblioteca *f* [bēblē·ōteˈkä] 121

license plate targa *f* [tärˈgä] 54

live: ~ **belt** cintura *f* di salvataggio [tshēntōōˈrä dē sälvätäˈjō] 76; ~ **jacket** giubetto *m* di salvataggio [jōōbeˈtō dē sälvätäˈjō] 71

liveboat scialuppa *f* di salvataggio [shälōōˈpä dē sälvätäˈjō] 75

liveguard bagnino *m* [bänyēˈnō] 185

lift: give s.o. a ~ dare un passaggio [däˈre ōōn päsäˈjō] 48

light *(adj.)* chiaro [kyäˈrō] 127; *(noun)* luce *f* [lōōˈtshe] 88

lighter accendino *m* [ätshendēˈnō] 140; ~ **fluid** benzina *f* per l'accendino [bendzēˈnä per lätshendēˈnō] 140; ~ **gas** ~ accendino *f* a gas [ätshendēˈnō ä gäs] 140

lighthouse faro *m* [fäˈrō] 76

lightning lampo *m* [lämˈpō] 27; ~ **system** impianto *m* elettrico [ēmpyänˈtō eleˈtrēkō] 54

like desiderare [desēderäˈre] 16; volere [vōleˈre] 23; piacere [pyätsheˈre] 14

lilacs lillà *m/pl.* [lēläˈ] 130

limbs arti *m/pl.* [ärˈtē] 167

linen lino *m* [lēˈnō] 137

lingerie biancheria *f* [byänkerēˈä] 134

liniment linimento *m* [lēnēmenˈtō] 161

lining fodera *f* [fōˈderä] 136

lip labbro *m* [läˈbrō] 167

lipstick rossetto *m* [rōseˈtō] 141

liqueur liquore *m* [lēkōō·ōˈre] 112

liter litro *m* [lēˈtrō] 193

little: a ~ un po' [ōōn pō'] 24

live vivere [vēˈvere] 119; *(in a place)* abitare [äbētäˈre] 14

liver fegato *m* [feˈgätō] 106; ~ **problem** problemi *m/pl.* di fegato [pröble'më dë fe'gätö] 170

living room salotto *m* [sälö'tö] 93

loafers mocassini *m/pl.* [mökäse̅'ne̅] 139

loan prestare [prestä're] 57

lobby atrio *m* [ä'tryö], hall *m* [äl] 92; ridotto *m* [re̅dö'tö] 177

lobster: ~ **cocktail** cocktail *m* di gamberetti [köktel' dē gämbere̅'-tē] 102; **rock ~/spiny ~** aragosta *f* [ärägö'stä] 105

local call chiamata *f* urbana [kyä-mä'tä ōōrbä'nä] 149

locate: be ~**d** essere situato [e'sere sētōō-ä'tö] 19

lock *(noun)* serratura *f* [serätōō'rä] 92; ~ **up** chiudere a chiave [kyōō'dere ä kyä've] 92

locker room spogliatoio *m* [spölyä-tö'yö] 186

locksmith fabbro *m* [fä'brö] 37

locomotive locomotiva *f* [lökömö-tē'vä] 67

long *(dimension)* lungo [lōōn'gö] 133; **how** ~ *(time)* quanto tempo [kōō-än'tö tem'pö] 18; ~ **distance express** rapido *m* [rä'pēdö] 60; ~ **wave** onda *f* lunga [ōn'dä lōōn'gä] 182

look: ~ **after** curarsi [kōōrär'sē] 48; ~ **for** cercare [tsherkä're] 15

loosen allentare [älentä're] 55

lose perdere [per'dere] 153

loss smarrimento *m* [zmärēmen'tö] 153

lounge sala *f* di soggiorno [sä'lä dē sōjōr'nö] 74

love *(noun)* amore *m* [ämö're] 184; *(verb)* amare; voler bene [ämä're/vōler' be'ne] 184

lovely simpatico [sēmpä'tēkö] 16

low basso [bä'sö] 169; ~ **pressure (system)** bassa pressione *f* [bä'sä presyö'ne] 27

lubricant lubrificante *m* [lōōbrēfē-kän'te] 54

lubrication servizio *m* lubrificazione

[serve̅'tsyö lōōbrēfēkätsyö'ne] 46

luck fortuna *f* [förtōō'nä] 23

luggage bagaglio *m* [bägä'lyö] 63; ~ **car** bagagliaio *m* [bägälyä'yö] 65; ~ **forwarding office** spedizione *f* bagagli [spedētsyö'ne bä-gä'lyē] 63; ~ **locker** armadietti *m/pl.* bagagli [ärmädye'tē bägä'lyē] 63; ~ **rack** rete *f* portabagagli [re'-te pörtäbägä'lyē] 67

lumbago lombaggine *f* [lōmbä'jēne] 171

lunch pranzo *m*; spuntino *m* [prän'-dzö/spōōntē'nö] 92

lung polmone *m* [pōlmō'ne] 107

M

macaroni maccheroni *m/pl.* [mäke-rö'nē] 104

macaroon biscotto *m* amaretto [bēskö'tö ämäre'tö] 114

mackerel sgombro *m* [zgöm'brö] 105

Madam Signora *f* [sēnyö'rä] 13

magazine rivista *f* [rēvē'stä] 182; **fashion** ~ rivista *f* di moda [rēvē'-stä dē mö'dä] 182

maid cameriera *f* [kämerye'rä] 92

maiden name nome *m* da ragazza [nö'me dä rägä'tsä] 79

mail posta *f* [pö'stä] 85; ~ **box** cassetta *f* per le lettere [käse'tä per le le'tere] 145; buca *f* delle lettere [bōō'kä de'le le'tere] 149

mailman postino *m* [pöstē'nö] 36

main: ~ **road/** ~ **street** strada *f* principale [strä'dä prēntshēpä'le] 43; ~ **station** stazione *f* centrale [stätsyö'ne tshenträ'le] 60

male organ organo *m* maschile [ör'-gänö mäskē'le] 167

malt liquor birra *f* al malto [bē'rä äl mäl'tö] 111

manager direttore *m* [dēretö're] 23

manicure manicure *f* [mänēkoō're] 156

manufacturer's spare parts pezzi *m/pl* di ricambio originali [pe'tsē dē rēkäm'byō orējēnä'lē] 50

many: how ~ quanti/quante [koō·än'tē/koō·änte] 18

map carta *f* (geografica) [kär'tä (je·ōgrä'fēkä)] 40, 130; **city ~** pianta *f* della città [pyän'tä de'llä tshē-tä'] 130; **road ~** carta *f* automobilistica [kär'tä outōmōbēlē'stēkä] 130; **street ~** carta *f* stradale [kär'tä strädä'le] 130

March marzo *m* [mär'tsō] 33

marinated in salamoia [ēn sälä-mō'yä] 107

marital status stato *m* di famiglia [stä'tō dē fämē'lyä] 79

marksmanship tiro *m* [tē'rō] 189

maroon rosso scuro [rō'sō skoō'rō] 194

marriage matrimonio *m* [mä-trēmō'nyō] 22

married sposato [spōzä'tō] 79

mascara mascara *m* [mäskä'rä] 141

mass messa *f* [me'sä] 125; **high ~** messa *f* solenne [me'sä sōle'ne] 124

massage *(noun)* massaggio *m* [mä-sä'jō] 175; *(verb)* massaggiare [mäsäjä're] 175

masseur massaggiatore *m* [mäsäjä-tō're] 175

masseuse massaggiatrice *f* [mäsä-jätrē'tshe] 175

mast albero *m* [äl'berō] 76

mat piattino *m* [pyätē'nō] 144

match *(sports)* partita *f* [pärtē'tä] 188

matches fiammiferi *m/pl* [fyämē'fe-rē] 140

material materiale *m* [mäteryä'le] 137

mathematics matematica *f* [mäte-mä'tēkä] 39

matte opaco [ōpä'kō] 132

mattress materasso *m* [mäterä'sō] 90

mauve color *m* malva [kōlōr' mäl'vä] 194

maxillary sinus cavità *f* mascellare [kävētä' mäshelä're] 167

maximum speed velocità *f* massima [velōtshētä' mä'sēmä] 42

May maggio *m* [mä'jō] 33

maybe può darsi [poō·ō' där'sē] 21

mayonnaise maionese *f* [mäyōne'-se] 101; **~sauce** salsa *f* di maionese [säl'sä dē mäyōne'se] 101

meal pasto *m* [pä'stō] 159

mean significare [sēnyēfēkä're] 18

meanwhile nel frattempo [nel frä-tem'pō] 32

measles morbillo *m* [mōrbē'lō] 171

meat: ~balls polpette *f/pl* [pōlpe'te] 107; **~loaf** polpettone *m* [pōl-petō'ne] 107

mechanic meccanico *m* [mekä'nē-kō] 36

mechanical engineering industria *f* meccanica [ēndoō'strē·ä mekä'-nēkä] 39

medical director direttore *m* medico [dēretō're me'dēkō] 172

medicine medicina *f* [medētshē'nä] 39

medium (done) cotto a metà [kō'tō ä metä'] 100

meet incontrarsi [ēnkōnträr'sē] 15; **~again** rivedersi [rēveder'sē] 16

melon melone *m* [melō'ne] 102; **honeydew ~** melone *m* [melō'ne] 110

watermelon cocomero *m* [kōkō'me-rō] 110; anguria *f* [ängoōr'yä] 110

membership card tessera *f* [te'serä] 95

memorial monumento *m* commemorativo [mōnoōmen'tō kōme-mōrätē'vō] 119

men's room (gabinetto *m* per) signori *m/pl* [(gäbēne'tō per) sē-nyō're] 92

menstruation mestruazione f [me-strōō·ätsyō'ne] 167
mention: don't ~it di niente [dē nyen'te] 21
menu lista f [lē'stä] 96
meringue meringa f [merēn'gä] 114
metabolism metabolismo m [metä-bōlē'zmō] 168
metalworker operaio m metal-mec-canico [ōperä'yō mētäl-mekä'nē-kō] 36
meter metro m [me'trō] 193
Methodist metodista m [metōdē'stä] 124
middle: in the ~(train) nel mezzo [nel me'dzo] 65; (thea.) al centro [äl tshen'trō] 176; **~ear inflamma-tion** infiammazione f dell'orec-chio medio [ēnfyämätsyō'ne delō-re'kyō me'dyō] 171
midnight mezzanotte f [medzänō'te] 31
midwife levatrice f [levätrē'tshe] 37
mile miglio m [mē'lyō] 193; **nautical ~** miglio m marittimo [mē'lyō mä-rē'tēmō] 193
mileage indicator contachilometri m [kōntäkēlō'metrē] 54
milk latte m [lä'te] 98; **condensed ~/ evaporated ~** latte m condensato [lä'te kōndensä'tō] 98, 114; **~ shake** frappè m di latte [fräpe' dē lä'te] 112
millimeter millimetro m [mēlē'me-trō] 193
miner minatore m [mēnätō're] 37
minerals acque f/pl minerali [ä'kōō·e mēnerä'lē] 175
miniature golf minigolf m [mē'nē-gōlf] 180; **~ course** campo m di minigolf [käm'pō dē mē'nēgōlf] 180
ministry ministero m [mēnēste'rō] 121
minute minuto m [mēnōō'tō] 86; **just a ~** un momento [ōōn mōmen'tō] 16

mirror specchio m [spe'kyō] 92
miss mancare [mänkä're] 23; (mo-tor) andare a strappi [ändä're ä strä'pē] 54
Miss Signorina f [sēnyōrē'nä] 13
mist foschia f [fōskē'ä] 27
molar molare m [mōlä're] 174
moment momento m [mōmen'tō] 87; **at the ~** adesso [äde'sō] 32
monastery monastero m [mōnäste-rō] 125
Monday lunedì m [lōōnedē'] 33
money denaro m [denä'rō] 151; sol-di m/pl [sōl'dē] 85; **~ exchange** cambio m [käm'byō] 60; **~ order** versamento m [versämen'tō] 146
month mese m [me'se] 32
monument monumento m [mōnōō-men'tō] 119
moon luna f [lōō'nä] 27
moped motorino m [mōtōrē'nō] 41
morning mattina f [mätē'nä] 31; mattinata f [mätēnä'tä] 31; **in the ~** di mattina [dē mätē'nä] 31; **this ~** stamattina [stämätē'nä] 31
mosaic mosaico m [mōsī'kō] 125
Moslem musulmano m [mōōsōōl-mä'nō] 124
motel motel m [mōtel'] 81
mother madre f [mä'dre] 35
mother-in-law suocera f [sōō·ō'-tsherä] 35
motion picture theatre sala f cine-matografica [sä'lä tshēnemätō-grä'fēkä] 122
motor motore m [mōtō're] 54; **~ oil** olio m motore [ō'lyō mōtō're] 46; **~ scooter** motoretta f [mōtōre'tä] 41
motorboat motoscafo m [mōtōskä'-fō] 75
motorcycle motocicletta f [mōtō-tshēkle'tä] 41; **to go by ~** andare in motocicletta [ändä're ēn mōtō-tshēkle'tä] 42
motorrail service littorina f [lētō-rē'nä] 60

mountain montagna f [mōntän'yä] 121; ~ **climber** alpinista m [älpēnē'stä] 189; ~ **climbing** alpinismo m [älpēnē'zmō] 189; ~ **range/** ~**s** montagne f/pl [mōntän'ye] 70, 121

moustache baffi m/pl [bä'fē] 157

mouth bocca f [bō'kä] 165

mouthwash colluttorio m [kōlōōtōr'yō] 141

move (verb) muovere mōō·ō'vere 164; ~ **in** traslocare in [träzlōkä're ēn] 92; ~ **out** traslocare da [träzlōkä're dä] 92; (noun) mossa f [mō'sä] 182

movie film m (a soggetto) [fēlm (ä sōje'tō)] 179; ~ **house/** ~**s** cinema m [tshē'nemä] 179

Mr. (name) Signor (name) [sēnyōr'] 13

Mrs. (name) Signora (name) [sēnyō'rä] 13

much: how ~ quanto/quanta [kōō·än'tō/kōō·än'tä] 18; **too** ~ troppo [trō'pō] 127

mucous membrane mucosa f [mōōkō'sä] 168

mud fango m [fän'gō] 175; ~ **bath** fare i fanghi [fä're ē fän'gē] 175; ~ **pack** mettere il fango/l'impacco [me'tere ēl fän'gō/l'ēmpä'kō] 175

muggy: it's ~ c'è afa [tshe ä'fä] 25

mumps orecchioni m/pl [ōrekyō'nē] 171

murder omicidio m [ōmētshē'dyō] 153

Muscatel moscato m [mōskä'tō] 110

muscle muscolo m [mōōs'kōlō] 168

museum museo m [mōōze'ō] 116

mushrooms funghi m/pl [fōōn'gē] 101

music: piece of ~ pezzo m di musica [pe'tsō dē mōō'zēkä] 110

musician musicista m [mōōzētshē'stä] 37

musicology musica f [mōō'zēkä] 39

mussels cozze f/pl [kō'tse] 105

mustard senape f [se'näpe] 101; ~ **jar** mostardiera f [mōstärdye'rä] 97

my mio/mia [mē'ō/mē'ä] 12; miei/mie [mye'ē'/mē'e] 14

N

nail unghia f [ōōn'gyä] 156; ~ **file** lima f per le unghie [lē'mä per le ōōn'gye] 141; ~ **polish** smalto m [zmäl'tō] 141; ~ **polish remover** dissolvente m per lo smalto [dēsōlven'te per lō zmäl'tō] 141; ~ **scissors** forbicine f/pl per le unghie [fōrbētshē'ne per le ōōn'gye] 141

name nome m [nō'me] 14; **first** ~ nome m di battesimo [nō'me dē bäte'zēmō] 79; **last** ~ cognome m [kōnyō'me] 79

napkin tovagliolo m [tōvälyō'lō] 97

narcotics narcotici m/pl [närkō'tētshē] 154

narrow stretto [stre'tō] 127

national park parco m nazionale [pär'kō nätsyōnä'le] 122

nationality nazionalità f [nätsyōnälētä'] 79; ~ **plate** targa f della nazionalità [tär'gä de'lä nätsyōnälētä'] 54

nausea nausea f [nou'ze·ä] 171

nauseated nauseato [nouze·ä'tō] 164

nave navata f [nävä'tä] 125

near here qui vicino [kōō·ē' vētshē'nō] 44

nearest più vicino [pyōō vētshē'nō] 45; prossimo [prō'sēmō] 19

near-sighted miope [mē'ōpe] 138

neck collo m [kō'lō] 168; **back of the** ~**/nape of the** ~ nuca f [nōō'kä] 168

backlace collana f [kōlä'nä] 133

need aver bisogno [äver' bēzō'nyō] 18

needle ago *m* [ä'gō] 136; **sewing ~** ago *m* da cucire [ä'gō dä kōō-tshē're] 136

negative negativo *m* [negätē'vō] 131

nephew nipote *m* [nēpō'te] 35

nephritis nefrite *f* [nefrē'te] 171

nerve nervo *m* [ner'vō] 168

neuralgia nevralgia *f* [nevräljē'ä] 171

neurologist neurologo *m* [ne·ōōrō'-lōgō] 162

neutral gear marcia *f* in folle [mär'-tshä ēn fō'le] 53

never mai [mī] 21

new nuovo [nōō·ō'vō] 50

news: television ~ telegiornale *m* [telejōrnä'le] 182

newsdealer giornalaio *m* [jōrnälä'yō] 129

newspaper giornale *m* [jōrnä'le] 182

next prossimo [prō'sēmō] 32; più vicino [pyōō' vētshē'nō] 40

nice simpatico [sēmpä'tēkō] 184

niece nipote *f* [nēpō'te] 35

night notte *f* [nō'te] 17; **all ~** tutta la notte [tōō'tä lä nō'te] 44; **at ~** di notte [dē nō'te] 31; **good ~** buonanotte! [bōō·ōnänō'te] 17; **~ club** night club [nīt klōōb] 180; **~ duty** servizio *m* notturno [ser-vē'tsyō nōtōōr'nō] 159; **~ shirt/ nightie** camicia *f* da notte [kä-mē'tshä dä nō'te] 134; **~'s lodging** alloggio *m* per una notte [älō'jō per ōō'nä nō'te] 92

nine nove [nō've] 28

ninepins birilli *m/pl* [bērē'lē] 189

no no [nō] 21

nobody nessuno [nesōō'nō] 49

non-swimmer non nuotatore *m* [nōn nōō·ōtätō're] 186

noodles pasta *f* asciutta [pä'stä äshōō'tä] 104

noon mezzogiorno *m* [medzōjōr'nō] 31; **at** a mezzogiorno [ä medzō-jōr'nō] 31; **this** oggi a mezzo-giorno [ō'jē ä medzōjōr'nō] 32

nose naso *m* [nä'sō] 168

nosebleed emorragia *f* nasale [emōräjē'ä näsä'le] 171

notary notaio *m* [nōtä'yō] 37

nothing niente [nyen'te] 21

novel romanzo *m* [rōmän'dzō] 130; **detective ~** giallo *m* [jä'lō] 130

November novembre *m* [nōvem'bre] 33

now adesso/ora [äde'sō/ō'rä] 32; **~ and then** di quando in quando [dē kōō·än'dō ēn kōō·än'dō] 32

nude nudo [nōō'dō] 185; **~ beach** spiaggia *f* per nudisti [spyä'jä per nōōdē'stē] 186

number numero *m* [nōō'merō] 65

nurse *(male)* infermiere *m* [ēnfer-mye're] 37; *(female)* infermiera *f* [ēnfermye'rä] 37; **night ~** infermiera *f* di notte [ēnfermye'rä dē nō'te] 172

nursery camera *f* per i bambini [kä'-merä per ē bämbē'nē] 93

nut: hazel ~s nocciole *f/pl* [nōtshō'-le] 110

nutmeg noce *f* moscata [nō'tshe mōskä'tä] 101

nylon nylon *m* [nē'lōn] 137

O

oarsman rematore *m* [remätō're] 189

observatory osservatorio *m* [ōser-vätōr'yō] 122

occupation professione *f* [prōfe-syō'ne] 79

occupied occupato [ōkōōpä'tō] 66

ocean oceano *m* [ōtshe'änō] 77

October ottobre *m* [ōtō'bre] 33

offer offrire [ōfrē're] 16

office: doctor's ~ ambulatorio *m* [ämbōōlätōr'yō] 163; **~ hours** orario *m* di visita [ōrär'yō dē vē'-zētä] 163

officer: deck ~ ufficiale *m* di coperta [ōōfētshä'le dē kōper'tä] 74; **first ~** ufficiale *m* in seconda [ōōfētshä'le ēn sekōn'dä] 76

off-side fuorigioco *m* [fōō·ōrējō'kō] 190

often: how ~ quante volte [kōō·än'te vōl'te] 72

oil olio *m* [ō'lyō] 46; **~ filter** filtro *m* dell'olio [fēl'trō delō'lyō] 54; **~ pump** pompa *f* dell'olio [pōm'pä delō'lyō] 54

ointment pomata *f* [pōmä'tä] 161; **boric acid ~** pomata *f* all'acido borico [pōmä'tä älä'tshēdō bō'rēkō] 160; **burn ~** unguento *m* per le scottature [ōōngōō·en'tō per le skōtätōō're] 160; **eye ~** pomata *f* per gli occhi [pōmä'tä per lyē ō'kē] 160

old vecchio [ve'kyō] 35

olives olive *f/pl* [ōlē've] 101

one uno [ōō'nō] 28; **~ way street** senso *m* unico [sen'sō ōō'nēkō] 59; **~ way ticket** biglietto *m* di andata [bēlye'tō dē ändä'tä] 62

onion cipolla *f* [tshēpō'lä] 101

open *(adj.)* aperto [äper'tō] 44; *(verb)* aprire [äprē're] 18; **~ market** mercato *m* [merkä'tō] 122

opera glasses binocolo *m* da opera [bēnō'kōlō dä ō'perä] 177

operate operare [ōperä're] 172

operation operazione *f* [ōperätsyō'ne] 172

operator telefonista *m/f* [telefōnē'stä] 149

optician ottico *m* [ō'tēkō] 37

oral surgeon medico *m* dentista [me'dēkō dentē'stä] 174

orange *(noun)* arancia *f* [ärän'tshä] 109; *(adj.)* arancione [äräntshō'ne] 194; **~ juice** succo *m* d'arancia [sōō'kō därän'tshä] 98

orangeade aranciata *f* [äräntshä'tä] 112

orchestra seats posti *m/pl* di platea [pō'stē dē pläte'ä] 178

orchids orchidee *f/pl* [ōrkēde'e] 130

order *(verb)* ordinare [ōrdēnä're] 115; *(noun)*: **in ~** in ordine [ēn ōr'dēne] 23; **to be out of ~** non essere a posto [nōn e'sere a pō'stō] 23; non funzionare [nōn fōōntsyōnä're] 50

organ organo *m* [ōr'gänō] 125

orthodontist ortodontista *m* [ōrtōdōntē'stä] 174

orthopedist ortopedico *m* [ōrtōpe'dēkō] 162

ounce oncia *f* [ōn'tshä] 193

overture preludio *m* [prelōō'dyō] 178

overheat riscaldarsi [rēskäldär'sē] 54

oysters ostriche [ō'strēke] 102

P

pack pacco *m* [pä'kō] 126

package pacco *m* [pä'kō] 149; **~ card** bolletta *f* di spedizione [bōle'tä dē spedētsyō'ne] 149

packet pacchetto *m* [päke'tō] 126

pad blocco *m* [blō'kō] 138; **scratch ~** blocco *m* per appunti [blō'kō per äpōōn'tē] 138; **sketch ~** blocco *m* da disegno [blō'kō dä dēse'nyō] 138

pail secchio *m* [se'kyō] 92

pain dolore *m* [dōlō're] 163

~ killer/ ~ pills compresse *f/pl* contro il dolore [kōmpre'se kōntrō ēl dōlō're] 173

paint job vernice *f* [vernē'tshe] 54

painter imbianchino *m* [ēmbyänkē'nō] 37; *(artist)* pittore *m* [pētō're] 37

painting pittura *f* [pētōō'rä] 39

pair paio *m* [pä'yō] 126

pajamas pigiama *m* [pējä'mä] 134

palace palazzo *m* [pälä'tsō] 119

palate palato *m* [pä'lätō] 168

pale chiaro [kyä'rō] 127

pancreas pancreas *m* [pan'kre·äs] 168

panties calzoncini *m/pl* da donna [kältsōntshē'nē dä dō'nä] 134

pants pantaloni *m/pl* [päntälō'nē] 134; ~ **suit** tailleur *m* pantalone [tä'yär päntälō'ne] 134

paper carta *f* [kär'tä] 132; ~ **napkins** tovaglioli *m/pl* di carta [tōvälyō'lē] dē kär'tä 144

paperback tascabile *m* [täskä'bēle] 130

papers documenti *m/pl* [dōkōō-men'tē] 78

paprika paprica *f* [pä'prēkä] 101

paralysis paralisi *f* [pärä'lēzē] 171

parcel pacco *m* [pä'kō] 145; **small** ~ pacchetto *m* [päke'tō] 145; **registered** ~ **with declared value** pacco *m* raccomandato con valore dichiarato [pä'kō] räkōmändä'tō kōn välō're dēkyärä'tō] 150

pardon: (I) beg your ~ scusi [skōō'zē] 22; **come dice** [kō'me dē'tshe] 20

parents genitori *m/pl* [jenētō'rē] 35

park (noun) parco *m* [pär'kō] 122; (verb) parcheggiare [pärkejä're] 43

parka giacca *f* a vento [jä'kä ä ven'tō] 134

parking parcheggio *m* [pärke'jō] 44; ~ **disc** disco *m* orario [dē'skō ōrär'yō] 42; ~ **lights** luci *f/pl* di posizione [lōō'tshe dē pōzētsyō'ne] 53; ~ **lot** parcheggio *m* [pärke'jō] 42; ~ **meter** parcometro *m* [pärkō'metrō] 42; **no** ~ divieto *m* di parcheggio [dēvye'tō dē pärke'jō] 42; ~ **space** box *m* [bōks] 44

parsley prezzemolo *m* [pretse'mōlō] 101

part (theat.) parte *f* [pär'te] 178; (hair) riga *f* [rē'gä] 157; ~ **of town** quartiere *m* [kōō·ärtye're] 122

party party [pär'tē] 183; ~ **games** giochi *m/pl* di società [jō'kē dē sō-tshetä'] 182

pass (noun) passo *m* [pä'sō] 42; (verb) passare [päsä're] 99; traversare [träversä're] 43

passenger passeggero *m* [päseje-rō] 77; viaggiatore *m* [vyäjätō're] 66; ~ **car** autovettura *f* [outōve-tōō'rä] 41

passing: no ~ divieto *m* di sorpasso [dēvye'tō dē sōrpä'sō] 42; ~ **out** svenimento *m* [zvenēmen'tō] 171

passport passaporto *m* [päsäpōr'tō] 78

pasta pasta *f* asciutta [pä'stä äshōō'tä] 104

pastime passatempo *m* [päsätem'pō] 182

patch (tube) aggiustare [äjōōstä're] 46

path cammino *m* [kämē'nō] 19; sentiero *m* [sentye'rō] 42

patient paziente *m* [pätsyen'te] 172

patio cortile *m* interno [kōrtē'le ēn-ter'nō] 92

patterned a fantasia [ä fäntäzē'ä] 137

pawn (chess) pedina *f* [pedē'nä] 181

pay (out) pagare [pägä're] 80, 152

payment pagamento *m* [pägämen'tō] 152

peas piselli *m/pl* [pēze'lē] 108

peach pesca *f* [pes'kä] 110; ~ **melba** gelato *m* con pesca sciroppata [jelä'tō kōn pes'kä shērōpä'tä] 114

pear pera *f* [pe'rä] 110

pearls perle *f/pl* [per'le] 133

pedal pedale *m* [pedä'le] 54

pedestrian pedone *m* [pedō'ne] 122; ~ **crossing** passaggio *m* pedonale [päsä'jō pedōnä'le] 122

pediatrician pediatra *f* [pedyä'trä] 162

pedicure pedicure *f* [pedēkōō're] 156

pelvis bacino *m* [bätshē'nō] 168

pen: ball point ~ biro f [bē'rō] 138; **fountain** ~ penna f stilografica [pe'nä stēlōgrä'fēkä] 138

penalty kick calcio m di rigore [käl'tshō dē rēgō're] 190

pencil matita f [mätē'tä] 138

pendant ciondolo m [tshōn'dōlō] 133

penis pene m [pe'ne] 168

pension pensione f [pensyō'ne] 81

people persone f/pl [persō'ne] 41

pepper pepe m [pe'pe] 101; ~ **mill** macinino m del pepe [mätshē-nē'nō del pe'pe] 97; ~ **shaker** portapepe m [pōrtäpe'pe] 97

peppermint menta f [men'tä] 161

peppers peperoni m/pl [peperō'nē] 108

peptic ulcer ulcera f gastrica [ōōl'-tsherä gä'strēkä] 171

perch pesce m persico [pe'she per'-sēkō] 105

performance spettacolo m [spetä'-kōlō] 176; rappresentazione f [rä-prezentätsyō'ne] 178

perfume profumo m [prōfōō'mō] 80

perhaps forse [fōr'se] 21

period periodo m [perē'ōdō] 119

permanent wave permanente f [per-mänen'te] 155

personal personale [persōnä'le] 80

petticoat sottoveste f [sōtōve'ste] 134

pharmacist farmacista m [färmä-tschē'stä] 37

pharmacy farmacia f [färmätshē'ä] 39, 159

pheasant fagiano m [fäjä'nō] 105

phone (noun) telefono m [tele'fōnō] 148; (verb) telefonare [telefōnä'-re] 78; **pay** ~ telefono m [tele'fō-nō] 148; ~ **book** elenco m telefonico [elen'kō telefō'nēkō] 147; ~ **booth** cabina f telefonica [käbē'-nä telefō'nēkä] 147; **make a** ~ **call** telefonare [telefōnä're] 85

photo (verb) fotografare [fōtōgräfä'-re] 132; (noun) foto f [fō'tō] 132

photocopies fotocopie f/pl [fōtōkō'-pye] 138

photograph fotografare [fōtōgräfä'-re] 132

photographer: ship's ~ fotografo m di bordo [fōtō'gräfō dē bōr'dō] 74; ~'**s studio** studio m fotografi-co [stōō'dyō fōtōgräfēkō] 129

physics fisica f [fē'zēkä] 39

piano recital recital m di pianoforte [retshētäl' dē pyänōfōr'te] 178

pickle/ ~**s** sottaceti m/pl [sōtätshe'-tē] 108

pickled (conservato) in salamoia [(kōnservä'tō) ēn sälämō'yä] 100, 107

picture (paint.) quadro m [kōō·ä'-drō] 119; (phot.) fotografia f [fōtō-gräfē'ä] 132; foto f [fō'tō] 144; (cin.) spettacolo m [spetä'kōlō] 179

piece pezzo m [pe'tsō] 126; (chess) pedina f [pedē'nä] 182

pier pontile m [pōntē'le] 77

pike/ ~-**perch** luccio m [lōō'tshō] 104

piles emorroidi f/pl [emōrō'ēdē] 171

pill pastiglia f [pästē'lyä] 161

pillar colonna f [kōlō'nä] 125

pillow cuscino m [kōōshē'nō] 87; ~ **case** federa f [fe'derä] 90

pilot pilota m [pēlō'tä] 71

pin (noun) spillo m [spē'lō] 136; **bobby** ~**s** forcine f/pl [fōrtshē'ne] 140; ~ **up** (verb) (hair) raccogliere su [räkō'lyere sōō] 155

pincers tenaglie f/pl [tenä'lye] 57

pineapple ananas m [ä'nänäs] 109

ping-pong ping-pong m [pēng-pōng] 181

pink rosa [rō'zä] 194

pinkie mignolo m [mē'nyōlō] 167

pint pinta f [pēn'tä] 193

pipe pipa f [pē'pä] 140; ~ **cleaner** nettapipe m [netäpē'pe] 140

piston pistone *m* pēstō'ne 54; ~ **ring** fascia *f* elastica [fä'shä elä'stēkä] 54

pity: what a ~! che peccato! [ke pekä'tō] 22

place *(seat)* posto *m* [pō'stō] 66; ~ **of birth** luogo *m* di nascita [lōō·ō'gō dē nä'shētä] 79; ~ **of residence** residenza *f* [resēden'tsä] 79

plaice pesce *m* passera [pe'she pä'serä] 105

plane aereo *m* [ä·e're·ō] 68; aeroplano *m* [ä·erōplä'nō] 71

plate piatto *m* [pyä'tō] 97; **bread ~** piattino *m* [pyätē'nō] 97; **soup ~** piatto *m* fondo [pyä'tō fōn'dō] 97

platform binario *m* [bēnär'yō] 60; marciapiede *m* [märtshäpye'de] 60

play *(verb)* giocare [jōkä're] 182; *(noun) (thea.)* opera *f* drammatica [ō'perä drämä'tēkä] 178

player giocatore *m* [jōkätō're] 189

playground campo *m* di giochi [käm'pō dē jō'kē] 95

playing cards carte *f/pl* da gioco [kär'te dä jō'kō] 144

playroom sala *f* da gioco [sä'lä dä jō'kō] 77

please per favore [per fävō're] 20

pleasure: with ~ con piacere [kōn pyätshe're] 21

plenty *(adv.)* abbastanza [äbästän'tsä] 127

pleurisy pleurite *f* [ple·ōōrē'te] 171

pliers pinze *f/pl* [pēn'tse] 57

plug spina *f* [spē'nä] 92

plumber stagnino *m* [stänyē'nō] 37

pneumonia polmonite *f* [pōlmōnē'te] 171

point punto *m* [pōōn'tō] 188

poisoning avvelenamento *m* [ävelenämen'tō] 171

police polizia *f* (stradale) [pōlētsē'ä (strädä'le)] 49; ~ **car** macchina *f* della polizia [mä'kēnä de'llä pōle-

tsē'ä] 154; ~ **station** questura [kōō·estōō'rä] 122; commissariato *m* di Pubblica Sicurezza [kōmēsäryä'tō dē pōō'blēkä sēkōō're'tsä] 154

policeman poliziotto *m* [pōlētsyō'tō] 122

political science scienze *f/pl* politiche [shen'tse pōlē'tēke] 39

pool hall sala *f* da biliardo [sä'lä dä bēlyär'dō] 180

pork maiale *m* [mäyä'le] 106; ~ **hock** garretto *m* di maiale [gäre'tō dē mäyä'le] 106

port porto *m* [pōr'tō] 72; *(side)* babordo *m* [bäbōr'dō] 77; ~ **fees** diritti *m/pl* portuali [dērē'te pōrtōō·ä'lē] 77

portal portale *m* [pōrtä'le] 125

porter facchino *m* [fäkē'nō] 64

portion porzione *f* [pōrtsyō'ne] 96

post: ~ **office** ufficio *m* postale [ōōfētshō pōstä'le] 116; ~ **office box** casella *f* postale [käze'llä pō'stä'le] 150

postage tariffa *f* postale [tärē'fä pōstä'le] 145; affrancatura *f* [äfränkätōō'rä] 150

postal: ~ **clerk** impiegato *m* postale [ēmpyegä'tō pōstä'le] 150; ~ **savings book** libretto *m* postale di risparmio [lēbre'tō pōstä'le dē rēspär'myō] 150; ~ **transfer** vaglia *m* postale [vä'lyä pōstä'le] 146

postcard cartolina *f* (postale) [kärtōlē'nä (postä'le)] 85, 145; **picture ~** cartolina *f* illustrata [kärtōlē'nä ēlōōsträ'tä] 85

postman postino *m* [pōstē'nō] 150

pot pentola *f* [pen'tōlä] 92; bricchetto *m* [brēke'tō] 96; brocca *f* [brō'kä] 97; **coffee ~** caffettiera *f* [käfetye'rä] 97; **tea ~** teiera *f* [teye'rä] 97

potatoes patate *f/pl* [pätä'te] 108, **boiled ~** patate *f/pl* lesse [pätä'te le'se] 108; **french-fries ~** patate

f/pl fritte [pätä'te frē'te] 108;
roasted ~ patate *f/pl* arroste [pätä'te ärō'ste] 108

poultry pollame *m* [pōlä'me] 105

pound mezzo chilo *m* [me'dzō kē'lō] 126; libbra *f* [lē'brä] 193

powder cipria *f* [tshē'prē·ä] 141; polverina *f* [pōlverē'nä] 161

power steering servo sterzo *m* [ser'vō ster'tsō] 54

practice allenamento *m* [älenämen'tō] 188

prawns gamberetti *m/pl* [gämbere'tē] 105; granchiolini *m/pl* [gränkyōlē'nē] 105

precipitation precipitazione *f* [pretshēpētätsyō'ne] 27

pregnancy gravidanza *f* [grävēdän'tsä] 168

prescribed: as ~ come da prescrizione medica [kō'me dä preskrē-tsyō'ne me'dēkä] 159

prescription ricetta *f* [rētshe'tä] 159

present regalo *m* [regä'lō] 80

press stirare [stērä're] 137

preview rassegna *f* dei film [räse'nyä de'ē fēlm] 179

previously prima [prē'mä] 32

price prezzo *m* [pre'tsō] 92

priest prete *m* [pre'te] 123

print *(noun)* foto *f* [fō'tō] 131

printed variopinto [väryōpēn'tō] 137
~ **matter** stampe *f/pl* [stäm'pe] 145

priority road (strada con) diritto di precedenza [(strä'dä kōn) dērē'tō dē pretsheden'tsä] 59

prison prigione *f* [prējō'ne] 154

probably probabilmente [prōbäbēlmen'te] 21

procession processione *f* [prōtshesyō'ne] 125

producer produttore *m* [prōdōōtō're] 178

production messa *f* in scena [me'sä ēn she'nä] 178

program programma *m* [prōgrä'mä] 178; ~ **schedule** orario *m* dei programmi [ōrär'yō de'ē prōgrä'mē] 182

pronounce pronunciare [prōnōōntshä're] 24

prophylactics profilattici *m/pl* [prōfēlä'tētshē] 141

Protestant protestante *m* [prōtestän'te] 124

psychiatrist psichiatra *m* [psēkyä'trä] 162

psychologist psicologo *m* [psēkō'lōgō] 162

psychology psicologia *f* [psēkōlōjē'ä] 39

public: ~ **garden** giardino *m* pubblico [järdē'nō pōō'blēkō] 122; ~ **rest room** gabinetti *m/pl* pubblici [gäbēne'tē pōō'blētshē] 122

pull *(tooth)* estrarre [esträ're] 173

pulpit pulpito *m* [pōōl'pētō] 125

pump room chiosco *m* delle acque [kyōs'kō de'le ä'kōō·e] 175

punch punch *m* [pōōntsh] 111

puncture foratura *f* [fōrätōō'rä] 47

pupil discente *m* [dēshen'te] 37; scolaro *m* [skōlä'rō] 37

purple color *m* porpora [kōlōr' pōr'pōrä] 194

purse borsellino *m* [bōrselē'nō] 144; borsetta *f* [bōrse'tä] 153

purser commissario *m* di bordo [kōmēsär'yō dē bōr'dō] 74

Q

quay banchina *f* [bänkē'nä] 77

quart quarto *m* [kōō·är'tō] 126

quarter quarto *m* [kōō·är'tō] 30; trimestre *m* trēme'stre] 32

queen regina *f* [rejē'nä] 181

quickly presto [pre'stō] 48

quinine chinino *m* [kēnē'nō] 161

R

rabbit coniglio *m* [kōnē'lyō] 106

race gara *f*, corsa *f* [gä'ra, kōr'sä] 187

racing car macchina f da corsa [mä'kē'nä dä kōr'sä] 187

radiation therapy terapia f dei raggi [teräpē'ä de'ē rä'jē] 175

radiator radiatore m [rädyätō're] 54; **~ grill** mascherina f del radiatore [mäskerē'nä del rädyätō're] 54

radio radio f [rä'dyō] 182; **~ play** radiocommedia f [rädyōkōme'dyä] 182; **~ room** stazione f radiotelegramma [stätsyō'ne rädyōtelegrä'mä] 74

rag straccio m [strä'tshō] 57

ragout stufato m [stōōfä'tō] 107

rail car automotrice f [outōmōtrē'-tshe] 60

railroad ferrovia [ferōvē'ä] 67; **~ crossing** passaggio m a livello [päsä'jō ä lēve'lō] 42; **~ man** ferroviere m [ferōvye're] 37; **~ station** stazione f [stätsyō'ne] 72

rain (verb) piovere [pyō'vere] 25; (noun) pioggia f [pyō'jä] 27

raincoat impermeabile m [ēmperme·ä'bēle] 134

raisins uva f passa [ōō'vä pä'sä] 101

rare (cul.) al sangue [äl sän'gōō·e] 100

rash esantema m [ezänte'mä] 171

raspberries lamponi m/pl [lämpō'nē] 109

raw crudo m [krōō'dō] 100

razor rasoio m [räzō'yō] 141; **~ blades** lamette f/pl. [läme'te] 141; **~ cut** taglio m a rasoio [tä'lyō ä räzō'yō] 157; **~ safety** rasoio m di sicurezza [räzō'yō dē sēkōōre'tsä] 141

reading room sala f di lettura [sä'lä dē letōō'rä] 74

ready pronto [prōn'tō] 50

real estate agency agenzia f immobiliare [äjentsē'ä ēmōbēlyä're] 129

rear: at/on the ~ in coda [ēn kō'dä] 65, 66; **~ lights** luci f/pl posteriori [lōō'tshē pōsteryō'rē] 53; **~ motor** motore m a trazione posteriore [mōtō're ä trätsyō'ne pōsteryō're] 54; **~ view mirror** specchietto m retrovisore [spekye'tō retrōvēzō're] 55

rear-end collision tamponamento m [tämpōnämen'tō] 49

receipt ricevuta f [rētshevōō'tä] 150

recently recentemente [retshentemen'te] 32

recommend raccomandare [räkōmändä're] 81

record disco m [dē'skō] 130; **~ player** giradischi m [jērädēs'kē] 182; **~ phonograph ~ disco** m [dē'skō] 144

recording tape nastro m (magnetico) [nä'strō (mänye'tēkō)] 144

recreation room soggiorno m [sōjōr'nō] 95

red rosso [rō'sō] 194; **bright ~** rosso chiaro [rō'sō kyä'rō] 194; **dark ~** rosso scuro [rō'sō skōō'rō] 194; **fire engine ~** rosso vivo [rō'sō vē'vō] 194; **~ cabbage** cavolo m rosso [kä'vōlō rō'sō] 108; **~ currants** ribes m rosso [rē'bes rō'sō'] 110

reduced fare ticket biglietto m tariffa ridotta [bēlye'tō tärē'fä rēdō'tä] 62

reduced rates riduzioni f/pl [rēdōōtsyō'nē] 83

referee arbitro m [ärbē'trō] 189

refill caricare [kärēkä're] 140

refreshments rinfreschi m/pl [rēnfres'kē] 65

refrigerator frigorifero m [frēgōrē'ferō] 92

regards saluti m/pl [sälōō'tē] 16

register fare una raccomandata [fä're ōō'nä räkōmändä'tä] 150; **~ed letter** raccomandata f [räkōmändä'tä] 150

registration immatricolazione [ēmätrēkōlätsyō'ne] 43

regret (noun) dispiacere m [dēspyätshe're] 22

regular benzina f normale [bendzë'-nä nörmä'le] 45

religion religione f [relējō'ne] 125

religious religioso [relējō'sō] 125

remedy rimedio m [rēme'dyō] 161

renew rinnovare [rēnōvä're] 79

rent *(noun)* affitto m [äfē'tō] 92; *(verb)* noleggiare [nōlejä're] 41

repair *(verb)* riparare [rēpärä're] 46; *(noun)* riparazione f [rēpärätsyō'ne] 142; **~ shop** officina f riparazioni-auto [ōfētshē'nä rēpärätsyō'nē-ou'tō] 48

replace sostituire [sōstētōō·ē're] 138

report denunciare [denōōntshä're] 153

reservation prenotazione f [prenō-tätsyō'ne] 71

reserve prenotare [prenōtä're] 82; riservare [rēservä're] 62; **~ fuel can** tanica f di riserva [tä'nēkä dē rēser'vä] 55; **~ wheel** ruota f di scorta [rō·ō'tä dē skōr'tä] 47

respiration respirazione f [respērätsyō'ne] 168

rest room gabinetto m [gäbēne'tō] 60; ritirata f [rētērä'tä] 66

restaurant ristorante m [rēstōrän'te] 60; **seafood ~** ristorante m con specialità di pesce [rēstōrän'te kōn spetshälētä' dē pe'she] 96

result risultato m [rēsōōltä'tō] 188

retailer commerciante m [kōmer-tshän'te] 37

retiree pensionato m [pensyōnä'tō] 37

return flight volo m di ritorno [vō'lō dē rētōr'nō] 71

reverse gear retromarcia f [retrō-mär'tshä] 53

rheumatism reumatismo m [re·ōō-mätē'zmō] 171

rhubarb rabarbaro m [räbär'bärō] 110

rib costola f [kō'stōlä] 168

ribbon nastro m [nä'strō] 136

rice riso m [rē'sō] 103

ricotta ricotta f [rēkō'tä] 109

ride cavalcare [kävälkä're] 189

rider cavalcatore m [kävälkätō're] 189

riding equitazione f [ekōō·ētätsyō'-ne] 189; **~ stable** scuderia f [skōōderē'ä] 180

rifle range poligono m di tiro [pōlē'-gōnō dē tē'rō] 189

right esatto [ezä'tō] 21; *(direction)* a destra [ä de'strä] 40; **~of way** precedenza f [pretsheden'tsä] 43

ring anello m [äne'lō] 133; **~s** *(gymn.)* anelle f/pl [äne'le] 188; **wedding ~** fede f [fe'de] 133

rise salire [sälē're] 25

river fiume m [fyōō'me] 70

road strada f [strä'dä] 19; **~ conditions** viabilità f delle strade [vyäbēlētä' de'le strä'de] 25; **~ sign** segnale m [senyä'le] 43; **~ under construction** lavori m/pl in corso [lävō'rē ēn kōr'sō] 43

roast arrosto m [ärō'stō] 106

roasted arrostito [ärōstē'tō] 100

rôle parte f [pär'te] 178; **leading ~** parte f principale [pär'te prēntshēpä'le] 178

roll panino m [pänē'nō] 98; *(paper etc.)* rotolo m [rō'tōlō] 126

Romance languages lingue f/pl. romanze [lēn'gōō·e rōmän'dze] 39

Romanesque romanico [rōmä'nēkō] 125

roof tetto m [te'tō] 55

rook *(chess)* torre f [tō're] 181

room camera f [kä'merä] 82; posto m [pō'stō] 94; **double ~** (camera f) doppia f [(kä'merä) dō'pyä] 82; **quiet ~** camera f tranquilla [kä'mera tränkō·ē'lä] 82; **single ~** camera f singola [kä'merä sēn'gōlä] 82

root radice f [rädē'tshe] 174; **~ canal work** trattamento m della radice [trätämen'tō de'lä rädē'tshe] 174

rope fune f [foo'ne] 77

roses rose f/pl [rō'ze] 130

rosemary rosmarino m [rōzmärē'-nō] 101

rouge rossetto m [rōse'tō] 141

rough seas mare m mosso [mä're mō'sō] 77

round rotondo [rōtōn'dō] 156

roundtrip giro m [jē'rō] 73; ~ **ticket** biglietto m per il giro [bēlye'tō per ēl jē'rō] 73

route itinerario m [ētēnerär'yō] 43; percorso m [perkōr'sō] 67

row fila f [fē'lä] 177

rowing canottaggio m [känōtä'jō] 189

rubber boots stivali m/pl di gomma [stēvä'lē dē gō'mä] 139

ruby rubino m [roobē'nō] 133

rucksack zaino m [tsī'nō] 144

rudder timone m [tēmō'ne] 77

ruin rovine f/pl [rōvē'ne] 122

rum rum m [room] 112

S

sacristan sagrestano m [sägrestä'-nō] 125

sacristy sagrestia f [sägrestē'ä] 125

saddle sella f [se'lä] 107

safety pin spilla f di sicurezza [spēl'-lä dē sēkoore'tsä] 136

sail (noun) vela f [ve'lä] 189; (verb) veleggiare [velejä're] 189

sailboat barca f a vela [bär'kä ä ve'lä] 75

sailing sport m della vela [spōrt de'-lä ve'lä] 189

sailing school scuola f di navigazio-ne a vela [skoō·ō'lä dē nävēgä-tsyō'ne ä ve'lä] 180

sailor marinaio m [märēnä'yō] 77

salad insalata f [ēnsälä'tä] 102

salesperson (male) commesso m [kōme'sō] 37; (female) commessa f [kōme'sä] 37

salmon salmone m [sälmō'ne] 105; **smoked** ~ salmone m affumicato [sälmō'ne äffōōmēkä'tō] 102

salt sale m [sä'le] 101; ~ **shaker** portasale m [pōrtäsä'le] 97

salted/salty salato [sälä'tō] 100, 115

salve unguento m [oōngoō·en'tō] 161

sanatorium sanatorio m [sänä-tōr'yō] 175

sandals sandali m/pl [sän'dälē] 139; **beach** ~ sandali m/pl da spiaggia [sän'dälē dä spyä'jä] 139

sandpaper carta f vetrata [kär'tä ve-trä'tä] 57

sanitary napkins assorbenti m/pl igienici [äsōrben'tē ēje'nētshē] 141

sapphire zaffiro m [dzäfē'rō] 133

sardines sardine f/pl [särdē'ne] 102

Saturday sabato m [sä'bätō] 33

sauce salsa f [säl'sä] 101; **cream** ~ salsa f alla crema [säl'sä ä'lä kre'-mä] 101

saucer piattino m [pyätē'nō] 97

sauerkraut crauti m/pl [krou'tē] 108

sauna sauna f [sou'nä] 175

sausage salsiccia f [sälse'tshä] 98

savings book libretto m di rispar-mio [lēbre'tō dē rēspär'myō] 152

Savoy cabbage verza f [ver'tsä] 108

say dire [dē're] 24

scalp massage frizione f [frētsyō'-ne] 157

scarf sciarpa f [shär'pä] 134

scarlet fever scarlattina f [skärlä-tē'nä] 171

scenery scenario m [shenär'yō] 178

scheduled flight aereo m di linea [ä·e're·ō dē lē'ne·ä] 71

scholar scienziato m [shentsyä'tō] 37

school scuola f [skoō·ō'lä] 38

sciatica sciatica f [shä'tēkä] 171

scissors forbici *f/pl* [fôr'bëtshë] 136

Scotch tape scotch *m* [skôtsh] 144

screen schermo *m* [sker'mō] 179

screenplay copione *m* [kōpyō'ne] 179

screw vite *f* [vē'te] 55

screwdriver cacciavite *m* [kätshävē'te] 57

scuba diving nuotare sott'acqua [nōō·ōtä're sōtä'kōō·ä] 186

scuba equipment attrezzatura *f* subacquea [ätretsätōō'rä sōōbä'kōō·e·ä] 186

scull barca *f* a remi [bär'kä ä re'mē] 189

sculptor scultore *m* [skōōltō're] 37

sea mare *m* [mä're] 77; **~ water** acqua *f* di mare [ä'kōō·ä dē mä're] 175

seasickness mal *m* di mare [mäl dē mä're] 75

season stagione *f* [stäjō'ne] 93

seasoned condito [kōndē'tō] 100

seasoning condimento *m* [kōndēmen'tō] 101

seat posto *m* [pō'stō] 62; sedile *m* [sedē'le] 55; **~ belt** cintura *f* di sicurezza [tshēntōō'rä dē sēkōōre'tsä] 55; **~ reservation** prenotazione *f* posti [prenōtätsyō'ne pō'stē] 62

second *(noun)* secondo *m* [sekōn'dō] 32; *(num.)* secondo [sekōn'dō] 29; **~ class** seconda classe *f* [sekōn'dä klä'se] 62

secretary segretaria *f* [segretär'yä] 37

security *(econ.)* titolo *m* [tē'tōlō] 152

see vedere vede're 12; visitare [vēzētä're] 118

self-service self-service *m* [selfser'vēs] 129

send spedire [spedē're] 63

sender mittente *m* [mēten'te] 150

September settembre *m* [setem'bre] 33

serious grave [grä've] 164

sermon predica *f* [pre'dēkä] 123

service servizio *m* [servē'tsyō] 83; *(eccl.)* funzione *f* religiosa [fōōntsyō'ne relējō'sä] 125; messa *f* [me'sä] 125; **~ charge** tassa *f* di servizio [tä'sä dē servē'tsyō] 93; **~ station** officina *f* riparazioni-auto [ōfētshē'nä rēpärätsyō'nē-ou'tō] 48

set *(noun) (hair)* messa *f* in piega [me'sä ēn pye'gä] 158

setting lotion fissatore *m* [fēsätō're] 158

settings *(theat.)* scenario *m* [shenär'yō] 178

seven sette [se'te] 28

severe forte [fôr'te] 163

shampoo shampoo *m* [shäm'pōō] 142

shape *(noun)* forma *f* [fôr'mä] 127

share of stock azione *f* [ätsyō'ne] 152

sharp pungente [pōōnjen'te] 163; **at eleven ~** alle undici in punto [ä'le ōōn'dētshe ēn pōōn'tō] 30

shave *(noun)* barba *f* [bär'bä] 158; *(verb)* radere [rä'dere] 157

shaving: ~ brush pennello *m* per la barba [pene'lō per lä bär'bä] 142; **~ cream** crema *f* da barba [kre'mä dä bär'bä] 142; **~ foam** schiuma *f* da barba [skyōō'mä dä bär'bä] 142; **~ soap** sapone *m* da barba [säpō'ne dä bär'bä] 142

sheet lenzuolo *m* [lentsōō·ō'lō] 90

shellfish crostacei *m/pl.* [krōstä'-tshe·ē] 105

sherbet sorbetto *m* [sōrbe'tō] 114; **lemon ~** sorbetto *m* di limone [sōrbe'tō dē lēmō'ne] 114; **orange ~** sorbetto *m* d'arancia [sōrbe'tō därän'tshä] 114

sherry sherry *m* [she'rē] 111

shin stinco *m* [stēn'kō] 168

ship nave *f* [nä've] 72; **~'s doctor**

medico *m* di bordo [me'dēkō dē bōr'dō] 77

shipboard party festa *f* a bordo [fe'stä ä bōr'dō] 77

shipping: ~ agency agenzia *f* di navigazione [äjentsē'ä dē nävēgätsyō'ne] 77; **~ company** compagnia *f* di navigazione [kōmpänyē'ä dē nävēgätsyō'ne] 77

shirt camicia *f* [kämē'tshä] 135

shock shock *m* [shōk] 171; **~ absorber** ammortizzatore *m* [ämōrtēdzätō're] 55

shoe scarpa *f* [skär'pä] 139; **~ horn** corno *m* per le scarpe [kōr'nō per le skär'pe] 139; **~ laces** lacci *m/pl* per le scarpe [lä'tshē per le skär'pe] 139

shoemaker calzolaio *m* [kältsōlä'yō] 37

shoot sparare, tirare [spärä're, têrä're] 189

shop negozio *m* [negō'tsyō] 122; **antique ~** antiquario *m* [äntēkōō·är'yō] 128; **barber ~** barbiere *m* [bärbye're] 128; **butcher ~** macelleria *f* [mätshelerē'ä] 128; **china ~** negozio *m* di porcellane [negō'tsyō dē pōrtshelä'ne] 128; **cobbler ~** calzolaio *m* [kältsōlä'yō] 128; **electrical ~** negozio *m* di apparecchi elettrici [negō'tsyō dē äpäre'kē ele'trētshe] 128; **flower ~** fiorista *m* [fyōrē'stä] 128; **hat ~** negozio *m* di cappello [negō'tsyō dē käpe'lō] 128; **lingerie ~** negozio *m* di biancheria [negō'tsyō dē byänkerē'ä] 129; **perfume ~** profumeria *f* [prōfōōmerē'ä] 129; **pet ~** negozio *m* di animali domestici [negō'tsyō dē änēmä'lē dōme'stētshē] 129; **photo ~** fotografo *m* [fōtō'gräfō] 129; **shoemaker's ~** calzolaio *m* [kältsōlä'yō] 129; **souvenir ~** negozio *m* di souvenir [negō'tsyō dē sōōvenēr'] 129; **tailor ~** sarto *m* [sär'tō] 129; **watch-**

maker's ~ orologiaio *m* [ōrōlōjä'yō] 129; **wine ~** negozio *m* di vini [negō'tsyō dē vē'nē] 129

shopping acquisto *m* [äkōō·ē'stō] 118; **~ mall** centro *m* d'acquisti [tshen'trō däkōō·ē'stē] 122

shore terra *f* [te'rä] 77

short corto [kōr'tō] 133; **~ circuit** corto circuito *m* [kōr'tō tshērkōō·ē'tō] 55; **~ sleeved** a maniche corte [ä mä'nēke kōr'te] 135; **~ subject** cortometraggio *m* [kōrtōmeträ'jō] 179; **~ wave** onda *f* corta [ōn'dä kōr'tä] 175

shorten accorciare [äkōrtshä're] 137

shorts shorts *m/pl* [shōrts] 135

shoulder spalla *f* [spä'lä] 107

show far vedere [fär vede're] 83; mostrare [mōsträ're] 20

shower doccia *f* [dō'tshä] 82

shrimps gamberetti *m/pl* [gämbere'tē] 102

shuffle *(cards)* mescolare [meskōlä're] 181

shut chiudere [kyōō'dere] 88

shutter otturatore *m* [ōtōōrätō're] 132; *(release)* scatto *m* [skä'tō] 132

sick malato [mälä'tō] 12; **~ bay** infermeria *f* di bordo [ēnfermerē'ä dē bōr'dō] 74

side lato *m* [lä'tō] 176; **~ road** strada *f* laterale [strä'dä läterä'le] 122; **~ wind** vento *m* di traverso [ven'tō dē träver'sō] 43

sideburns basette *f/pl* [bäze'te] 158

sidewalk marciapiede *m* [märtshäpye'de] 122

sights cose *f/pl* interessanti [kō'se ēnteresän'tē] 117

sightseeing giro *m* turistico [jē'rō tōōrēs'tēkō] 122

sign *(verb)* firmare [fērmä're] 146; **~ up** iscriversi [ēskrē'versē] 85

signature firma *f* [fēr'mä] 79

silk seta *f* [se'tä] 137; **artificial ~** seta f artificiale [se'tä ärtēfētshä'le] 137; ~ **thread** seta f da cucire [se'tä dä kōotshē're] 136

silver (adj.) argento [ärjen'tō] 194; (noun) argento m [ärjen'tō] 133; ~ **plated** argentato [ärjentä'tō] 133

since da [dä] 32

sincere: yours ~ly cordiali saluti [kōrdyä'lē sälōo'tē] 13

sinew tendine f [ten'dēne] 168

singer cantante m [käntän'te] 178

singing canto m [kän'tō] 178

single celibe, nubile [tshe'lēbe/nōo'bēle] 79

singles (tennis) singolare m [sēngōlä're] 190

sink lavandino m [lävändē'nō] 93

sister sorella f [sōre'lä] 35

sister-in-law cognata f [kōnyä'tä] 35

six sei [se'ē] 28

size taglia f [tä'lyä] 133; numero m [nōo'merō] 139

skate (verb) pattinare [pätēnä're] 188

skater pattinatore m [pätēnätō're] 188

skates pattini m/pl [pä'tēnē] 188

ski (verb) sciare [shē·ä're] 189; (noun) sci m [shē] 189; ~ **binding** attacco m [ätä'kō] 189; ~ **jump** trampolino m [trämpōlē'nō] 189; ~ **lift** sciovia f [shē·ōvē'ä] 189; ~ **pants** pantaloni m/pl. da sci [päntälō'nē dä shē] 135

skiing sport m sciistico [spōrt shē·ē'stēkō] 189

skin pelle f [pe'le] 168; ~ **disease** dermatosi f [dermätō'zē] 171; ~ **lesion** escoriazione f [eskōryätsyō'ne] 171

skirt gonna f [gō'nä] 135

skull cranio m [krä'nyō] 168

sky cielo m [tshe'lō] 26

slacks calzoni m/pl sportivi [kältsō'nē spōrtē'vē] 135

Slavic languages lingue f/pl slave [lēn'gōo·e slä've] 39

sled slitta f [zlē'tä] 144

sleep dormire [dōrmē're] 12

sleeper vagone m letto [vägō'ne le'tō] 61; ~ **reservation** prenotazione f vagoni letto [prenōtätsyō'ne vägō'nē le'tō] 62

sleeping: ~ bag sacco m a pelo [sä'kō ä pe'lō] 95; ~ **car** vagone m letto [vägō'ne le'tō] 61; ~ **pill** sonnifero m (in pastiglie) [sōnē'ferō (ēn pästē'lye) 161, 173

slice fetta f [fe'tä] 98

slide diapositiva f [dē·äpōzētē'vä] 132

sliding roof tetto m apribile [te'tō äprē'bēle] 55

slip (verb) slittare [zlētä're] 53

slippers: bedroom ~ pantofole f/pl [päntō'fōle] 139

slippery road strada f sdrucciolevole [strä'dä zdrōotshōle'vōle] 43

slow piano [pyä'nō] 24; adagio [ädä'jō] 42

small piccolo [pē'kōlō] 127

smallpox vaiolo m [väyō'lō] 78

smear sporcare [spōrkä're] 55

smoke fumare [fōomä're] 70

smoked affumicato [äfōomēkä'tō] 100

smoking (sign) fumatori m/pl [fōomätō'rē] 66; **no ~** (sign) non fumatori m/pl. [nōn fōomätō'rē] 66

smuggling contrabbando m [kōnträbän'dō] 154

snails lumache f/pl [lōomä'ke] 102

sneakers scarpe f/pl da ginnastica [skär'pe dä jēnä'stēkä] 139

snow (verb) nevicare [nevēkä're] 25; (noun) neve f [ne've] 27; ~ **chains** catene f/pl da neve [käte'ne dä ne've] 52; ~ **flurries** tempesta f di neve [tempe'stä dē ne've] 27; **it's ~ing** nevica [ne'vēkä] 27

soap sapone m [säpō'ne] 142; **cake of ~** saponetta f [säpōne'tä] 87

soccer calcio *m* [käl'tshō] 189; ~ **field** campo *m* di calcio [käm'pō dē käl'tshō] 186; ~ **game** partita *f* di calcio [pärtē'tä dē käl'tshō] 187; **play** ~ giocare a pallone [jōkä're ä pälō'ne] 190

sociology sociologia *f* [sōtshōlōjē'ä] 39

socket presa *f* (di corrente) [pre'sä (dē kören'te)] 93; ~ **wrench** chiave *f* fissa a tubo [kyä've fē'sä ä tōō'bō] 57

socks calzini *m/pl* [kältsē'nē] 135

soda: bicarbonate of ~ bicarbonato *m* di sodio [bēkärbōnä'tō dē sō'dyō] 160

soft morbido [mōr'bēdō] 100; ~ **drink** bevanda *f* analcolica [bevän'dä änälkō'lēkä] 112

solder saldare [säldä're] 55

sole *(verb)* risuolare [rēsōō·ōlä're] 139; *(noun) (shoe)* suola *f* [sōō·ō'lä] 139; *(anat.)* pianta *f* [pyän'tä] 168; *(fish)* sogliola *f* [sōl'yōlä] 105; **crêpe** ~ suola *f* di gomma crespata [sōō·ō'lä dē gō'mä krespä'tä] 139; **leather** ~ suola *f* di cuoio [sōō·ō'lä dē kōō·ō'yō] 139; **rubber** ~ suola *f* di gomma [sōō·ō'lä dē gō'mä] 139

solid color a tinta unita [ä tēn'tä ōōnē'tä] 137

solid-colored in tinta unita [ēn tēn'tä ōōnē'tä] 194

soloist solista *m* [sōlē'stä] 178

somebody qualcuno [kōō·äl'kōō'nō] 41

sometimes qualche volta [kōō·äl'ke vōl'tä] 32

son figlio *m* [fē'lyō] 14

son-in-law genero *m* [je'nerō] 35

song canzone *f* [käntsō'ne] 178; **folk** ~ canzone *f* popolare [käntsō'ne pōpōlä're] 178; ~ **recital** serata *f* di canto [serä'tä dē kän'tō] 178

soon presto [pre'stō] 16; fra poco

[frä pō'kō] 32

sore throat faringite *f* [färēnjē'te] 171

soup zuppa *f* [tsōō'pä] 103; **bean** ~ minestra *f* di fagioli [mēne'strä de fäjō'lē] 103; **clear** ~ brodetto *m* (brodino *m* leggero) [brōde'tō (brōdē'nō leje'rō)] 103; **cream of asparagus** ~ crema *f* di asparagi [kre'mä dē äspä'räjē] 103; **cream of mushroom** ~ crema *f* di funghi [kre'mä dē fōōn'gē] 103; **fish** ~ zuppa *f* alla marinara, [tsōō'pä ä'lä märēnä'rä] 103; zuppa *f* di pesce [tsōō'pä dē pe'she] 103; **leek** ~ brodo *m* di verdura [brō'dō dē verdōō'rä] 103; **noodle** ~ pastina *f* in brodo [pästē'nä ēn brō'dō] 103; **onion** ~ zuppa *f* di cipolle [tsōō'pä dē tshēpō'le] 103; **oxtail** ~ zuppa *f* di coda di bue [tsōō'pä dē kō'dä dē bōō'e] 103; **thick** ~ minestra *f* [mēne'strä] 103; **tomato** ~ zuppa *f* di pomodoro [tsōō'pä dē pōmōdō'rō] 103; **turtle** ~ brodo *m* di tartaruga [brō'dō dē tärtärōō'gä] 103; **vegetable** ~ minestrone *m* [mēnestrō'ne] 103

sour acido [ä'tshēdō] 115

souvenir souvenir *m* [sōōvener'] 80

spa stazione *f* balneare [stätsyō'ne bälne·ä're] 175

space: parking ~ box *m* [bōks] 44

spades *(cards)* picche *f/pl* [pē'ke] 181

spaghetti spaghetti *m/pl* [späge'tē] 104

spare: ~ **part** pezzo *m* di ricambio [pe'tsō dē rēkäm'byō] 50; ~ **wheel** ruota *f* di scorta [rōō·ō'tä dē skōr'tä] 55

spark scintilla *f* [shēntē'lä] 55; ~ **plug** candela *f* [kände'lä] 45

speak parlare [pärlä're] 15; **speaking!** *(teleph.)* pronto! [prōn'tō] 148

special: ~ **delivery** espresso *m* [espre'sō] 150; ~ **delivery letter** lettera *f* per espresso [le'terä per espre'sō] 150; ~ **issue (stamp)** francobollo *m* di emissione speciale [fränkôbô'lō dē emēsyō'ne spetshä'le] 146, 150

specialist specialista *m* [spetshälē'stä] 163; **ear, nose and throat** ~ otorinolaringoiatra *m* [ōtōrēnōlä-rēngōyä'trä] 162

spectacles occhiali *m/pl* [ōkyä'lē] 138

speed: ~ **limit** limite *m* (limitazione *f*) di velocità [lē'mēte (lēmētä-tsyō'ne) dē velōtshētä'] 43, 59

speedometer tachimetro *m* [täkē'-metrō] 55

spices condimento *m* [kōndēmen'tō] 101

spinach spinaci *m/pl* [spēnä'tshē] 108

spinal cord midollo *m* spinale [mēdō'lō spēnä'le] 168

spine spina *f* dorsale [spē'nä dōrsä'-le] 168

spleen milza *f* [mēl'tsä] 168

spoke razza *f* [rä'tsä] 55

sponge spugna *f* [spōō'nyä] 142

spoon: **soup** ~ cucchiaio *m* [kōō-kyä'yō] 97

sport: ~ **shirt** camicia *f* sportiva [kämē'tshä spōrtē'vä] 135: ~**s** **sport** *m/pl* [spōrt] 187; ~**s event** manifestazioni *f/pl* sportive [mänēfestätsyō'nē spōrtē've] 186; ~**s fan** fan *m* sportivo [fän spōr-tē'vō] 190

sportswear vestiti *m/pl* sportivi [vestē'tē spōrtē'vē] 135

spot remover smacchiatore *m* [zmäkyätō're] 144

sprain *(verb)* lussare [lōōsä're] 164; *(noun)* strappo *m* muscoloso [strä'pō mōōskōlō'sō] 171

spring *(tech.)* molla *f* [mō'lä] 55; *(season)* primavera *f* [prēmäve'rä] 33

squab piccione *m* [pētshō'ne] 105

square piazza *f* [pyä'tsä] 122; *(chess)* scacco *m* [skä'kō] 181

stadium stadio *m* [stä'dyō] 122

stage palcoscenico *m* [pälkōshe'nē-kō] 178; ~ **director** regista *m* [rejē'stä] 178

stain macchia *f* [mä'kyä] 137

staircase scala *f* [skä'lä] 93

stairwell tromba *f* delle scale [trōm'-bä de'le skä'le] 93

stake posta *f* [pō'stä] 182

stall interrompere [ēnterōm'pere] 55

stamp *(noun)* francobollo *m* [fränkōbō'lō] 85; *(verb)* affrancare [äfränkä're] 150; ~ **machine** distributore *m* francobolli [dēstrēbōō-tō're fränkōbō'lē] 150

star stella *f* [ste'lä] 27

starboard tribordo *m* [trēbōr'dō] 77

start *(noun)* partenza *f*, via *m* [pärten'tsä, vē'ä] 188; *(verb)* cominciare [kōmēntshä're] 176

starter starter *m* [stär'ter] 55; motorino *m* d'avviamento [mōtōrē'nō dävyämen'tō] 55

station stazione *f* [stätsyō'ne] 60; ~ **master** capostazione *m* [käpōstä-tsyō'ne] 65; ~ **wagon** macchina *f* familiare [mä'kēnä fämēlyä're] 41

Stations of the Cross Via *f* Crucis [vē'ä krōō'tshēs] 125

statue statua *f* [stä'tōō-ä] 119

stay fermarsi [fermär'sē] 78; restare [restä're] 154

steak: **rump** ~ bistecca *f* di filetto [bēste'kä dē fēle'tō] 106

steal rubare [rōōbä're] 153

steamed cotto a vapore [kō'tō ä vä-pō're] 100

steamer vaporetto *m* [väpōre'tō] 77

steep: ~ **downgrade** discesa *f* [dē-she'sä] 43; ~ **upgrade** salita *f* [sä-lē'tä] 43

steering sterzo *m* [ster'tsō] 56; ~ **wheel** volante *m* [vōlän'te] 56

stern poppa f [pô'pä] 77

stew: delicate ~ stufato m [stoōfä'-tō] 107

steward cameriere m [kämerye're] 77; **chief ~** capocameriere m di bordo [käpōkämerye're dē bôr'dō] 74

stewed cotto in umido [kō'tō ēn ōō'-mēdō] 100; stufato [stoōfä'tō] 107

still ancora [änkō'rä] 31

stitch in the side fitta f al fianco [fē'tä äl fyän'kō] 171

stock titoli m/pl [tē'tōlē] 152

stockings calze f/pl [kält'se] 135

stole stola f [stō'lä] 135

stomach stomaco m [stō'mäkō] 159; **~ pains** dolori m/pl. di stomaco [dōlō'rē dē stō'mäkō] 171

stop (noun) fermata f [fermä'tä] 58; (verb) smettere [zme'tere] 26; fermare [fermä're] 43; fermarsi [fermär'sē] 58; stare fermo [stä're fer'mō] 66

stopover scalo m [skä'lō] 71

stopped up otturato [ōtoōrä'tō] 88

stopping: no ~ divieto m di sosta [dēvye'tō dē sō'stä] 42

store magazzino m [mägädzē'nō] 12; **candy ~** pasticceria f [pästē-tsherē'ä] 128; **cigar ~** tabaccheria f [täbäkerē'ä] 128; **department ~** grande magazzino m [grän'de mägädzē'nō] 128; **drug ~** (cosmetics & sundries) drogheria f [drōgerē'ä] 128; **drug ~** (prescription pharmacy) farmacia f [färmätshē'ä] 128; **grocery ~** negozio m di alimentari [negō'tsyo dē älēmentä'rē] 128; **jewelry ~** gioielleria f [jōyelerē'ä] 128; **leather goods ~** pelletteria f [peleterē'ä] 129; **liquor ~** negozio m di liquori [negō'tsyo dē lēkōō-ō'rē] 129; **music ~** negozio m di musica [negōtsyo dē moō'zēkä] 129; **record ~** dischi m/pl [dē'skē] 129; **shoe ~** calzoleria f [kältsōlerē'ä]

129; **sporting goods ~** articoli m/pl sportivi [ärtē'kōlē spôrtē'vē] 129; **stationery ~** cartoleria f [kärtōlerē'ä] 129; **textile ~** abbigliamento m [äbēlyämen'tō] 129; **toy ~** giocattoli m/pl. [jōkä'tōlē] 129

storekeeper magazziniere m [mägädzēnye're] 37

storm tempesta f [tempe'stä] 27; burrasca f [boōräs'kä] 26

stormy: it's ~ c'è tempesta [tshe tempe'stä] 25

stove stufa f [stoō'fä] 93

straight ahead (sempre) diritto [(sem'pre) dērē'tō] 40, 116

strait (noun) stretto m [stre'tō] 77

strand frangetta f [fränje'tä] 158

strawberries fragole f/pl [frä'gōle] 109

street strada f, via f [strä'dä, vē'ä] 116

strict severo [seve'rō] 165

string spago m [spä'gō] 57

stroke apoplessia f [apōplesē'ä] 171

student studente m [stoōden'te] 37

study studiare [stoōdyä're] 15

stuffed farcito [färtshē'tō] 100; **~ animal** animale m di stoffa [änē-mä'le dē stô'fä] 144

stuffing ripieno m [rēpye'nō] 100

styptic pencil antiemorragico m [äntē-emōrä'jēkō] 161

subject materia f [mäter'yä] 39

subtitled con i sottotitoli [kōn ē sōtōtē'tōlē] 179

suburb sobborgo m [sōbôr'gō] 122

suburban train treno m suburbano [tre'nō soōboōrbä'nō] 60

subway metropolitana f [metrōpōlē-tä'nä] 123

suddenly improvvisamente [ēmprō-vēzämen'te] 55

suède pelle f scamosciata [pe'le skämōshä'tä] 139

suède coat soprabito m in pelle scamosciata [sōprä'bētō ēn pe'le skämōshä'tä] 135

suède jacket giacca *f* in pelle scamosciata [jä'kä ēn pe'le skämōshä'tä] 135

sugar zucchero *m* [tsōō'kerō] 114; **cube ~** zucchero *m* in cubetti [tsōō'kerō ēn kōōbe'tē] 114; **bowl** zuccheriera *f* [tsōōkerye'rä] 97

suit *(lady's)* tailleur *m* [täyär'] 135; *(man's)* completo *m* [kōmple'tō] 135

suitcase valigia *f* [väle'jä] 80

summer estate *f* [estä'te] 33; **~ dress** vestito *m* estivo [veste'tō este'vō] 135

sun sole *m* [sō'le] 26; **~ roof** tetto *m* apribile [te'tō äprē'bēle] 55; **~ tan cream** crema *f* solare [kre'mä sōlä're] 142; **~ tan lotion** lozione *f* solare [lōtsyō'ne sōlä're] 142; **~ tan oil** olio *m* solare [ō'lyō sōlä're] 142

sunburn scottatura *f* solare [skōtätōō'rä sōlä're] 171

sundae coppa *f* di gelato con frutta [kō'pä dē jelä'tō kōn frōō'tä] 114

Sunday domenica *f* [dōme'nēkä] 33

sunglasses occhiali *m/pl* da sole [ōkyä'lē dä sō'le] 138

sunlamp lampada *f* a raggi ultravioletti [läm'pädä a rä'jē ōōlträvyōle'tē] 175

sunrise sorgere *m* del sole [sōr'jere del sō'le] 27

sunset tramonto *m* (del sole) [trämōn'tō (del sō'le)] 27

sunstroke insolazione *f* [ēnsōlätsyō'ne] 171

supermarket supermercato *m* [sōōpermerkä'tō] 129

supplement supplemento *m* [sōōplemen'tō] 66

supplemental fare (ticket) supplemento *m* [sōōplemen'tō] 60, 62

suppository supposte *f/pl.* [sōōpō'ste] 161

suppuration suppurazione *f* [sōōpōōrätsyō'ne] 171

surcharge supplemento *m* [sōōplemen'tō] 83; **seasonal ~** aumento *m* stagionale [oumen'tō stäjōnä'le] 83

surgeon chirurgo *m* [kērōōr'gō] 163

surgery: plastic ~ chirurgia *f* plastica [kērōōrjē'ä plä'stēkä] 163

surroundings dintorni *m/pl* [dēntōr'nē] 123

suspenders bretelle *f/pl* [brete'le] 135

sweater pullover *m* [pōōlō'ver] 135

sweatshirt pullover *m* cottone [pōōlō'ver kōtō'ne] 135

sweets dolci *m/pl* [dōl'tshē] 114

swelling gonfiore *m* [gōnfyō're] 171

swim nuotare [nōō·ōtä're] 185; fare il bagno [fä're ēl bän'yō] 185

swimmer nuotatore *m* [nōō·ōtätō're] 186

swimming nuoto *m* [nōō·ō'tō] 190; **~ area** piscina *f* [pēshē'nä] 122; **~ pier** pontile *m* [pōntē'le] 186; **~ pool** piscina *f* [pēshē'nä] 74; **indoor ~ pool** piscina *f* coperta [pēshē'nä kōper'tä] 187; **outdoor ~ pool** piscina *f* all'aperto [pēshē'nä äläper'tō] 187; **no ~!** vietato bagnarsi! [vyetä'tō bänyär'sē] 185

swimsuit costume *m* da bagno [kōstōō'me dä bän'yō] 135

Swiss Francs franchi *m/pl* svizzeri [frän'kē zvē'tserē] 152

switch interruttore *m* [ēnterōōtō're] 56

swollen gonfio [gōn'fyō] 164

sympathy condoglianze *f/p* [kōndōlyän'tse] 23

symphony concert concerto *m* sinfonico [kōntsher'tō sēnfō'nēkō] 178

synagogue sinagoga *f* [sēnägō'gä] 116

system time table *(railroad)* orario

m ferroviario [ōrär'yō ferōvyär'yō] 61; *(planes)* orario *m* del volo [ōrär'yō del vō'lō] 71

T

table tavolo *m* [tä'vōlō] 93; ~ **tennis** ping-pong *m* [pēng-pōng] 182
tablecloth tovaglia *f* [tōväl'yä] 93
tablet compressa *f* [kōmpre'sä] 161
tailor sarto *m* [sär'tō] 37
take prendere [pren'dere] 83
taken occupato [ōkōōpä'tō] 96
take-off decollo *m* [dekō'lō] 71
talcum powder borotalco *m* [bōrō-täl'kō] 161
tampons tamponi *m/pl* [tämpō'nē] 142
tangerine mandarino *m* [mändä-rē'nō] 110
tape fettuccia *f* [fetōō'tshä] 136; ~ **measure** metro *m* a nastro [me'trō ä nä'strō] 136; ~ **recorder** magnetofono *m* [mänyetō'fōnō] 182
target bersaglio *m* [bersä'lyō] 189
tart, fruit ~ torta *f* di frutta [tōr'tä dē frōō'tä] 114
tartar tartaro *m* [tär'tärō] 174
taxi tassì *m* [täsē'] 64; ~ **stand** posteggio *m* dei tassì [pōste'jō de'ē täsē'] 116; posteggio-tassì *m* [pōste'jōtäsē'] 123
tea tè *m* [te] 98; ~ **with lemon** tè *m* con limone [te kōn lēmō'ne] 98; ~ **with milk** tè *m* con latte [te kōn lä'te] 98
teacher insegnante *m/f* [ēnsenyän'-te] 37
tease cotonare [kōtōnä're] 156
teaspoon cucchiaino *m* [kōōkyä·ē'-nō] 97
technical college istituto *m* tecnico [ēstētōō'tō tek'nēkō] 39
technician tecnico *m* [tek'nēkō] 37
telegram telegramma *m* [telegrä'-mä] 147; ~ **form** modulo *m* per

telegrammi [mō'dōōlō per tele-grä'mē] 147
telegraphic telegrafico [telegrä'fē-kō] 152
telephone telefono *m* [tele'fōnō] 93
television televisione *f* [televēzyō'-ne] 180; ~ **play** dramma *m* televi-sivo [drä'mä televēzē'vō] 183
tell dire [dē're] 20
teller cassiere *m* [käsye're] 152
temperature temperatura *f* [tempe-rätōō'rä] 27; ~ **chart** diagramma *m* della temperatura [dyägrä'mä de'lä temperätōō'rä] 172
temple *(anat.)* tempia *f* [tem'pyä] 168; *(archit.)* tempio *m* [tem'pyō] 123
temporarily per ora [per ō'rä] 32
ten dieci [dye'tshē] 28
tender tenero [te'nerō] 100
tenderloin filetto *m* di carne [fēle'tō dē kär'ne] 106
tendon tendine *m* [ten'dēne] 168; **pulled** ~ stiramento *m* [stērä-men'tō] 171
tennis tennis [te'nēs] 190; ~ **ball** palla *f* da tennis [pä'lä dä te'nēs] 190; ~ **court** campo da tennis [käm'pō dä te'nēs] 190; **play** ~ giocare a tennis [jōkä're ä te'nēs] 190
tent tenda *f* [ten'dä] 95
terrace terrazzo *m* [terä'tsō] 82
terrific! magnifico! [mänyē'fēkō] 21
tetanus tetano *m* [te'tänō] 172
thank *(verb)* ringraziare [rēn·grä-tsyä're] 21; **thanks** grazie *f/pl* [grä'tsye] 12; ~ **a lot** mille grazie [mē'le grä'tsye] 21; ~ **very much** tante grazie [tän'te grä'tsye] 21
thaw *(noun)* tempo *m* di sgelo [tem'-pō dēzje'lō] 27; *(verb):* **it's ~ing** sgela [zje'lä] 27
theater teatro *m* [te·ä'trō] 178; ~ **schedule** programma *m* [prōgrä'-mä] 178
theft furto *m* [fōōr'tō] 153

there là [lä] 40

thermometer termometro *m* [termō'metrō] 144

thermos bottle termos *m/inv.* [ter'mōs] 144

thermostat termostato *m* [termō'stätō] 56

thief ladro *m* [lä'drō] 154

thigh femore *m* [femō're] 167

thimble ditale *m* [dētä'le] 136

third terzo *m* [ter'tsō] 29

thorax torace *m* [tōrä'tshe] 168

thread filo *m* [fē'lō] 136; **(screw)** ~ madrevite *f* [mädrevē'te] 56

three tre [tre] 28

thriller giallo *m* [jä'lō] 130

throat trachea *f* [träke'ä] 168

through car carrozza *f* diretta [kärō'tsä dēre'tä] 64

throughway passaggio *m* [päsä'jō] 123

throw up rimettere [rēme'tere] 163

throw-in rimessa *f* in gioco [rēme'sä ēn jō'kō] 190

thumb pollice *m* [pō'lētshe] 166

thunder tuono *m* [tōō-ō'nō] 27

thunderstorm temporale *m* [tempōrä'le] 26

Thursday giovedì *m* [jōvedē'] 33

thyme timo *m* [tē'mō] 101

ticket: one way ~ biglietto *m* [bēlye'tō] 58; ~ **sales** vendita *f* dei biglietti [ven'dētä de'ē bēlye'tē] 178; ~ **window** biglietteria *f* [bēlyeterē'ä] 60; **transfer** ~ biglietto *m* di coincidenza [bēlye'tō dē kō-ēntshēden'tsä] 117

tie cravatta *f* [krävä'tä] 135

tight stretto [stre'tō] 51

tighten stringere [strēn'jere] 55

tights collant *m* [kōlän'] 135

time tempo *m* [tem'pō] 15; **any** ~ in ogni tempo [ēn ō'nye tem'pō] 32; **from** ~ **to** ~ di tanto in tanto [dē tän'tō ēn tän'tō] 32; **on** ~ in punto [ēn pōōn'tō] 32; ~ **table** orario *m* [ōrär'yō] 60

tincture tintura *f* [tēntōō'rä] 161

tint tingere [tēn'jere] 158

tire gomma *f* [gō'mä] 46; ~ **change** cambio *m* di una gomma [käm'byō dē ōō'nä gō'mä] 47; ~ **pressure** pressione *f* delle gomme [presyō'ne de'le gō'me] 47; ~**s** *(in general)* ruote *f/pl* [rōō-ō'te] 47

tissue fazzoletti *m/pl* di carta [fätsōle'tē dē kär'tä] 142

tobacco tabacco *m* [täbä'kō] 140

toboggan slitta *f* [zlē'tä] 190; ~**ing** sport *m* della slitta [spōrt de'lä zlē'tä] 190

today oggi [ō'jē] 31

toe dito *m* del piede [dē'tō del pye'de] 168

together insieme [ēnsye'me] 115

toilet toletta *f* [tōle'tä] 88; servizi *m/pl* [servē'tsē] 82; ~ **articles** accessori *m/pl* da toletta [ätshesō'rē dä tōle'tä] 142; ~ **kit** beauty-case *m* [byōōtē käs] 142; ~ **paper** carta *f* igienica [kär'tä ēje'nēkä] 142

toiletries accessori *m/pl* da toletta [ätshesō'rē dä tōle'tä] 142

tomato pomodoro *m* [pōmōdō'rō] 108; ~ **juice** succo *m* di pomodoro [sōō'kō dē pōmōdō'rō] 102

tomb tomba *f* [tōm'bä] 123

tomorrow domani [dōmä'nē] 17; **the day after** ~ dopodomani [dōpōdōmä'nē] 31; ~ **morning** domani mattina [dōmä'nē mätē'nä] 31

tongue lingua *f* [lēn'gōō-ä] 106

tonic tonico *m* [tō'nēkō] 161; acqua *f* tonica [ä'kōō-ä tō'nēkä] 112

tonight stanotte [stänō'te] 31; stasera [stäse'rä] 176

tonsillitis tonsillite *f* [tōnsēlē'te] 172

tonsils tonsille *f/pl* [tōnsē'le] 168

too *(degree)* troppo [trō'pō] 31

tool utensile *m* [ōōtensē'le] 57; ~ **box/kit** cassa *f* degli utensili [kä'sä de'lyē ōōtensē'lē] 57

tooth dente *m* [den'te] 168; ~ **brush** spazzolino *m* per i denti [spätsō-

lēʼnō per ē denʼtē] 142; ~ **cervix**
colletto *m* del dente [kōleʼtō del
denʼte] 174; ~ **paste** dentifricio *m*
[dentēfrēʼtshō] 142; ~ **pick** stuzzi-
cadente *m* [stōōtsēkädeʼnte] 97;
~ **powder** dentifricio *m* in polvere
[dentēfrēʼtshō ēn pōlʼvere] 142;
wisdom ~ dente *m* del giudizio
[denʼte del jōōdēʼtsyō] 174

toothache mal *m* di denti [mäl dē
denʼtē] 174

top *(car)* tetto *m* [teʼtō] 56

topless con il topless [kōn ēl tōples]
185

tough duro [dōōʼrō] 100; legnoso
[lenyōʼsō] 115

toupé tuppè *m* [tōōpeʼ] 158

tour: ~ **guide** guida *m* [gōō·ēʼdä]
74; ~ **guide office** ufficio *m* della
guida [ōōfētʼshō deʼlä gōō·ēʼdä]
74; **guided** ~ visita *f* guidata [vē-
ʼzētä gōō·ēdäʼtä] 118

tow rimorchiare [rēmōrkyäʼre] 48; ~
line cavo *m* di rimorchio [käʼvō dē
rēmōrʼkyō] 49; ~ **truck** rimorchiatore *m* [rēmōrkyätōʼre] 48; carro
m attrezzi [käʼrō ätreʼtsē] 49

towel asciugamano *m* [äshōōgä-
mäʼnō] 87; **bath** ~ asciugamano
m da bagno [äshōōgämäʼnō dä
bänʼyō] 142

tower torre *f* [tōʼre] 123

towing service servizio *m* traino-au-
to [servēʼtsyō trīʼnō ouʼtō] 49

town città *f* [tshētäʼ] 40; **old** ~ centro *m* storico [tshenʼtrō stōʼrēkō]
122

toy giocattolo *m* [jōkäʼtōlō] 144

track binario *m* [bēnärʼyō] 67; ~ **and
field** atletica *f* leggiera [ätleʼtēkä
lejeʼrä] 190; ~ **suit** tuta *f* sportiva
[tōōʼtä spōrtēʼvä] 135

traffic traffico *m* [träʼfēkō] 43; ~ **cir-
cle** rotatoria *f* [rōtätōʼryä] 43; ~
light semaforo *m* [semäʼfōrō] 43;
~ **regulations** codice *m* della
strada [kōʼdētshe deʼlä sträʼdä] 43

tragedy tragedia *f* [träjeʼdyä] 178

trailer rimorchio *m* [rēmōrʼkyō] 41;
roulotte *f* [rōōlōtʼ] 94

train treno *m* [treʼnō] 61; **suburban
express** ~ ferrovia *f* urbana [ferō-
vēʼä ōōrbäʼnä] 122

trainee apprendista *m/f* [äprendēʼ-
stä] 37

tranquilizer tranquillante *m* [trän-
kōō·ēlänʼte] 161

transfer rimessa *f* [rēmeʼsä] 152

translate tradurre [trädōōʼre] 24

translation traduzione *f* [trädōō-
tsyōʼne] 130

translater traduttore *m* [trädōōtōʼre]
37

transmission cambio *m* [kämʼbyō]
56

travel agency agenzia *f* viaggi [äjen-
tsēʼä vyäʼje] 82

travel reading letture *f/pl* per il viaggio [letōōʼre per ēl vyäʼjō] 130

tray vassoio *m* [väsōʼyō] 97

trick *(cards)* bazza *f* [bäʼtsä] 181

trim spuntare [spōōntäʼre] 157

trip gita *f* [jēʼtä] 43; viaggio *m* [vyäʼ-
jō] 43; **have a good** ~ ! buon viaggio! [bōō·ōn vyäʼjō] 17

tripe trippa *f* [trēʼpä] 107

trotting race corsa *f* al trotto [kōrʼsä
äl trōʼtō] 189

trousers pantaloni *m/pl* [päntälōʼnē]
135

trout trota *f* [trōʼtä] 105

truck autocarro *m* [outōkäʼrō] 41; ~
driver camionista *m* [kämyōnēʼ-
stä] 37

trump briscola *f* [brēʼskōlä] 181

trunk portabagagli *m* [pōrtäbä-
gälʼyē] 56

tube tubo *m* [tōōʼbō] 56; tubetto *m*
[tōōbeʼtō] 126

Tuesday martedì *m* [märtedēʼ] 33

tug rimorchiatore *m* [rēmōrkyätōʼre]
77

tulips tulipani *m/pl* [tōōlēpäʼnē] 130

tumor tumore *m* [tōōmōʼre] 172

tuna fish tonno m [tō'nō] 105

turbot rombo m [rŏm'bō] 105

turkey tacchino m [täkē'nō] 106

turn *(the car)* girare [jērä're] 43; ~ *(into a road)* voltare [vŏltä're] 43; ~ **off** spegnere [spen'yere] 183; ~ **off** *(a road)* cambiare strada [kämbyä're strä'dä] 43; ~ **on** accendere [ätshen'dere] 183

tweezers pinzette f/pl [pēntse'te] 142

two due [dōō'e] 28

two-piece due pezzi m/pl [dōō'e pe'tsē] 135

two-stroke motor motore m a due tempi [mōtō're ä dōō'e tem'pē] 54

typewriter paper carta f per scrivere a macchina [kär'tä per skrē'vere ä mä'kēnä] 138

typhoid fever tifo m [tē'fō] 172

U

ulcer ulcera f [ōōl'tsherä] 172

ultrasonics ultrasuoni m/pl [ōōlträsōō·ō'nē] 175

umbrella ombrello m [ōmbre'lō] 144; **garden ~** ombrellone m [ōmbrelō're] 91

umpire arbitro m [ärbē'trō] 190

uncle zio m [tsē'ō] 35

underpants mutande f/pl [mōōtän'de] 135

undershirt canottiera f [känōtye'rä] 135

understand capire [käpē're] 24

undertow correnti f/pl [kōren'tē] 185

underwear biancheria f intima [byänkerē'ä ēn'tēmä] 135

undisturbed indisturbato [ēndēstōōrbä'tō] 183

university università f [ōōnēversētä'] 38

unlock aprire con chiave [äprē're kōn kyä've] 92

unstamped non affrancato [nōn äfränkä'tō] 150

until fino a [fē'nō ä] 32

urgent urgente [ōōrjen'te] 147

urine urina f [ōōrē'nä] 168

urinalysis analisi f dell'orina f [änä'lēsē delōrē'nä] 165

urologist urologo m [ōōrō'lōgō] 163

use uso m [ōō'zō] 80

usher maschera f [mäs'kerä] 179

uterus utero m [ōō'terō] 168

V

vacant libero [lē'berō] 66

vaccinate vaccinare [vätshēnä're] 164

vaccination vaccinazione f [vätshēnätsyō'ne] 78; ~ **certificate** certificato m di vaccinazione [tshertēfēkä'tō dē vätshēnätsyō'ne] 78

vagina vagina f [väjē'nä] 168

valerian drops gocce f/pl di valeriana [gō'tshe dē väleryä'nä] 161

valid valido [vä'lēdō] 62

valley valle f [vä'le] 123

valuables oggetti m/pl di valore [ōje'tē dē välō're] 84

value declaration dichiarazione f del valore [dēkyärätsyō'ne del välō're] 150

valve valvola f [väl'vōlä] 47

vanilla vaniglia f [vänē'lyä] 101

vase vaso m [vä'zō] 130

vaseline vaselina f [väzelē'nä] 161

veal vitello m [vēte'lō] 107; ~ **knuckle** garretto m di vitello [gäre'tō dē vēte'lō] 106

vegetables verdura f [verdōō'rä] 108

vegetable market mercato m della verdura [merkä'tō de'llä verdōō'rä] 129

vehicle veicolo m [ve·ē'kōlō] 41

vein vena f [ve'nä] 168

velvet velluto m [velōō'tō] 137

venison capriolo m [käprē·ō'lō] 106

ventilation ventilazione f [ventēlätsyō'ne] 93

verdict sentenza f [senten'tsä] 154

vermouth vermut *m* [ver'mōōt] 110

vest panciotto *m* [päntshō'tō] 135

veterinarian veterinaio *m* [veterē-nä'yō] 37

veterinary medicine veterinaria *f* [veterēnär'yä] 39

victory vittoria *f* [vētōr'yä] 188

video cassette videocassetta *f* [vē-de-ōkäse'tä] 144

viewfinder mirino *m* [mērē'nō] 132

village villaggio *m* [vēlä'jō] 123; paese *m* [pä·e'ze] 123

vinegar aceto *m* [ätshe'tō] 101

vintage vendemmia *f* [vendem'yä] 111

violet *(adj.)* violetto [vyōle'tō] 194; **~s** *(noun)* violette *f/pl* [vyōle'te] 130

violin recital recital *m* di violino [retshētäl' dē vyōlē'nō] 178

visa visto *m* [vē'stō] 78

visit visitare [vēzētä're] 78; andare/venire a trovare [ändä're/venē're ä trōvä're] 184; *(chat)* fare quattro chiacchiere [fä're kōō·ä'trō kyä'kyere] 184

visiting hours orario *m* delle visite [ōrär'yō de'lle vē'zēte] 173

vocational school scuola *f* d'avviamento professionale [skōō·ō'lä dävvyämen'tō prōfesyōnä'le] 38

vodka vodka *m* [vōd'kä] 112

volleyball pallavolo *m* [pälavō'lō] 190

voltage voltaggio *m* [vōltä'jō] 86

volume volume *m* [vōlōō'me] 130

vomiting vomito *m* [vō'mētō] 172

voyage viaggio *m* in nave [vyä'jō ēn nä've] 77

W

wafers wafer *m/pl* [ōō·ä'fer] 114

wait aspettare [äspetä're] 87

waiter cameriere *m* [kämerye're] 37

waiting room sala *f* d'aspetto [sä'lä däspe'tō] 60

waitress cameriera *f* [kämerye'rä] 37

wake svegliare [zvelyä're] 86

walk: take a ~ fare una passeggiat [fä're ōō'nä päsejä'tä] 184

walking shoes scarpe *f/pl* bass [skär'pe bä'se] 139

wall muro *m* [mōō'rō] 123; parete [päre'te] 93

wallet portafoglio *m* [pōrtäfōl'yō 144

walnuts noci *f/pl* [nō'tshē] 110

want volere [vōle're] 21

ward corsia *f* d'ospedale [kōrsē döspedä'le] 173

warm caldo [käl'dō] 67

warning triangle triangolo *n* [trē·än'gōlō] 57

warship nave *f* da guerra [nä've d gōō·e'rä] 77

wash lavare [lävä're] 95; **~ clot** guanto *m* spugna [gōō·än't spōō'nyä] 142; **~ rooms** docc *f/pl* [dō'tshe] 94

washer *(tech.)* rondella *f* [rōnde'lä 56

watch orologio *m* [ōrōlō'jō] 142; **~ band** cinturino *m* [tshēntōōrē'nō 143; **pocket ~** orologio *m* d tasca [ōrōlō'jō dä täs'kä] 143 **stop ~** cronometro *m* [krōnō'me trō] 143; **wrist ~** orologio *m* d polso [ōrōlō'jō dä pōl'sō] 143

watchmaker orologiaio *m* [ōrōlō jä'yō] 37

water acqua *f* [ä'kōō·ä] 45; **~ glas** bicchiere *m* da acqua [bēkye'r dä ä'kōō·ä] 93; **~ skiing** sci *n* nautico [shē nou'tēkō] 185 **~ temperature** temperatura dell'acqua [temperätōō'rä delä kōō·ä] 186; **carbonated ~** acqua gassata [ä'kōō·ä gäsä'tä] 112 **distilled ~** acqua *f* distillat [ä'kōō·ä dēstēlä'tä] 45; **drinking ~** acqua *f* potabile [ä'kōō·ä pōtä'bē le] 95; **hot and cold running ~** a qua f calda e fredda [ä'kŌŌ-ä käl'dä e fre'dä] 82; **mineral ~** acqua f minerale [ä'kŌŌ-ä mēnerä'le] 112; **non-carbonated ~** acqua f naturale [ä'kŌŌ-ä nätŌŌrä'le] 112; **soda ~** seltz m [sels] 112

waterfall cascata f [käskä'tä] 123

wave onda f [ōn'dä] 77

way: no ~ in nessun caso [ēn nesŌŌn kä'zō] 21; **go by ~ of** passare per [päsä're per] 61

weather tempo m [tem'pō] 25; **~ prediction** previsioni f/pl del tempo [prevēzyō'nē del tem'pō] 27; **~ report** bollettino m meteorologico [bōletē'nō mete-ōrōlō'jēkō] 27

wedding matrimonio m [mätrēmō'nyō] 123

Wednesday mercoledi m [merkōledē'] 33

week settimana f [setēmä'nä] 31; **a ~ from now** oggi fra una settimana [ō'jē frä ŌŌ'nä setēmä'nä] 31

weekend weekend m [ŌŌ-ē'kend] 32

weekly ogni settimana [ō'nye setēmä'nä] 32

welcome! benvenuto! [benvenŌŌ'tō] 12; **You're ~** Prego, non c'è di che [pre'gō, nōn tshe' dē ke'] 21

well bene [be'ne] 12; **get ~ soon!** buona guarigione! [bŌŌ-ō'nä gŌŌ-ärējō'ne] 20; **~ done** ben cotto [ben kō'tō] 100

wet bagnato [bänyä'tō] 155

what (che) cosa [(ke) kō'sä] 15, 18; **~ for** per che cosa [per ke kō'sä] 18

wheel ruota f [rŌŌ-ō'tä] 47

when quando [kŌŌ-än'do] 15; **a che ora** [ä ke ō'rä] 15

where dove [dō've] 15; **~ from** di dove [dē dō've] 14; **da dove** [dä dō've] 18; **~ to** dove [dō've] 18

which quale [kŌŌ-ä'le] 18

whiskey whisky m [ŌŌ-ē'skē] 112

white bianco [byän'kō] 194

who chi [kē] 18

wholesaler grossista m [grōsē'stä] 37

whom chi [kē] 18; **to ~** a chi [ä kē] 18; **with ~** con chi [kōn kē] 18

whose di chi [dē kē] 19

why perchè [perke'] 18

wide largo [lär'gō] 127

widowed vedovo [ve'dōvō] 79

wife moglie f [mō'lye] 13

wig parucca f [pärŌŌ'kä] 156

win vincere [vēn'tshere] 188

wind vento m [ven'tō] 26; **east ~** vento m di levante [ven'tō dē levän'te] 27; **north ~** tramontana f [trämōntä'nä] 27; **south ~** vento m australe [ven'tō ousträ'le] 27; **west ~** vento m di ponente [ven'tō dē pōnen'te] 27

windbraker giacca f a vento [jä'kä ä ven'tō] 135

winding road serpentina f [serpentē'nä] 43

window finestra f [fēne'strä] 88; finestrino m [fēnestrē'nō] 65; **~ (pane)** vetro m [ve'trō] 47, 93; **~ seat** posto m al finestrino [pō'stō äl fēnestrē'nō] 67

windshield parabrezza m [pärä-bre'dzä] 47; **~ washer** impianto m lavacristallo [ēmpyän'tō läväkrēstä'lō] 56; **~ wiper** tergicristallo m [terjēkrēstä'lō] 56

windy: it's ~ c'è vento [tshe ven'tō] 27

wine vino m [vē'nō] 110; **~ list** lista f delle bevande [lē'stä de'le bevän'de] 96; **dessert ~** vino m liquoroso [vē'nō lēkŌŌ-ōrō'sō] 110; **dry ~** vino m secco [vē'nō se'kō] 110; **mulled ~** vin m brulé [vēn brŌŌle'] 110; **red ~** vino m rosso [vē'nō rō'sō] 110; **sweet ~** vino m dolce/amabile [vē'nō dōl'tshe/ämä'bēle] 110; **white ~** vino m bianco [vē'nō byän'kō] 110

wing ala f [ä'lä] 71

winter inverno m [ēnver'nō] 33

wire filo *m* metallico [fē'lō metä'lēkō] 57

wish augurare [ougōōrä're] 20

wisp ciocca *f* di capelli [tshŏ'kä dē käpe'lē] 158

withdraw ritirare [rētērä're] 152

within entro [en'trō] 32

witness testimone *m* [testēmō'ne] 49

wood carving scultura *f* in legno [skōōltōō'rä ēn le'nyō] 144

wool lana *f* [lä'nä] 136; **pure ~** lana *f* pura [lä'nä pōō'rä] 137; **pure virgin ~** lana *f* pura vergine [lä'nä pōō'rä ver'jēne] 137

word parola *f* [pärō'lä] 24

work *(noun)* opera *f* [ō'perä] 178; *(verb)* lavorare [lavōrä're] 15; funzionare [fōōntsyōnä're] 87

worker operaio *m* [ōperä'yō] 37

worsted lana *f* pettinata [lä'nä petēnä'tä] 137

wound ferita *f* [ferē'tä] 172; **~ salve** pomata *f* per una ferita [pōmä'tä per ōō'nä ferē'tä] 161

wrapping paper carta *f* da impacco [kär'tä dä ēmpä'kō] 138

wrench chiave *f* (inglese/per viti) [kyä've (ēngle'se/per vē'tē)] 57

wrestle lottare [lōtä're] 190

wrestler lottatore *m* [lōtätō're] 190

wrestling lotta *f* libera [lō'tä lē'berä] 190

wrist polso *m* [pōl'sō] 168

write scrivere [skrē'vere] 24

writer scrittore *m* [skrētō're] 37

writing paper carta *f* da scrivere [kär'tä dä skrē'vere] 138

X

x-ray *(verb)* fare una radiografia [fä're ōō'nä rädyōgräfē'ä] 173

Y

yacht yacht *m* [jäkt] 77

yard iarda *f* [yär'dä] 193

year anno *m* [ä'nō] 32; **Happy New Year!** Felice Anno Nuovo! [felē'tshe ä'nō nōō·ō'vō] 23

yellow giallo [jä'lō] 132

yes si [sē] 21

yesterday ieri [ē·e'rē] 31; **the day before ~** ieri l'altro [ē·e'rē läl'trō] 31

yield right of way dare precedenza *f* [dä're pretsheden'tsä] 59

young giovane [jō'väne] 35

youth: ~ group gruppo *m* di giovani [grōō'pō dē jō'väne] 95; **~ hostel** ostello *m* per la gioventù [ōste'lō per lä jōventōō'] 95; **~ hostel card** tessera *f* per l'ostello [tese'rä per lōste'lō] 95

Z

zebra crossing strisce *f/pl* pedonali [strē'she pedōnä'lē] 43

zero zero [dze'rō] 25

zipper cerniera *f* lampo [tshernye'rä läm'pō] 136

zoo zoo *m* [dzō'ō] 119

zoology zoologia *f* [dzō·ōlōjē'ä] 39